THE COMPLETE
ENCYCLOPEDIA OF

FOSSILS

THE COMPLETE ENCYCLOPEDIA OF

FOSSILS

A comprehensive guide
to Fossils from around the world

MARTIN IVANOV, STANISLAVA HRDLIČKOVÁ,
RŮŽENA GREGOROVÁ

REBO
PUBLISHERS

Explanation of abbreviations used

■   – sea
▣   – brackish water
□   – freshwater
●   – land

© 2001 Rebo International b. v., The Netherlands

Production and editing: Granit, s.r.o., Praha
Translation: Stephen Challacombe, Tony Langham and Plym Peters for Bookpros, UK
Cover design: Minkowsky Graphics, Enkhuizen, The Netherlands
Layout: Studio Granit
Text: Martin Ivanov, Stanislava Hrdličková, Růžena Gregorová
Photographs: Andreas Richter 200, Monika and Marek Kořínek 140, Bořivoj Záruba 97, Růžena
Gregorová 54, Jeffrey A. Scovil 45, the Moravian Museum in Brno 18, Zbyněk Roček 16, Anton
Gabert 7, Jiří Bursík 4, Jiří Mališ 3, Jozef Klembara 2, Studio Granit 20
Drawings: Petr Dočkal
Typesetting: Artedit, spol. s r.o., Praha

ISBN 90 366 15003

CONTENTS

Introduction

Our planet is in the region of 4.8 billion years old. The first life forms probably arose around four billion years ago in the form of primitive organisms resembling bacteria and cyanobacteria. During a period around 545 million years ago there was a massive growth in types of organisms with development of the first hard exteriors. From the start of the Paleozoic until the present day one can detect a massive degree of adaptation among all the organisms of the earth (diversification of a line of development in response to different living circumstances through environmental changes).

While biologists research living nature the study of and research into life in bygone eras is the subject of paleontologists. In contrast to biologists, the capacity to reconstruct is a fundamental study tool for the paleontologist. The scientist's fantasy also plays an important role.

The path taken by paleontology from its origins to the science as we know it today has been a complex one. It took many centuries before fossils ceased to be regarded merely as a "trick of nature" and were regarded as remains of long deceased life.

Fossils in the past

Fossils are more or less intact remnants of plants or animals that we find mainly in sedimentary rock from earlier geological eras.

The Neanderthal man was interested in fossils more than fifty thousand years ago. This is evidenced by a small collection of fossils found in caves in Burgundy in France. We shall never know what prehistoric humans thought about fossils. These early humans appear to have used them as amulets or to wear as necklaces.

Archaeological explorations in Egypt have uncovered fossilized shark and fish teeth from the Neolithic period. The enormous teeth of the precursor of today's man-eating shark, a member of the family of Procharodon, were discovered on Malta in the Bronze Age. Several archaeologists suggest that people used the shape of these shark teeth to form decorations in ceramics.

The Greek philosopher **Xenofanes of Colofon** (570–470 BC) knew the origins of fossils, especially those from the sea. He understandably had a problem with identifying large fossilized bones. In primeval times people placed fossilized bones of large vertebrate animals in the sacred places.

Empedocles (492–432 BC) described large bones that were deemed to have come from giants. We presume that the presence of elephant skulls in the Quaternary sediments of Sicily led to myths of the cyclops–single-eyed giants. Elephants have a very small eye socket compared with the very large nasal recess for their trunk. An interesting opinion concerning fossils comes from the greatest of the philosophers of classical antiquity, **Aristotle** (384–322 BC). He held that rocks possessed inner strength that created the forms. The Greek historian and geographer **Strabon** (64 BC–circa 20 AD), who was the first to describe Vesuvius as a volcano, was aware of marine fossils and turned the belief that nummulites were old coins on its head.

The Roman scholar and naturalist **Plinius the Elder** (23–79 BC) described the shark's teeth as "tongue teeth" or *glossopetrae*, saying that they fell from heaven during the dark period of the moon. This same scholar also gave us the name of the best known fossils – ammonites. He called them horn of the god Ammon, *cornu Ammonis*.

In the Middle Ages Aristotle was regarded by the church as an authority and hence his opinions

Homo diluvii testis
an error by J. Scheuchzer from the early 18th century.

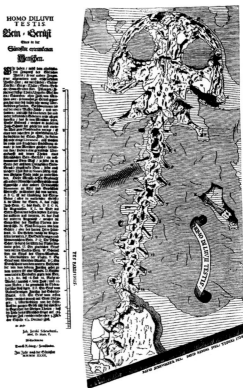

Left: *Tadarida* sp.
Upper Oligocene, Cereste, France

7

about fossils were adopted. Up to the eighteenth century fossils were hence regarded as tricks of nature and the stars. The Arab scholar **Avicenna** broadened this opinion around the year 1000 and the founder of German scholarship, **Albert Magnus** did likewise in the thirteenth century. In the sixteenth and seventeenth centuries fossils were officially deemed to be relics of the biblical flood, but there were scientists who kept their opinions to themselves to prevent problems with the church. The Italian scholar, philosopher, and artists, **Leonardo da Vinci** (1452–1519) noted his remarkably advanced opinions about the origins of fossils in secret writing in his diary. He found marine fossils in the mountains and logically concluded that they could not be relics of a flood brought about by extensive rainfall. At about the same time the French ceramicist, **Bernard Pallisy** correctly suggested that the imprints of fish and the shells of mollusks that he found in clay were the remnants of marine life from a sea that had retreated.

The first person to not only describe fossils but also to illustrate them in 1556 was the physician **Konrad Gesner** of Zurich. He correctly identified the tongue-form fossils as shark's teeth but he could find no explanations for larger fossils. Fossils were eagerly sought after specifically because of their "secretive origins". People believed that fossils had secret powers and in the eighteenth century they were used as an everyday medicine.

The Swiss doctor **Johan Jacob Scheuchzer** (1673–1733) made his fame through a mistake. He

One of the fossils from the book
Lithographiae wirceburgensis.

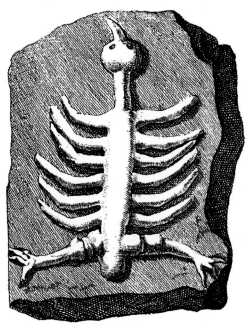

described a giant salamander as a human skeleton: *Homo diluvii testis* – witness to the flood. His error was only discovered a century later by the renowned French paleontologist **Georges Cuvier** (see below). The inappropriate beliefs about fossils only ended following a student prank. A professor in the medical faculty at Würzburg in Germany, **J.B. Beringer**, published the famous book *Litographiae wirceburgensis* in 1726. This featured illustrations of two hundred different types of fossils which students had retrieved from soft chalk and subsequently buried in a site where the professor collected them. The duplicity came to light immediately the book was published. The Beringer affair brought an end to the theories concerning the creative forces and tricks of nature.

An important individual in late eighteenth century biology was the gifted Swedish natural historian **Carl von Linné** (1707–1778), better known as Linnaeus. He regarded species as unchangeable and fossils as relics of species of previously living animals. He also still believed in the biblical flood and even in prehistoric giants. He did have the courage though to incorporate humans within his system of classification of all organisms and animals. His proposition of the immutability of the species though was challenged by **Georges Buffon** (1707–1788) who regarded change as degeneration (he said donkeys originated from horses and apes from humans). **Jean-Baptiste Lamarck** (1744–1828), a botanist, zoologist, and paleontologist, established the continuity of mollusk fossils found in the Paris basin at different levels of the strata. This resulted in astonishing thinking in respect of the historical development of living nature. In 1809 Lamarck wrote *Philosophie zoologique* in which he considered development as a creation of new species from existing ones through their perfection and metamorphosis.

The renowned French paleontologist **George Cuvier** (1769–1832) had access to all European fossil collections as a leading light at the court of Napoleon. He had excellent knowledge of anatomy and created paleontology as a discipline of its own. He became famous for his theory of the cataclysm – catastrophes on such a large scale that all life was exterminated, giving rise to entirely new replacement fauna.

The English geologist **Charles Lyell** (1797–1875) suggested that the geological changes the earth has undergone in its development were slow not cataclysmic and similar to contemporary events. According to Lyell the flora and fauna changed during the earth's development and fossils represented long since extinct organisms. Lyell's book, *Principles of Geology*, was of enormous influence upon the English natural historian **Charles Darwin** (1809–1882), who proposed the theory of evolution. In his ground-breaking book of 1859, *On the Origin of Species by Means of Natural Selection*, Darwin

Reconstruction of a lizard in an engraving of circa
the mid 19th century.

produced powerful evidence that species are not
immutable or permanent, but result from a long process of evolution that takes place through natural
selection. The existence of new and unknown species of animals within certain geological formations
he explained as the result of incomplete palaeontological recording.

Among the adherents to Darwin's theories was the
German zoologist **Ernst Haeckel** (1834–1919), who
gave rise to the term phylogenisis – the development
of a species or group of species through a succes-
sion of forms from their simplest to most advanced
forms and was the first to use the term "ecology."
The development of an individual he indicated as
ontogenisis and in doing so established the biological law that ontogeny is repetitive short-term phylogenisis.

In his search for the precursors of humans he placed his emphasis on comparative anatomy, comparative embryology, and paleontology. Another of the
leading proponents of Darwinian theory was **Henri
Fairfield Osborn** (1857–1935), a professor of paleontology at the University of Columbia in New
York. At his instigation, renowned palaeontological
expeditions to the deserts of Asia were organized,
which found many relics of dinosaurs in the Gobi
desert.

The development of biochemistry and molecular
genetics dates from the early 1950s. The foundation
had already been established by **Johan Gregor
Mendel** (1822–1884), who considerably expanded
the potential for research into the development
paths of the organic world.

The collection of fossils

Each fossil is an extremely important part of nature's history and a unique fragment, for only a remarkably small number of the total number of organisms that have existed become preserved as
fossils. The process of fossil forming is a complex
one of physics and chemistry enabling preservation
of deceased organisms. Among the requirements for
fossilization are structure of the organism's body
and rapid covering with a very fine sediment of the
right properties. The process is also influenced by
pressure, temperature, and the dissolved minerals
in sediments.

Fossils fascinate because they take us back to eras
millions of years ago. They are of incalculable value
in determining the age of strata in the earth's crust
and in particular in the search for inorganic com-
pounds. Many people have become so taken with
the beauty of fossils that they have established amateur collections of considerable importance.

True fossils are extremely rare, especially from early
geological periods. Most fossils are impressions of
the original form of the body or external part of it in
surrounding stone. The shell, external skeleton, or
skeleton is often dissolved in the process of fossilization by minerals such as calcium carbonate and
pyrites, usually leaving a perfect copy of the outer
form of the organism's body in the form of a **cast**.
If the cavity formed by the outer body is also penetrated by soft sediment as well as minerals a fossilized imprint of the inside is formed. It is important
to collect both positive and negative fossils for in

many cases the negative image provides a more precise means of identification. Fossils are not just of the organisms but also of traces of their existence such as their tracks or footprints, e.g. reptile tracks, worm chambers, rodent tracks etc. These are known as **bioglyphs.**

We do not regard forms of inorganic origin as fossils, such as branching aggregates of oxides and hydroxides of iron and manganese in fissures of strata, known as **dendrites**, which have the appearance of superbly preserved plants. Mineral substances can form around inorganic and organic origin in forms reminiscent of shells. These are **concretions** which together with dendrites are regarded as **pseudo-fossils**.

The best fossils are of marine origin formed from ultra-fine grain sediments of slate, ultra-fine sand, marl, chalk, and clay, found in cliffs, quarries, sand pits, clay pits, slagheaps, and such like. To collect fossils a suitable geological hammer is required and perhaps a pick, shovel, and trowel. For splitting thin layers a sturdy knife is necessary and stonemason's cold chisels are useful for slabs of rock. Where fossils are brittle, e.g. bones, the material should be conserved before chipping the fossil out with a hammer and chisel. Fine detail cleaning should be done with a special vibrating needle tool. With harder rock it is possible to emulate weathering by artificially heating and freezing the stone to separate the fossil by hand. Fragmented fossils require conservation. Broken or cracked fossils can be repaired with a suitable adhesive but it is essential to test the adhesive first on a small area. Epoxy or polyester resins or poly vinyl acetate adhesives (PVA) are suitable for strengthening fossils. Important collections should be protected from damage. Normally it is sufficient to wrap each piece and its impression in paper.

To find appropriate locations a large-scale detailed map or geological chart is a useful aid. With really interesting finds we use a loupe and a notebook is essential to record its location. If a camera is not available then a simple sketch of the fossil and its location are useful. Each fossil should be recorded with its precise location, date, strata in which it was found (if possible). If it is later possible to identify the fossil then its name and age are added to the data. We give our fossils a finds number in sequence, name of the collector, manner it was obtained, and date collected or added to the collection. We mark the fossil with the finds number in a way that does not detract from its aesthetic value. A catalogue of acquisitions completes the records. We note each fossil in order it was acquired, with a sequential number that complies with the number on the specimen and the finds location map. We store the marked fossils with the location map in cardboard boxes.

Amateur collectors know rare specimens should be made available to museums where they can be made accessible to as many people as possible. It is easy to take a cast using polyester resins. Good quality reproductions can be produced in plaster, or various proprietary products that are almost impossible to tell apart and can be the centerpiece of any palaeological collection.

Systematic classification of plants and animals

Life is diverse. The number of species increases through advances of knowledge and scientific research. Alongside additions from better knowledge of species die out through natural causes and humankind's activities. Paleontologists believe 99% of all organisms that ever existed have become extinct. The taxonomic system of genus and species used for naming organisms stems from Swedish naturalist Linnaeus. The systematic and internationally universal naming of species of all living organisms is done according to international rules. The starting date for zoological taxa is the tenth edition of Linnaeus' treatise *Systema naturae* published in 1758. The date for plant fossils is 1820 when Count Sternberg's *Flora der Vorwelt, Versuch, Fasc. I.* appeared.

This system is used for plants and animals and consists of a group of similar species in a sort of family (although that word is reserved for a higher grouping) known as a *genus* and the specific *species*. These are written in italics, with a capital initial letter for the genus, e.g. *Crocuta spelaea* = grothyena, or *Betula alba* = white birch. All taxonomic levels higher than the species name are written with a single word for the genus, family, order etc. The complete scientific name includes the name of the author who first described the species, with a comma separating the author's name from the year of that publication e.g. *Sao hirsuta* Barrande, 1846. Both author's name and date are usually omitted. With sub-species the additional name of the sub-species is added, e.g. *Burmirhynchia decorata decorata*. Zoological sub genera names are written in brackets between the genus and the species name, e.g. *Cymatium (Septa) affine*. With botanical taxonomy the taxa of sub genera that is higher in taxonomic hierarchy than the species name is not inserted in brackets but indicated with an abbreviation, e.g. subg. (sub-genus), sect. (section).

For both zoological and botanical taxonomy there is a hierarchy within seven fundamental classifications starting at the top with **kingdom** and descending through **phylum, class, order, family, genus,** to **species**.

In paleontology situations can occur in which it is not possible to precisely categorize a fossil to a specific taxon or scientific name. In these cases an abbreviation is used, with the most important being **aff.** from the Latin *affinus* or related to. This used when the fossil shows a slight deviation from the typical form, e.g. *Ptychoparia* aff. *striata* means that the fossil is similar to the species *P. striata* but a slight deviation suggests that it could be a different species; **cf** for the Latin *confer*, to compare, is used when it is almost certain a specimen is of that species but this is not established, e.g. *Spirifer* cf. *ventricosa*.

It is possible to encounter **quotation marks** e.g. '*Cidaris' forchhammeri*, where '*Cidaris*' is a broad genus comprising many smaller genera.

This system relates to natural plants and organisms. A parallel taxonomic system has been created for fossils recording traces of once living organisms, such as their tracks, or remnants of plants, with a genus outside the general taxonomic system.

Manganese dendrite (pseudo-fossil)
Late Jurassic, Solnhofen, Germany.

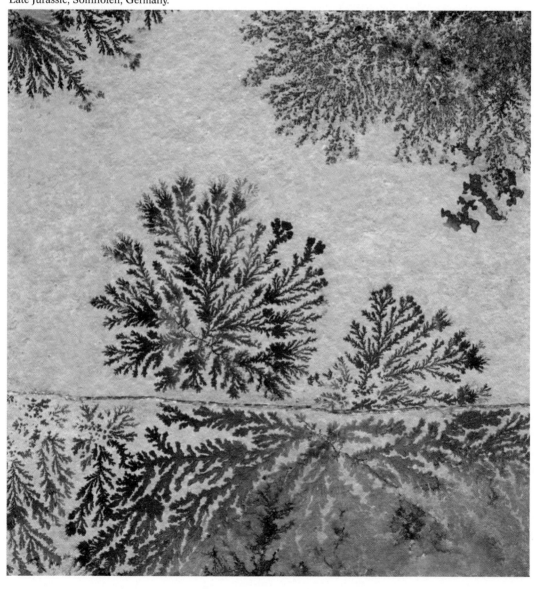

1. Plants

The plant kingdom of our planet came into existence many millions of years ago and has continuously developed with incredible rich and varied forms. The age of our earth is currently estimated at 4.8 billion years. Indications are that the first life emerged around 4 billion years ago. The first living organisms were the eobacteria which in turn gave rise to the development of more complex organisms. At first these were single-cell prokaryotes which lacked a true nucleus, possessing their DNA as a loop in the cytoplasm rather than as chromosomes. These were later followed by eukaryotes, organisms with a distinct nucleus with the cytoplasm separated by a double membrane and possessing chromosomes formed from DNA and proteins. The development of primitive single-cell organisms probably took much longer – of the order of 3.4 billion years – than the time taken for countless multicellular plants and animals to evolve – during the course of some 600 million years.

Plants are autotrophic organisms capable of taking in nutrients, growing, reproducing, and reacting to their environment. In contrast with animals they are not able to move actively because they are dependent on the soil in which they grow for their nutrition. The crucial difference though is the ability of most plants to derive their nourishment autotrophically, to change inorganic matter into organic matter through photosynthesis. By means of this chemical process a plant derives organic matter and oxygen from water and carbon dioxide by means of chlorophyll and the energy of the sun. No life would be possible in the form we know on earth without photosynthesis. Green plants form the key diet for herbivorous animals and therefore indirectly also of carnivores. The development of animals, which are heterotrophic (mainly relying on organic matter for food), is and always has been dependent on the development of green plants, not just for nutrition but also for oxygen which is essential for breathing. The development of an atmosphere rich in free oxygen was one of the important pre-requisites for the development of organisms. Towards the end of the Paleozoic the atmosphere merely contained some three percent of freely available oxygen compared with twenty-one percent today. The greatest role in enriching the atmosphere with oxygen in this time is attributed to the simple organisms of cyanobacteria and algae. Gradually an ozone layer was formed in the atmosphere which like water absorbs the short wave-length radiation of light (the ultra-violet component), which can have deadly consequences. This gave organisms that had previously only existed in water an opportunity to move ashore. The increase of the oxygen in the atmosphere was the fundamental influence on the evolution of life on earth. Although the development of organisms has not always been at a uniform pace and groups of organisms have existed in the geological past that were incapable of adapting quickly enough to the changes in their environment, there is ample fossil evidence to show evolution from simple organisms to more complex, from less well-adapted forms to more perfected ones. The relationship between these development stages is not necessarily readily apparent though when comparing individual plants and animals. The oldest fossils contain relics of organisms from 3.8 billion years ago that are prokaryotes. Also of great age are the irregular forms with a layered inner texture that record the earliest forms of bacteria, cyanobacteria (prokaryotes), and algae found in Australia. In strata of the Pre-Cambrian era one finds primitive single-cell and also multicellular organisms.

The largest proportion of the vascular plants probably evolved from green algae. The first group of primitive vascular spore-bearing plants were rhyniophytes with very rudimentary structures comprising a number of forked stems. Their fossil remains are found in the late Silurian through to Devonian eras. Plants evolved rapidly during the Carboniferous period and many different large groups of plants are found in these strata – fern-like (ferns, club moss, staghorn moss, horsetail), and plants with naked seeds (*Pteridosperm*, *Cycas*, *Cordaites*, and coniferous trees). Several of them, e.g. club and staghorn mosses, and horsetail types developed the zenith of

Leaf from a plant with covered seeds, Lower Miocene, Březánky – Jenišův Újezd, Czech Republic

Left: *Taxodium dubium*
Lower Miocene, Březánky, Czech Republic

Oncolite. The diameter of the ball-like structure is 10–20 mm ($1^3/_4-{}^{25}/_{32}$in).
Precambrian, Mesabi Range, Minnesota, USA

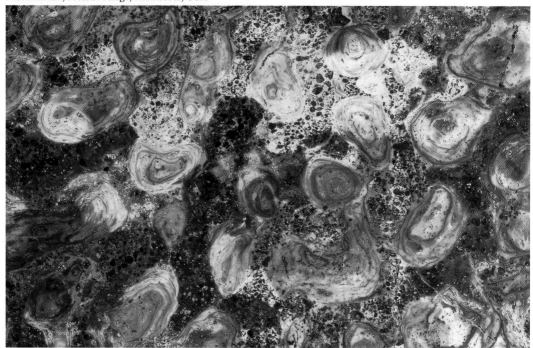

their evolution during this period. In the earlier period of the Mesozoic these plants are rarely found. Their original tree-like forms died out leaving only non-woody herb forms. Dominant plants in strata of this era are those without covered seeds *(Cycas, Gingkoopsida, conifers)*.

In the Cretaceous, at the end of the Mesozoic, plants evolved with covered seeds that developed rapidly, overtaking and crowding out both the fern-like plants and those with naked seeds to become the most dominant group of the plant world. Predecessors of both types of plants, with covered or naked seed can possibly be found among the fern-like plants. The reasons for the major changes in the animal kingdom were the significant changes in sea level, position of the continents, and the considerable mountain forming processes. This led to the formation of new barriers and changes in climate. The organisms were forced to respond to these differences in their environment. Either they evolved to form new and improved species or they became extinct.

Although efforts have been made throughout human history to understand and classify plants humankind has still not succeeded in creating a uniform and universally recognized system of scientific classification. The separate systems developed by important botanists still differ considerably from each other, both in terms of the classification within groups and in the naming. In this book we adhere to the evolutionary or phylogenetic system, based on the evolution of the plants and their relationships one to another. This starts by categorizing all organisms into two main groups, based on whether their cells have a nucleus or not: Eukaryotes with and Prokaryotes without.

Main group: Prokaryotes organisms without a nucleus

ARCHAEAN TO RECENT TIMES

In this category are the microscopic heterotrophic or autotrophic organisms without a nucleus (the genetic material formed by DNA strands is not separated from the cytoplasm by the membrane of a nucleus). These organisms live on their own or in colonies. Currently these are categorized as Bacteriophyta – bacteria or as Cyanophyta – cyanobacteria, and possibly also as Virophyta – viruses, but the taxonomic classification is exceptionally difficult because they differ greatly in character from typical plants.

Virophyta – viruses represented by extremely small specific life forms (the size of which is expressed in millimicrons), which always live as parasites in the living bodies of all manner of host organisms, and can only reproduce within their host organisms. They attack plants and animals, including humans, and are the origin of many dangerous diseases, or viral infections. Viruses do not form cells and exist in both formless plasma masses or as a body with the

Stromatolite *Collenia undosa*
Precambrium, Mesabi Range, Minnesota, USA

characteristic form of a crystal – paracrystals. Viruses themselves have not been found in fossil form but we know that they existed in previous geological eras from finds that had been infected with a virus such as fossils of misshapen leaves.

Bacteriophyta – bacteria are single-cell microscopic organisms that are clearly the most prolific forms of life, accounting for about half of all living matter on earth in terms of weight. Their cells have a characteristic form and very simple inner structure. The central mass is not concentrated in a nucleus but diffused throughout the cell. In terms of their nutrition they can by exception be autotrophic (they live through photosynthesis) or as is more usually the case heterotrophic (deriving their energy through chemical synthesis), they live parasitically, saprophytically, or symbiotically. Aerobic bacteria live in an oxygen-rich environment but anaerobic bacteria are not reliant upon oxygen.

Cyanophyta – cyanobacteria belong to the simplest and in terms of evolution to the earliest organisms on earth. Unlike bacteria their cell mass without a nucleus has a blue-green assimilating coloring. These were the first organisms on earth to photosynthesize and they are responsible for changing an atmosphere devoid of free oxygen into one rich in oxygen. These autotrophic organisms that live in water and on land generally form colonies. Most of them digest calcium, becoming encrusted with chalk, and with bacteria but mainly algae form part of the process of creation of organic sediments or *algolites*. These are bulbous clump-forming or irregular and often branched forms of chalk or silica, usually with a layered internal structure. If the algolites form distinct separate balls in the sediment we call them *oncolites*, and if they form large flat forms encompassing several metres then we call them *stromatolites*. Their most important period of development was during the Proterozoic, when they formed an important constituent of limestone. Their role in the formation of rock in the subsequent periods through to the present day rapidly became much less significant.

Stromatolite
Upper-Proterozoic, Mítov, Czech Republic.

Stromatolite
Upper-Proterozoic, Mítov, Czech Republic.

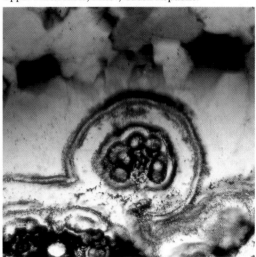

Main group: Eukaryotes – organisms with a nucleus

PROTEROZOIC – RECENT TIMES

This group encompasses all organisms with cells with a nucleus. On the basis of their internal structures we categorize them into kingdoms of fungi, plants, and animals. Those organisms that do not readily fall into one of these categories are incorporated in one of three taxa created specially for them.

Kingdom: Plantae – plants

PROTEROZOIC – RECENT TIMES

The plant kingdom mainly consists of single or multi-cell autotrophic organisms with assimilation coloring, that is usually green chlorophyll. Where this colorant is missing the plants exist heterotrophically as parasites or saprophytes. The oldest of the plants are algae that has existed for at least 2.5 billion years. Plants can be classified into higher or lower orders of plants on the basis of their method of reproduction and the extent to which their body has evolved.

Lower plants mainly reproduce by means of spores and they have simplified bodies. They also miss the chief characteristic of higher plants – water-filled vascular parts, having no true roots, stem, or leaves. Their simple body is known as *thallus* and they do not flower. These plants include algae. Formerly fungi and lichens were regarded as part of this group but they are now separately classified.

Higher plants reproduce by means of spores or seeds, have evolved roots, a stem, and leaves, and in most cases they flower (plants with covered seeds). The vascular spore-bearing plants, mosses, and seed-bearing plants are incorporated within this group.

Lower plants: Algae

PROTEROZOIC – RECENT TIMES

In common with cyanobacteria, algae are among the simplest and most primitive organisms on earth. These single-cell and multicellular organisms mainly live in their original environment of water. Because they are supported by the water they have never developed supporting tissue. The body or thallus of algae has not evolved roots and a stem and they have no water-absorbing and transporting tissue. Nutrients are absorbed from the water across their entire body. The bodies do contain assimilation colorants of different hues, and this is an important factor in their classification.

Solenopora jurassica
Upper-Jurassic, Thannay, France

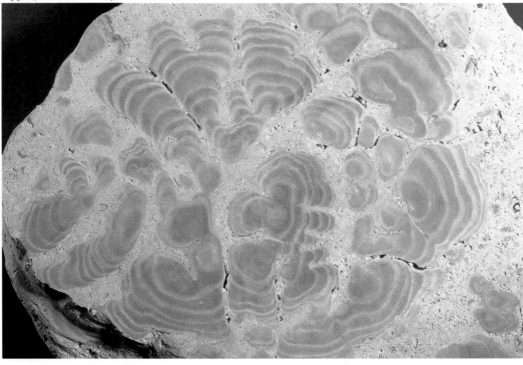

Teutloporella herculea
Lower-Triassic, Dobšiná, Slovakia

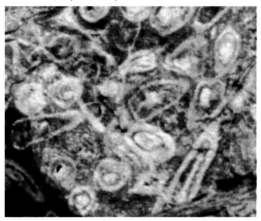

Solenopora ■

CAMBRIAN – JURASSIC

The genus *Solenopora* forms bulbous incrustations with a smooth or warty surface that can have a span of several centimeters. They belong to the group of red algae (Rhodophyta) and use a red assimilation colorant for their absorption of nutrients which also makes their bodies red. Their body is of the polyaxial type (the separate fibers radiate out in every direction) with readily apparent diagonal shoots between the different fibers. The intricate cross-section has the appearance of thin lattice-work. The bulbs of the genus *Solenopora* were spread almost over the entire world and are found in Cambrian to Jurassic strata. An outstanding example of the *Solenopora jurassica* species has a cross-section of 100 mm (4 in).

Teutloporella ■

PERMIAN – JURASSIC

Seaweed of the genus Teutloporella has an erect rod-like stem upon which irregular but densely packed side shoots (phyloides) grow like attachments. This genus belongs to the group of green seaweed (Chlorophyta), because its assimilation colorant is green chlorophyll. The genus *Teutloporella* was widespread throughout Europe during the Permian through to Jurassic periods but specifically during the Middle Triassic and is of important stratigraphic significance. The length of the illustrated specimen in chalk showing a seaweed thallus of the species *Teutloporella herculea* is 40 mm (1⁹/₁₆ in).

Higher plants: Telomophyta

UPPER-SILURIAN – RECENT TIMES

Mosses and vascular plants (both spore and seed-bearing) belong to the group of higher plants.

Division: Bryophyta – bryophytes

DEVONIAN – RECENT TIMES

This isolated group in the plant kingdom probably evolved from green algae. It comprises slender, terrestrial, moisture-loving plants with green colorant. Their body or thallus has not yet fully developed water-bearing vascular tissues.

A morphological division is made with the mosses between sexual and asexual generations in arriving at the appropriate gender. There is a set pattern of interchange between sexual generation (gametophyte) and asexual generation (sporophyte) in the reproduction of a new plant. Sexual generations, which are dominant over asexual ones, produce distinct stem-like stalks with readily apparent gender organs and cells. Among the mosses we include liverwort, mosses, and sphagnum moss. Liverwort is found in Devonian strata but sphagnum moss only appears from the Tertiary period on.

Riccia ☐ ●

MIOCENE – RECENT TIMES

The genus *Riccia* consists of both the terrestrial and aquatic liverworts, which possess a multi-layered flaky thallus with separated assimilation and basic tissues. These plants are almost devoid of transpiring pores. The genus *Riccia* is found throughout the world in strata from the Miocene onwards. The species *Riccia fluitans* has a branching thallus and is mainly found on the banks of still water. The specimen in argillite illustrated is 60 mm (2⁵/₈ in).

Riccia cf. *fluitans*
Miocene, Sokolov, Czech Republic

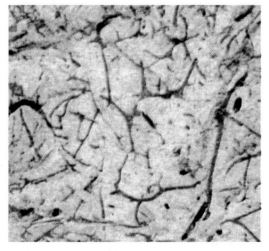

Psilophyton sp.
Middle-Devonian, Srbsko, Czech Republic

Lepidodendron aculeatum
Carboniferous, Karviná, Czech Republic

Tracheophyta – vascular plants

UPPER-SILURIAN – RECENT TIMES

Within this group are found the multicellular and predominantly terrestrial plants with a body that is separated into a stem, green leaves, and roots. A wide variation in cell structure has evolved, adapted to numerous functions. Water and nutrients are transported by means of the xylem and phloem tissues and the assimilating colorant is chlorophyll. The above ground part of the larger plants is protected by a hard impermeable skin or cuticle, within which there are pores that permit transpiration. Vascular plants are sub-divided into two groups:

Spore-bearing vascular plants – which reproduce through spores, do not flower, and therefore form no seeds. These include rhyniophytes, club moss, horsetails, and ferns.

Seed-bearing vascular plants that flower with male

Barrandeina dusliana
Middle-Devonian, Hostím, Czech Republic

plants or organs that produce pollen and female plants or organs that need to be fertilized. Following fertilization seeds are produced which enable the plant to reproduce or propagate itself. These plants are further sub-divided into those with naked or covered seeds. Both spores and pollen are extremely hard and consequently are discovered in sediments while other plant remnants are missing.

Division: Rhyniophyta – rhyniophytes

UPPER-SILURIAN – DEVONIAN

Rhyniophytes were the most primitive forms of vascular spore-bearing plants, that probably developed from algae. They mainly grew in areas of morass or on the banks alongside water and they formed low shrubs with branched and branchless shoots, generally without leaves. At the ends of these shoots they bore sporangia (receptacles of densely packed spores). Their water-bearing tissue was not highly developed. The group died out during the Devonian period.

Psilophyton ●

LOWER-DEVONIAN – MIDDLE-DEVONIAN

The genus *Psilophyton* consists of terrestrial herbaceous rhyniophytes, that thrived best in a wet swampy environment. The upper part of the plants consisted of a branched stem with pores that was either plain or bore thorn-like shoots resembling rudimentary leaves. The average thickness of the stems was of the order of 20–60 mm ($^3/_4$ –$2^5/_8$ in), and the plant could reach heights of some tens of centimeters. The genus closely resembles the well-known genus *Rhynia*, but is differentiated by the curled ends of the young shoots. The genus *Psilophyton* is found in Lower and Middle Devonian strata. The fossil of genus *Psilophyton* illustrated measures 60 mm ($2^5/_8$ in).

Division: Lycophyta – lycophytes

LOWER-DEVONIAN – RECENT TIMES

Among the lycophytes (club horn and staghorn mosses) are both herbaceous and tree-like forms with unsegmented but hollow stems or shoots. A shallow branching root system evolved to fasten themselves to the muddy ground in which they grew. They are known as *Stigmaria*. The dished leaves grew on an unusual leaf axil from which they were shed with age, leaving characteristic scars behind that today help us to establish the genus. The spores enclosed in sporangia were located within rod-like fruits. The lycophytes were an important part of primeval forest of the Carboniferous period, reaching heights of up to 40 metres (130 ft), and they contributed to the deposits of coal. Today only a few genera survive from this group of impressive structure.

Barrandeina ●

MIDDLE-DEVONIAN

The genus *Barrandeina* is one of the genera of plants from the Middle-Devonian period which remains not precisely classified. The appearance and anatomy have clear characteristics of rhyniophytes and lycophytes, but also of seaweed. These plants resembled a tree with regularly spaced branches of up to 1 m (39 in) high with wedge-shaped leaves that are lobed and notched at the front and carried on lengthy leaf stalks. Clear scars are left behind when the leaves are shed that are reminiscent of lycophytes. During the Middle-Devonian period, the genus *Barrandeina* was spread throughout Europe, North America and Asia.

Lepidodendron ●

CARBONIFEROUS

The trees of the genus *Lepidodendron* can reach up to 30 m (98 ft) in height with trunks of up to 2 m (6 ft 6 in) in diameter. The trunks bear diagonal markings of elongated but narrow leaves that were quickly shed. The bark is unusually hard. The trunks branched out to form spreading crowns and bore reproductive organs at the ends of the leaf-bearing twigs in the form of rod-like cones of 20–30 cm (8–12 in) known as *Lepidostrobus*. These formed on the branch itself or on separate twigs.

The genus *Lepidodendron* was spread throughout Europe and North America. Bark, leaf-bearing twigs, and also the cones have been preserved in the illustrated sample of the species *Lepidodendron simile*. It shows clear markings on the bark (25 mm/1 in).

Lepidodendron simile
Upper Carboniferous, Nýřany, Czech Republic

Sigyllaria cf. *ichthyolepis*
Upper Carboniferous, Graissesac, France

Sigillariostrobus sp.
Upper Carboniferous, Graissesac, France

Sigillaria ●

LOWER CARBONIFEROUS – LOWER PERMIAN

Sigillaria was another important genus of the tree-like lycophytes. The tall trunks were only moderately thick at their bases and they bore small and narrow crowns with elongated grass-like leaves. Unlike the *Lepidodendrons* there were no leaf axils as the leaves grew directly from the trunk, leaving clear markings behind that are generally distributed in elongated rows (with the true *Sigillarias – Eusigillaria*) or more widely dispersed in the case of *Subsigillaria*. The spore-bearing cones grew from the trunk on long stalks beneath the leafy crown. They were up to 30 cm (12 in) long. The genus *Sigillaria* was spread throughout Europe and North America from the

Lower Carboniferous to the Lower Permian. The species *Sigillaria* cf. *ichtyolepis* illustrated represents the *Subsigillaria* group. The width of the marking is 13mm ($^1/_2$ in). The second illustration shows a 6 mm ($^3/_4$ in) wide cone or *Sigillariostrobus* together with a horsetail of the most commonly found species *Annularia stellata*.

Division: Sphenophyta – horsetails

DEVONIAN – RECENT TIMES

Initially these were herbaceous types with a segmented stem but later also trees up to 20 m (65 ft) high, rooted in swampy soil with segmented roots or

Calamodendron,
cross-section of the stem of a horsetail imprinted in quartz. Tertiary, Libya

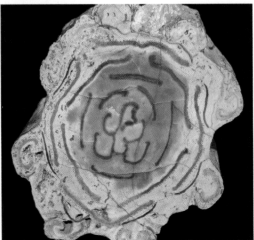

Annularia sp.
Upper Carboniferous, Rosice, Czech Republic

rhizomes. Side branches shoot from the joints in the segmented stem together with leaves arranged directly opposite each other. The position of the leaves helps to classify the different horsetails. The spores are encased in sporangia that are located within thin rod-like cones. Primitive forms of horsetail have been found from the Lower Devonian period with tree-like species from the Carboniferous and Triassic periods. There is only one surviving species. Some of the tree-like horsetails have been embedded in quartz and they are classified within "artificial" genera.

Annularia ●

UPPER CARBONIFEROUS – LOWER PERMIAN

Horsetails of the *Annularia* genus have single-veined dished leaves that are quite broad with skeletons on the undersides that merge. Horsetail leaves are arranged laterally and are generally of differing lengths. Thin cones are borne at the ends of the branches. The *Annularia* genus is found throughout the world from the Upper Carboniferous to the Lower Permian and is especially abundant in Europe. The *Annularia* horsetail illustrated has a diameter of 30–40 mm ($1^3/_{16}$–$1^9/_{16}$in).

Asterophyllites ●

UPPER CARBONIFEROUS – LOWER PERMIAN

Unlike *Annularia*, the genus *Asterophyllites* has single-veined dished leaves that are plain on the underside, as long as they are wide, and point towards the tip of the branch. The longest leaves are borne on the undersides of the longer branches and the shortest ones on the upper side.

Asterophyllites are found throughout Europe, North America, and Asia in strata of the Upper Carboniferous to the Upper Permian periods. The leaves of the most commonly found species, *Asterophyllites equisetiformis,* are of similar length to their stalks. The specimen shown is 100 mm (4 in).

Calamites ●

LOWER CARBONIFEROUS – LOWER PERMIAN

Calamites form part of the tree-like horsetails that reached heights of 30 m (100 ft). The trunks were smooth on the outside but hollow inside with many impressions of the inner stem having been found. These cores are grooved laterally and some if not all these grooves have branches that criss-cross each other. Where the branches join the main stem there are generally imprints of the pores of the leaf tissue. *Calamites* are found world-wide in Lower carboniferous and Lower Permian strata.

The photograph shows a typically grooved core of a *Calamites radiatus* horsetail measuring 120 mm ($4^3/_4$ in).

Asterophyllites equisetiformis
Upper Carboniferous, Graissesac, France

Calamites radiatus
Lower Carboniferous, Hainichen, Germany

Psaronius, cross-section of the stem of a fern, 90 mm (3⁹/₁₆ in)
Permian, Arizona, USA

Division: Pterophyta
– Ferns

DEVONIAN – RECENT TIMES

This is a group of herbaceous to small tree-like ferns
with unsegmented stems or trunks with abundant
fan-like foliage. The emergent leaves uncoil themselves and in the odd case are also protected by a different form of foliage. The small leaflets of each fan-like
frond grow on a common leaf stalk. The sporangia
containing the spores of the higher type ferns are formed on the underside of a number of fronds. These
are the fertile fronds, the rest of the spore-less fronds
being sterile. The sporangia open themselves by
means of thickened cells that form a ring or *annulus.* Two different types of spores – male and female
– had already developed with the higher forms of
ferns by the Upper Devonian period, and this process
eventually led with other plants to male and female
flower forms and seeds. Ferns are classified in three
groups: primitive, phyllophorate, and true ferns.
Impressions of fronds make up the most ubiquitous
fossils of plants. The sporangia of the ferns, which are
the chief characteristic for their classification, are either separate features or borne on the undersides of
the fronds. We mainly find fossils though of sterile

Tieta singularis, cross-section through the stem of a fern,
190 mm (7¹/₂ in) Permian, Araguaina, Brazil

Asterotheca cf. *arborescens*
Permian, Hilbersdorf, Germany

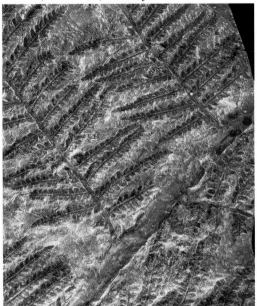

Pecopteris arborescens
Upper Carboniferous, Radnice, Czech Republic

fern fronds. For this reason we are not able to classify the great majority of fern fossils into their appropriate genus or even family. This also applies to the leaves of certain naked seed plants. For this reason the sterile fronds of ferns and the foliage from naked seed plants are incorporated within artificial taxa, in which the fronds or leaves are categorized solely on the basis of their shape and vein structure. Artificial genera are also used for impressions of fern stems in quartz.

Asterotheca ●

Pecopteris ●

CARBONIFEROUS – UPPER TRIASSIC

The true ferns of the natural genus *Asterotheca* and the artificial genus *Pecopteris* have large twin-fronded forms of foliage forming tongue-like "leaves" with branching veins. The sporangia, that do not form annuli take the shape of a star with four to six sporangia in groups on the undersides of the fronds in two rows on either side of the central vein.
The family of *Asterotheca* originates from the Upper Carboniferous to Upper Triassic when it must have been the most widespread fertile type of form in Europe, the USA, the Middle East, and Asia. It is found together with very many sterile ferns that are incorporated in the artificial genus *Pecopteris* from the Upper Carboniferous to Upper Triassic. The "cut-out" of the species *Asterotheca* cf. *arborescens* is 140 mm (5$^{1}/_{2}$ in) and the spe-

cimen of *Pecopteris arborescens* measures 110 x 90 mm (4$^{5}/_{16}$ x 3$^{9}/_{16}$ in).

Dactylotheca ●

UPPER CARBONIFEROUS – LOWER PERMIAN

The genus *Dactylotheca* primarily consists of true tree ferns with large multi-fronded forms of foliage and large aflebia. The generally slender sporangia are in proportion with these larger plants and they are carried separately on the lateral veins. The annulus formed by the sporangia is difficult to see. The important *Dactylotheca* genus from the Permian to Carboniferous period was widespread throughout present-day Europe.

Dactylotheca plumosa
Upper Carboniferous, Rakovník, Czech Republic

Marioperis sp.
Upper Carboniferous, Karviná, Czech Republic

Adiantites ternuifolius
Lower Carboniferous, Velká Střelná, Czech Republic

Gymnospermae
– gymnosperms

DEVONIAN – RECENT TIMES

In general, gymnosperms are trees, and much less often, plants. The tree trunks can be up to 1 m (39 in) in diameter. The leaves are pinnate and divided fans or simple, oval to needle-shaped. In spore-bearing vascular plants, the gametophyte forms independent plants and is significantly reduced in vascular, seed-bearing plants, and inextricably linked with the sporophyte. Reproduction is not carried out with spores, but with the ovum and pollen grains. When the ovum is fertilized, a seed develops which is not protected by a shell in Gymnospermae, but is "naked". Therefore no fruit forms.

Spenopteris hoeninghausi
Carboniferous, Saarbrücken, Austria

Class: Peteridospermopsida
– Pteridosperms

DEVONIAN – UPPER CRETACEOUS

Pteridosperms (former seed-ferns) are extinct, shrub-like plants or small trees, with trunks which could grow to a diameter of 10 cm (4 in). They produced multiple, pinnate fans. The kidney-shaped pollen cases and the ova grow either directly in the fans or have an independent shape. A distinction is made in the pteridosperms between natural and artificial genera.

Marioperis ●

UPPER CARBONIFEROUS

The representatives of the genus *Marioperis* had thin, distinctly liana-like stems with double-forking fans which were partly pinnate. The leaves had a thin, fork-like nervation, and therefore the edges were pointed and serrated, or indented with points. The oldest leaves on the side usually curved out in an interesting manner. The genus *Marioperis* was widespread during the Upper Carboniferous in Europe and North America. The part of the *Marioperis sp.* shown in the photograph is 13 cm (5 in) long.

Sphenopteris ●

DEVONIAN – JURASSIC

The artificial genus *Sphenopteris* has forking and pinnate fans with side leaves which are usually in the shape of an elongated triangle with rounded or comma-shaped indentations and a pinnate nervation. The genus *Sphenopteris* was widespread all over the world and has been identified in strata dating from the Devonian to the Jurassic. Many species of this genus are of stratigraphic significance for the Upper Carboniferous. The specimen shown in the photograph belongs to the species, *Sphenopteris hoeninghausi* , and is 11 cm (4^1/$_4$ in) long.

Callipteris conferta
Lower Permian, France

Neuropteris sp.
Upper Carboniferous, Illinois, United States

Adiantites ●

LOWER – UPPER CARBONIFEROUS

The fans of the artificial genus *Adiantites* are sometimes bipinnate, with relatively wedge-shaped leaves, which were rounded and often short, with thin leaf stalks. The genus *Adiantites* was particularly common in the Lower Carboniferous in Europe. The specimen with leaves belonging to the species *Adiantites tenuifolius* measures 9 x 7 cm ($3^1/_2$ x $2^3/_4$ in).

Callipteris ●

UPPER CARBONIFEROUS

The large, pinnate divided fans are characteristic of the artificial genus *Callipteris,* which had rounded, triangular, pecopterid lateral leaves (the whole base is attached to the leaf axis) with a pinnate nervation. The leaf axis is also characteristic, with striking leaflets growing between the fans of the last row. The genus *Callipteris* has been identified in strata dating from the Upper Carboniferous and Permian. Remains have been found in Europe, the United States and Asia. The most common species of this genus is the species illustrated here, *Callipteris conferta,* which is also of stratigraphic importance for Europe.

Neuropteris ●

LOWER CARBONIFEORUS – LOWER PERMIAN

The individual species of the artificial genus *Neuropteris* are only related by the nervation of the leaves. There is a single vein or mid-rib along the leaf, which either forks immediately to form a fan of small veins, or continues through the leaf as a mid-rib of differing lengths (depending on the species), finally branching out into curving side veins (in a fan shape at the end of the leaf). The leaves are large and neuropterid. The rounded, tongue-shaped leaves are in the leaf axis, with a narrow, rounded base, or with a short stalk). There are aphlebia on the base of the main leaf axis. Remains of the genus *Neuropteris*

have been found mainly in Europe, North America and Asia, dating from the Lower Carboniferous to the Lower Permian. The specimen in the photograph is 19.1 cm ($7^1/_2$ in) long.

Alethopteris ●

UPPER CARBONIFEROUS – LOWER PERMIAN

The artificial genus *Alethopteris* has multiple pinnate fans with alethopterid lateral leaves (the long, tongue-shaped, pointed or blunt rounded leaves are attached to the axis along their entire base, while the base extends to the next leaf). The leaves have a pinnate nervation. The genus *Alethopteris,* dating from the Upper Carboniferous to the Lower Permian has been found in Europe and North America. The majority of species are important from the stratigraphic point of view.

Alethopteris serlii
Upper Carboniferous, Svatý Kříž u Radnic,
Czech Republic

Pterophyllum brevipenne
Triassic, Lunz, Austria

Class: Cycadopsida – Cycads

UPPER CARBONIFEROUS – RECENT TIMES

Cycads are tree-like plants, with tall or short, sometimes conical trunks, which do not branch, usually with a pithy center, up to 50 cm (19$\frac{1}{2}$ in) diameter. Rigid leaves are long, narrow, and spiral when young, not indented and of simple pinnate shape. Flowers grow in the leaf axillae. Their important development was during the Jurassic, when they were widespread. A distinction is made between natural and artificial genera.

Gingko adiantoides
Paleocene, Morton County, South Dakota, United States

Pterophyllum ●

UPPER CARBONIFEROUS – UPPER CRETACEOUS

The artificial genus *Pterophyllum* has simple, pinnate leaves. These are divided into long, narrow leaves, which are attached to the main leaf axis along a broad base. The nervation runs along the length of the leaf. The genus *Pterophyllum* was widespread from the Upper Carboniferous to the Middle Cretaceous, and remains have been found in sediments in Europe and North America. The specimen illustrated here, with some of its leaves, belongs to species *Pterophyllum brevipenne* and measures 25 x 18 cm (9$\frac{3}{4}$ x 7 in).

Class: Ginkgopsida – Ginkgo

PERMIAN – RECENT TIMES

Ginkgoes are tree-like pants with ginkgoid leaves (rounded, wedge-shaped leaves, divided by indentations of different depths into lobed or comma-shaped pieces), which grow on short stalks, forming a thin brush. The nervation is fan-shaped. For this group, an artificial system is also used for the classification on the basis of the leaves. The most important development of this group took place during the Triassic and Jurassic. There are now only representatives of one genus of *Ginkgo* extant.

Ginkgo ●

UPPER TRIASSIC – RECENT TIMES

The shape of the ginkgoid leaves of the genus *Ginkgo* varies enormously, but broad, wedge-shaped, lobed leaves with a long stalk are characteristic. Specimens of the genus *Ginkgo* have been identified dating from the Upper Triassic, and impressions of the leaves are widespread throughout the world. The leaves of the species *Ginkgo adiantoides* cannot be distinguished from the present-day *Ginkgo biloba*. The fossilized leaf shown in the photograph is 8 cm (3 in) across.

Cordaites borassifolius
Upper Carboniferous, Stradonice, Czech Republic

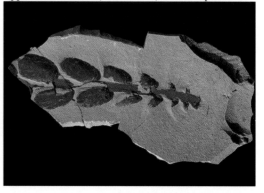

Araucaria mirabilis, Upper Jurassic – Lower Cretaceous, Cerro Quadrado, Argentina

Class: Cordaitopsida

UPPER CARBONIFEROUS – LOWER TRIASSIC

The Cordaitopsida were trees which grew to a height of 30 m (98 ft), with hollow trunks (with a maximum diameter of 50 cm/19^1/$_2$ in) and a strongly branching crown. The nervation of the rigid taeniopterid leaves up to 1 m (39 in) long (tongue-shaped or ribbon like, with differently formed bases and differently shaped tips) was lengthwise (as in the leaves of monocotyledonous angiospermous plants). The flowers formed thin cones. The Cordaitopsida were among the most important elements in the formation of coal. In this group there are also natural and artificial genera.

Cordaites ●

UPPER CARBONIFEROUS – LOWER PERMIAN

The genus *Cordaites* is typical of the Cordaitopsida. Its thick leathery leaves were so strong that they were likely to be well preserved in the form of good fossils. The leaves were up to 1 m (39 in) long and 20 cm (7^3/$_4$ in) wide, narrowing at the bottom and tip. The nervation is dichotomously branching along the length of the leaf. The leaves can be classified into three artificial genera on the basis of shape and the type of nervation (*Cordaites, Dorycordaites* and *Poacordaites*). The tall, thin trunks of the genus *Cordaites* were securely rooted in soft marshy soil with greatly branching, almost horizontally spreading roots called *Rhizocordaites*. The delicate flowers, grouped in long, thin ears or cones, are exclusively male or female. They grow in the leaf axilla, and are called *Cordaianthus*. The seeds are flat. The genus *Cordaites* was widespread all over the world from the Upper Carboniferous to the Lower Permian. The part of the leaf of the species *Cordaites borassifolius* shown in the photograph is 2.9 cm (more than 1 in) across.

Class: Pinopsida – conifers

UPPER CARBONIFEROUS – RECENT TIMES

Conifers are bushy, though usually tree-like plants with trunks that can grow more than 1 m (39 in) in diameter. In most cases the well-developed pith and the bark contain resin canals. The leaves are mainly single-veined, in the shape of needles or scales, and in primitive types divided into forks. The flowers form cones, varying in appearance and size. The wood of fossilized conifers, transformed into quartz, is classified on the basis of an artificial system. For example, primitive conifers, ferns and fern-like plants from the Upper Paleozoic and Mesozoic in Central Europe are classified as *araucaria*. The most important development of conifers took place during the Jurassic and Cretaceous. The number of angiosperms has declined from the Upper Cretaceous to the present day.

Torreya ●

JURASSIC – RECENT TIMES

The tree-like species of the genus *Torreya* belong to a group of conifers in which, unlike all the other conifers, there was no grouping of the male organs in a biaxial cone. The male cones grow in the axilla of the flat leaves; the female cones normally grow in pairs on the end of side branches. The oldest specimens found of the genus *Torreya* date back as far as the Jurassic. During the Miocene and Pliocene, they spread significantly across the northern hemisphere. The twig of the species *Torreya bilinica* shown in the illustration is 9 cm (3^1/$_2$ in) long.

Torreya bilinica
Miocene, Břežánky u Bíliny, Czech Republic

Lebachia piniformis
Permian, Lodève, France

Pinus sp.
Tertiary, Northern Czech Republic

Lebachia

UPPER CARBONIFEROUS – LOWER PERMIAN

The primitive genus *Lebachia* is one of the two natural genera of the artificial genus *Walchia*, classified
on the basis of the differences between the structure
of the cones and the air spaces which have been preserved. The trunks of these tree-like plants had a thin
medulla and a thick secondary bark. The branches
were arranged horizontally on the trunk like a horse's tail, branching in a pinnate pattern. Long, fine
needles grew on these twigs, divided into many forks
with sickle-shaped curved tips. The genus *Lebachia*
was widespread from the Upper Carboniferous to the
Lower Permian, and has been identified in Europe,
the United States and China. Some of the most common species include *Lebachia piniformis*. The twig
of this species shown in the photograph is 28 cm
(11 in) long.

Pinus

LOWER CRETACEOUS – RECENT TIMES

The appearance of the recent genus *Pinus* (pine) differs little from its ancestors dating from the Mesozoic
and Tertiary. The differences can only be seen in the
details, e.g., in the anatomical structure, and in the
arrangement of the needles and cones, and their
lengths and shapes. Fossilized remains have been

found all over the northern hemisphere dating from
the Lower Cretaceous. A great increase in the number of species took place from the Pleistocene. More
than a hundred species have now been identified.
The cone in the photograph is approximately 10 cm
(4 in) long.

Glyptostrobus

UPPER CRETACEOUS – RECENT TIMES

In general, the species of the genus *Glyptostrobus*
are very similar to the only recent species, *Glyptostrobus pensilis*, which only grows in a small area
of Southeast China. The leaves consisted of short
needles, pointing in every direction. However, the
genus *Glyptostrobus* was most widespread after the
Upper Cretaceous, and during the Oligocene and
Miocene in particular, it was one of the most common conifers in the northern hemisphere, which also
played the most important role in the formation of
lignite. The most common impressions of conifers
dating from the Miocene in Central Europe are of the
species *Glyptostrobus europaeus*. The photograph
shows a branch with cones, 8 cm (3 in) long.

Taxodium

UPPER CRETACEOUS – RECENT TIMES

Like the genera *Glyptostrobus* and *Pinus*, the genus
Taxodium is one of the higher genera of conifers.
The short needles spread out on two sides. Never-
theless, it is sometimes difficult to distinguish fossils

Glyptostrobus europaeus
Miocene, Břežánky u Bíliny, Czech Republic

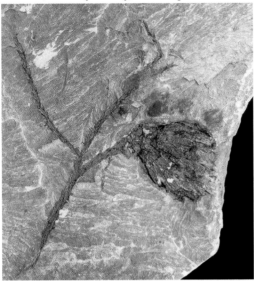

Taxodium dubium
Lower Miocene – Jenišův Újezd, Czech Republic

Widdringtonia ●

UPPER TRIASSIC – RECENT TIMES

The genus *Widdringtonia* comprises tree-like conifers, of which remains are often found, particularly in the form of impressions of young, leafy twigs or shoots. The oldest remains date back to the Upper Triassic, but specimens have also been found all over the northern hemisphere, dating as far back as the Cretaceous. Only five species of this genus have survived up to the present day, and these are found in Southeast Africa. The twig of the species *Widdringtonia reichii* shown in the photograph is 13 cm (5 in) long.

of the genus *Taxodium* from those of the genus *Glyptostrobus*. The genus *Taxodium* was widespread throughout the northern hemisphere from the Upper Cretaceous, and the species illustrated here, *Taxodium dubium*, was extremely common.

Widdringtonia reichii
Miocene, Břežánky u Bíliny, Czech Republic

Nyssa ornithobroma,
fruits of a dicotyledonous plant, Tertiary, Czech Republic

Angiospermae – angiosperms

LOWER CRETACEOUS – RECENT TIMES

Angiosperms, which are represented by both plants and trees, are a large group of the most developed species of vascular plants. Nowadays they account for the largest share of the earth's vegetation. In general, they are green and adapted to living on land. The body (sporophyte) is divided into the root system and the shoots (stem or trunk and leaves). The leaves have very varied shapes, and the individual leaves grow on a thin stalk. The nervation is branching or parallel. The plants form flowers which are usually hermaphrodite. The ova are concealed in a seed case, and when they have been fertilized, they ripen to form seeds which are protected by a fruit. The oldest fossilized remains of these plants (pollen grains) were found in strata dating from the Lower Cretaceous. Angiosperms underwent the strongest development from the Tertiary up to the present day. However, the origin of this development has still not been explained entirely satisfactorily. Angiosperms are divided into monocotyledonous and dicotyledonous plants, on the basis of the number of cotyledons in the seed.

Magnolia sp.
Upper Cretaceous, Maletín, Czech Republic

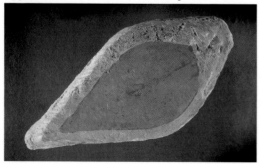

Class: Magnoliopsida – dicotyledonous plants

LOWER CRETACEOUS – RECENT TIMES

These are woody plants or plants which usually germinate with two seeds. The vascular bundles and medulla tissue (Cambrian) thicken at a secondary stage, which results in the actual trunks becoming thicker. The main root of the seed survives, and lateral roots also develop. The stalks of the leaves in many different forms, and with a dichotomously branching nervation, are often compound. The flowers usually have four or five petals, generally with a receptacle (calyx, corolla, sepals). Dicotyledonous plants are about four times as common as monocotyledonous plants. Transitional species between these two groups have also been identified, and therefore it is not possible to make a clear distinction between monocotyledonous and dicotyledonous angiosperms.

Magnolia

UPPER CRETACEOUS – RECENT TIMES

The genus Magnolia is one of the oldest dicotyledonous angiosperms. The genus comprises bushy and tree-like species, which generally have a branching crown. The leaves are not indented, and are shed. The shape varies from oval to lanceolate, and the flowers are hermaphrodite. Specimens of leaves of the genus *Magnolia*, which was widespread all over the world, have been found dating back as far as the Upper Cretaceous. Nowadays, they grow mainly in the tropical and subtropical regions of North and South America, Southeast Asia and Oceania. The leaf of the genus *Magnolia* in this photograph is 20 cm (7³/₄ in) long.

Daphnogene

EOCENE – MIOCENE

The leaves of the extinct genus *Daphnogene* have a nervation of the cinamomoid type, which is characterized by two strikingly elongated veins on the

Daphnogene ungeri
Upper Oligocene, Kučlín u Bíliny, Czech Republic

Platanus cuneiformis
Cretaceous, Kunštát, Czech Republic

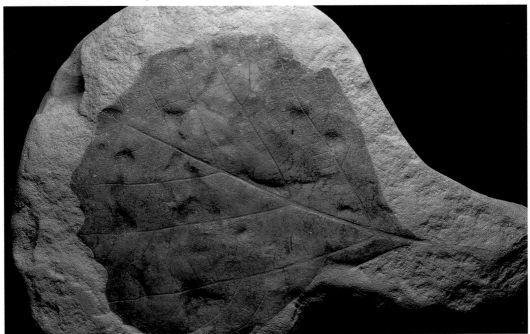

side, branching from the main vein on the bottom of the leaf and extending virtually to the tip (so-called three-veined leaves). They are very similar to the leaves of the genus *Cinnamomum* (cinnamon tree). The genus *Daphnogene* has been found throughout Europe in strata dating from the Eocene to the Miocene. The leaf of *Daphnogene ungeri* in the photograph is 4.5 cm (1³/₄ in) long.

Acer tricuspidatum
Lower Miocene, Bílina, Czech Republic

Acer ●

UPPER CRETACEOUS (?) PALEOCENE – RECENT TIMES

The genus *Acer* is characterized by a great diversity of species and the characteristic appearance of the leaves. They are unusually large, and broadly palmate, and are divided into several characteristic lobes, which may end in a number of pointed tips on the perimeter. Fruits may also be found with the leaves (flower heads). No fossil remains have been convincingly identified as dating from the Upper Cretaceous, though specimens have been identified with certainty as dating from the Paleocene. The genus was common in Europe, North America and parts of Asia. The photograph shows a leaf of *Acer Tricuspidatum*, measuring approx. 10 cm (4 in).

Platanus ●

UPPER CRETACEOUS – RECENT

Representatives of the genus *Platanus* (plane tree) are strong, monoecious trees, which are interesting because their bark comes off in thin flakes. The leaves are alternately palmate and coarsely indented with palmate nervation. The fruit is a hard capitulum. The genus mainly grew in the northern hemisphere, and fossils are common from the Miocene. The species in the photograph, *Platanus cuneiformis*, is distinct from the majority of species of the genus *Platanus* because of the shape of the leaf. The leaf measures 10 cm (4 in).

31

Alnus julianiformis
Lower Miocene, Březno u Chomutova, Czech Republic

Alnus julianiformis ●

UPPER CRETACEOUS – RECENT TIMES

The genus *Alnus* (alder) consists of monoecious deciduous trees or shrubs with alternating, simple, oval or broad lanceloate leaves, with a dichotomously branching nervation, often found together with conical fruits. The genus *Alnus* has been particularly widespread in the northern hemisphere since the Upper Cretaceous.

Comptonia acutiloba
Miocene, Břežánky u Bíliny, Czech Republic

Comptonia ●

TERTIARY – RECENT TIMES

The genus *Comptonia* belonged to the subtropical group of aromatic plants with long, deep and roughly lobed leaves with a pinnate nervation. Shrubs of the genus *Comptonia* were already common during the Tertiary, although the numbers declined during the Quaternary. Nowadays, they grow in temperate regions in North America. The leaf of the species *Comptonia acutiloba* shown in the photograph measures 9 cm ($3^1/_2$ in).

Juglans acuminata
Miocene, Moravská Nová Ves, Czech Republic

Quercus sp.
Oligocene, St. Bauzile en Privas, France

Juglans ●

UPPER CRETACEOUS (?) – TERTIARY – RECENT TIMES

The genus *Juglans* (walnut tree) comprises deciduous, monoecious trees with uneven, pinnate, serrated leaves, with or without indentations. The fruit is a nut. The oldest fossils remains have been identified, though not convincingly, in strata dating from the Upper Cretaceous. From the Tertiary, the genus *Juglans* was widespread throughout the northern hemisphere, and was most common in the later Oligocene and the Miocene. The leaf of the tree of the species *Juglans acuminata* in the photograph is 11.5 cm ($4^1/_2$ in) long.

Quercus ●

LOWER CRETACEOUS – RECENT TIMES

In terms of species, the genus *Quercus* (oak) is unusually diverse; six hundred species have been identified. They have very different long leaves with an unbroken edge or deeply indented, with lobes. Specimens of *Quercus* have been found dating from the Lower Cretaceous, particularly in the northern hemisphere. The photographed fossilized leaf of *Quercus* sp. (above), 6.5 cm ($2^1/_2$ in) long, is with recent species, *Quercus robur*.

Poacites aequalis
Upper Oligocene, Kučlín u Bíliny, Czech Republic

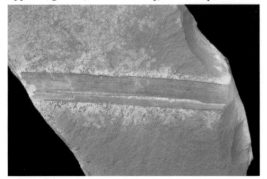

Class: Liliopsida – monocotyledons

LOWER CRETACEOUS – RECENT TIMES

These are usually plants in which the seed has one cotyledon. The vascular bundles are not able to grow any thicker, so that there is no secondary thickening of the stalks or trunks. The root system, with a rudimentary main root, is formed only of the replacement (adventive) roots. The comma-shaped or oval roots are directly placed on the trunk without a stalk, and the nervation runs across, without a central vein. The flowers consist mainly of three petals. All the important characteristics of monocotyledonous plants can be derived from dicotyledonous plants which are older in terms of development.

Poacites ●

TERTIARY – RECENT TIMES

The genus *Poacites* belongs to the grasses, a very extensive and old group of monocotyledonous plants in terms of development. The stem (stalk) is not branched but is segmented. The leaves are very long and narrow. The nervation runs across the leaf. The plant is pollinated by the wind. The fruit is a grass fruit. The genus *Poacites* was widespread all over the world from the Tertiary. The fragment of the species *Poacites aequalis* illustrated here measures 5 cm (2 in).

Phragmites ●

UPPER CRETACEOUS – RECENT TIMES

The genus *Phragmites* (reeds) is now one of the most common species of grass and can grow to a height of 2 m (6 ft 6 in). The extremely light fruits of these grasses are easily dispersed by the wind. Species of reeds develop in places where there is plenty of water and sufficient nutrients. The genus *Phragmites* has been found on almost all the continents in strata dating from the Upper Cretaceous. The fragment of *Phragmites oeningensis* illustrated here measures 15 cm (6 in).

Phragmites oeningensis
Miocene, Břežánky u Bíliny, Czech Republic

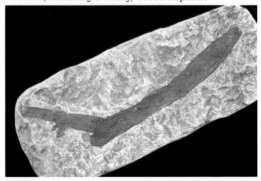

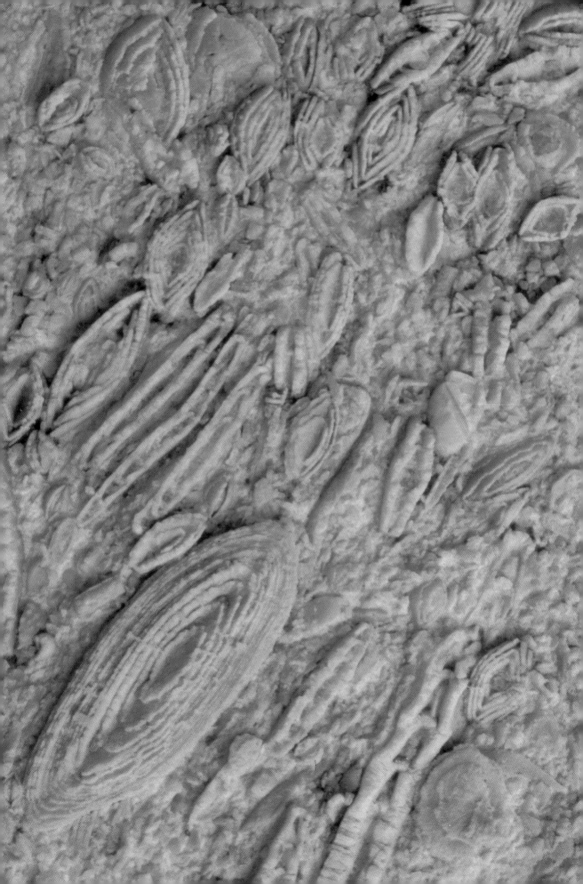

2. Animals – from protozoa to annelids

Kingdom: animalia – animals

PRECAMBRIAN – RECENT TIMES

The animal kingdom mainly differs from the plant kingdom because it relies on a different method of nutrition. Animal life forms are heterotrophic organisms with a separate nucleus *(Eukaryotes)*, and unlike plants, they are not capable of photosynthesis. Animals obtain organic substances from autotrophic organisms, i.e., plants. However, it is interesting to note that at the lowest level of the organic world, some single-cell organisms, e.g., a number of flagellates, contain an assimilation colorant and feed autotrophically like plants, while others have no chloroplasts, and are therefore heterotrophic, like animals. Therefore it is assumed that in the course of geological history, higher and increasingly perfect animals developed from heterotrophic flagellates, and that plants evolved from autotrophic forms. The uniform structure of the cells of plants and animals reflects the uniformity of the organic world.

The main criteria for the selection of different classes of animals are the methods of nutrition and reproduction. This was undoubtedly related to the adaptation to new environments. The transition from water to land and air served as further incentives for development. This development took place with the step-by-step control of fundamental functions, from mechanical problems related to metabolism, to the achievement of high levels of information gathering and regulation (perfecting the sense of sight, sonar in bats, and the sensitivity to electrical fields in fish).

In higher species, there was a trend towards shared life forms. At a higher level, this was repeated in the coordinated activity which resulted in the creation of multicellular organisms. The social community characteristic of arthropods led to the perfecting of the division of functions of the individual members.

Phylum: Protozoa – unicellular organisms

PRECAMBRIAN (?), CAMBRIAN – RECENT TIMES

Protozoa are single-cell organisms in which all the functions are performed by one cell. However, this cell has a more complicated structure and development than the cell of many multicellular organisms.

Left: Limestone consisting of nummulites
Eocene, Dalmatia, Croatia

Sometimes it can help itself by changing and performing the various different functions in stages in this way. For example, the flagellate settles and changes into a static cyst, and subsequently transforms into a different cell form by means of amoeba-like movements. Protozoa can also be distinguished from multicellular organisms by a different form of reproduction, respectively by the alternation of sexual and asexual regeneration. The great majority of unicellular organisms are solitary, although some form a sort of colony. The cell consists of *protoplasm* and one or more *nuclei*. The protoplasm of unicellular organisms contains different elements (chondriosomes), vacuoles and fatty or starch grains. In autotrophic single-cell organisms the protoplasm contains *chloroplasts*. The surface of the single-cell organisms often forms a thin membrane – the *pellicula*. Hairs, flagella, as well as other anorganic forms, appear on this membrane. In some organisms the protoplasm secretes a solid material, the *cuticula*, which can develop to become a strong shell. These groups are important in paleontology, and particularly for stratigraphy. They even have a practical use, because the accumulation of the shells of Acritarchs led to the formation of limestone or chalk. Single-cell organisms are rather limited in size. Usually they are no bigger than one millimeter. However, there are some representatives of Acritarchs from the Tertiary – nummulites – with a shell larger than 12 cm ($4^{3}/_{4}$ in). Single-cell organisms are prevalent throughout the natural world; they are found in oceans, lakes, marshes, rivers and wetlands.

Unicellular organisms are classified in a number of classes on the basis of the morphology of their cell nucleus, the structure of the organelles for movement, the method of reproduction and other characteristics. From the point of view of paleontology, there are four important classes: Flagellata – flagellates, Rhizopoda – rhizopods, Actinopoda and Ciliata – infusorians.

Class: Rhizopoda – rhizopods

CAMBRIAN – RECENT TIMES

The large majority of fossils of single-cell organisms are rhizopods. These marine single-cells organisms usually form a calcareous, chitinous or other shell, and rarely consist of naked protoplasm. A smaller number of rhizopods are classified as plankton, benthic species which move about with the aid of pseudopodia, which they also use to obtain food. The class of Rhizopoda consists of many orders; for paleontology, the order of Acritarchs, Foraminifera, is the most important.

Orbitolites – complanata
Eocene, Paris basin, France

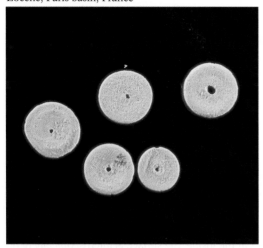

Pseudoschwagerina extensa
Lower Permian, Alps, Austria

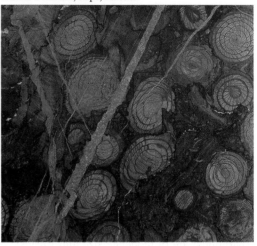

Order: Foraminifera

CAMBRIAN – RECENT TIMES

The body of the Foraminifera consists of a nucleus and cytoplasm and is usually protected by a calcareous shell. Some Foraminifera are agglutinating, i.e., they build a shell by cementing together foreign particles, or the shell consists of tectine, and is then transformed into quartz, in rare cases. The shell consists either of a single chamber (monothalamous), or more frequently, of several chambers (polythalamous). The organism spreads out in the shell with several chambers with the growth of the protoplasm over the chambers which are added. The shells are characterized by a large diversity of forms. They are subdivided into a number of groups: *uniserial* shells have chambers which are arranged in a line, one

Ammonia beccarii
Pliocene, San Gimignano, Italy

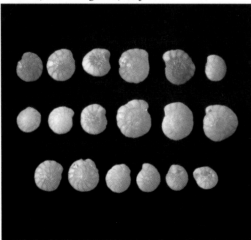

above the other, *biserial* chambers are arranged in two rows, and *triserial* chambers are arranged in three rows. If the case spirals at one level, this results in the *plano-spiral* form. and if the shell spirals, it is known as a *trochospiral* shell. A distinction can be made between the dorsal side, which reveals all the whorls, and the ventral, umbilical side. On the ventral side, there is a platform – the umbilicus. In planospiral (lens-shaped, disc-shaped) shells, in which the chambers are in concentric circles in one plane, there is a distinction between the *evolute type*, which reveals all the whorls from the side, and the *involute type*, in which the last whorl overlaps all the previous ones. There are a number of transitional forms for the shape and type of shell of Foraminifera.

Orbitolites

PALEOCENE – EOCENE

The genus *Orbitolites* represents Foraminifera, with a relatively large disc-shaped shell, which is thicker at the circumference than in the center. The starting stage is plano-spiral, but subsequently a concentrically structured shell is formed. In the shell, there are ring-shaped cylindrical chambers divided up into smaller chambers by radial undulating partitions. There is no communication between them, but the previous and subsequent chamber are linked. There are numerous foramina on the wall of the shell. The Foraminifera *Orbitolites* inhabited the warm seas in the Eocene. The size of the shell of the species illustrated here, *Ortibolites complanata*, varies from 4 to 6 mm.

Ammonia

UPPER CRETACEOUS – RECENT TIMES

The Foraminifera *Ammonia* has a simple spiral shell with an evolute spiraling side and an involute umbilical side. The umbilicus is covered by a wart, which is divided into small columns by slits. The calcareous shell is perforated and consists of a number of concentric layers which cover it completely and represent the periods of growth. There are dozens of *Ammonia* species from all over the world, dating from the Upper Cretaceous to today. The species illustrated here, *Ammonia beccarii,* is a benthic species of Forminifera, which inhabits a very shallow brackish environment up to today. The largest specimens in the photograph are 1.3 mm across.

Pseudoschwagerina ■

LOWER CRETACEOUS

The genus *Pseudoschwagerina* has a calcareous, cylindrical or bullet-shaped shell. At the surface, the wall consists of a thin layer of tectine (tectum) and a calcareous layer, the so-called keriotheca. The septa (partitions) are of moderate size and irregular in shape. They are quite far apart, and therefore do not generally form chambers. Chomata (deposits of calcium secreted at a secondary stage) are rarely developed or are altogether absent. The representatives of the Foraminifera of the genus *Pseudoschwagerina* are widespread in sediments dating from the Lower Permian in Europe, Asia, North Africa and North America. The species illustrated here, *Pseudoschwagerina extensa,* shows a cross section of the calcareous shells, the largest of which is 8 mm across.

Nodosaria ■

DEVONIAN (?) – RECENT TIMES

The genus *Nodosaria* has a calcareous, perforated and polythalamous shell. The individual oval or round chambers are arranged in one straight line, forming a uniserial shell. The shell has a terminal radiating mouth, and is usually ribbed, although it can occasionally also be smooth. There are examples of *Nodosaria* dating from the Devonian, but it only spread throughout the whole world in the Mesozoic and Kainozoic eras. It is interesting to note that the mesozoic and older representatives of these Foraminifera inhabited shallow seas, but they are now found below the levels where there is light, viz., lower than 200 m (656 ft). In the species illustrated here, *Nodosaria bacillum,* the length of the shell of the largest specimen is 11 mm (less than $^1/_2$ in).

Nummulites ■

PALEOCENE – OLIGOCENE

The genus *Nummulites* is extremely important; compared with single-cell organisms, these organisms can achieve gigantic dimensions. In fact, the diameter of the shell can be up to 12 cm ($4^3/_4$ in).
The calcareous case of nummulites is lens or disc-shaped, and the surface is smooth or slightly rough.

Nodosaria bacillum
Miocene, Southern Moravia, Czech Republic

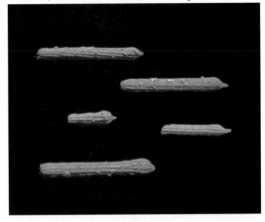

On the inside, the surface is microscopically perforated, and it is only on the edges that the holes do not go right through. The shell contains small chambers arranged in a spiral, which are particularly visible in cross sections of calcified nummulites. In Classical Antiquity, nummulites were seen as old lenses. This view was only overturned by the Greek traveler, Strabon.
The genus *Nummulites* flourished in the Middle Eocene. It was found in the area of Tethyda, the original ocean which divided the southern and northern continents in the Mesozoic. There are limestone formations consisting of accumulations of nummulite shells in Slovakia, Italy, Croatia, the Paris basin and northern Germany. The diameter of the shell of the representative of the genus *Nummulites* illustrated here is 1.5 cm ($^1/_2$ in).

Limestone consisting of nummulites
Eocene, Dalmatia, Croatia

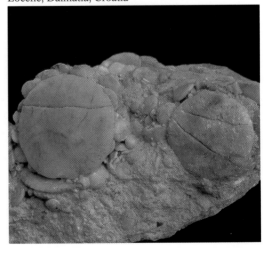

Mawsonietes spriggi
Precambrian, Ediacara, Australia

Metazoa
– multicellular organisms

PRECAMBRIAN – RECENT TIMES

The body of the first multicellular organism resembles a colony of protozoa, interrelated at the same level, lacking any deeper integration. It is very probable that multicellular organisms developed from these. They mainly differ from protozoa because of the larger number of cells and a greater degree of differentiation with regard to the execution of different functions. The ancestors of these multicellular organisms, which lived in the Precambrian, hundreds of millions of years earlier, did not produce any fossil

remains. In the 1940s, important fossils were discovered in Australia, representing the impressions of different forms of animal life, but no hard remains survived. The size of these fluctuates around one centimeter and they are disc or leaf shaped. These fossils also include, for example, *Dickinsonia costata*, *Mawsonites spriggi* and *Charnia masoni*, which are 580–560 million years old. Similar discoveries were later made in other areas in the county of Shropshire in Great Britain, in Namibia, Russia and Newfoundland. It is assumed that these fossils could represent the origins of many animal phyla, such as echinoderms, worms and arthropods.

Phylum: Porifera
– animal sponges

PRECAMBRIAN (?), CAMBRIAN – RECENT TIMES

Animal sponges mainly represent marine organisms attached to the sea bed. They are closest to the original organisms, and up to now have not developed specialized nerve cells. Sponges form a stage in the development of unicellular organisms to multicellular animals. Size varies from a few millimeters to 2 m (6 ft 6 in). Sponges differ enormously in shape, and within a species. They can be sac-shaped, round, cylindrical, disc-shaped, fan-shaped or conical. They usually form a colony, but are sometimes solitary. Primitive sponges form a hollow cylinder, cone or sac surrounding a central hollow *spongocel*. This is an

Dickinsonia costata
Precambrian, Ediacara, Australia

Charnia masoni
Precambrian, Charnwood Forest, Great Britain

asconoid sponge, linked with the inner cavity with an opening – the *osculum*. In higher forms the organization is *syconoid*, and the inner layer of cells is curved, forming many finger-shaped folds, increasing the active surface area, where digestive and respiratory processes occur. The highest type is the *leuconoid system*, with further expansion of the chambers from the central cavity. Instead of a single osculum, chambers are formed in the body, linked to the inner area by a large number of pores and canals – *ostia*. Nutrients are supplied by flagellate cells, and anything not digested is excreted through a joint opening. Sponges are reinforced with mineral and organic substances so the shape and canals can be maintained. In most species a solid calcareous or siliceous *skeleton* forms; in some species this is an organic mass of spongin, created by individual or interconnected needle-like *spicules*. These spicules secrete cells, called *scleroblasts*. Sponges can be subdivided into five basic morphological types: free monaxonic spicules (monaxonones), triaxonic spicules, tetraxonic spicules, polypxonic spicules and spheres – see illustrations.

The traditional system of classifying sponges is based on the chemical composition of the skeleton and morphology of the spicules. The phylum is divided into two basic classes: Calcarea – calcareous sponges, and Silicea – siliceous sponges.

The structure of animal sponges: A– asconoid, B – syconoid, C – leuconoid

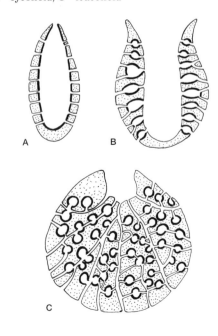

Spicules of sponges (the specimens are approximately 6 mm across) Upper Jurassic, Nattheim, Germany

Peronidella furcata
Upper Cretaceous, Kaňk, Czech Republic

Class: Calcarea
– calcareous sponges

CAMBRIAN – RECENT TIMES

Calcarea comprise animal sponges with spicules consisting of calcium carbonate. In most calcareous sponges the spicules are distributed freely around the body of the organism, and are therefore often found on their own in sediment. However, the skeletons of some species have also been found, because the spicules have fused together. Sponges can be all sorts of shapes: cylindrical, club-shaped, spherical, round or bushy. There are various types of structure (asconoid, syconoid and leuconoid). The oldest calcareous sponges date from the Cambrian and are still found today. They were extremely rare during the Paleozoic, widespread in the Jurassic and Triassic, and flourished prolifically during the Cretaceous, and declined during the Tertiary. Many calcareous sponges have been described which were found in the sediments of the Czech Cretaceous.

Peronidella (Peronella) ■

DEVONIAN – CRETACEOUS

The genus *Peronidella* is a representative of the order of Pharetronida, which comprises the most important of calcareous sponges, with structure of the leuconoid type. This genus comprises sponges with a rigid calcareous wall and a cylindrical shape, living in colonies and as solitary specimens. A small platform at the top, indicates the position of the osculum. About twenty species have been described in fossilized form, from marine sediments in Europe dating from the Devonian to the Cretaceous. The genus *Peronidella* illustrated here is represented by a colony of individuals with a diameter of 2 cm ($^3/_4$ in). This sponge is widespread in the Bohemian chalk basin of Korýčany.

Stellispongia ■

TRIASSIC – CRETACEOUS

The genus *Stellispongia* usually forms bulb-shaped bunches in colonies. When the sponges are solitary, they are round, semi-circular, club-shaped or cylindrical. Every specimen has a protruding upper section ending in one star-shaped mouth (osculum). The genus *Stellispongia* is common in Europe, North Africa and South America in sediments from the Triassic to the Cretaceous. Some species of this genus have also been found dating from the Czech Cretaceous.

Craticularia ■

UPPER JURASSIC – MIOCENE

Sponges of the genus *Craticularia* have a thick-walled, funnel-shaped skeleton. The surface on the inside of the skeleton has a regular structure of holes. The ostia are arranged in regular horizontal and vertical lines. The canals are short with closed ends. Almost twenty species of this sponge have been described in fossil form. The genus *Craticularia* is found in sediments dating from the Jurassic to the Miocene, in Europe and North Africa. Together with many other species of animal sponges, this species is also represented in the Czech Cretaceous.

Class: Silicea
– siliceous sponges

CAMBRIAN – RECENT TIMES

As the name suggests, the class of Silicea covers sponges with a skeleton consisting of spicules. Fossilized siliceous sponges can be divided into two subclasses: Demospongidia and Hexactinellidia. Specimens have been found dating from the Cambrian up to today.

Subclass: Demospongidia

CAMBRIAN – RECENT TIMES

The skeleton of the representatives of the subclass Demospongidia consists of siliceous spicules or spongin, and often of a combination of the two materials. Most of the fossilized representatives of these sponges belong to the Lithistida order; others are fairly rare.

Stellispongia tuberosa
Upper Cretaceous, Nákle, Czech Republic

Craticularia vulgata
Upper Cretaceous, Zbyslav, Czech Republic

Verruculina philipsi
Upper Cretaceous, Chrtníky u Choltic, Czech Republic

Order: Lithistida

CAMBRIAN – RECENT TIMES

The sponges in this order have very diverse shapes. They are solid, thick-walled species, with a complicated system of canals. The skeleton is composed of megasclera (large spicules), which are characteristic of this group, and so-called desmesids. These spicules have four rays which have developed into irregular, branching tubicles. These have fused to form a so-called lithistid skeleton, which is a characteristic feature of this group. Representatives of the Lithistida begin to appear in large numbers in the Ordovician, and reached a maximum distribution in the Cretaceous.

Verruculina ∎

MIDDLE CRETACEOUS – TERTIARY

From a palaeontological point of view, the siliceous sponge in the genus *Verruculina* belongs to the most important order of siliceous sponges, Listhida, subclass Demospongidia. This comprises sponges with a body of the leuconoid type with a skeleton of siliceous spicules or spongin. *Verruculina* is found in the shape of a leaf, ear, funnel or cup. The sponge has a short foot or is without a stalk. At the top of the

osculum there is a raised, wavy edge. The spicules can have different shapes and sizes, and also include a few smooth spicules. The genus *Verruculina* is widespread in sediments of the Upper Cretaceous in Europe, and in sediments from the Kainozoic in Australia. It is widely represented in chalk sediments dating from the Czech Cretaceous.

Coelocorypha obesa
Upper Cretaceous, Chrtníky u Choltic, Czech Republic

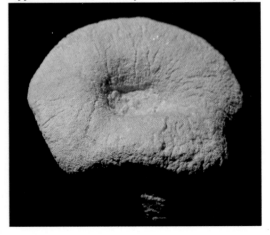

Coelocorypha ■

CRECATEOUS

The genus *Coelocorypha*, which also belongs to the Lithistida order, represents simple sponges or sponges composed of several individuals. They have different shapes, varying from oblong and cylindrical shapes to branching specimens. Occasionally they are spherical. The skeleton forms a thick wall. They have a rounded osculum with a tube-shaped spongocel, which can be very deep and reach down to the base, or, conversely, be very shallow (depending on the general shape of the sponge). The genus *Coelocorypha* is widespread in Cretaceous sediments in Europe, and is widely represented in the Czech limestone basin.

Siphonia ■

JURASSIC – TERTIARY

The siliceous sponge of the genus *Siphonia* has a pear or apple-shaped structure. The sponge usually has a long stem with a branching root. It has a fairly complicated system of canals. This genus has a deep spongocel. In the surface layer there are monaxonic and triaxonic spicules. The elements of the root of the skeleton correspond to the main elements of the skeleton, and only the collars of the spicules of some species with a very long ray are usually elongated.

More than ten species of the sponge of the genus *Siphonia* have been described, from sediments in Europe and Southern Australia dating from the Jurassic to the Tertiary. The sponge is also widely represented in the Czech limestone basin.

Subclass: Hexactinellidia

LOWER CAMBRIAN – RECENT TIMES

The structure is less strong that that of the representatives of the subclass Demospongidia. The sponges have a large and wide spongocel, often with a thin wall and a simple system of canals. These sponges have no spongin at all. The spicules are arranged in three pairs (six rays), which explains the name of this subclass.

Order: Lychniskida

TRIASSIC (?), JURASSIC – RECENT TIMES

The order Lychniskida represents one of the most common groups of fossil sponges. The arrangement of the spicules resembles lanterns with open sides (the name Lychniskida is derived from lychnos – lantern). The maximum distribution of Lychniskida sponges in the Cretaceous mainly occurred in Europe.

Siphonia geinitzi
Upper-Cretaceous, Nákle, Czech Republic

Ventriculites ■

MIDDLE CRETACEOUS – UPPER CRETACEOUS

The body of the genus *Ventriculites* often has a conical, cylindrical or cup-shape. This sponge has a broad spongocel and a thin, wavy edge. The folds are close together and are separated by vertical grooves, which run over the inside and outside of the sponge, and are visible on the surface as a regular sieve-like structure. The basic skeleton of the sponge is relatively narrow and is anchored by branching roots. The genus *Ventriculites* is particularly widespread in Cretaceous sediments of Europe and was also common in the Czech Cretaceous.

Ventriculites chonoides
Upper Cretaceous, Yorkshire, Great Britain

Phylum: Archaeocyatha

LOWER CAMBRIAN – MIDDLE CAMBRIAN

Archaeocyatha form an extinct group of multicellular, stemless organisms, which live in colonies and as solitary specimens. Occasionally they are seen as the common ancestor of calcareous sponges and textraxon-bearing sponges. They inhabited the bed of the warms seas of the Lower and Middle Cambrian, in areas which were not too far from the shore. Their widespread distribution over almost the whole world, as well as the diversity of the species, can be explained, amongst other things, by the fact that they were like plankton during the larval stage. The significant growth of this group in the Cambrian suggests that Archaeocyatha had already developed in the Precambrian, although there are no fossil remains from that time. However, after the Lower and Upper Cambrian, they were extremely important fossil guides. The types which lived in colonies formed extensive chalk cliffs at depths of 20–30 m (65 ft 6 in–98 ft). Solitary species also inhabited greater depths (up to approximately 100 m/328 ft).

Archaeocyatha usually forms a shell in the form of an inverse cone, with a height varying from 0.6 to 15 cm (6 in). There were often conical prominences at the pointed end, attaching the creatures to the bed. In primitive times, the calcium dioxide shells consisted of a porous *single wall*, while higher types had a *double wall*. Various structures developed in the *intervening space (intervallum)* between the walls, dividing up the whole space. These are *partitions (pseudosepta)*, arranged vertically or radiating outwards. Where they are attached to the outer walls of the shell, the surface of the outer wall has delicate grooves. There are also horizontal *bases (tabulae)*, which connect the septa.

The shell of Archaeocyatha: 1 – outer wall, 2 – inner wall, 3 – partitions (pseudosepta), 4 – intervening space (intervallum), 5 – pores, 6 – bases (tabulae), 7 – prominences on the roots

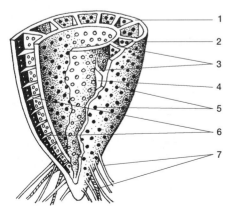

The systematic classification of Archaeocyatha is based on the morphology, the elements of the skeleton, and also on ontogenetic development.

Coscinocyathus ∎

LOWER-MIDDLE CAMBRIAN

The genus *Coscinocyathus* belongs to the most developed genera of Archaeocyatha. It is characterized by a double shell which is broadly conical or cylindrical. The intervallum is broad and has a regular pattern of septa and bases. All the elements have single perforations. In some shells, small spines are visible on the surface of the inside of the inner wall. More than fifty, mostly solitary species, have been identified. The genus *Coscinocyathus* was widespread all over the world in the Lower and Middle Cambrian. The photograph illustrates the vertical cross sections of the cup of individual specimens. At the bottom, the diameter reaches 1.4 cm ($^1/_2$ in).

Phylum: Coelenterata – coelenterates

PROTEROICUM – RECENT TIMES

The phylum of coelenterates only comprises aquatic, predominantly marine, multicellular organisms. They usually have a *ray-shaped (radial)* symmetry. They have a clearly visible *mouth*, which serves both for the ingestion of food and for excretion (there is no anal aperture). The supply of water with its nutrients, and its removal, are carried out by muscular contractions. Simple or springy hollow *tentacles* are usually placed around the mouth opening in one or several rings. They often have stinging cells (nematocysts), which are necessary to anaesthetize the food and protect the animal. The mouth opening opens into the closed body cavity *(coelenteron)*. This is divided up with radiating walls in a regular arrangement. These partitions run from one point in the center to the circumference of the cavity. The cavity is surrounded by the *body wall*. There is a middle layer of a varying thickness *(mezoglea)* between the outer body wall *(ectoderm)* and the inner body wall *(endoderm)*. In many coelenterates, the ectoderm or the mezoglea secretes a horny or calcareous skeleton. The nervous system is primitive, consisting only of a thin network of nerve cells in the body wall. There are no respiratory organs, blood or organs for circulation. The digestion of coelenterates is complicated: the food is ingested in its entirety, surrounded with mucus and then digested *outside the cells (extra-cellular)*. Coelenterates reproduce by means of sexual reproduction, or by alternating *sexual generation (polyp)* and *asexual generation (jellyfish)*. The stemless polyp, which reproduces by budding, usually represents the larval stage, while the mobile jellyfish represents the mature stage.

Coscinoyathus sp.
Lower Cambrian, Siberia, Russia

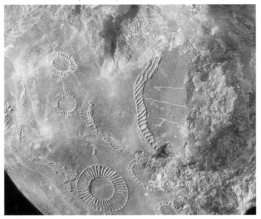

Coelenterates are among the most important organisms that form rocks. This was also the case in the distant geological past. From the stratigraphic point of view, they are one of the most important groups for paleontology.

They can be systematically classified into three classes on the basis of their inner structure, and by their methods of reproduction.

Class: Hydrozoa – polyps

LOWER CAMBRIAN – RECENT TIMES

Polyps represent the most primitive group of coelenterates. They usually grow to a size of 2–3 mm ($^1/_{16}$–$^1/_8$ in). They often live in colonies in seas. There are usually two genera, polyps and jellyfish. Individual polyps in a colony differ in shape, depending on their function (feeding, protection, reproduction). They are interconnected by a system of fine tubes *(cenosark)*, which distributes the digested food over the whole colony. The whole colony is reinforced by an inner chitinous, horny or calcareous skeleton *(perisark, periderm)*, which is secreted by the ectoderm. The periderm can create a cup-shaped skeleton around every polyp *(hydrotheca, polyparium)*, where the polyp can withdraw. Sometimes there is also a sort of lid. In some polyps the cenosark also secretes siliceous fibers, forming a fine porous system, the coenosteum. Only the polyps have survived as fossils. From the stratigraphic point of view, Stromatoporoidea and Chaetetida are important orders.

Order: Stromatoporoidea

CAMBRIAN – CRETACEOUS

Stromatoporoidea are exclusively fossilized organisms which probably had no stem and lived on the bed of warmer seas. Colonies of these created extensive limestone cliffs, mainly in the Paleozoic. The individual groups were solid, cylindrical, spherical, plate-shaped or branching, and could grow to a size from a few millimeters to several metres. The cylindrical colonies were attached to the bed with the whole of the base or with only a short stem. The polyps lived at the surface of a colony.

The actual skeleton of the stromatoporoidea *(cenosteum)* is a single skeleton, usually consisting of two structural elements – *horizontal plates (lamellae)* and *vertical columns (pilae)*, which have a round cross section, and may be long (crossing the plates), or short, connecting only the two adjacent plates. The surface of a colony is sometimes smooth, and sometimes grainy or even wart-like. Star-shaped elements *(astrorizes)* are visible on the warts on the surface of a colony, or directly on the lamellae, and fine branching rays connect these to the center, with a vertical canal running through them.

Amphipora ■

SILURIAN – PERMIAN

The genus *Amphipora* usually has a branching, cylindrical cenosteum with eight canals in the middle. On the edge of the usually rough surface, there are generally hollow blisters. There are no lamellae or astrorizes, and in this, *Amphipora* differs from the other Stromatoporoidea. The genus *Amphipora* was widespread from the Silurian to the Permian, and eleven species have been identified altogether. Fossilized specimens have been found in Europe, North America, Africa, Asia and Australia. The species illustrated here, *Amphipora ramosa*, is characteristic of the Middle Devonian in Moravia, where it forms amphiporous limestone in certain places. The diameter of the individual branches of the species *Amphipora ramosa* in the photograph is approximately 5–10 mm ($^5/_{16}$–$^3/_8$ in).

Amphipora ramosa
Middle Devonian, Adamov, Czech Republic

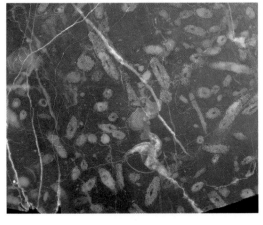

Actinostroma vastum
Lower Devonian, Koněprusy, Czech Republic

Actinostroma ■

CAMBRIAN – LOWER CARBONIFEROUS

The genus *Actinostroma* has a cenosteum with a clear net-like structure. The vertical columns uninterruptedly penetrate the lamellae over a long distance, in contrast with the well-developed lamellae, which are often interrupted. A cross section shows that the two elements together form a network of square eyes. The surface of the club-shaped colony is covered with small tubicles with astrorizes. The genus *Actinostroma* was widespread all over the world from the Cambrian to the Lower Carboniferous. The species illustrated here is 10.5 cm (4 in) long.

Order: Chaetetida

ORDOVICIAN – EOCENE

This group of extinct, marine, stemless coelenterates is characterized by the fact that they lived in massive colonies of different organisms, varying in size from a few centimeters to several decimeters. They formed skeletons consisting of calcium carbonate. The individual polyps had their own skeleton (polyparium), which was long and narrow. They had a striking fibrous structure, and there was a suture at the point of contact between two corallites. The colony grew by budding at the base, or by division of the partition. As they grew, polyps separated from the uninhabited part of the polyparia with horizontal plates. The Chaetetidiae inhabited shallow seas and were at their peak during the Carboniferous.

Barrandeolites ■

SILURIAN

The stemless, living colonies of corals of the species *Barrandeolites* are formed of narrow polyparia, compressed on the side, which are polygonal in cross section. Although they were very common in Europe in Silurian strata, this genus has not been accurately described up to the present day. The maximum width of the colony of the species *Barrandeolites bowerbanki* in the photograph is 8 cm (3 in). The colorful surface of the colony is the result of the mixing of volcanic ash in the sediment where the fossil was found.

Class: Scyphozoa – jellyfish

PROTEROZOIC – RECENT TIMES

Jellyfish mainly include solitary coelenterates which move about freely, and usually have a radial symmetry. There are stinging cells in the skin. There are two different body structures in the life history of an individual organism: the sexually immature, fixed polyp and the sexually mature, free-swimming jellyfish. Except in the extinct subclass Conularia, jellyfish do not have a hard skeleton, and consequently they were unlikely to survive. It is extremely rare to find impressions of the soft body of jellyfish. Only the subclass Conulata has greater significance for paleontology.

Barrandeolites bowerbanki
Upper Silurian, Amerika u Mořiny, Czech Republic

Subclass: Conulata – Conularia

MIDDLE CAMBRIAN – TRIASSIC

The position of this group in the classification is not entirely clear. Initially it was classified under snails. It was only in the early 1970s that it was classified under coelenterates as a specialist group of jellyfish, on the basis of detailed research into specimens which had been preserved in good condition.

The bodies of these exclusively marine organisms were covered by a thin, but strong and flexible chitinous skeleton (*periderm, exoskeleton*), partly reinforced with phosphorous carbonate. The skeleton is in the shape of an inverse cone or pyramid, with a polygonal, quadrilateral, diamond or triangular base. The angle at the top varies from 5° to 40°. The skeleton is usually a maximum of 10 cm (4 in) long, though some specimens reach a maximum length of 40 cm (15³/₄ in). The walls of the skeleton are elongated at the top to form triangular plates – *mouth lobes*, which fold down above the open end of the skeleton, forming *the mouth*. The walls of the skeleton cross each other in so-called *angular lines*. Usually there are parallel *side grooves* running along these lines. The middle of the walls is reinforced by lengthwise partitions, *septa*. On the surface these are visible as shallow grooves, or so-called *cardinal fossulae*. In this way every wall is divided in two.

The surface of the skeletons is usually richly sculpted with grooves running across and along the length. The surface was smooth in primitive forms. In some cases, a disc-shaped plate has survived at the top of the skeleton, which served to attach individuals of some species to the substratum. Mature specimens of Conularia floated freely like modern jellyfish. However, the mouth probably pointed downwards. Movement through water was probably achieved with the arms and mouth lobes. There is no information about soft tissue, and little is known about how they lived. Important development of Conularia occurred during the Paleozoic. They became extinct at the start of the Mesozoic. Classification of Conularia is based on skeleton shape, structure and sculpture of the walls, and shape of the cardinal fossulae.

Anaconularia ∎

ORDOVICIAN

The skeleton of the genus *Anaconularia* has a smooth surface, in the shape of a tall, slender pyramid, slightly twisted along its axis. The sides are sharp, without grooves. *Anaconularia* inhabited the shallow parts of the seas in the Ordovician in parts of present-day Europe. The height of the stone center of the species *Anaconularia anomala* shown in the photograph is 6.5 cm (2⁹/₁₆ in).

Anaconularia anomala
Middle Ordovician, Drabov u Berouna, Czech Republic

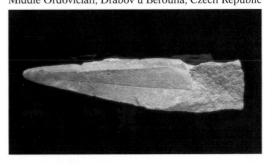

Pseudoconularia ∎

ORDOVICIAN – SILURIAN

Skeletons of *Pseudoconularia* are curious because they measure up to 40 cm (15³/₄ in) and for the striking decoration of the surfaces, consisting of regular rows of tubercles where transverse and lengthwise ribs cross. The lengthwise ribs are most visible. A cross section of the skeleton reveals a square shape. The case is tall and slender. The slightly curving walls curve out at an angle of 20–25° and are divided by a central cardinal fossula. *Pseudoconularia* has been identified in Ordovician and Silurian strata in Europe and America. The part of the broken case of *Pseudoconularia grandissima* illustrated here is 6.5 cm (2⁹/₁₆ in) long. Of the three Ordovician species of Conularia, this is the most common.

Pseudoconularia grandissima
Middle Ordovician, Vráž u Berouna, Czech Republic

Class: Anthozoa – corals

UPPER CAMBRIAN – RECENT TIMES

These include the best organized coelenterates, which only live in seas. No freshwater representatives have ever been identified. Rock-forming corals inhabit warm, tropical and subtropical shallow seas with clean water, rich in oxygen, where they often form gigantic reefs. Solitary species are found at any depth. Corals which only produce layers, but no rocks, inhabit both shallow and deep waters (up to more than 1,800 m/5,905 ft). They are most common at depths of 200–400 m (656–1,312 ft). Corals which form rocks inhabit warm, shallow waters with plenty of air and oxygen, where they usually grow on a strong limestone sea bed. It is characteristic of corals that they have only developed the polyp stage. They reproduce both sexually and asexually. Asexual reproduction is normal for colonial species. The colonies mainly develop by means of budding (e.g., on the sides, on the periphery or from partitions). They attach themselves to the sea bed and sometimes form entire colonies of the same flowers. This is the derivation of the scientific name of corals – Anthozoa (from the Greek anthos = flower, and zoon = animal). Corals generally have a cylindrical or conical shape. The mouth opening passes into a digestive canal which leads to the cavity, divided by fleshy partitions or *septa (mesenterium)*. Around the mouth, there is a ring of tentacles, and their number corresponds to the number of mesenteries. Some corals secrete isolated calcareous spicules or horny elements, – *spiculae* – which sometimes fuse to form a systematic skeleton. However, the majority of corals secrete an external skeleton with an ectodermic origin, known in solitary individuals as *corallite*, and for corals which live in colonies as the *polyparium*. When an external skeleton is secreted, vertical walls – *septa* – are formed at the same time. These are important for the classification of the coral. Fossilized corals are important indicators of the climate and the depth of the sea during various geological periods, and are therefore very important for paleontology.

The class of corals is systematically divided into five subclasses on the basis of the type of skeleton and the number and shape of the mesenterial partitions. We will only mention the three subclasses here which are of interest from a stratigraphic viewpoint.

Subclass: Zoantharia

ORDOVICIAN – RECENT TIMES

These are corals which either live as solitary individuals, or in colonies, and usually secrete a strong calcareous skeleton. They have single or divided tentacles, though these are never pinnate around the mouth. The size of the polyps fluctuates between 1 mm–3 cm ($^1/_{32}$–$1^3/_{16}$ in), though can achieve 30 cm (12 in). In the case of corallite, it is possible to di-

stinguish the lower *base*, a cylindrical or conical *stem*, and an upper *cup*, comprising a cavity (lumen) and the wall of the cup, as well as the plateau of the cup at its base. There is great variety in the shapes of corallites. Some form colonies which are either branching or solid. The branching types can be *bushy (dendroid)* if the individual corallites grow in radiating lines, or in bunches, if they grow parallel to each other. Two types can be distinguished in solid colonies, the *ceroid* type, in which individual are separated by a calcareous wall *(ephiteca)*, and the *plokoid* type, where the *epitheca* is not developed and the individual corallites are interconnected only by septa. The epitheca, which separate and protect the side walls of the polyp, connect with the first cup-shaped skeleton *(protheca)*, consisting of a disc at the base, with which the coral larva attaches itself to the sea bed. In massive types living in colonies, a common epitheca (or *holotheca)* is developed. The space in the corallite is divided by vertical and horizontal elements of the skeleton. These are vertical calcareous dividing plates known as *septa* or *sclerosepta,* which support fleshy mesenteries. The basic building blocks consist of vertical calcareous fibers *(trabecula)*. Horizontal elements form regular bases *(tabulae)* and small bases *(disepimenta)*. These are thin, horizontal, concave or convex lamellae, which partly or entirely fill the inside space of the corallite, forming a *tabularium*. The small bases are formed of tissue containing air bubbles. This space is known as the *disepimentarium.* In some cases, cylindrical or spiny prominences develop on the sides of the septa. These are *synapticula*, which can connect the individual septa. In some corals there are axial structures such as a column *(columela)*, which fills the axis of the corallite and usually penetrates the base of the cup protruding from this, or a *stereocolumela*, which develops because the axis of the septa is consolidated. The secondary walls *(pseudotheca)* which develop in the individual corallites sometimes

Acanthophyllum sp.
Devonian, Čelechovice, Czech Republic

resemble *epitheca*. This could be the *septotheca*, developed when septa fuse, or *sclerotheca*, which develops when disepimenta fuse. Zoantharia comprise two orders of stratigraphic importance: Rugosa and Scleractinia.

Order: Rugosa (Tetracorallia) – rugosa corals (radial symmetry)

ORDOVICIAN – PERMIAN

Rugose corals exclusively comprise Paleozoic corals which were usually solitary. The relatively strong outer wall, which is roughly sculpted, is characteristic. The name is derived from the Latin, *rugosus* or rough. When corals formed colonies, they retained considerable independence, as revealed by the outer walls which have survived (epitheca). Sclerosepta are secondary. They have well-developed vertical septa, and a distinction can be made between *major septa* and *minor septa*, respectively *septa I, II, and III*. Horizontal dividing plates (bases) are less developed, and usually combined with a diagonal tissue filled with air bubbles or there are none. Sclerosepta are arranged in bilateral or radiating symmetry. The number of septa is four-fold. In some radial symmetric corals the cup cavity was covered with a calcareous lid. Solitary corals usually reproduced sexually, while colonial corals reproduced asexually, budding to produce new coral, except for the primary individual which was at the origin of the community. Rugose corals lived in shallow seas since the Ordovician. They were a strongly developed group of coelenterates, and multiplied most rapidly during the Silurian. The first primitive representatives were very simple, and did not have disepimenta. These developed at the start of the Silurian, when more perfect rugose corals evolved. The columela appeared during the Carboniferous. Varieties with septa in six groups, appeared during the Permian.

Acantophyllum ■

DEVONIAN

Acantophyllum comprises solitary corals, in which the corallite is almost cylindrical with clearly walls and grooves. The cup is shallow. Only the septa in order I. reach the axis, where they coil in a spiral. The base contains pockets of air and is generally curved down on the sides. Specimens have been identified from the Devonian in Europe. The coral illustrated is 15 cm (6 in) long.

Calceola sandalina
Middle Devonian, Germany

Calceola ■

DEVONIAN

The calceolid shape of the corallite is characteristic of the representatives of the genus *Calceola*. In cross section it is semicircular. The lid which covers the cup also has this shape. The flat side normally lies on the sea bed. The arrangement of septa consists of a large number of thin inflated septa, which form fine grooves on the surface of the cup. The genus *Calceola* was common all over the world during the Devonian. The species *Calceola sandalina* is the most important Middle Devonian fossil. The specimen illustrated here measures 2 cm ($^3/_4$ in).

Phillipsastrea ■

DEVONIAN

The genus *Phillipsastrea* comprises colonial species. There are no walls between the individual corallites in the colony; they are linked together by septa or disepimenta. The septa become broader, especially on the inside of the disepimentarium. The corals of the genus *Phillipsastrea* made an important contribution to building Devonian rocks. They have been found in Europe, Asia and Australia. The colony consisting of the species *Phillipsastrea* cf. *ananas* which is illustrated here measures 15 cm (16 in).

Phillipsastrea cf. ananas
Middle Devonian, Erfoud region, Morocco

49

Hexagonaria percarinata
Middle Devonian, Hungry Hollow, Canada

Dohmophyllum cyathoides
Middle Devonian, Eifel, Germany

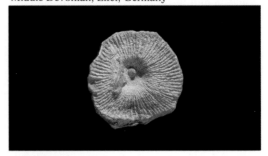

Hexagonaria ■

DEVONIAN – LOWER CARBONIFEROUS

The corals of the genus *Hexagonaria* form massive, loaf-shaped colonies, with strong walls between the corallites. The exceptionally long, prismatic corallites, which touch along the entire length of the side walls, usually have an hexagonal cross section, which explains the name of this genus. The many septa are long and thin, and in some species they extend to the axis form a pseudocolumela. The disepimenta are thin, but numerous. During the Devonian, the genus *Hexagonaria* was common throughout the world.

Goniophyllum ■

SILURIAN

The genus *Goniophyllum* is a clearly visible solitary corallite in the shape of a broad square-based pyramid. The short cup has rounded sides and is slightly curved, often with wart-like extensions on the top. The cup has a lid which consists of four triangular plates. The septa are thick, usually interconnected, and as long as the disepimentarium is wide. There are numerous bases and false bases, and they are usually reinforced. The genus *Goniophyllum* has been identified in Silurian strata in Europe and North America. The photograph shows a specimen of *Goniophyllum pyramidale*, seen from above (right) and the side (left). The corallite is 2.4 cm (1 in).

Goniophyllum pyramidale
Upper Silurian, Dudley, Great Britain

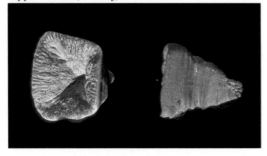

Dohmophyllum ■

MIDDLE DEVONIAN

The solitary corals of the genus *Dohmophyllum* are fairly striking, because of their large cups in the shape of a curved horn. The many major septa are long, reinforced and cylindrical. They extend as far as the central axis and coil around each other in a spiral, curving and becoming thicker. The bases are flat, with an irregular curve towards the base in the center. There are a large number of small disepimenta on the periphery. Representatives of the genus *Dohmophyllum* have been identified dating from the Middle Devonian in Europe, the Urals and Australia. The photograph of the specimen of the species *Dohmophyllum cyathoides* clearly shows a flat, shallow cup with a diameter of 5.6 cm (2 in).

Order: Scleractinia (Hexacorallia) – corals with septa in groups of six

MIDDLE TRIASSIC – RECENT TIMES

These corals usually form colonies. They have a calcareous external skeleton, secreted by the ectoderm. They usually have a cylindrical structure with a radial parallel symmetry. There are tentacles around the mouth, in multiples of six. The calcareous partitions (septa) and the other supporting systems which form the skeleton of these corals are arranged in groups of 6, 12, 24 etc. The majority of the structural elements correspond to those of corals with septa in groups of four. In contrast, calcareous structures are often visible in these corals *(cenosteum, cenenchym)*, which fill up the spaces between the individual corallites in a colony. The cenosteum can be massive or porous, and forms both horizontal and vertical structural elements.

It is possible to reconstruct the environment of these corals on the basis of their recent ancestors. They live in light, shallow seas, usually up to a depth of 45 m (147 ft), where the temperature does not fall below 18.5 °C (65.3 °F). They require sunlight, and one of the necessary conditions of life is a lot of movement in the sea water, that must be rich in oxygen and supply nutrients in the form of fine plankton, at the same time as removing assault on the colonies. Solitary specimens inhabit significantly deeper waters, usually between 200–500 m (656–1,640 ft). Some specimens have been identified at depths of 600 m (1,968 ft), and are therefore adapted to much lower temperatures and to darkness.

The first fossils of corals with groups of six septa date from the Middle Triassic. These lived in colonies. They developed quickly from the Middle Jurassic in Europe, and the rock-forming variety in particular developed from the Upper Jurassic. They are some of the most important rock-forming organisms dating from the Jurassic up to the present day. Because of their great sensitivity to changes in the environment, corals play an important stratigraphic role.

Meandrina

UPPER CRETACEOUS – RECENT TIMES

This genus of corals with groups of six septa forms massive colonies with a characteristic appearance. They consist of long, meandering colonies which developed as a result of the asexual budding of the corallites, when new polyps grow in the arms, and the corallites remain interconnected.

The many septa are thin and short. *Meandrina* has been found in Europe and America in strata dating

Meandrina sp.
Upper Cretaceous, Gosau, Austria

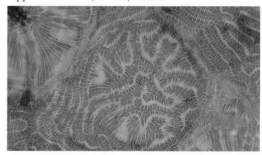

from the Upper Cretaceous to the present day. The individual, winding strips of the colony in the photograph are approximately 0.3 cm (0.1 in).

Dendrophyllia

EOCENE – RECENT TIMES

The corals of the genus *Dendrophyllia* form colonies of the dendroid type, which multiply by means of asexual budding, if the individual polyps do not grow between the arms, but outside. The corallites are isolated in the colony and are far apart. They have a strong coenosteum. The representatives of the genus *Dendrophyllia* appeared in the Eocene and spread all over the world. They still exist today. The coral colony illustrated here, *Dendrophyllia cornigera*, is 2.5 cm (1 in) across.

Dendrophyllia cornigera
Middle Miocene, Pauvrelay, France

Enallhelia compressa
Upper Jurassic, Schnaitheim, Germany

Enallhelia ■

MIDDLE JURASSIC – LOWER CRETACEOUS

The genus *Enallhelia* comprises several species of coral with groups of six septa, which form colonies of the dendroid type. The individual branches of these extensively branching colonies are fairly thin, and tend to develop in one plane. The polyparia are small and are only divided by a small number of septa. Generally they grow in an alternating pattern along the branches. The genus *Enallhelia* has been identified dating from the Middle Jurassic to the Lower Cretaceous in present-day Europe, Asia and South America. The coral group of the species *Enallhelia compressa* measures 6 cm ($2^3/_8$ in).

Thecosmilia ■

MIDDLE TRIASSIC – CRETACEOUS

Corals of the genus *Thecosmilia* form solid colonies of the fascelloid type. The individual corals are free-standing, or form short, thick branches with two to three specimens. They are virtually cylindrical with many thin septa which widen at the top. There is either no columela, or it is rudimentary. Corals of *Thecosmilia* multiply by budding. They have been identified from the Middle Triassic to the Cretaceous. The genus *Thecosmilia* was particularly widespread all over the world in the Jurassic. The colony of corals of the species *Thecosmilia trichotoma* in the photograph measures 6 cm ($2^3/_8$ in).

Thecosmilia trichotoma
Upper Jurassic, Schnaitheim, Germany

Thecosmilia costata
Jurassic, Switzerland

Aulosmilia ■

UPPER CRETACEOUS – EOCENE

The genus *Aulosmilia* consists of solitary corals, usually in the shape of a fan-shaped wedge, because the widened cup is generally compressed on the sides. The cup contains a large number of septa and is pointed at the bottoms or has a short stem. There are also a large number of disepimenta. The columela contains lamellae. Corals of *Aulosmilia* species have particularly been identified in Cretaceous strata in Western and Central Europe. The size of the individual corals of the species *Aulosmilia archiaci* (formerly *Placosmilia vidali)* shown in the photograph varies around 5.5 cm (2 in).

Balanophyllia ■

EOCENE – RECENT TIMES

The corals of the genus *Balanophyllia* are solitary, forming independent, virtually cylindrical cups with a broad encrusted base. The columela is spongy and the septa are closely grouped and often fuse. Representatives of the genus *Balanophyllia* appeared in the Eocene and are still found today. Their fossilized remains are mainly found in Central Europe. The photograph shows a coral of the species *Balanophyllia inaequidens* which measures 1.5 cm ($^5/_8$in).

Balanophyllia inaequidens
Lower Oligocene, Weinheim, Germany

Aulosmilia archiaci
Upper Cretaceous, Santa Maria, Spain

53

Cyclolites macrostoma, seen from above
Upper Cretaceous, Gosau, Austria

Cyclolithes macrostoma, seen from below
Upper Cretaceous, Gosau, Austria

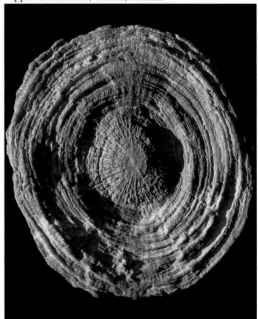

Cyclolithes ■

CRETACEOUS – EOCEEN

The genus *Cyclolithes* comprises solitary corals, in which the corallites are in the shape of a low, rounded loaf. The flat bottom is covered with a wrinkled epitheca, and the top is rounded. There are numerous thin, perforated septa which cross each other in an extended groove. They are interconnected by synapticula and lateral pieces. The edges of the septa are indented. The genus *Cyclolithes* was widespread from the Cretaceous to the Eocene. Fossilized remains have mainly been found in the Cretaceous strata of present-day Eurasia, North Africa and the Caribbean. The specimen of the species *Cyclolithes macrostoma* shown here measures approximately 5 cm (2 in).

Porites ■

JURASSIC – RECENT TIMES

The genus *Porites* consists of corals with septa in groups of six which form massive branching colonies. The individual corallites have a fine structure and are arranged close together, but do not have an outer wall; they are connected by porous calcareous walls *(cenenchym)*. They have only a small number of septa and the columela consists of a small number of columns. The genus *Porites* is one of the most important rock-forming corals. Fossils of this genus have been found dating from the Jurassic, and they are found virtually all over the world.

Montlivaltia ■

MIDDLE TRIASSIC – CRETACEOUS

The corals of the genus *Montlivaltia* are solitary. Their corallites are usually large, and in the shape of a virtually cylindrical or trochoid dome. The many septa are indented on the edges and touch each other, forming a long groove. There is often no epitheca. The columela is only primitively developed. The genus *Montlivaltia* was present from the Middle Triassic to the Cretaceous, and then became widespread across the whole world during the Triassic and Jurassic. The coral of the species *Montlivaltia lessneuri* illustrated here, is 7 cm ($2^3/_4$ in) tall.

Madrepora ■

EOCENE – RECENT

The genus *Madrepora* forms colonies of the dendroid type. The small corallites have a round shape and are interconnected by a well-developed, solid cenosteum. The number of septa varies from six to twelve, and they are thick and wedge-shaped. When there is a columela, it is spongy. The genus has been common all over the world since the Eocene. It is an important rock-forming coral in the oceans now, living at depths from 200–1,550 m (656–5,085 ft). The fragment of the colony of the species *Madrepora solanderi* shown in the photograph is 46 mm ($1^3/_4$ in) tall.

Porites pusilla
Miocene, Sabkhat Ghuzayil, Libya

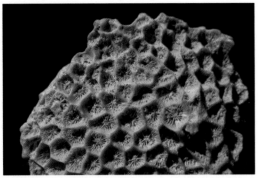

Halysites catenularia
Middle Silurian, Wenlock, Great Britain

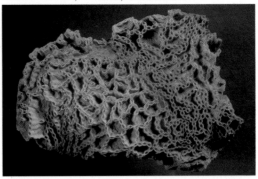

Subclass: Tabulata
– Tabulate corals

UPPER CAMBRIAN – PERM

Tabulate corals live exclusively in colonies. They have small angular or tubular corallites with a diameter of 0.5–4.0 mm (0.02–0.15 in), which incline together with the whole of their side walls, or are arranged one behind the other. In contrast with corals with septa in groups of four, the septa of tabulate corals are very primitively developed, although the two types of coral lived in the same way. The dominant structural elements in the corallite are horizontal dividing plates – bases *(tabulae)*, which can be complete or incomplete. Tabulate corals hardly ever have disepimenta, synapticula or a columela.

Colonies of tabulate corals consist of a large number of individuals and are fairly large, growing to an average size of 1 m (39 in). They are massive, branching like a bush, and multiply gradually. They reproduced most often by means of budding, forming carpets of growth on the shallow sea bed. The oldest tabulate corals date from the Upper Cambrian. They reached the peak of their development in the Silurian and Devonian. Their numbers declined from the Car-

boniferous, and they apparently became extinct during the Permian, although some uncertain specimens have been found dating from the Mesozoic. It is an important stratigraphic group, particularly from the Silurian to the Lower Carboniferous.

The systematic classification of tabulate corals is not entirely clear. It appears that they are related in some way to the Stromatoporoidea, as well as to animal sponges.

Halysites ■

UPPER ORDOVICIAN – UPPER SILURIAN

The corals of *Halysites* are curious and easily recognizable tabulate corals. They form bushy fascelloid colonies. The long, cylindrical polyparia are compressed on the side, and are only interconnected by small, virtually oblong tubes on their narrow sides. In this way, they form characteristic, irregularly curving chains, in cross section. There are no pores in the walls, and there are not usually any in the septa either. There are many horizontal or concave bases. *Halysites* was widespread all over the world from the Middle Ordovician to the Upper Silurian. The species *Halysites catenularia* in the photograph was described first in Great Britain and Sweden by Linneaus in 1767.

Montlivaltia lessneuri
Upper Jurassic, Le Havre, France

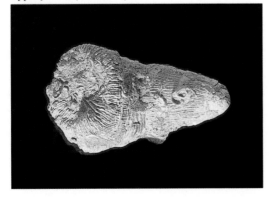

Madrepora solanderi
Eocene, Antwerp, Belgium

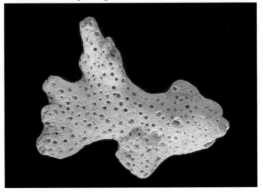

55

Catenipora escharoides
Lower Silurian, Gotland, Sweden

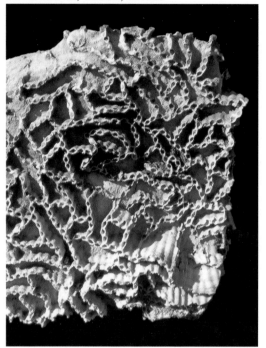

Favosites sp.
Silurian, Dudley, Great Britain

Catenipora ■

UPPER ORDOVICIAN – UPPER SILURIAN

The genus *Catenipora* is extremely similar to the genus *Halysites*, although there are no connecting tubes between the equally large corallites. However, the genus *Catenipora* was not as widespread as the genus *Halysites*. The photograph shows part of a colony of the species *Catenipora escharoides,* which is 7.5 cm (3 in)wide.

Favosites ■

MIDDLE ORDOVICIAN – PERMIAN

The genus *Favosites* probably belongs to the most widespread and most common varieties of tabulate corals. It forms solid, irregular bulb-shaped colonies with a diameter of 50 cm (19$^1/_2$ in), consisting of prismatic polyparia, polygonal in cross section, arranged closely together. The walls are usually thin with large pores, generally arranged in single rows. The septa are reduced to so-called septal thorns. The large number of horizontal or curving bases are complete. The genus *Favosites* was common all over the world, from the Ordovician to the Permian. It is worth noting that this genus was described by Lamarck as long ago as 1816, at a time when most interest was focused on trilobites.

Pleurodictyum ■

UPPER SILURIAN – MIDDLE DEVONIAN

The small disc-shaped or semi-spherical colonies of the genus *Pleurodictyum* are formed by narrow polyparia closely clumped together, which are polygonal or almost cylindrical in cross section. The rather thick walls are perforated by numerous pores. The septa are usually rudimentary and in the shape of spines. The bases may be incomplete or even entirely absent. The genus *Pleurodictyum* was common from the Upper Silurian to the Middle Devonian, and fossils have been found in Europe, Asia and Africa. It is curious to note that the genus is often found together with spores of the worm *Hicetes*, as can be seen in the cross section of the coral colony of the species *Pleurodictyum problematicum* in the photograph. The colony's diameter is 1.7 cm($^{11}/_{16}$ in).

Syringopora ■

UPPER ORDOVICIAN – LOWER PERMIAN

Colonies of the fascelloid type of the genus *Syringopora* consist of cylindrically formed polyparia which do not usually touch, but are connected by thin, randomly arranged lateral tubes (stolones). The thick walls of the polyparia do not have any pores. There are no septa, or they have developed in the form of a row of spines. The funnel-shaped bases are very thick. The genus *Syringopora* was found all over

Pleurodictyum problematicum
Lower Devonian, Oberstadtfeld, Germany

the world, from the Upper Ordovician to the Lower Permian. The colony of the species *Syringopora serpens* illustrated here is 10.5 cm (4¹/₄ in) across.

Aulopora ■

ORDOVICIAN – PERMIAN

The genus *Aulopora* forms small, creeping or standing colonies. The whole of the bottom is attached to the sea bed. The individual polyparia are in the shape of short horns and have thick walls. Sometimes there are septal spines.
The horizontal bases are often missing, and when

they have developed at all, frequently incomplete. The genus *Aulopora* was common all over the world from the Ordovician to the Permian. The colonies of the species *Aulopora serpens* illustrated here, attached to a specimen of the Stromatoporoidea, is 6 cm (2³/₈ in) tall.

Aulopora serpens
Middle Devonian, Gerolstein, Germany

Syringopora serpens
Upper Silurian, Dudley, Great Britain

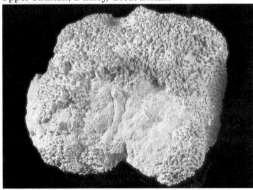

Subclass: Heliolitoidea – Heliolitida

MIDDLE ORDOVICIAN – MIDDLE DEVONIAN

This group consisted of colonial corals without stems. The massive, semi-circular, disc-shaped, plate-shaped or loaf-shaped colonies consist of small corallites. Every corallite contains a cup, with twelve septa, or septa in multiples of twelve, although they can also be entirely absent. The bases are well developed. The cylindrical corallites – *autopory* – are arranged in a delicate lattice work *(cenenchym, cenosteum)*, consisting of polygonal bars *(siphonopora)*.

The oldest known Heliolitida date from the last part of the Middle Ordovician. They developed most strongly during the Silurian. Together with tabulates and corals with septa in groups of four, the Heliolitida were widespread all over the world, inhabiting warm, shallow seas with sufficient calcium carbonate. This can be deduced from the development of the cenenchym of the tabulate corals, which forms the basis for the whole system of the Heliolitida.

Heliolites ■

UPPER ORDOVICIAN – MIDDLE DEVONIAN

The genus *Heliolites* forms solid bulb-shaped or semi-spherical colonies. The individual polyparia are cylindrical, rounded or rose-shaped in cross section, and they are separated by the cenenchym, which developed in the shape of thin polygonal tubes. The septa are usually formed by twelve septal spines. The horizontal bases are complete. The genus *Heliolites* was common all over the world, and specimens have been found dating from the Upper Ordovician to the Middle Devonian. The largest diameter of the colony of the species *Heliolites interstinctus* illustrated here is 7.5 cm (3 in).

Heliolites interstinctus
Lower Silurian, Visby, Sweden

Serpula socialis
Upper Cretaceous, Česká Třebová, Czech Republic

Phylum: Annelida – Annelids

PROTOROZOIC – RECENT TIMES

Annelids represent the most important phylum of the so-called higher worms. They are the oldest multi-cellular organisms with a bilaterally symmetrical body. This bilateral symmetry of the body was most probably the result of the transition from a life form without a stem to a life form with free movement.

The body of annelids is divided into a head *(prosoma)*, a digestive tract *(metasoma)* and tail section *(pygidium, telzon)*. The elongated body is segmented, and the individual segments are visible at the surface and in the body, separated from each other by partitions. There are small, muscular parapodia with chitinous bristles on the side of each segment, which, in combination with the parapodia, enable the worm to move forward.

Nerve centers were concentrated in the head – the brain, the sensors – eyes, feelers, and an organ to ingest food. The mouth served to take in the food, and there was an excretory aperture at the other end of the body so that the digestive system was no longer a closed cavity. Annelids had developed a respiratory system and a complete vascular system (they had already developed a heart), which made it possible to transport oxygen through the whole body. The body consists of a large number of rings (up to eight

Serpula proteus
Upper Cretaceous, Kent, Great Britain

hundred). The tail section is not divided into rings.
Annelids are both aquatic animals (mainly marine animals) and land animals, and live in virtually all geographical areas. Some crawl along the sea bed, while others dig themselves into the mud. However, there are also species which resemble plankton and nekton. Annelids feed in extremely different ways. They can feed on organic waste matter, and they can be vegetarian, carnivorous or parasitical.

Annelids have different sexes or they are hermaphrodite. In benthic species a transparent *larva (trochofora)* develops from the egg, which initially floats in the sea water as part of plankton. After a few weeks it descends down to the sea bed, where it continues to grow to become a mature organism.

It is assumed that annelids developed from coelenterates. There is very little palaeontological information available regarding the development of this group of animals, which was important in terms of numbers and from the phylogenetic point of view, because they did not form a skeleton that could be fossilized. Therefore they were not of stratigraphic importance. Fossilized representatives mainly belong to the class of Polychaeta.

Class: Polychaeta
– brush worms

PROTEROZOIC – RECENT TIMES

These are almost exclusively marine annelids, most of which live in coastal strips at depths up to 40 m (131 ft), mainly on the sea bed *(bentos)*. Only a small number live in the open sea *(pelagic)*. Their soft, segmented body is sometimes protected by a horny, agglutinated or calcareous skeleton, which can have a lid. The digestive tract usually has a biting mechanism.

Fossilized brush worms have been identified by their fossilized calcium carbonate skeletons, brushes, and chitinous mandibles. In addition, traces of gnawing and tracks of crawling have survived on or in sediments.

Serpula ■

SILURIAN – RECENT TIMES

Representatives of the genus *Serpula* formed calcareous tubular skeletons up to 10 cm (4 in) long. They have an irregular coil or spiral shape, and are ring-form in cross section. The skeleton is attached to the sea bed at the bottom of the tube. The top of the tube is more or less vertical, and the surface of the skeleton is decorated with fine, concentric rings. The lid is horny or calcareous. The genus existed all over the world and is found in Silurian strata, but became more common from the Jurassic. The long, straight tubes, interconnected in bunches or bundles, are characteristic of *Serpula socialis*, which existed in the Jurassic and Cretaceous. The bunch of tubes of the species shown in the photograph is 6 cm (2³/₈ in)long, the diameter of the individual tubes is 0.7 mm (0.02 in). The diameter of the spiraling part of the tube of the other species, *Serpula proteus*, is 1.5 cm.

Spirorbis ■

ORDOVICIAN – RECENT TIMES

The genus *Spirorbis* is characterized by fine calcareous skeletons, coiled like a snail. The skeleton is attached to the sea bed with the bottom of the older part, and the newer whorls are usually free. On the surface of the skeleton, there are often concentric grooves or rings, as well as thorns. The genus *Spirorbis* was widespread all over the world, originally in salt water and fresh water, but now inhabits only the sea. Specimens have been found dating from the Ordovician onwards. The diameter of the skeletons of the species in this photograph, *Spirorbis pusillus*, is a maximum of 2 mm (¹/₁₆ in).

Spirorbis pusillus
Upper Carboniferous, Holzwickede, Germany

3. Arthropods

There is an exceptionally large number of species of arthropods (Arthropoda), which have evolved from annelids. Furthermore, they are the most numerous and extensive class of invertebrates. Nowadays, almost 80 % of invertebrate animal species described up to the present belong to this family. The oldest fossilized remains of arthropods date from the end of the Proterozoic. At the beginning of the Paleozoic, in the Lower Cambrian, there were representatives of all the main groups of arthropods, except insects. Fossilized insects have only been found dating from the Devonian. Arthropods were originally marine animals. Of all the invertebrates, they were best able to adapt to extremely different environments during the course of the geological periods. In addition to marine environments, they also live in brackish and fresh water, on land, and some also in the air. They are found at every geographical latitude. Mature arthropods reach a size from 0.2 mm to 4 m/0.07 in to 13 ft (the present-day Japanese giant crab).

The bodies of arthropods are bisymmetrical, and consist of 8 to 180 segments, which can only be seen on the surface of the body. The segmented body and the limbs of arthropods are their most important characteristic. The three basic parts of the body developed as a result of the gradual grouping of various numbers of original segments in larger specialist units – *the head (caput), the thorax and the abdomen*. The thorax consists of a varying number of hard or flexible jointed segments. The abdomen usually has a different number of moving parts which form a so-called *tail segment (pygidium)* when they are fused. In some cases, the thorax merges with the head in a *cephalothorax*, and in others, the thorax fuses with the abdomen.

The body of arthropods is covered with a strong carapace – *the chitinous carapace* – which is usually reinforced (encrusted) by calcium carbonate or calcium phosphate. This forms a very strong skeleton – *the exoskeleton*, although this restricts the growth of the body. However, the carapace is regularly cast off *(ecdysis)*. For the short period before the new carapace is formed and reinforced, the animal experiences a spurt of intensive growth. The body is joined to the exoskeleton by a number of muscles. The segments of the body generally have limbs which are usually in pairs and are also divided into segments, and are attached with joints. These appendages develop on the basis of their function (movement, respiration, biting, orientation in space).

The important sensory organs are located on the head, which has a well-developed nerve center: smell, touch and sight. There are simple eyes *(ocelli)*

Left: *Paradoxides gracilis*
Middle Cambrian, Jince, Czech Republic

and compound eyes. Ocelli are the original type and are often found with compound eyes, which are more common. The digestive system starts at the bottom of the head with a mouth, which opens into the digestive tube. This runs straight through the body, or turns in a variety of ways and ends in the last segment of the abdomen.

The vascular system of arthropods is open, and the heart tube is at the back. Primitive small aquatic arthropods breathe with the whole body surface. Larger marine arthropods have developed gills, usually with a flaky character, placed on the limbs. In land arthropods, these are *trachea*, distributed over the surface of the body, or *spiracles*.

In general, arthropods multiply by means of sexual reproduction. The hard chitinous exoskeletons of arthropods were – and still are – unusually strong, both physically and chemically. This means that many have survived in the form of fossils up to the present day. For this reason, arthropods are extremely important for paleontology.

Arthropods are classified into several subclasses on the basis of the way the body is segmented and the structure of the limbs. For paleontology, there are four important subclasses: Trilobitomorpha, Chelicta, Crustacea and Tracheata.

Subclass: Trilobitomorpha – trilobites

CAMBRIAN – PERMIAN

Trilobites are the oldest completely extinct group of extremely primitive aquatic arthropods. The back of the body was protected by a chitinous exoskeleton, usually consisting of three oblong lobes (hence the name trilobite). There was a pair of simple feelers on the head on the ventral side, and four pairs of jointed limbs. The limbs on the remaining two parts of the body were also jointed. The inner limb *(endopodite)* and the outer limb *(exopodite)* were extensions of the base *(coxopodite)*. The inner limb served to perform a walking movement, while the outer limb was used for swimming and breathing, as it has filaments which serve as gills.

Class: Trilobita – trilobites

CAMBRIAN – PERMIAN

Trilobites are a very old and widespread group of animals which do not have any close relatives in present-day fauna. This totally extinct category of marine arthropods is often found together with fossils of typically marine animals, such as echinodermata, corals and organisms with tentacles. The structure of their fossilized remains provides information about the way they lived, as does the development (facie) of the sediments of which they are part. They usually inhabited shallow waters not far from the coast, and are generally found in fine sand, limestone shale, chalk rocks or quartz. Their flat bodies, eyes placed on the back, and absence of organs which allow for rapid movement, indicate that trilobites were not good swimmers. They usually moved over the sea bed, digging themselves into the mud or swimming close to the bed. They fed on small organisms or on dead organic matter. There are also species which were active swimmers. There is interesting information available about the characteristics of some trilobites – they were able to turn their carapace to protect themselves against enemies in this way. Nevertheless, they were fairly easy prey for cephalopoda, echinodermata, and eventually also for the first vertebrates, fish. The development of these animals in the seas during the Silurian and the Devonian meant the end of the trilobites. Trilobites were exclusively Paleozoic animals. They already existed in the Lower Cambrian. They reached their peak during the Upper Cambrian and Ordovician. Growth slowed during the Silurian, but in the Devonian the group evolved again and new species developed. In the Carboniferous there was a considerable decline in the number of species and specimens. Only one family is known from the Permian, the Phillipsidae, though it had disappeared by the end of the Paleozoic when trilobites became extinct.

The body of mature trilobites reached a size of between 5 mm to 75 cm ($^3/_{16}$–3 in), though it was most often between 2–10 cm ($^3/_4$–4 in). The back of the body was covered with a hard carapace, divided across and lengthwise into three parts. The body can be divided across into the *carapace for the head (cephalon), the thorax and the pygidium*. The carapace is bilaterally symmetrical on a plane along the axis. This part is separated by two transverse furrows from the two parts on the side, which consist of individual *ribs (pleurae)*. The front edge of the cephalon always curves down so that it covers the ventral part, resulting in a *twofold division (doublure)*. At the bottom of this doublure there is usually a single plate, *the rostrum*, joining a lobe, *the hypostoma*, which covers the mouth. If the rostrum is not developed, the hypostoma is directly connected with the doublure of the cephalon. The protruding axial part of the cephalon is known as the *glabella*. At the base of the glabella, the occipital ring is separated from the rest of the glabella. Other furrows can divide the glabella into *lobes* (front, side and back lobes, etc.). The facial sutures separate the glabella from the sides, or cheeks.

Cheeks can normally be divided into inner cheeks (fixed cheeks), which lie against the glabella, and external cheeks (free cheeks). They are separated by the *facial sutures*, which consist of the *front (preocular), middle (periocular)* and *back (postocular) sections*. The type of facial suture is determined by the place where the suture crosses the posterior border of the cephalon. The *opisthoparian suture* crosses the posterior border of the cephalon, the *proparian suture* ends forward of the genal angle. The backs of the free cheek are either rounded or stretched into a number of long genal spines. The eyes are set on the borders of the cheeks. In some trilobites the eyes were reduced or disappeared completely. In this case, the facial sutures also disappeared. The thorax consists of 2 to 44 segments, though usually of between 8 to 16. The moving, joint-like connections between the segments means that the carapace can be rolled up. The number of segments of the mature animal, which is

The exoskeleton of a trilobite, the back seen from above: A – cephalon, B – thorax, C – pygidium, 1 – preglabellar field, 2 – border, 3 – glabella, 4 – eye, 5 – outer cheek (free), 6 – inner cheek (fixed), 7 – pleural furrow, 8 – occipital ring, 9 – genal spine, 10 – axial ring, 11 – rib (pleura), 12 – preocular limb, 13 – periocular limb, 14 – postocular limb.

Cephalon of trilobite, ventral side: 1 – rostrum, 2 – hypostoma, 3 – doublure

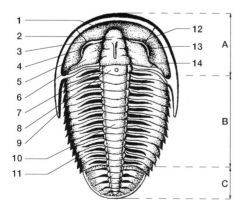

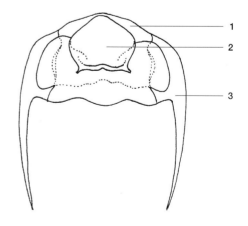

Peronopsis interstrictus
Middle Cambrian, House Range, Utah, United States

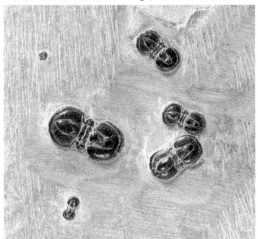

Phalagnostus nudus
Middle Cambrian, Skryje, Czech Republic

permanent for individual species, is one of the most important characteristics for classification. The ventral part of the body has only survived in very exceptional cases. This also applies to the antennae and appendages, because they were only covered with a thin cuticula. The pleura are normally curved back at the outside, and are either bluntly rounded, or extend in spines of different lengths and different shapes. The pygidium is normally round, semi-circular, or a rounded triangular shape. It developed from the fusion of a number of different segments of smaller sizes. Its fundamental structure corresponds to the structure of the thorax, although the segments are generally less striking. The outer edge of the pygidium is either straight or indented in various ways, and provided with spines. In some cases a thorn can be seen along the axis of the pygidium, referred to as a *pygidial spine*.

Trilobites could be classified into diverse genera with a degree of certainty. The regular molting of the carapace was characteristic of the entire ontogenisis (ecdysis). The systematic classification of classes is more or less artificial. It is based on the shape of the exoskeleton. The chief characteristics are the shape of the cephalon, particularly the glabella, the number and structure of the parts of the thorax, the shape of the pygidium, etc.

Order: Agnostida

LOWER CAMBRIAN – UPPER ORDOVICIAN

This includes very small, miniature trilobites, usually 6–10 mm ($^3/_4$–$^3/_8$ in) long, with two or three body rings. The relatively large cephalon and the pygidium are virtually the same size and formed in the same way, which means they are difficult to identify. Normally they had no eyes, and the great majority were blind. There is no ring on the back either. They

have been found all over the world, and are therefore important fossil guides.

Peronopsis ■

MIDDLE CAMBRIAN

Characteristic features of this genus include the oblong shape of the exoskeleton, which is usually 5–7 mm ($^3/_{16}$–$^3/_4$ in) long, the carapace on the head with small border, and glabella with striking square frontal lobe. The genus has no facial suture or eyes. The relatively long central axis of the pygidium reaches almost to the end, and it is just possible to distinguish three rings. *Peronopsis* was extremely widespread in the Middle Cambrian. It has been found in Europe, Asia, North America and Australia. In areas of the Barrandien, in layers of the Middle Cambrian, and the area of Jince, species of this genus are the most common agnostid trilobites. The specimen illustrated is 8 mm ($^5/_{16}$ in) long.

Phalagnostus ■

MIDDLE CAMBRIAN

Trilobites of the genus *Phalagnostus* are characterized by a simple exoskeleton with a semicircular, smooth cephalon without a border. The glabella is not usually visible, and the pygidium closely resembles the cephalon. The genus *Phalagnostus* is found in Middle Cambrian strata in Europe, Asia, North America and Australia. The complete exoskeleton of the species illustrated here, *Phalagnostus nudus*, which is 8 mm ($^5/_{16}$ in) long, clearly shows that the thorax consists of two segments with a broad axis. The pygidium can be distinguished from the cephalon by a short, unobtrusive axis, and a more or less rounded border. The surface is colored with limonite, which is characteristic of trilobites in the shale strata of Skryje.

63

Paradoxides gracilis
Middle Cambrian, Jince, Czech Republic

Class: Redlichiida

LOWER MIDDLE CAMBRIAN

This group of trilobites is characterized by an oval or oblong, slightly convex exoskeleton. The semicircular cephalon has a striking glabella, usually with numerous glabellar furrows. In most cases, there is a striking body ring, sometimes with a tubercle. The eye sockets are often arched. The broad free cheeks end in long genal spines. The facial sutures are opisthoparian. The body consists of 12 to 25 narrow segments, and the pygidium is extremely small. This order includes most of the trilobites which inhabited the oceans of the Lower and Upper Cambrian.

Paradoxides ■

MIDDLE CAMBRIAN

Together with the other characteristic genera, such as *Hydrocephalus* and *Eccaparadoxides,* the genus *Paradoxides* is one of the so-called paradoxical trilobites. These reached lengths of up to 30 cm (12 in) and were widespread throughout the world in the Middle Cambrian. For this reason they became important fossils for collectors and from the stratigraphic point of view. The genus *Paradoxides* is characterized by the pear-shaped glabella which has two pairs of connecting glabellar furrows, long genal spines, a narrow body consisting of 19 to 21 segments and a small, simple pygidium with a segmented axis. The hypostoma and the rostrum are fused. Trilobites of the genus *Paradoxides* have been identified in

Europe, North America and North Africa.
The species illustrated here, *Paradoxides gracilis,* is one of the most common trilobite species. Its slender, long, flat carapace covers a body consisting of twenty segments. The free cheeks and the edges of the pleura end in spines which curve back like sabers. The pygidium with its short central axis is extremely small. In the Barrandien area, it is mainly found in Jince. The specimens shown in the photograph are 5–9 cm (2–3^1/$_2$ in) long.

Hydrocephalus ■

MIDDLE CAMBRIAN

The genus *Hydrocephalus* can be distinguished from the previous *Paradoxides* by a broader body, consisting of seventeen to eighteen segments. Its pear-shaped glabella has four pairs of glabellar furrows and the hypostoma is fused with the rostrum. The pygidium is short. The trilobites of this species lived on the sea bed or dug themselves into the shallow mud. They were certainly not very good swimmers. They are found in Middle Cambrian strata in Europe, Asia (Siberia) and North America. Although the species *Hydrocephalus carens* is very common in the Barrandien region, complete specimens are rarely found there. The size of the specimen of the genus *Hydrocephalus* shown below comes from the Ginselyelli area and is 12 cm (4^3/$_4$ in) long.

Hydrocephalus carens
Middle Cambrian, Skryje, Czech Republic

Hydrocephalus lyelli
Middle Cambrian, Jince, Czech Republic

Elipsocephalus ∎

LOWER – MIDDLE-CAMBRIAN

One of the most important genera of trilobites dating from the Cambrian is the genus *Elipsocephalus*. It has an oval shape with a semicircular cephalon, and a striking, usually smooth glabella which broadens out at the front. The genal angles of the cephalon are rounded. The small cheeks are bordered by opisthoparian facial sutures. The eyes are large. The thorax consists of twelve segments, which become gradually narrower towards the short pygidium. The genus is found in layers of the Lower and Middle Cambrian in Europe, Asia and North America.

The species *Elipsocephalus hoffi* is probably the best known and most common redliichid trilobite in the Jince region. It was one of the first trilobites to be described by the German paleontologist, Schlotheim, as long ago as 1823. Its total length is usually not above 3 cm (1³/₄ in); usually the specimens which are found are whole and well-preserved, often in groups, which is not normally the case for other trilobite species.

Elipsocephalus hoffi
Middle Cambrian, Jince, Czech Republic

Ptychoparia striata
Middle Cambrian, Jince, Czech Republic

Sao hirsuta
Middle Cambrian, Skryje, Czech Republic

Order: Ptychopariida

LOWER CAMBRIAN – PERMIAN

This is the largest order, and comprises trilobites which differ significantly in terms of shape (polymorphous). They are often also very different as regards their development. However, they cannot be classified in the other specialized orders of which the representatives have developed in more or less corresponding ways.

The exoskeletons of ptychoparid trilobites are oval in shape and can become significantly narrower at the back. The glabellae can have very different shapes, and the facial sutures are usually opisthoparian. Some of the genera are blind. The thorax consists of 6 to 25 segments. The pygidium is usually clearly distinguishable and small in the most primitive species. Many hundreds of species of this group are found all over the world, dating from the whole of the Paleozoic.

Ptychoparia ■

MIDDLE CAMBRIAN

Trilobites of this genus have an oval exoskeleton which narrows towards the back. The semicircular cephalon has large eyes, with a rounded trapezium-shaped convex glabella with four pairs of single glabellar furrows. The free cheeks, with a fine nervation visible on the front, end in short genal spines. The facial sutures are opisthparian. The body consists of fourteen segments with a convex axis which becomes noticeably narrower towards the pygidium. This consists of five segments and has a convex segmented axis. The trilobites of the genus *Ptychoparia* inhabi-

ted muddy or sandy, usually shallow sea beds, and were therefore also found along shallow coasts. They are common trilobites in the Middle Cambrian deposits of Central Europe. The specimen illustrated here of the species *Ptychoparia striata* is 7 cm (2³/₄ in) long.

Conocoryphe ■

MIDDLE CAMBRIAN

Collectors often confuse trilobites of this genus with trilobites of the previous genus *Ptychoparia*, because they are very similar. The main difference is the absence of eyes and the blunt conical shape of the three pairs of glabellar furrows of the representatives of the genus *Conocoryphe*. In contrast with the previous genus, trilobites of the genus *Conocoryphe* dug themselves into the muddy sea bed. This is reflected in the fact that they were blind and are now only found in shale dating from the Middle Cambrian in Europe and Morocco. The specimens of the species *Conocoryphe sulzeri* shown in the photograph are 7 cm (2³/₄ in) long.

Sao ■

MIDDLE CAMBRIAN

This is the only well-known representative of this genus. It has a long, oval body. The cephalon is semicircular and has sharp genal angles. The glabella is narrow and conical, narrowing slightly towards the front. Three pairs of deep glabellar furrows cross each other on the glabella. The eyes are an average size. The exoskeleton of a mature specimen grows to a length of 3 cm (1³/₄ in). The whole surface of the back is covered with small tubercles close together, arranged in lines across the back, and with hollow conical spines, arising from the occipital ring and every axial ring. This accounts for the name of the species (the Latin word 'hirsutus' means bristly). The thorax consists of seventeen segments. The very small pygidium comprises only one segment.

Representatives of the genus *Sao* have been found dating from the Middle Cambrian in Europe. In 1852, the well-known French paleontologist Joachim Barrande, who spent most of his life engaged in geological and palaeontological research in the very interesting area of Barrandien in Bohemia, wrote a detailed description of the whole ontological development of the trilobite from the first stage as a small larva, which was actually based on the species, *Sao hirsuta.*

Agraulos ■

MIDDLE-CAMBRIAN

The relatively small representatives of this genus are usually characterized by the regular, elliptical shape of the body. However, they have a surprisingly large cephalon with a short, wide, flat glabella, which does not go up to the edge of the cephalon, and which has four pairs of glabellar furrows. There is a striking broad, flat (cranidial) suture at the front of the cephalon. The eyes are small. The thorax consists of sixteen segments with a striking axial section. The

Agraulos ceticephalus
Middle Cambrian, Skryje – Luh, Czech Republic

very small pygidium comprises only one segment. Specimens of the genus have been identified dating from the Middle Cambrian in Europe. The species identified here, *Agraulos ceticephalus*, has been found in the Barrandien region. The specimen in the photograph is 3 cm ($1^3/_4$ in) long.

Conocoryphe sulzeri
Middle Cambrian, Jince, Czech Republic

Asaphus expansus
Lower Ordovician, Sweden

Asaphus (Neoasaphus) delphinus
Ordovician, Putilova, St. Petersburg, Russia

Asaphus ∎

ORDOVICIAN

Representatives of the order of Ptychopariida belong to the curious group of asaphid trilobites, which include one of the largest trilobites. In some species the broad, oval body can reach a length of 50 cm (19¹/₂ in). The front of the cephalon is narrow and rounded, and finely segmented. The smooth glabella widens at the front and is convex. It is usually unob-

trusively separated from the fixed cheeks, and goes up to the front edge of the cephalon, which has broad doublure. The thorax usually consists of only eight segments, and the axis is spherical. The pygidium has indistinct transverse furrows, but may also be entirely smooth. Its shape is similar to that of the cephalon. The finely segmented exoskeleton and the strikingly large protruding eyes, as well as the almost disc-shaped cross section of the body of some of these trilobites, reveal that they were probably also

Asaphus kovalvskii
Ordovician, St. Petersburg, Russia

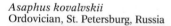

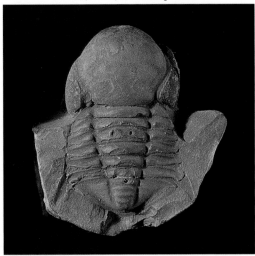

able to float and swim freely in the waters of shallow, warm seas with deposits of sand or clay. Asaphid trilobites were one of the most common groups of trilobites from the Upper Cambrian to the end of the Ordovician. The genus, which also includes the species illustrated, *Asaphus expansus*, reveals the capacity of some trilobites to roll up in a ball. In this way they protected their vulnerable ventral side against enemies. Representatives of the genus have mainly been identified from the Lower and Middle Ordovician in Northwest Europe. The specimen of *Asaphus expansus* illustrated is 6.7 cm (2¹/₂ in) long. In the other trilobite illustrated (*Asaphus kovalvskii*), the most striking feature is the appearance of the eyes. Some asaphid trilobites had large, almost round eyes on stalks, which enabled them to orient themselves when they dug into the sea bed. This specimen is 5.3 cm (2 in) long. The other photograph shows the species *Asaphus (Neoasaphus) delphinus*, which measures 7.5 cm (3 in).

Pricyclopyge ■

ORDOVICIAN

Trilobites of the genus *Pricyclopyge* are closer to the group of asaphid trilobites. Their exoskeleton can grow up to 5 cm (2 in) long and has an interesting appearance. It is oval with a broad, semicircular cephalon, with a wide, convex, smooth glabella. The large eyes, consisting of some 3,500 lenses are striking. The body consists of only six broad segments. In the last segment before the pygidium the ends of the pleurae extend to form short, sturdy spines. The pygidium is in the shape of a broad triangle. The broad axis of the body and the pygidium narrows considerably at the back, forming a striking conical shape. Individual specimens of the *Pricyclopyge* had

exoskeletons which could grow to 5 cm (2 in). They inhabited the cold seas of the Ordovician in Europe and North America. They probably swam with their legs pointing up (like the present day Limulus – the last surviving genus of the class of Merostomata: horseshoe crabs and sea scorpions). Another characteristic of this genus is the presence of two symmetrical hollows on the third axial segment, which are considered to be where there were luminous organs. The exoskeleton of the specimen illustrated is of *Pricyclopyge prisca* (4.5 cm /1³/₄ in/ long).

Radioscutellum ■

LOWER DEVONIAN

The genus *Radioscutellum* belongs to another curious-looking group of trilobites in the order of Ptychoparida. The genus is characterized by a large and broad cephalon and a glabella which broadens into a triangle at the front in a striking way. It has three pairs of glabella furrows which run forwards and backwards from the base. The free cheeks are large, and the kidney-shaped eyes can consist of four thousand lenses. The thorax is composed of ten segments. The strikingly large pygidium, which is bigger than the cephalon, is fascinating and has the shape of an open fan. Trilobites of the genus Radioscutellum have been identified in Lower Devonian strata in Europe. The species *Radioscutellum intermixtum* (formerly *Bojoscutellum paliferrum*) is one of the largest trilobites and could reach a length of 30 cm (12 in). Often only a collection of pygidia is found. The pygidia of the specimens illustrated here are approximately 5 cm (2 in) long.

69

Prionopeltis striata
Upper Silurian, Beroun – Kosov, Czech Republic

Deanaspis senftenbergi
Ordovician, Beroun, Czech Republic

Prionopeltis ∎

SILURIAN – MIDDLE DEVONIAN

The genus *Prionopeltis* belongs to another remarkably large group of ptychopariid trilobites, which already existed in the Lower Ordovician. It reached a peak during the Silurian and Devonian. It is one of the few groups of trilobites that only became extinct at the end of the Paleozoic. *Prionopeltis* are small, opisthoparian trilobites with a slightly convex exoskeleton. The semi-circular cephalon has a small border around the short and clearly defined glabella, and there is a broad preglabellar field. The eyes are set in the back half of the cephalon. The broad, free cheeks end in long genal spines. The elongated body consists of ten segments with pointed pleurae. The relatively large pygidium is strikingly segmented and has pleural spines. Specimens of the genus have been

Aulacopleura konincki
Lower Silurian, Loděnice, Czech Republic

found from the Silurian to Middle Devonian. The specimen illustrated here, which belongs to the species *Prionopeltis striata* is 1.2 cm ($^{1}/_{2}$ in) long.

Aulacopleura ∎

MIDDLE ORDOVICIAN – MIDDLE DEVONIAN

The genus *Aulacopleura* is classified in the same group as the previous genus, *Prionopeltis*, because the composition of the exoskeleton is extremely similar. Furthermore, they have often survived in their entirety. Sometimes they cover the whole surface, as in the species *Elipsocephalus hoffi* in the order of Redlichiida. This makes them interesting from the collector's point of view. The genus *Aulacopleura* comprises small trilobites with an oval shape and a cylindrical glabella which goes halfway up the cephalon. There is a broad preglabellar field in front of this. The cephalon has a narrow border along the edges, ending in narrow genal spines. The eyes are large. The body can comprise as many as 22 segments. The axis is narrow, and the long ends of the pleurae are rounded. The wide pygidium is very short and has a smooth outline. The genus *Aulacopleura* is found in Europe and Africa in layers dating from the Middle Ordovician to the Middle Devonian. The specimen illustrated here belongs to the species *Aulacopleura konincki*, and is approximately 2 cm ($^{3}/_{4}$ in) long.

Deanaspis ∎

ORDOVICIAN

The genus *Deanaspis* belongs to another group of ptychopariid trilobites, which have an exoskeleton with such a characteristic appearance that even fragments can be easily identified. Trilobites of the genus *Deanaspis* are small, usually 1.5–2.5 cm ($^{1}/_{2}$–1 in) long, and the exoskeleton is approximately as long as it is wide. The large semi-circular cephalon has a strongly convex glabella. The broad border around the head is perforated by parallel lines of openings arranged in almost regular lines. When the organisms lay on the sea bed and dug themselves in, these were probably used to look for food. The genal spines are often three times as long as the trilobite's own exoskeleton. It has no eyes. The body is composed of six narrow segments. The narrow and triangular pygidium with a long axis is segmented in a very unobtrusive way. Specimens of trilobites of the genus *Deanaspis* dating from the Ordovician have been found all over the world. The above-mentioned Ordovician species, *Deanaspis senftenbergi*, is a very common trilobite in the Barrandien area. The larval stage has also been identified, although specimens have only been found in certain shale layers dating from the Lower Ordovician. The specimen illustrated here is approximately 2 cm (1³/₄ in) long.

Order: Phacopida

LOWER ORDOVICIUM – UPPER DEVONIAN

This is a very extensive group of small to medium-sized trilobites, which became particularly common all over the world in the seas of the Silurian and the Devonian. In most specimens the carapace is divided into the cephalon, thorax and pygidium in a very striking way. The clearly defined glabella can assume all sorts of shapes and is broader at the front. Usually there are three pairs of clearly visible transverse glabellar ribs, though these do not touch each other. The facial sutures are often proparian. The arched compound eyes are usually striking, and only a few species are blind. The thorax is composed of eight to nineteen segments. The pygidium is relatively large and semicircular, sometimes with spines.

Phacops rana
Middle Devonian, Ontario, United States

Reedops cephalotes
Lower Devonian, Tetín, Czech Republic

Phacops ■

SILURIAN – DEVONIAN

The genus *Phacops* comprises typical phacopid trilobites with a virtually identical skeletal structure, which is generally no larger than 10 cm (4 in). It has an oval shape, and the semicircular cephalon is covered with wart-like tubercles. In most cases the exceptionally large glabella, which broadens to the front, overlaps the cephalon. The convex cheeks are relatively small, and the facial sutures are proparian. The eyes are very striking, arched and protruding. The body is composed of eleven wide segments with rounded pleurae. The large semicircular pygidium is segmented in a way that is clearly visible. The structure of the appendages and the digestive system of this species have been revealed using X-rays. The genus *Phacops* was widespread all over the world during the entire Silurian and Devonian. The specimen illustrated here belongs to the species *Phacops rana*, and is shown in a position with a rolled-up carapace. This phenomenon is seen relatively often in trilobites of this group. They grow up to 1.5 cm (¹/₂ in) long.

Reedops ■

SILURIAN – DEVONIAN

In contrast with the genus *Phacops*, this other, very common, typical phacopic genus *Reedops* has a relatively narrow exoskeleton with a smooth, extremely convex glabella and an indistinctly segmented pygidium. From the Silurian to the Devonian, the genus particularly inhabited deep-sea beds, as is shown by the fact that entire exoskeletons have been found in fine-grained sediments. Like the genus *Phacops*, the genus *Reedops* was also very widespread geographically; it has been identified in Europe, Asia, North America and North Africa. The species illustrated here, *Reedops cephalotes*, has also assumed a rolled-up position.

Dalmanitina ■

ORDOVICIAN – SILURIAN

Trilobites of the genus *Dalmanitina* are representatives of a large group of phacopid trilobites which is of great stratigraphic importance. In view of the characteristic structure of the exoskeleton, fragments can easily be identified. The whole exoskeleton, which has a diameter of 4–7 cm ($1^1/_2$–$2^3/_4$ in), is slightly convex, and the cephalon is semicircular or parabolic. The pear-shaped glabella becomes wider towards the front, covering the front of the cephalon. The glabella always bears three pairs of clearly visible glabellar furrows. The large mosaic eyes are also striking, the facial sutures are proparian, and the genal angles end in short genal spines. The body is composed of eleven segments. The relatively large pygidium, with six to eight pairs of ribs on the side lobes, often ends in a striking pygidial spine. The genus *Dalmanitina* was widespread all over the world during the Ordovician and Silurian in different seas and different climates. The photograph shows the complete exoskeleton of a specimen of the species *Dalmanitina socialis*. The next photograph shows an accumulation of specimens of the species *Dalmanitina proeva*, which died on a massive scale.

Dalmanitina socialis
Ordovician, Trubín, Czech Republic

Dalmanitina proeva
Upper Ordovician, Drabov, Czech Republic

Odontochile hausmanni
Lower Devonian, Prague-Podolí, Czech Republic

Odontochile ∎

LOWER – MIDDLE DEVONIAN

The phacopid genus *Odontochile* belongs to the same group of trilobites as the genus *Dalmanitina*. These trilobites are oval with a semicircular cephalon with a broad border and strong genal spines. The glabella has three pairs of lateral furrows and does not extend to the front of the cephalon. The semicircular eyes are large. The thorax is composed of seven segments and the pointed pleurae are curved backwards. Twelve to fifteen striking pairs of ribs arise from the large, rounded, triangular pygidium. The axis narrows quickly and ends in a short spine. The surface of the whole carapace is usually covered with small tubercles or thorny bristles. The trilobites of this genus tended to inhabit the deeper areas of the tropical seas of the Devonian in Europe, North and South America, Africa and Australia. The species *Odontochile hausmanni* is a typical and very common trilobite in Devonian layers in the Barrandien area, although usually only in the form of pygidia found on their own. Ondotochile pygidia are amongst the oldest fossils in Central Europe.

Colpocoryphe ∎

LOWER ORDOVICIAN – MIDDLE DEVONIAN

The genus *Colpocoryphe* belongs to another group of phacopid trilobites. Its representatives have an elliptical, solid, strongly convex exoskeleton, usually 6–8 cm ($2^3/_4$–3 in) long. The thick raised front of the semicircular cephalon is characteristic. The broad glabella with deep glabellar furrows, narrows at the front. The small eyes are usually at the front, though their size can vary considerably from species to species. The free cheeks are very small. The body has a broad axis, and is composed of twelve to thirteen segments. The triangular pygidium is small, and its convex axis can consist of eight rings, reaching to the end of the pygidium. The genus *Colpocoryphe* has been identified in layers of the Lower Ordovician to the Middle-Devonian in Europe, Asia, Africa and North America.

Colpocoryphe declinata
Upper Ordovician, Králův Dvůr, Czech Republic

Placoparia barrandei
Lower Ordovician, Prague – Šárka, Czech Republic

Placoparia ■

ORDOVICIAN

Placoparia has an oval, but slender body with a se-micircular cephalon with a glabella which gets slightly broader towards the front, and has three pairs of deep lateral furrows. There is a narrow bor-der around the cephalon. The opisthoparian facial sutures often run along the edge of the head, and are frequently extremely indistinct. They separate the convex, fixed cheeks and the narrow free cheeks. There are no eyes. The body has a broad central axis and is composed of twelve convex rings. The small pygidium is also deeply segmented in this way, with six blunt spines on the periphery.

Acanthopyge haueri
Middle Devonian, Koněprusy, Czech Republic

The entire surface of the carapace is covered with small tubercles. The trilobites of the genus *Pla-coparia* inhabited fairly shallow sea beds in warm and colder regions. Specimens have been found dating from the Ordovician in Europe and North Africa.

The complete exoskeleton of the trilobite illustrated here, which belongs to the species *Placoparia bar-randei,* is 4 cm (1¹/₂ in) long and has survived in the strata which developed when the dead specimen was covered with sediment.

Order: Lichida

LOWER ORDOVICIAN – UPPER DEVONIAN

This is a group of curiously shaped trilobites which reached large average sizes. It includes the largest known species of trilobites in the world, with an exoskeleton which could grow up to 75 cm (3 in) long. The extremely broad glabella had complicated glabellar furrows. The sickle-shaped eyes are small and difficult to distinguish. The free cheeks are nar-row and always extend to the back, forming long, saber-like spines. The separate parts of the body also end in spines. The axial part is broad, convex, and indicates a well- developed musculature. This means they were probably good climbers and swimmers. The pygidium was flat, with a shorter central axis and three pairs of leaf-shaped ribs, also ending in spines. The whole surface of the carapace was covered with striking tubercles or warts. They usually lived in shal-low seas.

Acanthopyge ■

SILURIAN – MIDDLE DEVONIAN

The trilobites of the genus *Acanthopyge* are almost always found as pygidia or parts of the cephalon, which are conical in shape. The second and third glabellar furrows on the side are connected, and the eyes are on stalks. The narrow cheeks end in long spines. The body consists of eleven segments. The relatively large, moderately curved pygidium has th-ree pairs of ribs, ending in long spines. They mainly inhabited shallow seas, together with corals, and were widespread all over the world from the Silurian to the Middle Devonian. The illustration shows a fragment of the exoskeleton of the species *Acanthopyge haueri*, the 2.6 cm (1 in) long pygi-dium.

Order: Odontopleurida

MIDDLE CAMBRIAN – LOWER DEVONIAN

A large group of interesting, small spiny trilobites, with a body composed of eight to ten segments. This type of exoskeleton is found in a large number of spe-cies and sizes. The spines also grew on the cephalon and on the small triangular pygidium. The trilobites probably used this spiny 'equipment' as an organ for maintaining their balance when they moved. It allowed them to swim or float in the water freely. In addition, it was clearly also a useful protection against enemies.

Selenopeltis ■

MIDDLE – LOWER ORDOVICIAN

This is one of the best-known Ordovician genera of the order Odontopleurida. The genus is characterized by a moderately curved exoskeleton, which can reach a length of 12 cm ($4^3/_4$ in). The cephalon is short, oblong and rounded. The relatively broad glabella is segmented in a complicated way. The free cheeks end in long genal spines. The body is composed of nine segments. The ribs end in short spines which protrude forwards, and long spines which curve backwards. The pygidium has a short axis with three rings. The ribs of the pygidium also end in long spines. The trilobites of the genus *Selenopeltis* lived in the central and western part of Europe, and their remains have also been found in parts of Africa.

The species *Selenopeltis buchi* is a typical representative of this genus. We can be certain that this predator was an active swimmer. Echinoderms often attached themselves to their carapaces, e.g., specimens of the genus *Argodiscus*.

Miraspis ■

SILURIAN

Representatives of the genus *Miraspis* have a broad oval body with a semicircular cephalon, decorated with long, thin, fine spines. There are also spines on the genal angle. The body is composed of nine segments, which also bear spines. The pygidium is narrow, and has eleven pairs of spines on the border, the third pair of which is the longest. The large number of spines growing from the carapace in every direction, indicates that these trilobites cannot have been good swimmers, and that they therefore probably

Selenopeltis buchi
Ordovician, Trubín, Czech Republic

crawled over the sea bed. They were particularly common in the shallow seas of the Silurian in Europe.

Leonaspis ■

LOWER SILURIAN – DEVONIAN

The genus *Leonaspis* is another genus of the order of Odontopleurida, characteristic of the Lower Silurian. These small trilobites had a rounded oblong cephalon with a broad glabella. The spines on the cephalon, the body and the pygidium, can be straight or curved. The remains of exoskeletons dating from the Devonian are often found in coarse-grained limestone. This proves that these trilobites were able to inhabit shallow seas with strong currents. Fossils of this genus have been found dating from the Lower Silurian to the Devonian in Europe and North and South America.

Miraspis mira
Lower Silurian, Loděnice, Czech Republic

Leonaspis roemeri
Lower Silurian, Loděnice, Czech Republic

Eurypterus fischeri
Upper Silurian, Buffalo, New York, United States

Subphylum: Chelicerata – chelicerates

CAMBRIAN – RECENT TIMES

Chelicerates form a very specialized group of arthropods, in which the original segmented body changed when several segments fused. Their body was then formed by only two parts: the *cephalothorax (prosoma)* and the *abdomen (opistosoma)*. The cephalothorax consists of six fused segments and bears six pairs of appendages with one branch. The first pair developed into the upper jaws – *pincer-like parts of the mouth (chelicera)*. These are in front of the mouth, i.e., pre-oral. They are part of the mouth, as are the second pair, the lower jaws – the *maxilipalpa* or *pedipalpa*. These are situated behind the mouth, i.e., they are post-oral. The four other pairs are used for locomotion, and the last pair have sometimes evolved into *swimming limbs*. In addition, these appendages had developed in older fossils into *chewing organs*. The respiratory organs of chelicerates are extremely varied (gills, respiratory tubes, spiracles). Chelicerates reproduce with eggs or bear live young. The young specimens always resemble

mature specimens. The oldest chelicerates probably developed at the same time as the trilobites from common ancestors, and it is almost certain that they only inhabited the sea.

Class: Merostomata – horseshoe crabs

PRECAMBRIAN – RECENT TIMES

This group of crabs originally lived in salt water and gradually adapted to fresh water. The body of the horseshoe crab consists of a cephalothorax and an abdomen. Of the six pairs of appendages on the cephalothorax, the first pair developed into pincers used to pick up food. The other pairs were used for walking, and the last pair for swimming. The *coxae* of every pair were usually serrated, and used for chewing. The abdomen was divided into a front *preabdomen*, (*mezosoma*) and a back *postabdomen*, (*metasoma*). The preabdomen bears six or seven pairs of appendages. Apart from the first pair which can develop into small *plates (chilaria)*, the others can fork into a middle and side branch. There are gills on the side branches. The characteristic apertures of the genus, are on the second abdominal segment. The postabdomen, which does not have any appendages, ends in a differently shaped *spine (telson)*. Horseshoe crabs developed strongly during the Paleozoic. Only one family survives to the present day – Limulidae of the subclass Xiphosura (sea scorpions). A large number of extinct species of horseshoe crabs grew to enormous sizes (up to 3 m/10 ft long). In fact, they were the largest invertebrates in the history of life on earth. The class of Merostomata has two subclasses.

Subclass: Eurypterida – sea scorpions

ORDOVICIAN – PERMIAN

Sea scorpions represent a group of extinct chelicerates, which could grow to a length of 3 m (10 ft). They played an important role particularly in the fauna of the Upper Silurian and the Lower Devonian. The large, serrated pincers and spiny coxae of the swimming limbs indicate that they were dangerous predators in the seas at that time. They were good swimmers. They probably only adapted to a brackish environment later on, and inhabited a freshwater environment in the Permian and Carboniferous. The large cephalothorax was fairly convex, with a square or oblong shape. A pair of single eyes was placed in the middle of the back of the cephalothorax. There were two large oval or kidney-shaped compound eyes on the sides. Of the six pairs of appendages, the first pair developed as pincers, the last pair as powerful swimming limbs. The other pairs were used for walking, and always consisted of only

Eurypterus remipes
Silurian, Herkimer Co., New York, USA

one branch. On the ventral side there is a large, oval *metastoma*, indented at the front, which is characteristic of sea scorpions. This protects the inner part of the coxae of the last part of the appendages of the cephalothorax. The abdomen had a small number of segments and ended in differently shaped *telsons* (straight, curved or fin-like), which could also contain a *poison gland*. Sea scorpions were divided into genera. The second segment of the abdomen *(genital segment)* bore a double *plate (operculum)* which covered the exits of the genital organs. They could have different shapes in different species, and differed in male and female specimens. Usually only the relatively solid parts of the bodies of sea scorpions are found – the chelicera and the serrated coxae. Specimens which have survived intact are very rare.

Eurypterus

ORDOVICIAN – CARBONIFEROUS

The genus *Eurypterus* has an elongated body which narrows significantly towards the back. The cephalothorax is almost square, with rounded corners. On the sides, there is a pair of compound eyes, and in the middle a pair of simple eyes. The metastoma on the

ventral side is not convex and has an oval shape. The chelicera are short and unremarkable. The front walking legs are usually covered with spines. The swimming legs become wider, and are shaped like paddles. The telson is in the shape of a solid, straight spine. *Eurypterus* included some good swimmers. It was widespread in Europe, North America and Asia from the Ordovician to the Carboniferous. The complete specimen illustrated here belongs to the species *Eurypterus remipes*. It is 22.6 cm (8³/₄ in) long and is very well preserved. This is very unusual for sea scorpions, because their external chitinous skeleton was thin and not very mineralized, in contrast with that of the trilobites. That is why fossils of sea scorpions are seldom found, and then usually only as fragments.

Pterygotus

ORDOVICIAN – DEVONIAN

The exoskeletons of the species of the genus *Pterygotus* generally grew to considerable sizes (more than 2 m/6 ft 6 in long). On the rounded, almost square cephalothorax, there are large compound eyes on the front. In contrast with the genus *Eurypterus*, this genus has very long chelicera with large, serrated pincers. The slender walking legs are small, without any spines. The coxae of the swimming legs are large, with eleven to fifteen striking serrations. There is a raised line across the entire dorsal area of the abdomen, or there may be a number of spines. The telson is wide and paddle-shaped, and also has a raised rim and a number of spines. From the Ordovician to the Devonian, they first inhabited deep salt water, but later also lived in brackish waters, and they were good swimmers. Fossils have been found in Europe, North America, Spitsbergen and Australia. The species *Pterygotus bohemicus* is the most common species of the genus *Pterygotus*. The chelicera illustrated here are 13.5 cm (5³/₄ in) long.

Pterygotus bohemicus
Upper-Silurian, Prague – Velká Chuchle, Czech Republic

Mesolimulus walchi
Upper Jurassic, Solnhofen, Germany

Microlas sternbergi
Upper Carboniferous, Chomle, Czech Republic

Mesolimulus ■

This genus of horseshoe crabs belongs to the order of Xiphosurida. It includes horseshoe crabs with a relatively flat, three-lobed cephalothorax, which is much broader, and sometimes also longer, than the abdomen. The two parts are covered with a one piece exoskeleton. The abdomen tapers towards the back, and consists of six to ten segments which can be fused. The telson is dagger shaped, and usually longer than the abdomen. Like most Merostoma, *Mesolimulus* probably inhabited the sandy sea bed of littoral regions in the tropical and subtropical seas of the Upper Jurassic. It was widespread in Europe and North America. However, the best fossils have been found in lithographic limestone areas in Bavaria. The average size of the exoskeleton fluctuates between 15–20 cm (6–7³/₄ in). The specimen illustrated measures 19 cm (7¹/₂ in). Mesozoic representatives differ little from more recent examples. These are relatively common in the seas of our times, but represented by one only genus, *Limulus*.

Subclass: Xiphosura – horseshoe crabs

LOWER CAMBRIAN – RECENT TIMES

Horseshoe crabs have an oval or slightly elongated body, 2–60 cm (³/₄–23¹/₂ in) long. The hard chitinous exoskeleton normally consists of three lobes on the dorsal side. The cephalothorax usually looks like a broad, unsegmented shield. The glabella and the genera can be identified here. On the dorsal side of either side of the cephalothorax, there are two large compound eyes. There are usually two simple eyes in the middle. In most Paleozoic species the abdomen is composed of eight to twelve segments, ending in a long, moving, dagger-like telson. In geologically later species, this clear segmentation gradually becomes less apparent. On the ventral side the abdomen has seven pairs of appendages. The first pair are the *chilaria*, the second pair are genitalia *(operculum)* and the last five pairs are swimming legs which bear flaky gills. Horseshoe crabs inhabited salt water. From the Carboniferous a few species also adapted to live in fresh water. The oldest representatives of horseshoe crabs to be discovered date from the Lower Cambrian. They are now relatively strongly represented by one species, *Limulus* (order of Xiphosurida), particularly in the Atlantic Ocean and in Indo-Atlantic areas.

Class: Arachnida – arachnids

MIDDLE SILURIAN – RECENT TIMES

The spider family mainly comprises terrestrial animals. The body is normally divided into two parts, a cephalothorax and an abdomen.
If eyes have developed, they are usually placed on the cephalothorax, together with six pairs of unbranched appendages. The first pair *(chelicera)* consists of two

Eophrynus presticii
Upper Carboniferous, Great Britain

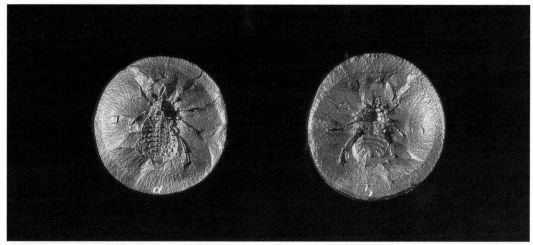

of three segments, ending in pincers or claws. The second pair *(pedipalps)* usually consists of six segments, develops in different ways and is used for the sense of touch. The other four pairs of appendages, which usually consist of seven segments, are used for walking. The segments of the abdomen, which number up to a maximum of twelve, are usually fused together. The mouth is at the front of the cephalothorax. Arachnids breathe through *trachea*. Few arachnids are adapted to living in water. Most are carnivorous. They are the oldest arthropods capable of breathing in air.

Microlabis ●

CARBONIFEROUS

This genus of scorpions is one of the most important orders of the subclass Latigastra. The broad connecting suture between the cephalothorax and the abdomen is characteristic of this genus. The group includes scorpions with an elongated, clearly segmented body. Their appearance is reminiscent of sea scorpions. They have a short cephalothorax, a broad elongated abdomen consisting of segments, and a long postabdomen consisting of five segments. There are poison glands at the end of the telson. The chelicera are short and end in pincers. The pedipalps end in powerful moving pincers, which are used to pick up food. Scorpions have been identified in Silurian strata. At that time they lived in water, but later moved ashore. They flourished during the Carboniferous. The genus *Microlabis* has been identified only in Carboniferous layers in Europe.

Eophrynus ●

UPPER CARBONIFEROUS

This genus of arachnids belongs to the only order of

the subclass Soluta. Arachnids are more developed than scorpions. Their body is no longer protected by a rigid carapace, and therefore the external skeleton is greatly reduced. The segmentation of the body has disappeared, as has the telson. The cephalothorax is always smaller than the abdomen, and can have different shapes. In the genus *Eophrynus*, it is triangular, while the abdomen is composed of nine segments, which are visible on the dorsal side. It has an elongated oval shape with a striking axis and four spines on the edge furthest back. It is decorated with countless tubercles. The rough dorsal side of the abdomen is large and relatively broad. The genus *Eophrynus* has been identified in layers of the Upper Carboniferous in Europe. The species *Eophrynus prestvicii* illustrated here has rarely survived intact. It is 2.5 cm (1 in) long. Fossilized spiders dating from later geological eras are most often found in amber.

Spider in amber, Eocene, Poland

Eoleperditia sp.
Lower Silurian, Slite, Gotland, Sweden

Leperditia sp.
Lower Silurian, Gotland, Sweden

Subclass: Crustacea – crustaceans

LOWER CAMBRIAN – RECENT TIMES

This is a group of virtually exclusively aquatic arthropods. The body consists of a *head (cephalon)*, *thorax* and an *abdomen*, protected either by a strong exoskeleton, usually permeated with mineral salts, or by a chitinous or calcareous skeleton, consisting of two shells or calcareous plates. In some cases the cephalon is fused with the thorax to form the *cephalothorax*. The body and limbs are segmented. The cephalon is always composed of five segments and five pairs of limbs. The first pair, *small feelers (antenullae)* have one joint. The second pair – *feelers (antennae)* comprise the organs for the senses of smell and touch. Like the other limbs, they have a two-branched structure, with an *inner branch (endopodite)* and an *outer branch (exopodite)*. The other two pairs form a chewing mechanism consisting of one pair of *upper mandibles (mandibulae)* and two pairs of *lower mandibles (maxillulae)*. The thorax consists of a varying number of segments; more developed species have eight. The limbs on the thorax are used for movement, and the first three pairs have usually evolved as mandibles *(maxilipeds)*. The abdomen is composed of seven segments. When there are limbs, these are also in two branches, and the sixth segment has usually developed as *broad plates (uropoda)*. The last segment, or *telson*, has no limbs. Crustaceans usually breathe with gills and are divided into two genera. Because mature crustaceans differ widely, classification is based on the study of the larval stage, when similarity is apparent.

Class: Ostracoda – ostracods

LOWER CAMBRIAN – RECENT TIMES

Ostracods are small crustaceans which inhabit seas, fresh water and brackish water. Their oval body is covered by a strong, chitinous, sometimes calcareous, two-lobed *skeleton (carapax)*. The shells of the carapax are connected by muscles on the dorsal side. The size of the shells of most species varies from 0.4–1.5 mm (0.01–0.05 in). Only some freshwater species grow to a size of 5 mm ($^3/_{16}$ in), and only free-swimming marine species can grow to almost 6 cm ($^3/_4$ in) in exceptional cases.

The soft body has seven pairs of appendages. The body ends in a fork-like spine, the *furka*, which enables the animal to move forward. The carapax of ostracods consists of two shells – a left and a right shell, which are usually bilaterally symmetrical. In some species this symmetry disappears entirely.

The shape of the skeleton can also vary considerably: from oval to elongated and bean-like shapes. The morphology of the skeleton of ostracods reveals a significant similarity to the skeletons of mollusks. A distinction can be made between a flexible chitinous *binding material (ligament)*, which moves the shells apart, and a joint-like connection of the shells, a *hinge* in all sorts of species, etc.

The eyes of ostracods are rarely entirely absent. In some cases only one eye develops on the cephalon. Marine species also have two eyes set on the sides. Ostracods breathe through the entire surface of the body, and a few species have separate gills. They prefer a quiet, aquatic environment, swim close to the surface or crawl along the bed. They feed on small organisms and organic matter. They are divided into two genera.

The systematic classification of living ostracods is based on the shape of their appendages. For fossils, the system is based on the structure of the hinge, the impressions of muscles, the shape of the skeleton and the structure of the surface. Fossilized representatives are found in large numbers in Kenozoic marine sediments. They are stratigraphically very important.

Eoleperditia ■

ORDOVICIAN

The genus *Eoleperditia* has a thick, oval, smooth skeleton up to 1 centimeter long, which broadens out at the back. The right shell is larger and covers the left shell on the free ventral side. On the right front there is an eye socket on the dorsal side, with muscle imprints below it. The edge of the hinge is straight, and it is not serrated. The genus *Eoleperditia* was widespread all over the world during the Ordovician. The skeleton in the photograph is 1.5 cm ($^1/_2$ in) long.

Leperditia ■

SILURIAN – DEVONIAN

The genus *Leperditia* has a broad, oval skeleton with a straight edge along the hinge, and the right shell is larger, overlapping the ventral edge of the left shell. The edge of the back of the shell is more convex and higher than the shell at the front. The muscle impressions are well developed under the eye socket and are divided into two branches. Some species have an indented hinge. They have been found in Silurian and Devonian strata in Europe. The average size of the cases is 0.5–3 cm (0.19–$1^3/_4$ in). The specimen illustrated here belongs to the genus *Leperditia*, and the shells, which are photographed from both sides, measure 0.9 – 1.2 cm ($^3/_4$–$^1/_2$ in)

Class: Cirripedia

CARBONIFEROUS – RECENT TIMES

This is a group of exclusively marine crustaceans, which grow to a length of between a few millimeters and 60 cm ($23^1/_2$ in). They are very mobile when they are young, but permanently immobile when they are mature. The shape of the body is similar to that of mollusks.

The body of Cirripedia is usually covered by an *exoskeleton (capitulum)*. This consists of freely moving calcareous plates (in animals which are attached to the substratum with a stalk). The limbs are fine, and coil in a spiral with two branches, and there are a maximum of six pairs. They are placed behind the mouth and churn up the water, pick up food, and are used for breathing. The abdomen is usually rudimentary with no limbs, but with a long organ for copulation. Unlike other crustaceans, Cirripedia are hermaphrodites. They are only of limited stratigraphic importance.

Balanus concavus
Miocene, Eggenburg, Germany

Balanus ■

EOCENE – RECENT TIMES

Cirripedia of the genus *Balanus* have an external skeleton. This consists of firmly interlinked plates on the side, which serve as a reinforcement in the form of irregularly truncated cones. There is no stalk, and consequently the case is directly attached to the substratum. The cone-like opening is protected by a lid, formed by two pairs of moving plates *(scutum and tergum)*, which are linked by a joint. They often inhabit areas with steep cliffs where the waves break, and the Cirripedia protect themselves from drying out by closing the lid. The genus *Balanus* was widespread all over the world from the Eocene, and still exists today. The species illustrated here, *Balanus concavus,* grows to a size of almost 1 cm ($^3/_4$ in). Specimens of the class of Cirripedia are often found attached to the shells of mollusks. A good example of this is shown in the other photograph of the specimen of the species *Balanus*, which is attached to the mollusk, *Clavatula interrupta,* and is 6 cm long ($2^3/_4$ in).

Balanus sp.
Pliocene, Oliveto, Italy

Creusa phryxa
Lower Pliocene, Almería province, Spain

Creusia ∎

MIOCENE – RECENT TIMES

The genus *Creusia* has a very long skeleton which is cylindrical or conical in shape, ending in a low cone at the top. The skeleton consists of four plates. Individual specimens attach themselves to coral colonies. Representatives of the genus *Creusia* have been identified from the Miocene to the present day. The largest example of the species *Creusia phryxa*, illustrated here, measures 1.5 cm ($^{1}/_{2}$ in).

Class: Malacostraca – malacostracans

LOWER CAMBRIAN – RECENT TIMES

This is an extremely old group which mainly comprises animals which lived in water, at different depths, predominantly marine animals. Some species swim about freely; others dig themselves in the mud. They feed on large and small organisms and organic matter. The species which live on land also feed on vegetable matter. The large majority of malacostracans have a body consisting of twenty segments. The head is normally fused with the thorax. This is covered by an extremely strong chitinous *exoskeleton (carapax)*, because it consists of calcareous minerals. There are five pairs of extremities *(antenulae, antennae, mandibulae, first and second maxillae)*. The extremities on the thorax *(maxipeda and pereiopoda)* can have several functions. The last pair of limbs *(pleopoda)*, are on the abdomen. They have developed into broader extremities *(uropoda)*. Together with the telson, they form the caudal fins. Malacostracans are not very important from the stratigraphic point of view.

Ceratiocaris ∎

CAMBRIAN – PERM

This malacostracan belongs to the important subclass of Phylocarida. This comprises species with a relatively large, oval, bivalve exoskeleton, which

Aeger longirostis
Upper Jurassic, Solnhofen, Germany

protects the thorax and the front segments of the abdomen. There is a moving plate (rostrum) at the front. The thorax extremities have two branches and have a broad leaf. There are no limbs on the abdomen. It is composed of a furca (a telson which develops with different shapes and has two fork-like appendages, cerci). The genus *Ceratiocaris* has an elongated exoskeleton, which is strikingly divided in the middle into two valves in the shape of a leaf. The cerci are shorter than the elongated telson. Specimens of the genus *Ceratiocaris* have been identified, dating from the whole of the Paleozoic, in Europe and North America. Some species of this genus grow to a length of 70 cm ($27^1/_2$ in). The photograph shows only the last part of the abdomen (furca) of a specimen of the genus *Ceratiocaris*.

Aeger ■

TRIASSIC – JURASSIC

The malacostracan of the genus *Aeger* belongs to the subclass Eucarida. This comprises species in which, unlike all other malacostracans, the exoskeleton fused with all the segments of the thorax. The compound eyes grow on stalks. They are marine and freshwater animals. The genus *Aeger* usually has a body which is compressed sideways, with long antenullae and antennae, five pairs of long slender legs for walking, pereiopoda, with pincers on the third pair which are never larger than those on the first and second and pairs. The abdomen is longer than the exoskeleton

Ceratiocaris sp.
Upper Silurian, Slivenec, Czech Republic

Aeger tipularius
Jurarassic, Solnhofen, Germany

and has well-developed uropoda. The pleopoda are also well developed, and help the animal to swim. As regards its development, the genus Aeger belongs to the oldest super family of the order of decapods (Decapoda). The genus *Aeger* lived in Europe from the Triassic to the Jurassic. The species illustrated here, *Aeger logirostris*, is 10 cm (4 in) long.

Antrimpos ■

PERMIAN/TRIASSIC – CRETACEOUS

The malacostracan of the genus *Antrimpos* is another representative of the oldest super family of decapods. However, in contrast with the genus *Aeger*, this genus already existed from the transition of the Permian and the Triassic to the Cretaceous. Fossils of the genus *Antrimpos* have been found in Europe. The specimen illustrated here belongs to the species *Antrimpos killiani*, and is 13.4 cm ($5^3/_4$ in) long.

Antrimpos killiani
Jurassic, Solnhofen, Germany

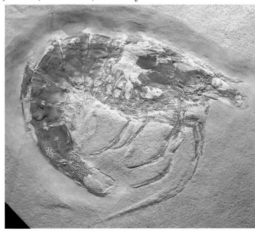

Glyphea regleyana
Jurassic, Haute Saone, France

Glyphea ∎

UPPER TRIASSIC

The decapods of the genus *Glyphea* have a cylindrical, elongated exoskeleton. The edge on the side is sharp and the rostrum is small. Transverse ribs are visible on the front of the exoskeleton. The pereiopoda do not have pincers, but end in claws. The first pair of pereiopoda are always larger and stronger than the other pairs. The first segment of the abdomen, which is always well developed, is shorter than the other segments. Remains of the genus *Glyphea* have been identified, dating from the Upper Triassic to the Cretaceous, but the majority of species date from the Jurassic. The genus *Glyphea* was particularly widespread in Central Europe. The specimen illustrated here, *Glyphea regleyana,* is 10 cm (4 in) long.

Eryon arctiformis
Jurassic, Solnhofen, Germany

Eryon ∎

JURASSIC – RECENT TIMES

The exoskeleton of the genus is dorsoventrally compressed, with a grooved surface and sharp edges on the side. There is no rostrum. They have well-developed eyes. The first four pereiopoda have characteristic pincers, and the first pair of walking legs are noticeably long. There is a raised area across the whole of the central part of the abdomen. Fossilized remains of the genus *Eryon* have been found in Europe dating from the Jurassic and the Lower

Eryma modestiformis
Jurassic, Solnhofen, Germany

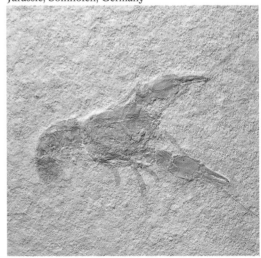

Eryon bilobatus
Jurassic, Solnhofen, Germany

Cretaceous. The recent representatives of this genus, which comprises many species, lived in deep seas and are hardly any different from their Mesozoic ancestors, which inhabited shallow waters. The specimen illustrated here belongs to the species *Eryon arctiformis* and is 9 cm (3¹/₂ in) long. The other specimen belongs to the species *Eryon bilobatus* and has an entirely intact dorsal section.

Enoploclytia ■

UPPER JURASSIC – UPPER CRETACEOUS

The decapods of the genus *Enoploclytia* have a large, elongated exoskeleton, that appears to be divided into several parts by three transverse furrows and a suture in the middle. The rostrum is long and indented. The pereiopoda of the first pair have long, narrow pincers, the second and third pairs have only small pincers. The well-developed abdomen with well-developed pleiopoda is just as long as the exoskeleton. The surface of the whole body is covered with small tubercles. The genus *Enoploclytia* was a well-known extremely common genus from the Upper Jurassic to the Upper Cretaceous. It has been found in Europe, North America, West Africa, Madagascar and Australia.

The illustration of the species *Enoploclytia leachi* reveals the well-preserved pincers which are 9 cm (3¹/₂ in) long.

Eryma ■

LOWER JURASSIC – UPPER CRETACEOUS

The genus *Eryma* belongs to the same super family as the previous species, *Enoploclytia leachi*. With its powerful, slender pincers at the front, it makes just as much of an impression as the genus *Enoploclytia* at first sight. The genus existed from the Lower Jurassic to the Upper Cretaceous. It is common in the lithographic limestone in Solnhofen in Central Europe. The specimen illustrated here belongs to the species *Eryma modestiformis*, and is 7 cm (2³/₄ in) long.

Enoploclytia leachi
Upper Cretaceous, Hrádek, Czech Republic

Prosopon sp.
Upper Jurassic, Rothenstein, Germany

is dorsoventrally compressed and broader than it is long. The exoskeleton is generally strongly calcareous, and therefore survives well when it is fossilized. The front pair of pereiopoda always end in strong pincers, and the other four pairs are used for movement. The genus *Prosopon* belongs to a group of very diverse, small primitive crabs. The exoskeleton has a square or oblong shape, and is strongly convex with a rounded edge and two distinct, but different deep furrows. The surface is covered in tubercles. It has not developed a rostrum, or eye sockets. The last pair of legs are reduced.

The genus *Prosopon* has been found in Europe in Jurassic and Lower Cretaceous strata. The specimen of genus *Prosopon* illustrated here is 1.2 cm (¹/₂ in) long.

Portunus ■ ▣

OLIGOCENE – RECENT TIMES

The genus *Portunus* belongs to another group of crabs with a hexagonal exoskeleton, with a particularly broad front part. The exoskeleton is characterized by three to six indentations on the front edge. The back, flat broader pereiopoda are used for rowing. The last segment of the strong pincers is oblong and flattened. Specimens of the genus *Portunus* have been found in Europe, dating from the Oligocene to the present day.

The exoskeleton of the species illustrated here, *Portunus granulatus,* is 7.5 cm (3 in) across.

Prosopon ■

JURASSIC – LOWER CRETACEOUS

The genus *Prosopon* belongs to a clearly different group of decapods, the crabs. Crabs constitute a very varied group of crustaceans. Their abdomen is noticeably reduced and is below the exoskeleton, which

Portunus granulatus
Miocene, Sardinia, Italy

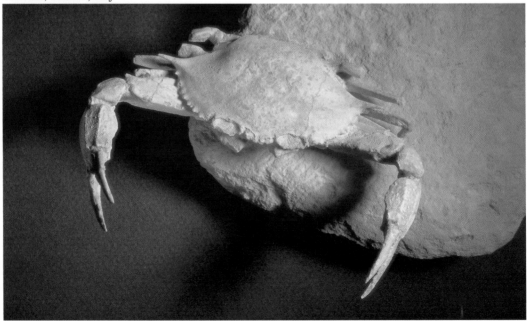

Harpactocarcinus punctulatus
Eocene, Arosa, near Verona, Italy

Harpactocarcinus

EOCENE

The genus *Harpactocarcinus* belongs to the same group of crabs as the above-mentioned genus, *Portunus*. It also has a broad, convex, hexagonal exoskeleton with an almost smooth surface. The front and side edges have regular indentations. The powerfully developed strong pincers are very curious. Fossilized remains have only been found dating from the Eocene in Europe, North America and East Africa. The specimens illustrated here belong to the species *Harpactocarcinus punctulatus*, and are 9 and 8.1 cm (3$^{1}/_{2}$ and 3 in) across.

Harpactocarcinus punctulatus
Eocene, Arosa, near Verona, Italy

Subclass: Tracheata – tracheates

SILURIAN (?), DEVONIAN – RECENT TIMES

This is the largest group of terrestrial arthropods, or arthropods which subsequently made the transition to an aquatic environment. They breathe in the oxygen in the air through *trachea*, a system of branching, chitinous tubes opening onto the surface of the body via apertures known as *stigmata*. The segmented body is always divided into a head, thorax and also an abdomen. On the head there is only one pair of antennae. The system of tracheae is based on the segmentation of the body, on the construction of the thoracic extremities and on the course of the ontogenetic development. The nervation of the wings is particularly important for the systematic classification of the insects.

Class: Diplopoda – diplopods

DEVONIAN – RECENT TIMES

Diplopods have a cylindrical, elongated and segmented body, reinforced with calcareous minerals. The head is clearly separated from the body. The first segment of the thorax and the last segment of the abdomen do not have extremities. The other three segments each have one pair, and the double segments of the abdomen each have two pairs of single-branched extremities. Diplopods breathe through trachea or the surface of the body. They feed on vegetable matter. They were common in jungles of the Carboniferous. It is not clear how their development relates to present-day diplopods.

Euphoberia ●

UPPER CARBONIFEROUS

The representatives of the genus *Euphoberia* have a cylindrical body with a large, broad, square head. The eyes are composed of a large number of simple eyes, close together. Behind the head, there are short thoracic segments, each with one pair of limbs. With the exception of the last segment, the segments of the oblong abdomen all have two pairs of limbs and a pair of short spines on the dorsal side. They lived in the Upper Carboniferous and fed on vegetable matter. A few specimens reached a length of 50 cm (19$^{1}/_{2}$ in). Fossilized remains dating from the Carboniferous are rare, but have been found in Western and Central Europe and in the United States.

Euphoberia hystrix
Upper Carboniferous, Nýřany, Czech Republic

The wings of a dragonfly (order of Odonata)
Miocene, Habartov, Czech Republic

Class: Insecta – insects

DEVONIAN – RECENT TIMES

These are the highest organized arthropods, usually adapted to life on land. They are the only group of invertebrates which conquered the air by learning to fly.

The body of the insect is divided into a head, thorax and abdomen, and is protected by a chitinous membrane. On the head there is a pair of usually compound eyes, three simple eyes, a pair of antennae and three pairs of appendages on the mouth. The thorax consists of three segments, with a pair of limbs growing from each one.

The majority of insects have wings on the dorsal side of the thorax. The front wings are on the second seg-

Mayfly in amber (order of Ephemeroptera)
Eocene, Poland

Aphid in amber (order of Homoptera)
Eocene, Bitterfeld, Germany

Larva of a beetle in amber (order of Coleoptera)
Eocene, Bitterfeld, Germany

Ant in amber (order of Hymenoptera)
Eocene, Poland

ment of the thorax, the back wings on the last segment. The wings can be reduced to one pair, but can also be entirely absent. The reproductive organs are in the abdomen.

Insects are divided into two genera. The develop-

ment of almost all insects involves metamorphosis. Only primitive insects developed without metamorphosis. Fossilized insects are usually found in fine grained shale or marl that was in fresh water. These are mainly insect wings, which are very thin

Fungus gnat with eggs in amber (order of Diptera)
Eocene, Bitterfeld, Germany

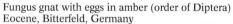

Flies in amber (order of Diptera)
Eocene, Bitterfeld, Germany

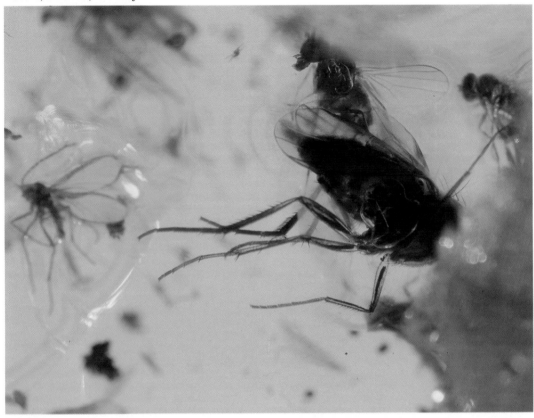

and delicate, but are, nevertheless, strong and durable. That is why they are the most frequently found remains of insects. Insects which are preserved intact in amber, the fossilized resin from cuts in conifers are particularly valuable. The insect is caught in the resin, which sets over time and changes into amber.

Water fly in amber (order of Trichoptera)
Eocene, Poland

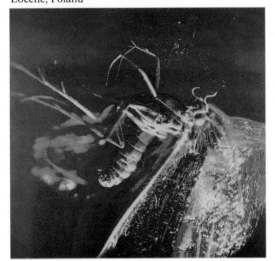

Copulation of gnats (order of Diptera) in amber
Eocene, Bitterfeld, Germany

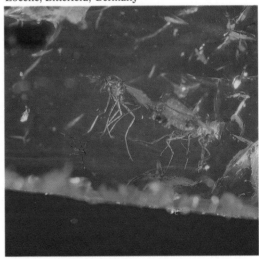

Petalia longiolata
Upper Jurassic, Solnhofen, Germany

Petalia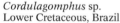

UPPER JURASSIC – RECENT TIMES

The genus *Petalia* belongs to the dragonflies. This group comprises large predatory insects with a long abdomen, consisting of ten or eleven segments. The moving head has a strong biting mechanism and large compound eyes. The long, narrow wings are transparent and membranous and do not fold over the abdomen when the insect is at rest. This is characteristic of primitive winged insects in the group of Paleotera. Both pairs of wings have the same structure and rich nervation, which is an important de-

termining characteristic of individual species of insects. The larvae of dragonflies live in the water, and their development includes an incomplete metamorphosis. The genus *Petalia* has been identified from the Upper Jurassic to the present day. Its fossilized remains have been found in Europe.

Cordulagomphus

LOWER CRETACEOUS

The representative of the genus *Cordulagomphus* illustrated here is another representative of dragonflies, whose chief characteristics were described for the genus *Petalia*. It lived in the Lower Cretaceous and is 7.7 cm (3 in) long.

Bojophlebia

UPPER CARBONIFEROUS

The genus *Bojophlebia* belongs to the order of mayflies, i.e., the group which comprises species with a small head and short antennae. The wings are wide, and the back wings are shorter. The straight nervation across the wings is unremarkable. On the abdomen the body ends with a pair of long, segmented appendages (cerci), which resemble antennae, and a single long appendage (paracercum).
Some sorts of mayflies had wings which could grow

Cordulagomphus sp.
Lower Cretaceous, Brazil

to a span of 45 cm (17³/₄ in), approaching the size of the dragonflies of the genus *Meganeura*. These were the largest insects of all time, with wings which could have a span of up to 75 cm (29¹/₂ in).

Etoblattina ●

UPPER CARBONIFEROUS

The genus *Etoblattina* belongs to the order of cockroaches. Like dragonflies and mayflies, cockroaches are one of the oldest groups of insects, but unlike them, they developed further and belong to the groups of Neoptera. They have a compressed body and there is a biting mechanism on the head. The front wings have a convex edge at the front, and a covering membrane. When the insect is at rest, these are folded over the abdomen. In some Carboniferous species, the wings were still membranous, like the back wings. Their development included a complete metamorphosis. Cockroaches were the most frequently found insects, dating from the Upper Paleozoic, particularly their wings. The oldest cockroaches to be found date back to the Carboniferous, when they developed to reach their peak. They have not changed in any essential way since that time. The wing illustrated here belongs to the genus *Etoblattina*, and is 3.5 cm (1³/₄ in) long.

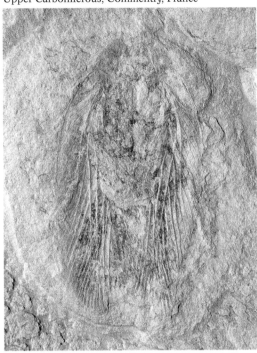

Etoblattina sp.
Upper Carboniferous, Commentry, France

Bojophlebia prokopi
Upper Carboniferous, Kladno, Czech Republic

93

4. Mollusks

An enormous number of fossils dating from the Cambrian era, as well as living species, belong to the phylum of mollusks (Mollusca). Almost 200,000 species have been described. Mollusks are characterized by a great diversity of species, as well as an enormous range of shapes. The sizes vary from microscopically small to more than 20 m (65 ft) across. They can weigh several tons; the largest invertebrates ever to live on the planet belong to this phylum.

Mollusks have soft, unsegmented bodies that are generally bilaterally symmetrical. It is usually possible to distinguish *the head, visceral hump* and the muscular *foot*. The foot is an organ for movement, but is also used for digging or swimming. The important internal organs like the heart, liver and digestive system are on the back of the intestinal tract. The digestive system starts at the mouth in the head, which opens into the gut. There is a rasp on the tongue called a *radula*, which scrapes up the food. The intestinal tract is covered on the dorsal side and on the side by a mantle. The space between the intestinal tract and the mantle contains the respiratory organs. (In aquatic mollusks these are gills.) One of the characteristic features of mollusks is the strong, usually external shell which is secreted by the mantle. The shell can consist of several plates, two shells, or just one piece. The wall of the shell usually consists of three layers. Mollusks multiply by means of sexual reproduction. Some are divided into gender, but there are also rare hermaphrodite species. The development of terrestrial mollusks and freshwater mollusks is a direct process. In marine species, the eggs first produce larvae. Less developed mollusks bear live young, and some species care for their young.

In general, marine mollusks are only adapted to a particular level of salt in the water. They represent a significant proportion of bethic organisms (organisms which inhabit the sea bed), or they are nektonic (active swimmers) or planktonic (floating passively). They are found at all depths; some even at depths of approximately 8,000 m (26,246 ft). Freshwater mollusks live in lakes, rivers, marshes or springs. Terrestrial species are found from tropical to arctic regions, and have even been discovered at heights of almost 6,000 m (19,685 ft). Mollusks comprise vegetarian and carnivorous species. Some feed on vegetable and animal waste, others are parasitic. For the classification of mollusks into seven classes, the structure of the shell and the morphology of the soft parts is important (although, with very few exceptions, the soft parts have not been preserved as fossils). The classes are: Aplacophora – worm mollusks, Polyplaco-

phora – chitons or coat-of-mail shells, Monoplacophora – Monoplacophorans, Gastropoda – gastropods, Scaphopoda – tusk-shells, Bivalvia – bivalves, Cephalopoda – cephalopods. With some reservations, two further classes of fossils can also be included: Tentaculita – tentacled animals and Hyolitha – hyolithids.

Class: Polyplacophora

Polyplacophora are primitive chitons or coat-of-mail mollusks that are bilaterally symmetrical. They inhabit shallow sub-littoral waters where they attach to rocks or crawl over the bottom; some species have been fished from great depths. They feed on seaweed or vegetable waste. The body is covered by interconnected, moving (dorsal) plates (usually eight), which more or less overlap. The head is separated and the ventral foot is adapted to crawling. There are numerous gills in the ventral groove between the foot and the material connecting the dorsal part. The group comprises organisms which are very old in geological terms, but rather conservative from a morphological point of view. They have never been important in the composition of fauna and probably developed from annelids at the start of the Cambrian era, at the same time as the Monoplacophorans. They are usually subdivided into the orders of Paleoricata and Neoloricata and are classified in a group of uncertain systematic origin, *incertae sedis*.

Helminthochiton ■

LOWER ORDOVICIAN – CARBONIFEROUS

Helminthochiton belongs to the most developed order of chitons, Neoloricata, the representatives of

Flabellipecten beudanti
Middle Miocene, Bordeaux, France

Left: *Douvilleiceras mammilatum,*
Troyes, France

95

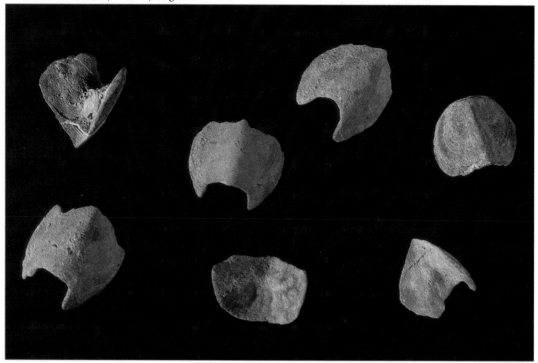

which developed a shell with a more or less complicated structure. The dorsal cover is segmented. In
a complete individual, it consists of eight convex,
thin, smooth plates with a rounded back across the
whole transverse axis of the organism's dorsal cover.
The internal plates are almost square, while the plates on the edge are rounded. In the fossils, there are
often only individual plates. Specimens of *Helminthochiton* have been identified in Europe and North
America, from the Ordovician to the Carboniferous.
The largest plate of the illustrated specimen of *Helminthochiton priscus* measures 19 mm ($^3/_4$ in).

Class: Monoplacophora – monoplacophorans

CAMBRIAN – RECENT TIMES

Monoplacophorans represent a small group of primitive marine mollusks, with bilaterally symmetrical
calcareous shell, which covers the dorsal side of the
body. The shell can have different shapes, but is often in the form of a hood or spoon, or broadly conical; in more developed species it can be curved like
a cornet. The top of the shell curves forwards, and is
close to the organism's head. On the inside of the
shell, parallel impressions of muscles are arranged in
pairs (which can be preserved in the fossil). The shell
has a smooth surface, or a net-like structure. It is for-

med by radial ribs which transect the concentric zo-
nes of the parts that have grown on. The soft body
of present-day species consists of a more or less separate head, a visceral hump and a foot. The body is
covered by a mantle. Between the foot and the
mantle, there is a space containing five pairs of leaf-
shaped ribs. Appendages like feelers are arranged
around the mouth, which is at the bottom of the
head. The impressions of muscles found on the inner
surface of the shell of fossilized examples indicate the
body was composed of a varying number of segments. Monoplacophorans represent a group of extremely primitive mollusks related to annelids and
coelenterates. They represent the basic form of gastropods and with an adaptation of the shell, also snails. The presence of feelers around the mouth may
have been the origin of the development of arms in
cephalapoda. They form a group of mollusks which
has survived without visible evolution. Changes took
place only in the form of a reduction to the muscle
impressions, or the extension or torsion of the shell.
Monoplacophorans were considered to be extinct. It
was only in 1952 that a Danish expedition found
a recent example of *Neopilina* off the coast of Me-
xico at a depth of 3,500 m (11,482 ft). The oldest
found date back to the Lower Cambrian. They were
common during the Silurian, and in the Devonian
they represented a significant proportion of benthic
organisms. Now, they are subdivided into three

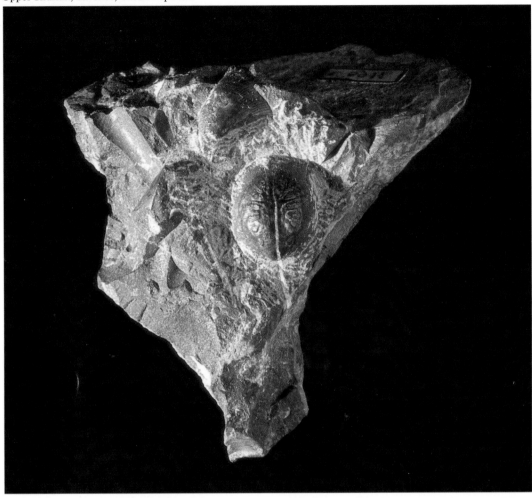

orders: Triblidioidea, Archinacelloidea and Stenothecoidea.

Order: Triblidioidea

CAMBRIAN – RECENT TIMES

This includes the largest group of monoplacophorans, mostly with spoon-shaped shell with the top is pushed forward. A few have convex or cornet-shaped shells with two pairs of muscle impressions. Others have five to eight pairs of these impressions.

Drahomira ■

UPPER SILURIAN

The genus *Drahomira* has a long, spoon-shaped shell with a weakly developed top at the front. The internal surface of the thin, walled shell has fine concentric wavy grooves, but usually only the internal fossilized center is found. Seven pairs of symmetrically arranged internal muscle impressions can be found in these. In the center, they are preserved as molds, which protrude in the shape of narrow walls. The animal moved forwards slowly over the muddy bed of shallow bays. Specimens of the genus *Drahomira* have been found in European seas dating from the Upper Silurian, but similar varieties are also described in North Africa.

The specimen shown here belongs to the species *Drahomira rugata*, and the plate is 1.6 cm ($^1/_2$ in) long.

Class: Gastropoda
– gastropods

LOWER CAMBRIAN – RECENT TIMES

Snails have now reached the peak of their development. At the same time, they represent the most extensive group of mollusks with more than 130,000 species (of which more than 40,000 are recent). They live mainly in a marine environment. Only a few snails have moved onto land, and are the only mollusks to breathe in the oxygen in the air. The body of snails is usually asymmetrical, and is normally covered with a single calcareous, helically-coiled *shell.* The shell is usually coiled in three-dimensional space; plano-spirally coiled shells are less common. The soft body has a clearly defined *head, an intestinal tract,* often coiled the same way as the shell, and a *foot.* In some snails, there is a gland at the top of the foot which secretes a calcareous or horny cover. The shells are formed on the exterior surface by an organic layer similar to chitin *(periostracum),* which contains the coloration. However, in fossilized remains it is rarely possible to identify the original colors. The lowest solid layer consists of $CaCO_3$ either consisting of the less stable material aragonite, or a less common, stable modification, calcium carbonate. The anorganic layer on the inside *(hypostracum)* consists of very fine, scaly aragonite crystals, usually with a pearly appearance resulting from the dispersion of white light. The hypostracum is only developed in a few, usually primitive snails.

The shells of the most primitive snails are not coiled in a spiral, and their shells resemble that of the representatives of the monoplacophorans. It starts to grow from *the top (apex),* though this is in an eccentric position. The base of the shell which is opposite is the mouth *(apertura).* The mouth of these non-helical conical shells sometimes has a narrow notch at the front, the so-called *sinus,* which corresponds with the position of the anal aperture and is therefore also known as the *anal slit.* This can go up to the top, but sometimes this opening is restricted to the upper part, in which case it is known as the *apical slit.* In later varieties, the lower conical shell of primitive snails changes to a high conical shape with a pointed end *(apical angle).* The shells are normally dextrally coiled. The direction of the spiral of the case can be determined holding it with the top pointing upwards and the mouth facing the viewer. If the mouth of the shell is on the right, it is dextrally coiled. In plano-spiral shells, there is a platform or *fistula (umbilicus)* between the edges on the inside of the last whorl on either side of the shell. Its width depends on the extent to which the whorls overlap. Fistulas also have insufficiently narrowly coiled helicoid shells. In some shells the first (larval) whorls differ from the other whorls in terms of shape and sculpture, and the axis of the whorl does not have to

correspond with the axis of the remaining whorls. A shell coiled around 360° is called a *whorl.* The last whorl, which contains the body of the snail or the body whorl, and the other whorls together form the *spira.*

Shells with irregular whorls or unrolled whorls are extremely rare. *Evolute* shells are those in which the whorls just touch, while *convolute* shells are those in which the whorls more or less overlap. In *involute* shells the last whorl overlaps all the previous whorls. The whorls touch in helical lines, referred to as *sutures.* In tightly coiled shells, a calcareous *columela* develops around the axis of the shell. This is flat or folded into columelar folds.

An *outer* and *inner lip* develop around the edge of the mouth which is at the end of the last whorl of the coiled shell. The outer lip differs in appearance and can be smooth or indented, thin, though sometimes reinforced, and may have spiny or finger-like appendages. The inner lip is near the axis of the shell and is usually reinforced with calcareous secretions known as *calus.* The upper *(parietal)* part of the inner lip contains a *parietal groove.* When the inner and outer lips merge together, this forms a *holostomatous* mouth, encompassing the whole rim. If the lips are separated by a notch, groove or canal, this forms a *siphonostomatous* mouth. During the snail's life, this canal protects either a fleshy, tube-like organ which supplies water to the cavity *(the incurrent siphon),* or an organ which removes water low in oxygen *(the excurrent siphon).* The canals tend to fill in, and because of the variation in the sculptured surface, a thin layer is formed, referred to as *selenizone* near the incurrent siphon, or *fasciola,* near the excurrent siphon.

Snails nearly always have sculptured shells, from the simple fused lines of primitive specimens to the radial ribs or tubercles, extensions and spines of the most

Morphology of the shell : 1 – body whorl, 2 – outer lip, 3 – mouth, 4 – anal fold, 5 – spira, 6 – apex, 7 – siphonal notch, 8 – umbilicus – fistula, 9 – columelar folds, 10 – inner lip, 11 – columela, 12 – radial (transverse) rib, 13 – spiral (lengthwise) rib, 14 – suture

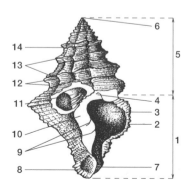

developed species. In addition to the radial elements which radiate from the top, lengthwise *(spiraling)* ribs can also develop. The combination of both types results in a woven or net-like sculpture.

Many snails with a spiraling shell develop a calcareous or horny cover at the foot, the *operculum*. This covers the mouth when the animal withdraws into its shell. These are also often found in fossilized form. The systematic classification of recent snails is based on the study of the soft parts. Fossilized representatives are studied on the basis of morphological characteristics of the shells. They are usually divided into three subclasses: Prospbrancha, Opisthobranchia and Pulmonata.

Subclass: Prosobranchia

CAMBRIAN – RECENT TIMES

These snails exhibit torsion for the gills, the anal opening, the heart and the intestinal tract, so that the nerve paths are in the form of a figure of eight. The most primitive representatives have two gills, but in more developed species, the right part of the gills has disappeared. The majority of snails in these subclasses have developed dextrally coiled, helical shells, and some have also developed an operculum. The other representatives of the class of gastropods developed from these eldest snails, which are still common today.

Order: Archaeogastropoda

CAMBRIAN – RECENT TIMES

These are the most primitive snails with two gills and a holostomatous mouth, which may have an anal slit on the inner lip. The shells have a small number of whorls, and may be plano-spirally or helically-coiled. In many cases the surface of the shell is coated with a pearly layer. Most of the development of the Archaeogastropodi took place as long ago as the Paleozoic era, and they still inhabit a marine environment today. Only a few freshwater varieties have been identified.

Praenatica ■

SILURIAN – DEVONIAN

The genus *Praenatica* is characterized by thick helically-coiled shells of different sizes. The shell is more or less round, with a very low spiral which has a blunt apex and whorls rapidly but evenly, increasing in size. The last, biggest whorl overlaps all the preceding whorls. The surface of the shell is smooth, or some virtually straight growth lines may be visible. The mouth is very wide and semicircular. The genus *Praenatica* was common throughout Europe from the Silurian to the Devonian. The specimen of the species *Praenatica gregaria* illustrated here measures 5 cm ($^3/_{16}$ in).

Praenatica gregaria
Middle Devonian, Koněprusy, Czech Republic

Orthonychia ■

SILURIAN – LOWER PERMIAN

The genus *Orthonychia*, is often seen as a subfamily of the genus *Platyceras*. It is characterized by conical shells almost 10 cm (4 in) long, which are wholly or partly uncoiled, and are in the shape of a hood. The walls of the shells have a smooth surface with pronounced wavy lines across the shells, or with irregular wavy grooves. Like the genus *Platyceras*, the representatives of the genus Orthonychia lived symbiotically with large echinoderms. They fed on their excrement. With their very broad, wavy mouth, they would settle on the roof of the echinoderm's - calyx at the place of the anal opening, and were able to avoid their arms. Specimens of the genus *Orthonychia* have been found dating from Silurian to the Lower Permian, in areas of Europe, Asia, North America and Australia. The fragment of the specimen of the species *Orhonychia anguis* shown here is 5 cm (2 in) tall.

Orthonychtia anguis
Upper Silurian, Zadní Kopanina, Czech Republic

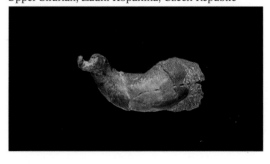

Sinuites sowerbyi
Lower Ordovician, Prague-Šárka, Czech Republic

Tropisodiscus pusillus
Lower Ordovician, Prague-Vokovice, Czech Republic

Sinuites ■

ORDOVICIAN

The rather small shells of the genus *Sinuites* are symmetrical and coiled in a spiral. The last whorl partly overlaps the older whorls. The outer lip has a deep U-shaped notch, which contains the siphonal tube. The inner lip is reinforced, and the umbilicus is covered. The surface sculpture usually consists of fine radial or lengthwise grooves. The classification of the genus *Sinuites* is not entirely clear. It is possible that the representatives of this genus could belong to the class of Monoplacophora. A large number of these species have been found Ordovician marine deposits in areas of Europe, Asia and North America. The specimens illustrated belong to the species *Sinuites sowerbyi*, which are approximately 2 cm ($^3/_4$ in) long.

Bellerophon ■

ORDOVICIAN – PERMIAN

The fairly small, solid shell (usually approximately 2 cm/$^3/_4$ in long) of the genus *Bellerophon* is a bilaterally symmetrical and spherical, plano-spirally coiled with a striking last (involute) whorl. The center of the whorls is transsected by a striking selenizone, bordered by a sharply serrated anal sinus in the

Bellerophon cf. *striatus*
Middle Devonian, Linde, Germany

outer lip. The umbilicus is usually covered with a distinct deposit of slime on the inner lip. The surface sculpture of the shell is most often formed by rings which indicate the specimen's age. The numerous representatives of the genus *Bellerophon* inhabited shallow seas all over the world from the Ordovician to the Permian. The larger of the two specimens illustrated here has a shell 1.3 cm ($^1/_2$ in) long.

Tropidodiscus ■

LOWER ORDOVICIAN – DEVONIAN

The genus *Tropidodiscus* is characterized by small shells with a diameter of 5–10 mm ($^3/_{16}$–$^3/_8$ in), which are common or extremely numerous in sediments dating from the Ordovician. The shells are flat, disc-shaped, coiled in a spiral with whorls increasing in size, and a sharp break line on the inner dorsal side. On the surface of the shell, there is a fine growth line, but there are no spiraling lines. The mouth aperture is wide, and a cross section reveals its triangular shape.

Spirina tubicina
Upper Silurian, Prague – Jinonice, Czech Republic

100

The walls of the shell are smooth, or covered with fine growth lines. Representatives of the genus *Tropidodiscus* have been found dating from the Lower Ordovician to the Devonian in areas of Europe, Asia and America. The specimens illustrated here belong to the species *Tropidodiscus pusillus*, and are 5 mm ($^5/_{16}$ in), across. The larger fragment of the shell belongs to the species *Sinuites sowerbyi*.

Spirina ■

MIDDLE SILURIAN – MIDDLE DEVONIAN

The shells of the genus *Spirina* are fairly large, symmetrically or helically-coiled, with sharp ribs. The spiral is flat, and the last whorl rapidly increases in size towards the mouth aperture. The umbilicus has various sizes and is oval in cross section. A large diversity of species of the genus *Spirina* has been described for many areas of Europe, dating from the Middle Silurian to the Middle Devonian. The specimen of *Spirina tubicina* shown here has a diameter of 3.8 cm ($1^1/_2$ in).

Theodoxus ■

OLIGOCENE – RECENT TIMES

Representatives of the genus *Theodoxus* are characterized by small, semi-spherical, involute shells with a large last whorl, and a low rudimentary helical shape. The shells have strong walls, and have a smooth, shiny surface. It is often possible to note traces of the original coloration. The mouth aperture is semicircular in cross section. This genus includes both freshwater and marine species. *Theodoxus*, which has survived up to the present day, existed as long ago as in the Oligocene, and was very common in the Miocene, Panon level in Central Europe. The largest specimen shown here of the species *Theodoxus isseli* has a diameter of approximately 1 cm ($^5/_8$ in).

Turbonitella ■

MIDDLE DEVONIAN – LOWER CARBONIFEROUS

The genus *Turbonitella* is characterized by a small to medium, thick-walled, rounded, low-spired shell, coiled in a spiral, a small number of whorls and a flat base. The whorls are more or less trapezoid in cross section, and the large whorl for the body broadens strikingly towards the mouth aperture. There is no umbilicus. The surface sculpture consists of striking transverse ribs. The mouth aperture is round or oval, and the inner lip is reinforced. Representatives of the genus *Turbonitella* inhabited shallow seas and were common in areas of Europe from the Middle Devonian to the Lower Carboniferous. The shell of the species *Turbonitella subcostata* shown here is 3 cm ($1^3/_4$ in) high. Because the shells are thick, fossilized remains of this species are often well preserved.

Turbonitella subcostata
Middle Devonian, Paffrath, Germany

Oriostoma dives
Upper Silurian, Prague – Podolí, Czech Republic

Euomphalus pentalugatus
Lower Carboniferous, St. Douglas, Ireland

Neritopsis ■

TRIASSIC – RECENT TIMES

The thick-walled shell of *Neritopsis* is small to average (approx. 2 cm/1³/₄ in) and characterized by a very low spire with a small number of whorls. The body whorl is large and has a convex conical shape. The inner lip is significantly widened, and the cross section of the round mouth aperture is smooth and reinforced. Sometimes it contains a broad, angular notch. In some cases the outer lip has a finely indented edge. The surface sculpture is usually characterized by a network of spiraling and radial ribbing or tubercles. Specimens of *Neritopsis* have been identified from the Triassic. They reached their peak in the Jurassic, and more than 150 species have been identified. Fossils of the *Neritopsis* have been found all over the world; nowadays they live in the Indian and Pacific Oceans. The species *Neritopsis asperata* shown has a shell which is 2.2 cm (³/₄ in) in diameter.

Nertopsis asperata
Upper Miocene, Vienna basin, Austria

Oriostoma ■

UPPER SILURIAN – LOWER DEVONIAN

The shells of the genus *Oriostoma* are relatively large, with a maximum diameter of approximately 5 cm (2 in). The low turreted shell is helically-coiled, and the whorls become broader towards the mouth aperture. There is a broad umbilicus at the base. The surface sculpture is composed of radial grooves or ribs, often with tubercles consisting of rows of fine triangular plates overlapping like scales. The mouth of the shell is round or square and rounded. It is often covered by a solid calcareous cover. The genus *Oriostoma* has a large number of species and representatives have been found and described in many areas of Europe and North America, dating from the Upper Silurian to the Lower Devonian. The fragment of the specimen shown here belongs to the species *Oriostoma dives* and is 5 cm (2 in) in diameter.

Euomphalus ■

SILURIAN – PERMIAN

The average or large shell (5 cm/2 in) of the genus *Euomphalus* is low and disc-shaped, coiled in a spiral consisting of seven to eight whorls. Near the top edge of all the whorls there is a distinct slit band. The umbilicus lies between the freely coiled whorls and is broad and shallow. The surface sculpture consists of growth lines. The mouth of the shell is in the shape of a rounded polygon. Some paleontologists have identified this genus as the genus *Straparollus*. The species of the genus *Euomphalus* are very similar. They were found on many continents, from the Silurian to the Permian.

Tubina armata
Lower Devonian, Koněprusy, Czech Republic

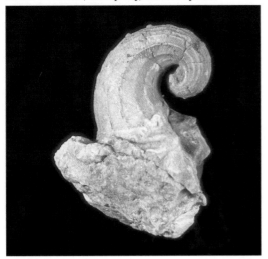

Turbo stenlai
Upper Cretaceous, Březno, Czech Republic

Tubina ■

LOWER DEVONIAN

The shell of the genus *Tubina* is relatively small, almost symmetrically coiled, and in mature specimens the body whorl is free. The surface sculpture consists of a combination of indistinct growth lines and clearly visible spiraling ribs. Long, thin, hollow spines arranged in a spiral are characteristic, but these are rarely preserved and are usually broken off. The mouth of the shell is round or square and rounded. Some of the species of the genus *Tubina* are particularly common in the Lower Devonian limestone rocks in the central Czech Republic (Barrandien region). These snails lived on the cliff sides there, together with corals, Stromatoporoidea, animals with tentacles, echinoderms and other organisms. The species *Tubina armata* illustrated here is 2.3 cm (1 in) across.

Turbo ■

TRIASSIC – RECENT TIMES

The genus *Turbo* is characterized by a thick-walled shell with a fairly low spire and a large whorl for the body. The whorls are convex and the surface sculpture sometimes consists of striking radial ribs which are thicker, and at the same time furthest apart on the whorl for the body. However, the surface of the shell is often completely smooth, and a patchy coloration can sometimes be distinguished. The mouth of the shell is almost round, and sometimes there is also a solid lid. The genus *Turbo* is represented by many different species. The first of these date from the Triassic and have been found in Europe, Africa, Asia and North America. Specimens of this genus are now found only in the Indian and Pacific Oceans.

Symmetrocapulus ■

JURASSIC – LOWER CRETACEOUS

The shells of the genus *Symmetrocapulus* are large, bilaterally symmetrical, with a low or very low bell shape, and a round or oval circumference. The apex is in the middle, coiling towards the front in a spiral. The surface structure consists of waving radial ribs and thick growth lines. A large number of Jurassic to Lower Cretaceous species are found in many parts of Europe. The specimen shown here belongs to the species *Symmetrocapulus rugosus* and has a shell 3.2 cm (1³/₄ in) long.

Symmetrocapulus rugosus
Middle Jurassic, Minchinhampton, Great Britain

Obornella plicopunctata
Middle Jurassic, France

Bathrotomaria reticulata
Upper Jurassic, Podpilany, Poland

Obornella ∎

JURASSIC

Representatives of the genus *Obornella* are characterized by a low conical or lens-shaped shell with a slightly convex base and a narrow fistula. The surface sculpture consists of a combination of spiraling and thick radial ribs. The mouth of the shell is short, like a slit, and there is a short, deep sinus on the outer lip for the excurrent siphon which has a clearly visible selenizone. The representatives of the genus *Obornella* still belong to the family of Pleurotomariidae, which were thought to be extinct for a long time. It was only in 1855 that a living specimen was found and named *Pleurotomaria quoyana*. Up to now, approximately thirty living species

Pleurotomaria constricta
Middle Jurassic, Heimbacht, Germany

have been found, considered to be 'living fossils'. Like the representatives of the Pleuromariidae family, which lived until recently, the genus *Obornella* also inhabited the deep seas and was a predator which attacked marine sponges. The extinct genus *Obornella* has been found in many Jurassic locations in Europe.

Pleurotomaria ∎

TRIASSIC – RECENT TIMES

The genus *Pleurotomaria* is characterized by a broad conical shell with a blunt spire. There is a sinus band in the upper part of the whorls. The surface sculpture normally consists of fine spiraling ribs which can be smooth or grainy. Often there are also transverse ribs, or the surface of the shell may be smooth. The mouth of the shell is oval, or a rounded diamond shape, and a clearly visible anal sinus has developed on the inner lip. Representatives of the genus *Pleurotomaria* have been found in Europe, Asia, Africa, Indonesia and New Zealand dating from the Triassic to the present day. They were widespread throughout the world during the Jurassic and the Cretaceous and are found today on the coasts of Japan and Western India. The specimen of the species *Pleurotomaria constricta* illustrated here has a shell 9 cm ($3^1/_2$ in) in diameter.

Bathrotomaria ∎

JURASSIC – CRETACEOUS

The average-sized shell (approximately 3 cm/$1^3/_4$ in) of the snails of the genus *Bathrotomaria* has low to average low whorls. The whorls are solid and convex and the umbilicus is narrow. The protruding slit-like spout covering the excurrent siphon forms a clearly visible slit band on the outer edge of the whorls. The cross section of the whorls reveals a rounded pentagon.

Leptomaria seriogranulata
Upper Cretaceous, Prague-Bílá Hora, Czech Republic

Pyrgotrochus conoideus
Middle Jurassic, Bayeux, France

The surface structure consists of a combination of a striking, spiraling slit band, numerous short, fine spiraling lines, as well as fine growth lines. The mouth of the shell is a short slit. Specimens of the genus *Bathrotomaria* dating from the Jurassic to the Cretaceous are found all over the world. The specimen shown here belongs to the species *Bathrotomaria reticulata* and has a shell 3 cm (1³/₄ in) across. The mouth of the shell has not been preserved.

Leptomaria ■

MIDDLE JURASSIC– UPPER CRETACEOUS

The shells of the genus *Leptomaria* are relatively low and conical, with slightly convex whorls which are oval in cross section. On the surface of the shell, the sculpture consists of a network of spiraling and radial ribs. On the top half of the whorls there is a narrow, spherical line instead of a suture. In the middle of the outer lip, there is a relatively long, narrow sinus, which merges into an indistinct sinus band. The sinus band often runs halfway along the length of the last whorl. A number of species of the genus *Leptomaria*, which is found all over the world, date from the Middle Jurassic to the Upper Cretaceous, and are found in Europe and North America. The species *Leptomaria seriogranulata* shown here has a shell with a diameter of 6.8 cm (2¹/₂ in).

Pyrgotrochus ■

JURASSIC– MIDDLE CRETACEOUS

The shells of the genus *Pyrgotrochus* are of average size, relatively high, and with a conical shape. The base of the shell is flat, and the umbilicus is completely covered. The sides of the whorls end in a striking slit band with a large number of small tubercles. The surface sculpture is characterized by a slit band coiled in a spiral, and fine, short spiraling lines above the fine growth lines.

The genus *Pyrgotrochus* lived in shallow waters in the period from the Jurassic to the Middle Cretaceous, and its representatives are found all over the world. The shell of the specimen of the species *Pyrgotrochus conoideus* shown here is 3 cm (1³/₄ in) high.

Haliotis ■

CRETACEOUS – RECENT TIMES

The genus *Haliotis* has a shell with an unusual ear-like shape, a large flat whorl for the body, and a spire that is not very clearly developed. In the lower part of the whorl for the body, there are round apertures representing the vestiges of a notch in the inner lip. This notch served as a spout for the anal siphon and was not completely filled with a calcareous mass. The genus *Haliotis* first appeared during the Cretaceous, and has survived up to the present day, with representatives all over the world. The specimen shown here belongs to the species *Haliotis lamellosa*, and has a shell with a diameter of 8.5 cm (3³/₄ in).

Haliotis lamellosa
Pliocene, Poggibonsi, Italy

Diodora sp.
Miocene, France

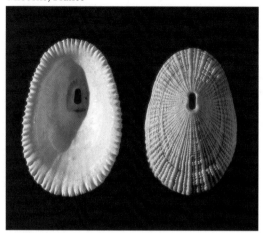

Calliostoma podolica
Upper Miocene, Mallersdorf, Germany

Diodora ■

UPPER CRETACEOUS – RECENT TIMES

The genus *Diodora* is characterized by a thick shell, almost 3–4 cm ($1^3/_4$–$1^1/_2$ in) across, with a relatively small oval opening at the top. On the outside of the shell, there are striking radial ribs which vary in thickness, becoming larger from the apex towards the broad oval mouth. They alternate with thinner radial and spiraling ribs, often resulting in a characteristic sieve-like sculpture. The genus *Diodora* has survived from the Upper Cretaceous to the present day, and is characteristic of the rocky coast of shallow tropical seas. Many fossil species from all over the world have been described and found in Europe, Africa, Asia, America and New Zealand. Nowadays, representatives are found mainly in the warm seas of the Caribbean. The shells of the genus *Diodora* shown here are 3.2 and 3.3 cm ($1^3/_4$ in) diameter.

Eucyclus capitaneus
Lower Jurassic, La Verpilière, France

Eucyclus ■

TRIASSIC – EOCENE

The genus *Eucyclus* is characterized by a thin-walled shell with an almost turreted whorl. The sides of the whorls are convex, and frequently there are a maximum of five slit bands coiled in a spiral and covered with small tubercles. The base of the shell spreads outwards and there is no umbicus. The mouth is round with an indented inner lip. A large number of species have been described, dating from the Triassic to the Eocene. The genus has been found in Europe, Africa, and North and South America. The incomplete shell shown here belongs to the species *Eucyclus capitaneus*, and is 3.4 cm ($1^3/_4$ in) high. The reddish-brown coloration is not the result of the original color, but occurred during fossilization, and is caused by the presence of a large amount of iron oxide in the rock.

Calliostoma ▣

MIOCENE – RECENT TIMES

The genus *Calliostoma* has a relatively small, broad conical shell (2–2.5 cm/$1^3/_4$–2 in), with a flattened base and indistinct sutures between the flat whorls. The columela is smooth, and the narrow, slit-like umbilicus is covered by an enlarged part of the shell. The mouth of the shell is a square with rounded corners. The surface of the shell is smooth, or the surface sculpture consists of a spiraling slit band with tubercles and slightly less striking helical whorls. The large number of specimens of the genus *Calliostoma* living today date back to the Miocene. They inhabit shallow freshwater coastal areas, and feed on microscopic algae. Their fossils have been found all over the world. The species shown here, *Calliostoma podolica*, has a shell 1.9 cm ($^3/_4$ in) high.

Neriea visurgis
Upper Jurassic, Hildesheim, Germany

Melanopsis sp.
Upper-Miocene, Hodonín, Czech Republic

Nerinea ■

JURASSIC – CRETACEOUS

Snails with very slender, high, twisted spires and a large number of whorls, belong to the genus *Nerinea*. The whorls are flat or concave, so that the sutures between the individual whorls may be just visible in relief. The side walls are smooth or have a spiraling sculpture, in the form of small tubercles. The mouth is wide and oblong, with a very short siphonal canal. The cavity in the whorls is made narrower by a few spiraling folds on the columela. The number and arrangement of these folds are important characteristics for the classification of species. The genus *Nerinea* was widespread from the Jurassic to the Cretaceous. A fairly large number of species have been described. During the Mesozoic the genus was common all over the world in shallow seas. In some places the shells of these cephalopods have even been significant in rock formation. The specimen shown here is of a 5 cm (2 in) tall fossilized center of the species *Nerinea visurgis*.

Order: Mesogastropoda – Mesogastropods

ORDOVICIAN – RECENT

The Mesogastropoda are an important group of snails, in which only the left part of the gills has survived. The helical coils are characterized by a holostomatous or unobtrusive siphonostomatous mouth. The pearly layer has not been developed. They normally live in the sea. They were very common from the Mesozoic and reached the peak of their development in the Eocene.

Melanopsis ▣

CRETACEOUS – RECENT TIMES

The genus *Melanopsis* is characterized by a helically-coiled shell with a low spire, in which the whorl for the body takes up most of the length. The wall of the shell is usually thin or of an average thickness. The

surface is usually smooth, and in many species the surface sculpture is covered with transverse ribs, sometimes with spines. The genus *Melanopsis* is found on many continents, mainly in strata dating from the Cretaceous to the present day. In the western Carpathians, this genus is particularly characteristic of the brackish sediments of the Upper Miocene (Panon level).

Turritella ■

CRETACEOUS – RECENT TIMES

The shells of this genus are narrow and turreted, with varying lengths and a large number of whorls (up to thirty). These are flat or slightly convex and smooth on the sides, or have a mainly spiraling sculpture. The mouth is holostomatous, circular or oval. The first representatives of the family belonging to the genus *Turritella* date back to the Devonian. The genus *Turritella* has existed since the Cretaceous; this genus is now viewed as a source of information, because it comprises a number of other related genera. Fossilized representatives have been found all over the world. In Central Europe they date mainly from the Neogene, and are found in the area of the Vienna basin. The genus is now found virtually everywhere, except in the Arctic and Antarctic. The largest specimen in the picture has a shell measuring 11 cm (4³/₄ in).

Turritella carinifera (tops to the right), *Turritella imbricataria* (top to the left),
Middle Eocene Gisors, France

Tenagodes anguinus
Pliocene, Italy

Gyrodes gentii
Upper Cretaceous, Březno, Czech Republic

Tenagodes ■

TRIASSIC – RECENT TIMES

The genus *Tenagodes* is characterized by an average-sized tubular shell (usually measuring 7–10 cm/ /2³/₄–4 in), which coils in a free spiral in the oldest whorls. The more recent part of the shell is completely uncoiled. The mouth of the shell has a striking sinus and sinus band on the inner lip, with a sort of chain of small apertures. The inner surface of the shell is smooth or finely ribbed. Approximately thirty species of this deviating type of snail have been described, which emerged for the first time in the course of the Triassic. Fossilized representatives have been found in Europe, North Africa and North America. Nowadays, the genus *Tenagodes* lives in fairly large areas of the Indian and Pacific Oceans, where it feeds on plankton. The specimen of *Tenagodes anguinus* in the illustration has a shell 7.3 cm (2³/₄ in) tall.

Vermetus arenaria
Upper Miocene, Vienna basin, Austria

Vermetus ■

MIOCENE – RECENT TIMES

The oldest part of the average-sized, solid shell of the deviating variety of snail of the genus *Vermetus* coils in a spiral. The whorls then become less regular, until there is a completely irregular pattern reminiscent of the skeleton of tube-worms of the genus *Serpula*. The mouth is round, without a sinus in the outer lip. On the inside of the surface of the shell, there are often traces of a spiraling sculpture, consisting of tubercles and growth lines. The genus *Vermetus* first appeared in the Miocene and was widespread all over the world during the Tertiary. Nowadays, representatives of this genus live in the Mediterranean and the Pacific. The shell of the specimen shown here belongs to the species *Vermetus arenaria* and measures 6 cm (2³/₄ in).

Gyrodes ■

UPPER-CRETACEOUS

The shell of the genus *Gyrodes* is conical or almost spherical. The whorl for the body is more or less flattened at the top. The spire is very low. The mouth of the shell is wide and oval, and the thin outer lip is much shorter than the axis. The edge of the inner lip is narrow. The umbilicus is rounded and has a sharp edge. The outside of the shell has a wrinkly sculpture. The representatives of the genus *Gyrodes* lived in the Upper Cretaceous, and many different species have been described which were found in Europe, Asia, Africa and North America.

Ampullina lavallei
Lower Palaeocene, Vigny-en-Vexin, France

Ampullina ■

LOWER JURASSIC – MIOCENE

The spires of the skeletons have low, convex whorls, while there is a generally fairly deep, or even canal-shaped suture along the individual whorls. The mouth is pear-shaped in cross section, with a striking parietal spout. The outer lip is thin, and in many species of this genus it is sharp. The curved edge of the inner lip lies closest to the surface of the shell. In other places this edge is thicker near the fistula, and may even partly or entirely overlap it. On the shell there are thick diagonal growth lines, elsewhere there are spiraling grooves. Specimens of the genus *Ampullina* have been found dating from the Lower Jurassic to the Miocene, and nowadays there are

Natica larteti
Lower Cretaceous, Algeria

a large number of species found all over the world. The fossilized center of the specimen illustrated here belongs to the species *Ampullina lavallei* and measures 7.5 cm (3 in).

Natica ■

LOWER CRETACEOUS – RECENT TIMES

The genus is characterized by an average-sized, more or less spherical, thick-walled shell (3–4 cm/ /$1^3/_4$–$1^1/_2$ in across), with a small number of whorls for the body and a greatly reduced spire. The last involute whorl is extremely concave and encloses the base of he shell. There is a false umbilicus at the bottom of the shell. The whorls of the shell are fairly rounded and smooth and have a striking structure of grooves, which indicate the growth. The mouth is large and wide, semi-spherical or broadly pear-shaped in diameter, often with slime at the inside of the edge of the mouth. The genus which has survived up to the present day dates back to the Middle Cretaceous and specimens are very common in marine sediments of the Mesozoic and Kenozoic of southern areas.

Neverita ■

CRETACEOUS – RECENT TIMES

The shells of the genus *Neverita* are spherical or oval. The mouth has a broad par shape, but can also be triangular. The outer lip is thin and straight, or wavy in cross section. The edge of the inner lip is massive and may have two slightly divided or undivided, thickened growths. The growth near the fistula is always more massive. Specimens of the genus *Neverita* have been found dating from the Cretaceous, and it is now very common throughout the world. The species illustrated here, *Neverita josephinia*, has a shell 3 cm ($1^3/_4$ in) in diameter. A sea acorn has attached itself to the surface.

Neverita josephinia
Pliocene, Oliveto, Italy

Megatylotus ■

EOCENE – MIOCENE

The shells are large and massive and have low, flat whorls separated by a canal-shaped suture. The mouth of the shell has a rounded triangular shape and curves towards the axis of the whorl. The outer lip does not have any characteristic features, the edge of the inner lip is completely spread over the flattened base and wholly covers the umbilicus. On the inside of the surface of the shell there are grooves which coil in a spiral, or small indentations in a spiral. Sometimes the shell is completely smooth. The representatives of the genus *Megatylotus* belong to very different species. Specimens have been found dating from the Eocene to the Miocene, all over Europe, Africa, Asia and America. The species illustrated here, *Megatylotus crassatinus*, has a shell measuring 6.5 cm ($2^{1}/_{2}$ in).

Tympanotomus ■

UPPER CRETACEOUS – RECENT TIMES

The genus *Tympanotomus* has more or less turreted shells with a high spire. The rounded oblong mouth is in the shape of a broad funnel with a thicker edge. The outer lip is hooded at the front, with a sharp notch in the back. The surface structure consists of transverse and spiraling lines of numerous small tubercles. Representatives of the genus *Tympanotomus* are still found on the west coast of Africa today. A large variety of species has been described. They were widespread all over the world during the Upper Cretaceous, and subsequently in particular during the early Tertiary. The specimen of the species *Tympanotomus margaritaceus* in the picture has a shell 4.2 tall. The representatives of this species belong to the very common European species which can be important for rock formation.

Megatylotus crassatinus
Lower Oligocene, Weinheim, Germany

Tympanotomus margaritaceus
Oligocene, Vienna basin, Austria

Cerithium ■

CRETACEOUS – RECENT

The shells of the genus *Cerithium* are usually high and turreted, and consist of a large number of whorls. The thick-walled shells are characterized by the round or angular walls of the whorls. The sculpture consists of ribs and spiraling lines of tubercles or there is a grainy effect. The broad, sloping mouth is oval. The short, deep siphonal canal is clearly curved. The outer lip is often wrinkled on the inside. The oldest representatives of this genus date back to the Cretaceous. Nowadays, the genus *Cerithium* inhabits all warm areas. This illustration shows the 13 cm ($5^{3}/_{4}$ in) tall, fossilized center of a large representative of the genus *Cerithium*.

Cerithium sp.
Lower Palaeocene, Vigny-en-Vexin, France

Terebralia bidentata
Upper Miocene, Grussbach, Germany

Serratocerithium serratum
Middle Eocene, Grignon, France

Terebralia ∎

The thick-walled shell of the genus *Terebralia* is average-sized and turreted, though not particularly slender. The whorls are smooth on the side. The mouth is broad and oval, and at a slant in relation to the axis of the shell. The thin, fragile outer lip has indentations and tubercles, the columela and columelar part of the mouth are wrinkled. The siphon is like a broad spout or shallow depression. The surface sculpture consists of striking tubercles arranged in a spiral. A large number of species has been described in this genus. The oldest specimens date from the Cretaceous. In geological history, the genus *Terebralia* was found all over the world. Nowadays, they are particularly common in the Indian and Pacific Oceans. The fragment of the shell shown here belongs to the species *Terebralia bidentata* and is 4.5 cm (1³/₄ in) tall.

Serratocerithium ∎

EOCENE

The average-sized shells of the genus *Serratocerithium* are turreted and have numerous oblong whorls in cross section. There is a parallel slit band directly below the sutures on the sides of the whorls. This consists of large, spiraling, relatively sharp tubercles with a broad base. The irregular, oval, broad mouth is at an angle to the axis, and the siphonal canal is short. Specimens of the genus *Serratocerithium* have been found mainly in Eocene marine sediments in Western Europe. The specimen of the species *Serratocerithium serratum* illustrated here has a shell which measures 6.7 cm (2¹/₂ in).

Campanile ∎

CRETACEOUS – RECENT TIMES

The genus *Campanile* is characterized by unusually large turreted shells (measuring approximately 50 cm/19¹/₂ in), with numerous stepped whorls with smooth sides. Usually there are a number of large, spiraling, button-like raised areas immediately below the suture, between the individual whorls. In relation to the axis of the shell, the very broad mouth is short and has a short, curved siphonal canal. The outer lip is shaped like a wing and is widely indented at the top. The rim of the inner lip is wrinkled. Not many species of this genus have been described up to now. Fossilized specimens of the genus *Campanile* have been identified in Europe dating as far back as the Cretaceous. Important discoveries dating from the Middle Eocene were made in the Paris basin. The fragment of the shell shown here belongs to the species *Campanile giganteum* and measures 19 cm (7¹/₂ in).

Campanile giganteum
Middle Eocene, Paris, France

Cymatium (Septa) affine
Pliocene, Oliveto, Italy

Anchura (Dicroloma) subpunctata
Middle Jurassic, Heiningen, Germany

Cymatium ■

CRETACEOUS – RECENT TIMES

The genus *Cymatium* is characterized by cylindrical shells with well-developed siphonal canals. The mouth is narrow and pear-shaped in cross section, and the inside of the area around the mouth is sharply indented. The surface on the inside of the shell has a spiraling sculpture, which can be simple or complicated, consisting of numerous tubercles. A large number of species of the genus *Cymatium* have been described. Specimens have been found dating from the Cretaceous, and nowadays they are extremely common in warm climates. The shell illustrated here belongs to the species *Cymatium (Septa) affine* and measures 4.5 cm (1³/₄ in).

Strombus ■

UPPER CRETACEOUS – RECENT TIMES

The genus *Strombus* comprises representatives with thick-walled helically oiled shells. Some grow to a considerable size. The spire is relatively low and the whorls are convex, often with a slit band. The last whorl is unusually large and forms the base of the shell. The siphonostomatous mouth is oval, and so-

Strombus coronatus (left), Pliocene, Poggibonsi, Italy
Strombus pugilis (right), recent, Western India

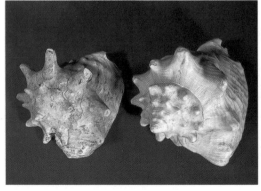

metimes has an elongated oblong shape. The inner lip is thicker, sometimes even broadening into a wing-like shape, and curving back to the surface of the shell. The surface on the outside of the shell is sometimes smooth, but more often the surface sculpture consists of spiraling tubercles or spines on the side of the whorls. The genus *Rombus* dates back to the Upper Cretaceous, and a large number of fossilized species have been found in Africa, Europe and Asia. Nowadays, representatives of the genus *Rombus* live in the Indian and Pacific Oceans, Western India and Japan. The specimen of the species shown here, *Strombus coronatus* has a shell which measures 12 cm (4³/₄ in). It is shown next to a recent representative of the species *Strombus pugilis*, which is found on the coast of Western India.

Anchura ■

JURASSIC – RECENT TIMES

The genus *Anchura* is characterized by fairly tall shells, with whorls with a more or less well-developed slit band. The mouth of the shell is characteristically thin and curved, often with a very good rostrum and a wing-shaped, broad outer lip in the shape of a hammer-like appendage. The surface on the outside of the shell has spiraling ribs, sometimes combined with transverse ribs. The genus *Anchura* has survived from the Jurassic to the present day, and many species have been described from Europe, Asia, and North and South America. The shell of the species *Anchura (Dicroloma) subpunctata* shown here measures 4 cm (1¹/₂ in).

Aporrhais ■

LOWER CRETACEOUS – RECENT TIMES

The genus *Aporrhais* is characterized by a thick-walled, turreted shell, with thick, coiled whorls. The large whorl of the body overlaps the base of the penultimate whorl. The slit-shaped siphonostomatous mouth has a long siphonal canal. The outer lip of the area around the mouth ends in a few long, finger-like shapes, each one of which has developed a spout on the inside. The inner lip is thickened. The surface of the shell has a pattern of transverse and spiraling ribbing. They have slit bands developed to varying degrees, normally with transverse tubercles. Representatives of the genus *Aporrhais* date back to the Lower Cretaceous. Many species have been described in Europe, Asia and North and South America. The shells of the species *Aporrhais uttingeriana* illustrated here measure approximately 3.5 cm (1³/₄ in).

Perissoptera ■

LOWER CRETACEOUS – UPPER CRETACEOUS

Representatives of the genus *Perissoptera* are very similar to the genus *Aporrhais*. The relatively large, massive shell is cylindrical, and the spire consists of numerous convex whorls. On the surface on the outside, there are striking, mainly radial ribs, often accompanied by thin, spiraling grooves. The mouth is narrow, with a long straight siphonal canal. The outer lip broadens out into a wing shape. Representatives of the genus *Perissoptera* have been found dating from the entire Cretaceous in areas of Europe, Africa, Asia, North and South America, and New Zealand. Only part of the spire has survived of the specimen illustrated here, which belongs to the species *Perissoptera megaloptera*. The mouth of the shell is missing.

Hippochrenes ■

UPPER CRETACEOUS – OLIGOCENE

The shells of the representatives of the genus *Hippochrenes* are large. The last whorl is large and convex. The mouth is long and narrow, and the rostrum is pointed and curved. The spout at the back reaches to the top of the mouth. The outer lip is in the shape of a large, flat wing, and the upper edge so-

Aporrhaius uttingeriana
Pliocene, Castell'Arquato, Italy

Perissoptera megaloptera
Upper Cretaceous, Březno, Czech Republic

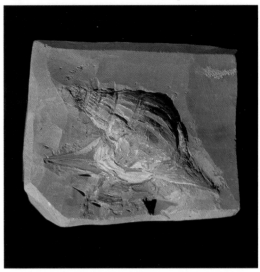

metimes extends to the top or even beyond. The surface on the outside of the lip is usually smooth. The genus *Hippochrenes* inhabited warm seas from the Upper Cretaceous to the Oligocene. Many species have been described which lived in areas of Europe and Asia. The shell of the specimen illustrated here belongs to the species *Hippochrenes fissura* and measures 5.3 cm (2 in).

Hippochrenes fissura
Middle Eocene, Neuilly-en-Thelle, France

Rimella fissurella
Middle Eocene, Paris basin, France

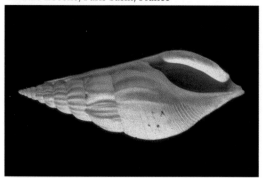

Drepanocheilus speciosus
Middle Oligocene, Gothen, Germany

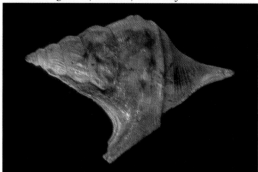

Rimella ■

UPPER CRETACEOUS – RECENT TIMES

The small shells of *Rimella* are bobbin-shaped with relatively high spire and tall, almost spherical body whorl. The mouth is elongated and oval. The outer lip looks like a turned-back cuff, or can be thicker at the edge, like a small wall. The siphonal canal is short and broad. At the top of the inner and outer lip, there is a small spout which reaches to the top, or the area next to it. The surface of the shell consists of striking transverse ribs, or various appendages. Sometimes there are spiraling ribs. Many species of *Rimella* have been described, and the oldest dates to the Cretaceous. During the Tertiary this genus was widespread, and nowadays it is found throughout the Indian and Pacific Oceans. The shell of the *Rimella fissurella* illustrated measures 1.5 cm ($^1/_2$ in).

Drepanocheilus ■

UPPER CRETACEOUS – PLIOCENE

In terms of shape, size and sculpture, the shell of the genus *Drepanocheilus* is fairly similar to the shell of the genus *Aporrhais*. It is turreted, with a whorl that is not too spherical for the body. On the sides of the whorls there are two spiraling slit bands, often with tubercles, which are most clearly visible on the whorl for the body. The outer lip broadens into the shape of a wing and has one or two finger-like appendages. The siphonal tube is narrow and short, and the anal canal is curved and considerably extended. The surface structure consists of a number of transverse and spiraling ribs and small tubercles. A large number of species of *Drepanocheilus* have been found in areas of Europe, Africa, Asia and North America, dating from the Upper Cretaceous to the Pliocene. The specimen of the *Drepanocheilus speciosus* shown has a shell 3.5 cm ($1^3/_4$ in) tall.

Pseudomelania heddingtonensis
Upper Jurassic, Heersum, Germany

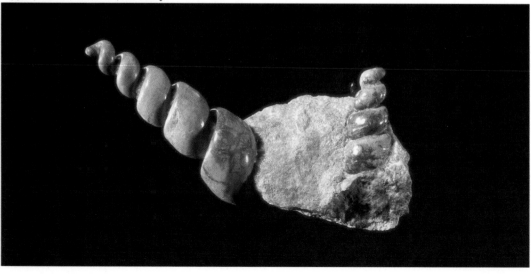

Volutispina scalaris
Middle Eocene, Damery, France

Pseudomelania ■

TRIASSIC – CRETACEOUS

The thick-walled shells of the genus *Pseudomelania* are turreted, and the smooth sides of the whorls are slightly convex or completely flat. In some cases there are brownish transverse stripes on the surface of the outside; these are traces of the original color. The sutures of the whorls are very deep, the columela is thickened. The mouth is round and does not curve to the surface of the shell. The genus *Pseudomelania* dates from the Triassic to the Cretaceous and a large number of species have been found in Europe, Asia and North America. The largest of the two fossilized centers of the specimen shown here, which belong to the species *Pseudomelania heddingtonensis*, measures 8 cm (3³/₄ in).

Volutispina ■

CRETACEOUS – RECENT TIMES

The helically-coiled shell of the genus *Volutispina* coils in a spiral and is characterized by a relatively tall spire which consists of a small number of whorls. The whorls are separated by steps. The upper part of the whorls have sharp but clearly visible spines on the edge. From these spines there are axial ribs which are combined with striking spiraling ribs. In comparison with the spire, the whorl of the body is much larger. The siphonal mouth of the shell is long, narrow and rounded at the end. The genus *Volutispina* dates back to the Cretaceous, and has survived up to the present day. Fossils mainly date from the Paleocene and are found in Western Europe (the Paris basin), where they were very common. The shell illustrated here belongs to a specimen of the species *Volutispina scalaris* and measures 7 cm (2³/₄ in).

Viviparus □ ▣

MIDDLE JURASSIC– RECENT TIMES

Representatives of the genus *Viviparus* grow to an average size, and are characterized by oval shells with a small number of whorls. The relatively large whorl for the body does not overlap the other whorls. The sides of the whorls are spherical or angular, and the sutures between the folds are deep. The shells have a broad holostomatous mouth with a semi-circular or wide oval shape. There is no umbilicus. On the surface of the shell there are fine growth lines, and sometimes also a more clearly distinct line. The genus *Viviparus* is characteristically found in freshwater or brackish water environments, and is very common in Tertiary freshwater sediments. Representatives of this genus have been found dating from the Middle Jurassic onwards, mainly in the northern hemisphere and in Africa. The species *Viviparus suevicus* illustrated here has a fossilized center as well as complete shells measuring 3 cm (1³/₄ in). The colored specimen belongs to the recent species, *Viviparus viviparus.*

Viviparus suevicus
Middle Miocene, Unterkirchberg, Germany

115

Tulotoma notha
Pliocene, Nova Gradiška, Croatia

Bayana lacteal
Middle Eocene, Grignon, France

Tulotoma □

PALAEOCENE – RECENT TIMES

The average-sized shells of the genus *Tulotoma* are thick-walled and conical. The umbilicus is narrow or may be entirely absent. The whorls are more or less angular with two striking slit bands on the side. Sometimes ribs of tubercles are visible on the surface of the whorls. The irregular, oval mouth is set at an angle to the axis. This genus is mainly found in very salty marine sediments. A large number of species of the genus *Tulotoma* has been described dating from the Paleocene. They were found throughout the northern hemisphere in Europe, North America and the Far East. Nowadays this genus is found in North America and China. The specimen of the species *Tulotoma notha* shown here has a shell measuring 2.7 cm (1 in).

Gyrineum (Aspa) marginatum
Pliocene, Oliveto, Italy

Gyrineum ■

PLIOCENE – RECENT TIMES

The shells of the genus *Gyrineum* are oval with a narrow mouth. The parietal spout is linked with a groove by the last spine. The siphonal canal is straight, relatively long and very narrow. The mouth is wrinkled on the inside. The outer lip is framed to varying degrees with long thorns. On the outside of the shell there are thick spines and ribs with tubercles on the surface. There are many species of the genus *Gyrineum*, and the oldest representatives date from the Pliocene. Nowadays, the genus *Gyrineum* in found in areas of the Indian Ocean. The specimen shown here belongs to the species *Gyrineum (Aspa) marginatum* and has a shell measuring approximately 3 cm ($1^3/_4$ in).

Bayana ■

EOCENE

The relatively small, turreted or bobbin-shaped shells of the genus *Bayana* have slightly convex whorls on the side, with a pattern of thin transverse ribs. These ribs are transsected by spiraling grooves. The surface sculpture of the outside can mainly be seen on the upper part of the shell near the top. The mouth of the shell is not particularly wide, and is pear-shaped in cross section. Not many species have been described of the genus *Bayana*. Representatives of the genus date only from the Eocene in Europe. The specimen shown here belongs to the species *Bayana lactea* and has a shell measuring 1.5 cm ($^1/_2$ in).

Trivia ■

UPPER EOCENE – RECENT TIMES

The shells of the genus *Trivia* are not large (approximately 2 cm/$^3/_4$ in). They are spherical with a blunt end. The spire is hidden. The mouth of the shell is narrow and slit-shaped, with a relatively broad and deep siphonal and anal canal. The surface on the

Trivia dorsolaevigata
Oligocene, Europe

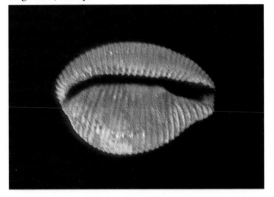

Zonaria lanciae
Miocene, Lapugy, Romania

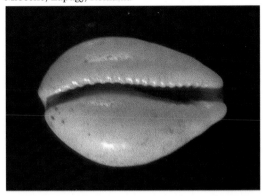

outside of the shell is covered with fine, spiraling ribs. There are many species of the genus *Trivia* dating from the Upper Eocene. In the geological past, it was widespread all over the world. Nowadays this genus is found in the Atlantic Ocean. The specimen illustrated here belongs to the species *Trivia dorsolaevigata* and has a shell 1.7 cm ($^1/_2$–$^3/_4$ in) long.

Zonaria

MIOCENE – RECENT TIMES

The genus *Zonaria* is characterized by small to average-sized oval or pear-shaped shells. The shells are narrower at the front. The spire is very low and has a slightly smaller number of whorls. The mouth of the shell is narrow and slit-shaped, and the outer and inner lip have a large number of notches, and the siphonal canal is very short. The surface on the outside of the shell is completely smooth, and it is often possible to see traces of the original color. Representatives of the genus *Zonaria* have been found dating from the Miocene, and a small number of species has been described which were found in Europe, Africa, Asia and North America. Nowadays, this genus is found in the Mediterranean and in the Atlantic and Pacific Oceans. The shell of the specimen illustrated here belongs to the species *Zonaria lanciae* and is 2.6 cm (1 in) long.

Phalium

EOCENE – RECENT TIMES

The genus *Phalium* is characterized by shells of an average size, generally with a very low spire and a spherical whorl for the body which is higher than it is broad. The circumference of the mouth is an elongated pear shape. The siphonal canal is deep, becomes narrower, and is very curved, and the anal slit is narrow. The outer lip looks like a rounded wall, and the edge is sometimes indented. The innermost fold is extremely wide and wavy at the front. The surface sculpture of the shell consists of broad, sometimes

unobtrusive spiraling ribs, which may have tubercles. Many species have been described of the genus *Phalium*, the oldest of which dates from the Eocene. In geological history, the genus was common all over the world, and it is still found all over the world today. The specimen illustrated here belongs to the species *Phalium saburon*, and has a shell measuring 4.8 cm ($1^3/_4$ in).

Phalium saburon
Upper Miocene, Vienna Basin, Austria

Ficus ■

PALAEOCENE – RECENT TIMES

The average-sized shell of the genus *Ficus* is pear-shaped and has a large, almost spherical whorl for the body. The mouth opens wide and ends in a relatively long, slightly curved siphonal canal. On the inside, the smooth outer lip is very thin, like the curved edge of the inner lip. The surface sculpture is like a grille, usually consisting of fine, axial and spiraling ribs which cross each other. However, the spiraling ribs are sometimes thicker, like the slit band, or may even be striking slit bands, usually with tubercles. The genus *Ficus* first appeared during the Palaeocene. Nowadays there are many species of this genus which are widespread in the warm seas all over the world. The shell illustrated here belongs to the species *Ficus reticulata* and measures 5.4 cm (2³/₄ in).

Order: Neogastropoda – Neogastropods

UPPER CRETACEOUS – RECENT TIMES

These snails also lost the right part of the gills, as in the order of Mesogastropoda. Unlike that order, the mouth of the shells of neogastropods is always siphonostomatous, often with a long siphonostomous canal. The shells are conical. The last whorl is high, but the spire is low. The oldest representatives date from the Cretaceous, and this continues to be a large group of snails up to the present day.

Ficus reticulata
Pliocene, Sicily, Italy

Fasciolaria (Pleuroploca) fimbriata
Pliocene, Oliveto, Italy

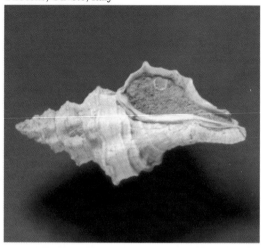

Fasciolaria ■

UPPER CRETACEOUS

The genus *Fasciolaria* is characterized by large oval or bobbin-shaped shells and a long body whorl. The whorls of the spire are relatively low, slightly spherical, or even angular. The whorl for the body is spherical. The mouth of the shell is fairly wide, and the narrow siphonal canal is very well developed, and curved to a greater or lesser extent. The outer lip is narrow, with a slight curve, and there are shallow wrinkles on the inside of the mouth. The surface of the shell is smooth, or has an indistinct sculpture. Fossilized specimens of the genus *Fasciolaria* have been found dating from the Upper Cretaceous. Most of the species to be described come from North America and Europe. Nowadays this genus is found in the Indian and Atlantic Ocean. The specimen illustrated here belongs to the species *Fasciolaria (Pleuroploca) fimbriata* and has a shell measuring 4.3 cm (1¹/₂ in).

Turricula ■

CRETACEOUS – RECENT TIMES

The shells of the genus *Turricula* grow to an average size. They are narrow and turreted, and have a very high spire. The whorls of the spire are slightly spherical, the whorl for the body is large, and the back broadens out. The mouth is elongated, broadening at the top and ending at the bottom in a narrow siphonal canal. The outer lip is thin, and it is possible to distinguish a deep, symmetrical or triangular sinus in a depression in front of the suture. The sinus of the suture is separated by a surrounding frame. The surface of the outside of the shell has a spiraling sculpture with a number of small tubercles, and some species have transverse ribs. The genus *Turricula* dates

Turricula dimidiata
Pliocene, Oliveto, Italy

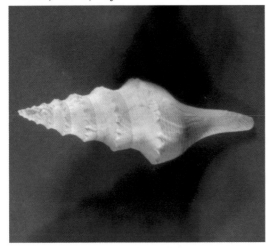

Conus (Chelyconus) pelagicus
Pliocene, San Gimignano, Italy

back to the Cretaceous. It is found all over the world and a large number have been described. The shell of the species *Turricula dimidiata* in the picture measures 4 cm (1¹/₂ in).

Conus ■

EOCENE – RECENT TIMES

The genus *Conus* comprises a large number of snails with a moderately large shell in the shape of a double cone. The whorl for the body accounts for about four-fifths of the height of the shell, and narrows towards the lower edge. The spire is very low and has a smaller number of step-shaped whorls which partly overlap. The top edge of the whorls is usually entirely smooth, and sometimes it is possible to distinguish a few tubercles. The mouth of the shell is a slit which runs the whole length of the last whorl. The mouth has a straight edge at the front and opens into a broad area with a siphonal notch. The surface of the shell is smooth, or has spiraling grooves. Occasionally it is possible to see traces of the original color. The genus *Conus*, which has survived to the present day, dates back to the Eocene and a large number of species have been described from all over the world. The shell of the *Conus (Chelyconus) pelagicus* shown here measures approximately 3 cm (1³/₄ in), and the colors have been retained very well.

Leptoconus ■

UPPER CRETACEOUS – RECENT TIMES

The thin-walled shells of the genus *Leptoconus* are of an average size and are rather similar to the representatives of the important genus *Conus*. The spire is relatively low, and the shell has the shape of a broad cone, with the individual step-shaped whorls overlapping each other. The upper edges of the whorls are

smooth. There are usually some tubercles near the top. The whorl for the body takes up about four-fifths of the height of the shell, becoming conical and narrower towards the lower edge. The mouth is narrow, like a slit, and has parallel edges. The siphonal canal is short and wide. The surface structure is generally made up of spiraling grooves, and the shell is completely smooth. Representatives of the genus *Leptoconus* which are found all over the world, first appeared in the Upper Cretaceous. The specimen shown here belongs to the species *Leptoconus diversiformis* and has a shell measuring 4.1 cm (1¹/₂ in).

Leptoconus diversiformis
Middle Eocene, Grignon, France

Nassarius obliquatus
Pliocene, Oliveto, Italy

Nassarius ■

EOCENE – RECENT TIMES

The shells of the genus *Nassarius* are small, with an oval or broad bobbin-like shape, and a large whorl for the body. The walls of the whorls are convex, coiled in steps, and separated by striking sutures. The mouth does not broaden out, and has an oval shape, curving away slightly from the axis of the shell. The outer lip is indented, and opens into a short siphonal canal at the lower edge. The edge of the inner lip is broad and sharply defined. The siphonal band is clearly developed. The outside surface of the shell usually has a sculpture consisting of predominantly spiraling ribs and numerous tubercles, but there are also completely smooth shells. Fossilized specimens date back to the Eocene and most of the species which have been described come from Europe and North America. Nowadays, the genus *Nassarius* is found in the seas of the Indian and Pacific Oceans, but also in the colder seas of northern Europe and North America. The specimen shown here belongs to the species *Nassarius obliquatus,* and has shell measuring approximately 3.5 cm (1³/₄ in).

Hinia (Uzita) clathrata
Pliocene, Oliveto, Italy

Hinia ■

EOCENE – RECENT TIMES

The genus *Hinia* is characterized by oval or bobbin-shaped shells with a large bullet-shaped whorl for the body and a mouth with a short siphonal canal. Because of the structure of the shell, representatives of the genus *Hinia* are so similar to those of the genus *Nassa* that the genus *Hinia* was considered a subgenus. The combination of thick transverse ribs and numerous spiraling ribs forms a net-like sculpture on the surface. The numerous fossilized representatives of the genus *Hinia* date back to the Eocene and are found particularly in many Tertiary locations in Europe. The two specimens shown here belong to the species *Hinia (Uzita) clathrata* and have a shell measuring approximately 2.5 cm (1 in).

Murex ■

PALAEOCENE – RECENT TIMES

The genus *Murex* is characterized by large shells in the shape of broad cones, with high spires, and large whorls for the body. The whorls are separated by deep sutures. The walls of the whorls are convex. The side walls are richly sculptured with striking ribs and tubercles, and there are often thin spines. The mouth of the shell is small, round or oval, and the outer and inner lip are slightly thicker. The siphonal canal is very long. A large number of species have been described. The genus *Murex* dates back to the Palaeocene and is still found to this day.

Murex conglobatus
Pliocene, Astigione, Italy

Pterynotus ■

EOCENE – RECENT TIMES

The genus *Pterynotus* is characterized by beautiful shells of an average size with thick walls and an irregular oval shape. The low pyramid-shaped spire has a small number of whorls. The whorl for the body reaches approximately halfway up the shell, or is slightly higher. The mouth of the shell is round or oval, and the siphonal canal is long and deep. The outer lip is indented, the inner lip has a broad fold. The surface sculpture of the shell consists of numerous sharp spiraling walls and transverse ribs at some distance from each other. The long, sharp spines which complete the sculpture have broken off in the fossils. *Pterynotus* is one of the predatory snails which bore their way through the shells or cases of other snails. The spiny shell protects it from other predators. The genus *Pterynotus* appeared in the Eocene and is very common in Tertiary sediments all over the world. The specimen of the species *Pterynotus tricarinatus* illustrated here has a shell measuring 4.5 cm (1³/₄ in).

Olivancillaria ■

EOCENE – RECENT TIMES

The shells of the genus *Olivancillaria* are usually pear-shaped, with a very low spire. The sutures are in a narrow spout. The mouth broadens towards the front and has a narrow siphonal notch at the front and back. The edge of the inner lip is thicker at the front and back. At the front of the thicker edge of the inner lip, there are sometimes a number of diagonal folds towards the axis. On the shell there is an indistinct central striped area which is not covered with a shiny layer. This genus dates from the Eocene, but

Pterynotus tricarinatus
Middle Eocene, Grignon, France

Olivancillaria plicaria
Lower Miocene, Saucats, France

up to now, not very many species have been found. Fossilized representatives of the genus *Olivancillaria* have been found in Europe and Asia, and nowadays there are species which live on the shores of Brazil and Africa. The shell of the largest specimen of the species *Olivancillaria plicaria* illustrated here measures 5 cm (2 in) and has a porcelain-like sheen.

Narona ■

PALEOCENE – RECENT TIMES

The shells of the genus *Narona* are shaped like bobbins and have a high spire. The last whorl is high and convex. The mouth is oval and pear-shaped. The columela generally consists of two or three slightly developed folds. The umbilical slit on the surface is visible, but the wall of the siphonal band is absent. Usually there are sharp transverse ribs on the surface of the outside of the shell, but the spiraling ribs are not very striking. The genus *Narona* first appeared during the Palaeocene, and up to now a large number of species have been described which originate from Western Europe. The specimen shown here of the species *Narona (Sveltia) varicosa* has a shell measuring 3.5 cm (1³/₄ in).

Narona (Sveltia) varicosa
Pliocene, Oliveto, Italy

Baryspira glandiformis
Upper Miocene, Mikulov, Czech Republic

Tudicla rusticula
Middle Miocene, Grund, Austria

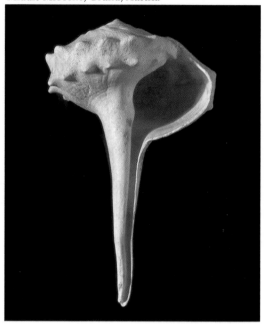

Baryspira

OLIGOCENE – RECENT TIMES

The average-sized shells of the genus *Baryspira* resemble the representatives of the other important genus *Ancilla*. The shells are elongated and oval. They are pointed at the top. The sutures between the whorls are not visible, because they are hidden under a shiny layer which also develops on the slime. The mouth of the shell is broader at the front, and has a broad and deep siphonal canal. The anal slit is narrow and shallow. The genus *Baryspira* dates back to the Oligocene and has survived up to the present day. Specimens are very common in Tertiary sediments all over the world. The specimen of the species *Baryspira glandiformis* shown here has a shell measuring 4.3 cm (1¹/₂ in).

Tudicla

UPPER CRETACEOUS – RECENT TIMES

The shell of the genus *Tudicla* is of an average size or large (usually measuring approximately 8 cm/ /3³/₄ in). It has a low, disc-like shape and a very low conical spire. The whorl for the body is large, broad and convex. The whorls have smooth walls with a spiny or spiraling sculpture with tubercles on the edges. The mouth has a broad oval shape and opens at the bottom into an unusually long, flat and sometimes slightly curved, narrow siphonal canal. The outer lip can be wrinkled on the inside. The inner lip has a thick fold.

The extremely curved columela has one to three folds. The surface sculpture of the shell consists of two rows of spiraling ribs, often without any tubercles. Sometimes the shell is completely smooth. Fossilized representatives of the genus *Tudicla*, which dates from the Upper Cretaceous have been found in Europe, Africa, Asia, North and South America, and Australia. The specimen shown here, which belongs to the species *Tudicla rusticula*, has a shell measuring 8.3 cm (3¹/₄ in).

Cancellaria

MIOCENE – RECENT TIMES

The genus *Cancellaria* is characterized by thick-walled, average-sized, bobbin-shaped shells with a low conical spire, and a large whorl for the body. The walls of the whorls are convex. The large mouth of the shell is rounded, and triangular or oval. The outer lip is indented, like the columelar area, where three folds have developed. On the surface of the shell there may be a net-like sculpture, consisting of thicker, often rounded, axial and more sharply spiraling ribs which cross each other. The oldest representatives of the genus *Cancellaria*, which has survived up to the present day, date from the Miocene, and a large number of species of this genus are found all over the world. The shell of the specimen illustrated here, which belongs to the species *Cancellaria cancellata*, measures 3.1 cm (1³/₄ in).

Cancellaria cancellata
Middle Pliocene, Sicily, Italy

Aquilofusus semioglaber
Upper Miocene, Gram, Denmark

Aquilofusus ■

TERTIARY

The genus *Aquilofusus* is characterized by a relatively slender shell with a turreted spire, and a very high whorl for the body. The sides of the whorls are extremely convex. The mouth of the shell is oval to pear-shaped, and ends in relatively short, broad siphuncle canals. On the surface of the shell, there are striking spiraling lines, and occasionally there are also axial ribs. Fossilized representatives of the genus *Aquilofusus* have only been recorded in Tertiary strata, particularly in regions of Central and Northern Europe. The shell of the specimen illustrated here, *Aquilofusus semioglaber,* measures 4.5 cm (1³/₄ in).

Fusinus ■

UPPER CRETACEOUS – RECENT TIMES

The genus *Fusinus* is characterized by average-sized to very large, slender shells (approximately 25 cm/9³/₄ in), with a relatively high turreted spire and an extremely high body whorl. The sides of the whorls are convex. The umbilicus is clearly visible in some specimens. The mouth of the shell is oval to pear-shaped, and ends in a very long, straight or slightly curved siphuncle canal. The surface sculpture consists of closely packed whorls and spiraling ribs. A pattern of spiraling tubercles is arranged along a line in the middle of the whorls on the spire and usually also on the body whorl. These form axial ribs which are re-

latively far apart. Representatives of the genus *Fusinus* are characteristic of the depths of warm seas, and date from the Upper Cretaceous. Nowadays they are found only in areas of the Indian and Pacific Oceans. The specimen shown here belong to the species *Fusinus longirostris* and has a long siphuncle canal, part of which has broken off. The fragment of the shell measures 4.5 cm (1³/₄ in).

Fusinus longirostris
Upper Miocene, Baden, Austria

Trochactaeon conicus
Upper Cretaceous, Gosau, Austria

Subclass: Opisthobranchia

CARBONIFEROUS – RECENT TIMES

This subclass includes snails which usually have a single gill behind the heart. The overlapping bunches of nerves disappeared with the torsion of the visceral organs. During the course of phylogenesis there was some reduction or even disappearance of the shell. For this reason, there is a small number of fossilized representatives. The mouth is narrow and slit-shaped, and the last whorl overlaps all the others, or at least the majority of the previous whorls. Opisthobranchia are virtually all marine species. Most of the shells which are found belong to the order of Tectibranchia, because these have a great potential for being fossilized. In the order of Pteropoda the shells are very thin and unsuitable for fossilization, or they are completely absent. Pteropoda are planktonic. The accumulation of their shells on the ocean floor resulted in so-called pteropodic layers.

Trochactaeon ■

LOWER CRETACEOUS – UPPER CRETACEOUS

The massive shells of the genus *Trochactaeon* are large (approximately 10 cm/4 in), bilaterally conical or a rounded conical shape. The body whorl is large and overlaps virtually all the older whorls. The mouth of the shell is oblong and narrow, broadening

out at the base, and sometimes thicker there. There are three folds on the columela at the front. The outer lip is broader on the inside, forming a wall. Deposits of calcium carbonate are secreted on the upper half of the whorls, on the inner walls and on the columela. A large number of species of the genus *Trochactaeon* have been recorded in many areas throughout the northern hemisphere. The illustration shows the fragment of a shell of the species *Trochactaeon conicus*, 10.2 cm (4 in) in diameter. It reveals a gradual reduction of the shell which took place during the lifetime of the specimen concerned.

Subclass: Pulmonata – pulmonates

CARBONIFEROUS – RECENT TIMES

In this subclass the inner wall of the mantel cavity contains a network of capillaries, creating a respiratory organ with which the snail breathes. Most air-breathing snails have developed a calcareous shell, though this can be rudimentary, or even completely absent. They are normally terrestrial or inhabit a freshwater environment. They probably first developed during the Carboniferous, but were most common in the Tertiary, and are found particularly in Quaternary deposits.

Gyraulus trochiformis
Middle Miocene, sand quarry near Steinheim, Germany

Gyraulus $\square$

LOWER EOCENE – RECENT TIMES

The genus *Gyraulus* comprises snails which grow to a small size (approximately 7 mm/³/₄ in). The shell consists of four or five rapidly growing whorls, is usually plano-spirally coiled, though sometimes the spire can be slightly higher. The body whorl is clearly broader near the mouth. The mouth is broad and oval, and sometimes there is a fold like a slit band. Only fine growth lines appear on the surface of the shell. Representatives of the genus have been found dating from the Lower Eocene in stagnant freshwater environments, and large numbers have been found in sediments of lakes and marshes. They are found all over the northern hemisphere. The illustration reveals a large number of specimens of the species *Gyraulus trochiformis* in sandstone. The largest specimen measures 5 mm (³/₁₆ in).

Galba $\square$

JURASSIC– RECENT TIMES

The small to medium-sized, thin-walled shell of the genus *Galba* are oval or bobbin-shaped and have a high spire. The whorls are spherical, gradually getting bigger, and the body whorl is the largest. The sutures are at an angle to the vertical axis of the shell.

Galba subpalustris
Upper Miocene, Velká Lípa, Czech Republic

Pupilla loessica
Pleistoceen, Prague-Bulovka, Czech Republic

The surface sculpture consists of fine growth lines. Representatives of the genus *Galba* first developed during the Jurassic, and nowadays there is a large variety of species. They inhabit small lakes and marshes across the entire northern hemisphere. The specimen shown here belongs to the species *Galba subpalustris* and has a shell measuring 2.5.

Pupilla ●

OLIGOCENE – RECENT TIMES

The genus *Pupilla* comprises very small terrestrial snails characterized by a thin-walled shell. The lower part of the shell is low and cylindrical, and the rest consists of a few convex whorls and a blunt, rounded apex. The umbilicus is narrow. The mouth of the shell is small, oval or semicircular, and the area around the mouth is slightly thicker. The surface sculpture consists of only fine growth lines. Various species of this genus have been recorded in Oligocene strata, but they only became common during the Quaternary. Nowadays they inhabit many areas throughout the northern hemisphere. The illustration shows how the important species *Pupilla loessica* has been deposited and is contained in loess. The shell measures 2–3 mm (¹/₁₆–¹/₈ in).

Helix insignis
Upper Miocene, Steinheim, Germany

Helix ●

The genus *Helix* is characterized by a medium-sized, thin-walled, usually spherical shell with a low, blunt spire and a small number of whorls. The body whorl is large. The shape of the fistula and the mouth can vary, which is helpful for the classification of a large number of species. The mouth is usually semicircular or oval. The area around the mouth forms a striking fold, so that that calus wholly or partly covers the fistula. The surface sculpture consists of a fine growth line. Representatives of these terrestrial snails of the genus *Helix* have been recorded dating from the Oligocene, and they are common in many Quaternary locations throughout Europe. Nowadays, they are most common in areas around the Mediterranean and Black Sea. The specimen shown here belongs to the species *Helix insignis* and has a shell measuring 2.6 cm (1 in).

Class: Scaphopoda
– Tusk shells

ORDOVICIAN (?), DEVONIAN – RECENT TIMES

Tusk shells are bilaterally symmetrical marine mollusks which belong to the small group of exclusively benthic organisms They have a tube-shaped extended shell of calcareous aragonite, which gradually narrows towards the back. Usually the shell is slightly curved (concave), but the ventral side (venter) is convex. They dig into marine sediments on the venter. The mollusk places the small posterior opening into the water to suck up the water needed for respiration. The length of the shell varies from 2–6 cm ($^3/_4$– $2^3/_4$ in). Some shells are broader in the middle resulting in

a barrel shape. The surface of the shell is smooth or has transverse or lengthwise ribs. The shell is open at each end. It secretes a mantle with the same shape, in which the left and right valves can grow together ventrally. There is an opening in the front of the mantle for a long, cylindrical, retractable foot, and an opening at the back to excrete undigested food. The head is rudimentary, and there are no eyes. There are a large number of tentacles around the mouth which serve to catch food. Behind the mouth, there is a radula. There are no gills, and the whole of the surface of the body is used for respiration.

Tusk shells can be divided into two families on the basis of the shape and the surface sculpture of the shell, the morphology of the radula and the anatomy of the foot. Only two genera have been recorded in Paleozoic strata, both dating from the Devonian (there are doubts about Ordovician specimens). Tusk shells flourished during the Cretaceous. Nowadays, there are approximately 150 species. They are found both in shallow coastal waters and at depths of several thousands of metres. They have characteristics in common both with snails and with bivalve mollusks.

Dentalium ■

CRETACEOUS – RECENT TIMES

The creature is enclosed in a slightly curved shell which is concave at the back. The shell is round or polygonal in cross section. The surface is sculpted with striking transverse ribs, but can also be smooth. The shell tapers from the back, and the diameter is largest at the front. The back opening is closed simply, with no special notches. This genus is found all over the world and dates to the Cretaceous. The specimens shown belong to the species *Dentalium elephantinum* and are 6–6.2 cm ($2^1/_4$–$2^1/_2$ in) long.

Dentalium elephantinum
Middle Miocene, Baden, Austria

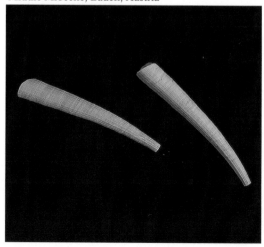

Class: Bivalvia – bivalves

CAMBRIAN – RECENT TIMES

Bivalves are bilaterally symmetrical aquatic organisms, with a flattened body and without a clearly separate head. The body is enclosed in two usually symmetrical valves. The front part ends in a muscular foot, which the organism not only uses for locomotion, but also for digging itself into the mud. In bivalves which are attached to the substratum, the foot is reduced and there is a byssal gland in the front part. This secretes a substance which hardens in water (*byssus*), with which the organism attaches itself to the substratum. At the back of the valve there are *siphons*, which let water in and out of the mantle cavity. The mantle consists of two lobes. They contain lamellar gills, the foot and the organs. The lobes grow together on the dorsal side of the mantle cavity. The edges and surface of the mantle secrete a calcareous shell consisting of three layers. The thin layer on the surface, the *periostracum*, consists of the organic mass, conchioline, which gives the shell its color. Under this layer there is a calcareous layer, the *ostracum*. This consists of calcium carbonate and aragonite and forms multi-surfaced prismatic crystals perpendicular to the surface of the shell. The inner layer, the *hypostracum*, has crystals of aragonite placed parallel to the surface of the shell. The individual shells are connected by muscles which close the whole shell. The so-called *ligament*, consisting of an organic mass of conchioline, which comes from the outer layer, the periostracum, opens the shell. Later an inner ligament developed as well – the *resilium*. This consists of an elastic cushion in a narrow groove on the dorsal side, which contracts when the shells shut and relaxes when they open. For these reasons, the shells found in sediments are usually separated (in contrast with those of tentacle animals). In places where the muscles are attached to the shell, two muscle scars have usually survived on the inside of the shell. When the shell shuts, the edges of the mantle pull together, forming a so-called *mantle (pallial) line*. In higher bivalves the ventral edges of the mantle grow together, forming a mantle tube, which can protrude from the shell at the back to serve as a siphon. This sort of extension is visible in a striking fold in the pallial line, known as a *sinupalliate line*. In the case of *integripalliate* shell lines, the sinus is not developed. The shells of bivalves can have all sorts of shapes, depending on the lifestyle. Some benthic bivalves crawl on the sea bed, and have two identical valves (*Glycymeris, Arca*). Others lie in one of the valves, and the lower valve is usually rounder (*Pecten*). Bivalves in shallow waters often attach themselves to the substratum with byssus (*Mytilus, Chlamys*). Other species which inhabit warm seas attach themselves to the substratum with *cement*. The lower valve is clearly larger, and also thicker and rounder (*Spondylus, Ostrea*). This characteristic is developed to an extreme extent in 'rudists', which have a cornet-shaped lower valve, while the top valve has developed into a lid. Therefore there are shells which are equivalve and valves which are *equilateral*. Conversely, there are inequivalve shells and inequilateral valves. The surface on the outside of the shells can either be smooth or sculpted. However, they all have concentrically arranged growth lines. The surface sculpture usually consists of ribs, radiating from the umbo to the edges, or arranged concentrically and parallel to the growth lines. This combination of lines can result in a net-like sculpture. Furthermore, the ribs can have all sorts of tubercles, indentations and spines. For the description, the shell is held with the umbo pointing up and the anterior edge forwards. The umbo is the part from which the shell begins to grow. Usually it points towards the anterior, i.e., the umbo is *prosogyral*, to the posterior, *opisthogyral* or upwards, *orthogyral*. There are areas with a different sculpture in front of the umbo (*lunula*) and behind the umbo (*area*). The valves are connected by a hinge plate consisting of teeth, with sockets opposite them into which they fit. The structure of the hinge plate is important for classification. More than fifteen types of dentition have been distinguished. The most primitive type is the *taxodont* dentition, in which the teeth and sockets alternate regularly in one or two rows. In contrast, the *dysodont* dentition is characterized by a reduction or absence of teeth. The most common type is the *heterodont* type of dentition, which is characterized by a few important (*cardinal*) teeth placed below the umbo, and a few smaller front and back *lateral* leaf-shaped teeth (on the side), which are parallel to the edge of the shell.

The classification of fossilized bivalves is based primarily on the structure of the dentition and the morphology of the shell, the shape of the pallial line and the muscle scars. This classification is often distinct from the zoological classification, which also takes the soft parts of the body into account.

Internal structure of the right half of the shell of a bivalve: 1 – ligament pit, 2 – hinge teeth, 3 – anterior muscle scar, 4 – posterior muscle scar, 5 – ligament, 6 – pallial line

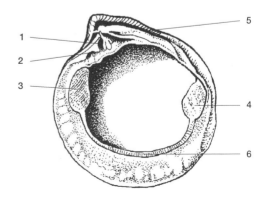

Panenca bohemica
Upper Silurian, Lochkov, Czech Republic

Order: Paleoconcha

CAMBRIAN – RECENT TIMES

The order comprises primitive bivalves, usually dating from the Paleozoic era; some genera have survived up to the present day (*Solemya*). They had an equivalve shell, and an imperfect dentition with hinge teeth that have not developed very much. The oldest representatives of this genus date from the Cambrian, and they were very common during the Silurian and the Devonian.

Panenca ■

SILURIAN – DEVONIAN

Panenca belongs to a Paleozoic group of bivalves, and the fossils were given a beautiful Czech name by Joachim Barrande. *Panenca* has a thin, symmetrical, slightly oval or round shell with radiating ribs, divided only by slightly wider grooves. The small

umbo of the shell is strikingly inclined towards the hinge plate, and slightly pointing towards the anterior part of the valve. The lunula is small, the edge of the hinge plate is straight or slightly broken up. The dentition is imperfect and the teeth are only slightly developed. The genus *Panenca* was widespread in Europe and America during the Silurian and the Devonian. Barrande described and illustrated 231 species in Bohemian Silurian strata. The shells of the species shown here, *Panenca bohemica*, have an average length of 6 cm (2¼ in) and a width of 5 cm (2 in).

Order: Schizodonta

ORDOVICIAN – RECENT TIMES

As the name suggests, the order comprises species with a schizodont type of dentition. This consists of two teeth in the right valve which grow from the umbo; there are three in the left valve. The shell can consist of two valves of the same or different sizes. Some species have an inner layer of mother of pearl or nacre. The two muscle scars are close to the posterior edge of the valves. This order mainly comprises marine bivalves; very few live in freshwater environments.

Trigonia ■

TRIASSIC – RECENT TIMES

The genus *Trigonia* has an interesting shell with an uncharacteristic shape and rather thick opisthogyral umbos towards the anterior and a ligament on the outside. The dentition of the right valve consists of two teeth with grooves that are very far apart. The dentition of the left valve consists of one strong middle tooth, and on each side, one long, grooved tooth. The surfaces of the valves have a different sculpture. The areas are divided by edges which run down from the umbo to the free edge. The area by the ligament and the side of the valve have concentric radiating or divergent ribs, or rows of tubercles. The genus is found in Triassic to Cretaceous sediments in every part of the world. Nowadays, a few last taxa still live in the seas around Australia.

The species shown here, *Trigonia intelaevigata*, is 7.1 cm (2¼ in) tall.

Unio □ ▣

TRIASSIC(?), UPPER JURASSIC – RECENT TIMES

A bivalve with a thick-walled shell with a diagonal oval or trapezium-shaped appearance. The surface is smooth, with clearly visible growth areas or concentric walls.

The hypostracum is made of mother of pearl. The dentition consists of teeth below the umbo, which

Trigonia intelaevigata
Middle Jurassic, Bielefeld, Germany

Unio atavus
Neogene, Gbely, Czech Republic

are usually weakly developed, and are known as pseudocardinal teeth. The teeth at the side are parallel to the edge of the hinge plate, and are known as pseudolateral teeth. The ligament is below the umbo (opisthodental ligament), which is characteristic of most representatives of schizodontal bivalves. Fossilized representatives of the genus *Unio* have been recorded in Mesozoic and Tertiary strata in Europe, Asia, Africa and America. This bivalve now lives in freshwater environments in lakes and rivers. It has been found in freshwater sediments in the Czech Republic.

Order: Taxodonta

CAMBRIAN (?), ORDOVICIAN – RECENT TIMES

This order comprises mollusks with a taxodont type of dentition, which consists of large teeth alternating with sockets in one or two rows. They have the same valves with a simple mantle line. The muscle scars are more or less the same. The order mainly comprises marine mollusks and representatives date back to the Ordovician and have survived up to the present day.

Glycimeris pilosus
Middle Miocene, Bulhary, Czech Republic

Chama gryphoides
Middle Miocene, Židlochovice, Czech Republic

Glycimeris ■

CRETACEOUS – RECENT TIMES

This genus is characterized by a large, thick-walled equivalve shell. The valves are round and have a curved hinge plate and two identical muscles. The anterior edge of the posterior muscle scar is surrounded by a wall. The numerous teeth of the taxodont type of dentition join in the middle of the valve. They can be absent in the middle part of the hinge plate. Under the umbo, there is a triangular area with broken grooves. The surface sculpture consists of growth lines. The inner layer has striking radiating ribs which also appear on the surface of the valve when it is mechanically polished. It is a free-living bivalve which wanders about on the sea floor. It dates back to the Cretaceous and is still found all over the world today. The species shown here, *Glycimeris pilosus*, is 10.6 cm (4¹/₄ in) tall.

Anadara sp.
Middle Miocene, Mikulov, Czech Republic

Anadara ■

TRIASSIC – RECENT TIMES

This is a bivalve with a taxodont type of dentition, and an oval equivalve shell, though the valves are inequilateral with an umbo in the anterior part. Beneath the umbo, there is a large, three-lobed area around the ligament covered with broken grooves. The hinge plate is narrow and straight, and the teeth point towards the middle of the valve. The surface sculpture consists of striking radial ribs. The genus *Anadara* has been recorded in Tertiary sediments in Europe and North and South America. Nowadays, these bivalves are found in warm seas all over the world. The species shown here, *Anadora sp.*, is 5.5 cm (2¹/₄ in) long.

Order: Heterodonta

SILURIAN – RECENT TIMES

Representatives of this order have a type of dentition consisting of cardinal teeth and lateral teeth. The shell is usually equivalve with muscle scars of the same size. Approximately half of all the bivalves that exist now belong to this order. Most of these are marine species; a smaller number live in brackish or freshwater environments.

Chama ■

CRETACEOUS – RECENT TIMES

This bivalve is characterized by an irregular, round, thick-walled shell with prosogyral umbos which coil in a spiral. The left valve is firmly attached to the substratum. The heterodont dentition consists of two strong cardinal teeth in the right valve and one on the left valve. Occasionally lateral teeth are developed to some extent. The pallial line is straight, without any folds. The shells are sculpted with concentric growth walls, often adorned with spines, tubercles or scales.

The genus *Chama* has inhabited warm seas since the Cretaceous. It has been recorded in sediments in Europe and America; in the Czech Republic the genus was common in the marine Miocene. The species shown here, *Chama Gryphoides,* measures 5 cm (2 in).

Venus ■

JURASSIC – RECENT TIMES

Circomphalus is one of the many subgenera of the genus *Venus,* and is represented by the important family of Veneridae. The rounded, triangular, thick-walled shell equivalve shell has laterally asymmetrical valves. The umbo of the valve is prosogyral. The surface of the shell has a striking concentric sculpture parallel to the growth areas. The dentition consists only of cardinal teeth, or also a lateral tooth at the back. The pallial line has developed a sinus fold. The inner edges of the shell are finely indented. The genus *Venus* was common all over the world, and fossils have been recorded in Jurassic sediments. The genus has survived up to the present day and there are many subgenera. The species show here, *Circomphalus plicata,* is 3.6 cm (1¹/₂ in) long.

Pelecyora ■

EOCENE – MIOCENE

The genus *Pelecyora* has an oval or rounded triangular shell, with a concentric or sometimes radiating surface sculpture and a prosogyral umbo. The edges of the valves are smooth or finely indented. The hinge plate is broad, with three simple teeth spaced some distance apart. The lunula is clearly visible. The pallial line is developed, and a short, round sinus fold is visible on it. The genus *Pelecyora* has been recorded in Eocene to Miocene strata in Eurasia and Africa. The species *Pelecyora gigas* was common in the Vienna basin during the Neogene. The shell of the specimen shown here belongs to the species *Pelecyora gigas* and is 9.5 cm (3³/₄ in) long.

Venus (Circomphalus) plicata
Middle Miocene, Mikulov, Czech Republic

Pelecyora gigas
Middle Miocene, Bulhary, Czech Republic

Megaxinus ■

PALEOGENE – RECENT TIMES

The genus *Megaxinus* has a flat shell with a round circumference and a fine concentric sculpture. It has a striking prosogyral umbo and an internal ligament in a narrow groove. The dentition is heterodont; in the left valve there are two front and two back lateral teeth in addition to the cardinal teeth. The muscle scars are different: the anterior one is narrow and elongated, the posterior one is oval. The pallial line does not contain a sinus and is therefore integripalliate. The genus Megaxinus was widespread all over the world from the Lower Tertiary. The curved edges on both sides of the shell are characteristic of the species shown here, *Megaxinus (Megaxinus) bellardiana.* The larger shell is 4.2 cm (1¹/₂ in) long.

Megaxinus (Megaxinus) bellardiana
Middle Miocene, Mikulov, Czech Republic

Linga (Linga) columbella
Middle Miocene, Mikulov, Czech Republic

Gryphaea arcuata
Lower Jurassic, Balingen, Germany

Linga ■

JURASSIC– RECENT TIMES

The genus *Linga* is extremely similar to the genus *Megaxinus* (both are members of the Lucinidae family). This bivalve has a slightly more convex shell with only a posterior fold. It is also slightly smaller, measuring on average 2 cm ($^3/_4$ in). The genus *Lingua* has been recorded in Tertiary sediments in Europe, Asia and America.

Cardita sp.
Middle Miocene – Mikulov, Czech Republic

Cardita ■

BOVEN-TRIASSIC – RECENT TIMES

The genus *Cardita* has a thick-walled, round to oval, strongly convex shell with a prosogyral umbo. It is equivalve, but the valves are not symmetrical (inequilateral). The surface structure consists of striking, radiating ribs which extend up to the umbo. The muscle scars are virtually identical. There are teeth on the lower edge of the valves. Usually no lateral teeth have developed at the back.

Cardita has been widespread all over the world from the Triassic to the present day. In the Carpathians they are found in marine Miocene strata. The shell of the species shown here, *Cardita sp.* is approximately 3 cm ($1^1/_4$ in) long.

Order: Dysodonta

ORDOVICIAN – RECENT TIMES

This order comprises bivalves in which the dentition is reduced, or has even disappeared altogether. The valves are different sizes. The posterior muscle scar is much more developed than the anterior one. There are usually no folds in the pallial line. The order mainly comprises marine bivalves which attach themselves to the substratum with byssus or cement. It also includes the important group of oysters.

Gryphaea ■

JURASSIC – PALEOGENE

This order has a thick-walled inequivalve shell with an oval shape. The left valve is strongly convex and the umbo clearly points to the anterior. The right valve is flat, in the shape of a lid. In a young bivalve the shell is attached at the umbo of the left valve. Later on, it is free. The surface sculpture consists of striking symmetrical lamellae.

The genus *Gryphea* has been mainly recorded in

Jurassic sediments in Europe, Asia and America. There are no recent representatives. The specimen shown here belongs to the species *Gryphaea arcuata* and measures 6.5 cm (2¹/₂ in).

Exogyra ■

JURASSIC– CRETACEOUS

Exogyra is the bivalve representative of oysters. The genus has a massive shell, consisting of very different valves, with an umbo turned to the posterior (opisthogyral). It is attached with the left valve, which is clearly more convex. The anterior edge of the shell is curved and the umbo turns dextrally to the join of the valves. The surface of the valves is usually smooth, but sometimes parallel growth lines can be discerned. The genus *Exogyra* was widespread all over the world during the Jurassic and the Cretaceous, and was represented by a large number of species. The shell of the specimen shown here, which belongs to the species *Exogyra columba*, is 7.8 cm (3 in) long.

Exogyra sigmoidea is a small oyster (measuring approximately 3 cm/1¹/₄ in), in which the left valve is helically coiled and entirely attached to the rocky substratum. Fossilized specimens are not found very often. The right valve is flat and narrow, with a spiraling umbo coiled to the posterior, turning into a

Exogyra columba
Upper Cretaceous, Kutná hora, Czech Republic

radial cone. This valve consists of a narrow, extremely sloping anterior, and a broad slightly inclined posterior. The edges are framed on the inside with small tubercles *(chomata)*. This species is common in limestone sediments in Europe.

Exogyra sigmoidea
Upper Cretaceous, Korycany, Czech Republic

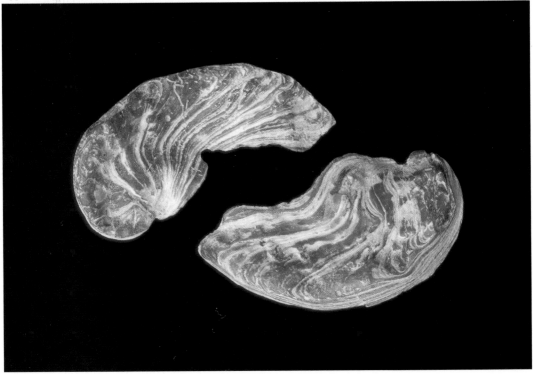

Pinna decussata
Upper Cretaceous, Vinary, Czech Republic

Cubitostrea multicostata
Eocene, Libya

Pinna ■

CARBONIFEROUS – RECENT TIMES

The shell of the genus *Pinna* is wedge-shaped or triangular, slender and with terminal umbos. There are two muscle scars, and the anterior umbo is larger than the posterior umbo. There are no teeth on the hinge plate, and the ligament is only developed on the inside. The shells are buried in the sediment with the umbo, and attached with byssus, which comes through the slit between the valves behind the umbo. Some shells grow to a length of one meter. The surface sculpture consists of radiating ribs and concentric walls, often covered with scales and chomata. They are often discovered on their own in the sediment because they form a thick prismatic layer. This genus has been common all over the world since the Carboniferous. Recent representatives live at depths of up to one hundred metres.

Deltoideum sowerbyanum
Upper Jurassic, Le Havre, France

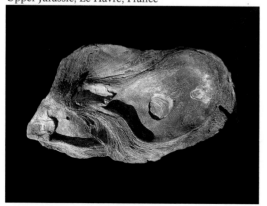

Deltoideum ■

JURASSIC

The shell of this oyster is large to average-sized, narrowing significantly towards the umbo. The regular triangular circumference is broken by a deep notch in the posterior edge. The two valves are similar and equally flat, although the right valve is slightly smaller. The surface on the outside of the shell is smooth. The genus *Deltoideum* was widespread in Europe in the Middle and Upper Jurassic. The shell of the specimen shown here, which belongs to the species *Deltoideum sowerbyanum*, consists of two specimens which have fused, and measures 17 cm ($6^3/_4$ in).

Cubitostrea ■

EOCENE – OLIGOCENE

The genus comprises oysters with a small or average-sized, sickle-shaped, half-moon or triangular shell. The sculpture of the surface on the outside of the two valves consists of concentric growth lines. The left valve has striking, narrow, sometimes forked, branching radial ribs. The edge of the left valve is finely crenellated; the edge of the right valve is smooth. Chomata have developed on both sides of the umbo on the inside of the shell. This oyster has been recorded in Eocene to Oligocene sediments in Europe and North America.

Oscilopha ■

CRETACEOUS

An oyster with an average-sized to large, biconvex, radially ribbed shell, with an oval or round circumference. The ribs are usually sharp, sometimes ending in spiny extremities. The edge is wavy or indented. On the inside there is a large, oblong or sickle-shaped muscle scar. Chomata have developed on the inside of the shell. This oyster was widespread during the Cretaceous in areas of Europe, North Africa and the Middle East.

Spondylus ■

PERMIAN – RECENT TIMES

The genus *Spondylus* is characterized by its thick-walled, inequivalve shell, with small wings, ribs arranged in a spiral, and many spines or lamellae The umbo is central or oposthogyral. The area is slightly developed. The dentition comprises two teeth, both placed to the side of the ligament pit. The right valve is larger and the oyster is attached to the substratum with this valve. This genus is widespread all over the world and dates back to the Permian. It was extremely common in the Miocene Carpathians, and is represented by the species shown here, *Spondylus crassicosta*. The specimen in the illustration measures 6.5 cm (2¹/₂ in).

Inoceramus ■

JURASSIC– CRETACEOUS

Inoceramus comprises bivalves with flat, round or oval thick-walled shells, of larger sizes, with a striking concentric sculpture that is characteristic of this genus.
The umbos of the more or less inequivalve shell have moved to the anterior edge. The hinge plate is very reduced in size, or entirely absent. *Inoceramus* was widespread all over the world during the Jurassic and

Spondylus crassicosta
Middle Miocene, Židlochovice, Czech Republic

the Cretaceous, but reached its peak during the Cretaceous. The numerous species of genus *Inoceramus* are of great stratigraphic importance. In the North Czech Cretaceous, the species *Inoceramus labiatus* is known as a fossil guide for the Lower Turon (Upper Cretaceous).

Inoceramus ianjonaensis
Upper Cretaceous, Ghadámes, Libya

Oscilopha dichotoma
Upper Cretaceous, Hodna, Algeria

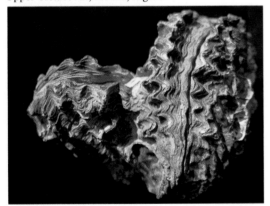

Posidonia ■

SILURIAN – JURASSIC

The shells of this genus are flat and inequilateral, with a slanted oval circumference and the umbo towards the anterior. The hinge plate is short, and there are no teeth. The wings around the umbo are slightly developed. The surface sculpture consists of concentric, regularly arranged ribs. *Posidonia* is an extinct genus, and has been recorded all over the world in Silurian to Jurassic sediments. This genus is very important for stratigraphy, i.e., to determine the relative age of sediments, particularly in the Lower and Middle Carboniferous and the Lower Jurassic. The specimen illustrated here belongs to the species *Posidonia becheri* and measures 6 cm ($2^1/_4$ in).

Neithea acuminata
Upper Cretaceous, Lobkovice, Czech Republic

Neithea ■

CRETACEOUS

The shell of this genus is extremely inequivalve, with a very striking convex, spiraling lower valve, while the upper left valve is flat. Small identical ears have developed on the valves. The hinge plate has two teeth on each side of the ligament, on the inside. The surface sculpture consists of strong radial ribs (4–6), with finer ribs between them. This genus was widespread all over the world during the Cretaceous. It belongs to the family of Pectinacea, which are attached to the substratum with byssus. The shell of the species *Neithea acuminata* shown here measures 7.8 cm (3 in).

Pecten ■

TRIASSIC(?), JURASSIC – RECENT TIMES

This genus is a typical representative of the important Pectinidae family. The shell is virtually round and equilateral, but not equivalve. The right valve is convex, while the left valve is flat or slightly concave. The ligament pit is triangular and central, like the umbo. Wings have developed on the sides, which are both the same, without a byssal indentation. The hinge plate consists of only slightly developed lamellae, which is characteristic of representatives of the Dysodonta order. The posterior muscle scar lies behind the center of the valve. The surface sculpture consists of striking radiating ribs. The arrangement of the ribs is also a characteristic feature of the individual species.

The genus *Pecten* dates back to the Triassic, but they only spread significantly all over the world in the Jurassic. The species *Pecten besseri* shown here measures 4.5 cm ($1^3/_4$ in).

Posidonia becheri
Lower Carboniferous, Velké Valteřice, Czech Republic

Congeria sp.
Upper Miocene, Hodonín, Czech Republic

Congeria ▣

TERTIARY – RECENT TIMES

This genus is important from the stratigraphic point of view, and is characterized by equivalve, thick-walled shells which are spherical or a rounded oblong shape with coiled prosogyral umbos. It has a dysodont type of dentition. There is a spoon-shaped extremity behind the anterior muscle scar, where the byssal muscle attaches the shell to the substratum. The pallial line does not have a sinus fold. The surface sculpture consists of visible growth lines. The genus *Congeria* is most common in Tertiary sediments in areas of Europe, Asia, Africa and America. In Moravia the genus is important in Pliocene strata. The specimens shown here belong to the species *Congeria* sp. and measure 5 cm (2 in).

Lima ■

UPPER CARBONIFEROUS – RECENT TIMES

The shell of this genus is slightly convex and slopes significantly at the back. The pointed umbos are relatively far apart, and have small, inequilateral wings without indentations. The surface sculpture consists of radiating ribs, but the shell can also be smooth. The hinge plate is not indented, but there may be small teeth. Freely moving species move by opening and shutting the valves quickly, while others are attached to the substratum with byssus in larger communities. This genus has been widespread all over the world from the Upper Carboniferous to the present.

Lima striata
Triassic, Germany

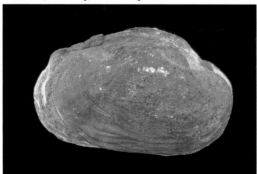

Order: Desmodonta

CAMBRIAN (?), ORDOVICIAN – RECENT TIMES

The genus comprises mollusks which bore or dig themselves in, often with an open equivalve or inequivalve shell. The dentition is not very developed or is entirely absent, depending on the inner ligament, which can be very thick, and is characteristic of species which dig themselves in.

Panopea ■

JURASSIC– RECENT TIMES

Bivalves of the genus *Panopea* have a relatively large and thick-walled equivalve shell, with convex oval to cylindrical valves, in which the edges separate away at the anterior and posterior ends (in front of the foot and the siphons). A large fold has developed on the mantle on the inside of the shell. One tooth has developed beneath the strongly opisthogyral – but small – umbos of each valve. The bivalve lives dug into the sediment of the sea bed, and therefore the shell is constantly open. The sculpture consists of striking growth lines. The genus is represented by many species in fossilized form. It has been recorded in Jurassic to Cretaceous strata in Eurasia, in Paleocene strata in Europe, and all over the world in Upper Tertiary strata. The specimen of the species *Panopea menardi* shown here is 8.6 cm ($3^1/_4$ in) long.

Order: Pachyodonta

JURASSIC – CRETACEOUS

The genus comprises extinct bivalves, which are clearly distinct from the majority of representatives of this class. This highly specialized group is often given the name of rudists. The shells of rudists are very similar to those of the solitary corals, and originally they were classified as such. They can grow to a size of 1.5 m (5 ft) and consist of two unequal valves. The umbo of the largest conical valve is usually coiled and grows down; the other half of the shell serves as a lid,

and is therefore more or less flat. The dentition consists of two strong cardinal teeth. The Pachyodonta appeared in the Upper Jurassic and became extinct in the Cretaceous. They lived in shallow bays.

Hippurites ■

UPPER CRETACEOUS

The genus includes bivalves attached to the substratum with a thick-walled shell of an unusual shape. They are attached by the right valve, which is conical or cylindrical in shape. They are up to one meter tall. The dentition consists of a large divided tooth in the right valve and two long, strong teeth in the left valve. So-called hippurite limestone is found in regions of the western Carpathians. This is an accumulation of shells of individual specimens. The genus existed only in the Upper Cretaceous.

Biradiolites

CRETACEOUS

The right valve is robust and thick-walled, irregularly conical and often coiled. There are striking concentric folds in the upper part. The left valve is lid-shaped and convex, or occasionally flat or even concave. The ligament is not developed. The dentition consists of two strong teeth which are found only on the left valve, while the sockets are in the right valve (unlike the hippurites).

This genus was widespread virtually all over the world during the Upper Cretaceous. More than fifty species have been recorded dating from the Creta-

Hippurites radiosus
Upper Cretaceous, Charente, France

ceous in Southern Europe, Trans-Caucasia, Central Asia, North Africa and America. The shell of the species illustrated here, *Biradiolites cornuspastoris,* measures 13.5 cm (5¹/₄ in).

Class: Cephalopoda – cephalopods

MIDDLE CAMBRIAN – RECENT TIMES

The class of cephalopods comprises the most highly organized predatory mollusks, which live exclusively in a marine environment, with a normal saline concentration. They include the largest invertebrates of all time, e.g., the squid that still exists today, belonging to the genus *Architeuthis,* which can grow to a size of 16 m (52 ft 6 in), the Ordovician member of the Endoceratoidea, *Cameroceras,* which was up to 10 m (33 ft) long, and the gigantic Cretaceous ammonite of the species *Pachydiscus seppenradensis,* with a shell which could be up to 3 m (10 ft) in diameter! In connection with their predatory lifestyle, the cephalopods developed a very advanced nervous system, unparalleled amongst invertebrates.

With a few exceptions, their body is bilaterally symmetrical and covered with a mantle. The head is usually separated from the rest of the body by a narrower neck. On the sides of the head there are highly developed eyes (in some two-gilled species, these have a diameter of 40 cm (15³/₄ in), which makes these eyes the largest in the animal kingdom). The mouth has a radula and also often has jaws. Tentacles develop around the mouth – there may be eight or ten of these, or even ninety. The tentacles are used mainly to catch food and for locomotion. In the cephalopods the original lobes of the foot developed into a funnel-shaped *hyponome,* and the narrower conical part protrudes from the bottom of the body. The broader part ends in the mantle cavity. Water sucked in through this cavity is regularly expelled through the hypònome. The cephalopod can move with the force of the flow of water resulting in this way, with the posterior part pointing forwards. The mantle secretes a calcareous shell. Normally the shell which develops is on the outside; occasionally it is on the inside. Sometimes the shell is absent altogether. The soft body of the cephalopod is located in a living chamber which takes up a quarter to a third of the whole shell. Behind this there are a number of *septa,* dividing hydrostatic chambers from each other. The posterior parts of the valves of cephalopods are known as the *phragmocone.* The septa are perforated, and while the cephalopod is alive, there is a fleshy band which passes through them known as the *siphon.*

The oldest cephalopods date from the Middle Cambrian, and were most common during the Upper Paleozoic and then the Mesozoic era. Nowadays there are about 650 species of cephalopods. The

Biradiolites comupastoris
Cretaceous, Dordogne, France

number of extinct species is difficult to estimate, and the figure of 11,000 is merely an approximation.

The systematic classification of cephalopods is complicated and far from uniform up to today. Recent cephalopods can be divided into two groups, depending on the number of gills: Tetrabranchiata – with four gills, and Dibranchiata with two gills. Fossilized species are normally classified on the basis of cephalopods with an external shell (Ectocochlia) and an internal shell (Endocochlia). Cephalopods are normally divided into five subclasses, on the basis of the morphology of the shell: Nautiloidea, Actinoceratoidea, Endoceratoidea, Ammonioidea (external shell, with four gills) and Coleoidea (internal shell with two gills). Some newer classifications are based on only two subclasses: Palcephalopoda and Neocephalopoda.

The so-called Orthocerataceae, which have resisted any attempt at sensible classification, are understandably a taxonomist's nightmare. In some classifications they are classified as an independent subclass of Orthoceratoidea, but the majority of classifications used up to now include the Orthocerataceae in the subclass Nautiloidea, and this is how we will classify them too.

Subclass: Nautiloidea

UPPER CAMBRIAN – RECENT TIMES

This is the only group of cephalopods recorded in Paleozoic strata to have survived to the present day. The best-known of the Nautiloidea is the genus *Nautilus*. We use its anatomy to determine the composition of the soft tissue of fossilised species. The body is contained in a mantle with a large mantle cavity. The musculature and the cable-like fleshy end of the visceral system, the so-called *siphon*, serves to attach the soft body to the shell on the outside. The siphon runs through all the chambers and is attached to the bottom of the cavity. There are a large number of tentacles around the mouth on the head, arranged in two rings. The mouth has a *radula* and strong beak-like jaws with calcareous ends, which can also survive in a fossilized state. The shells are found in all sorts of states and consist of three parts: an outer layer of conchioline, a thinner layer of porcelain and a thicker inner layer of mother of pearl. The most primitive shells are straight and conical, known as *orthoceraconi*, which are round or oval in cross section. The curved shells are described by the term *cyrtoceraconi*. Shells which are coiled in a spiral in one plane are described as *gyroceraconi,* and if the whorls are not compressed together but do touch, the shell is described as *tarphyceraconi*. Shells coiled in one plane, so that the oldest whorls are covered by the younger ones are described as *nautiliconi*. These can be *evolute* (the younger whorls barely overlap the older ones), *convolute* (the whorls are at least partly visible), or *involute* (the last whorl completely covers the previous whorls). Shells which are helically coiled are known as *trochoceraconi*. The whorls touch each other along a spiraling line known as the suture on the helically coiled shells. There is a funnel-shaped platform in the middle of the spiral, the so-called *umbilicus*. The width depends on the degree of overlap by the older whorls. The shell has a mouth *(apertura)*, surrounded by an area which can be different shapes *(peristome)*. The outside of the helically coiled shell is the ventral side (venter), the other side is the dorsal side. In straight shells the position of the venter is determined by the notch in front of the hyponome *(hyponomic sinus)*, which is on the mouth opening. On the inside, the shells are divided into chambers by *septa*. The septa are always secreted by the posterior edge of the mantle when the creature grows and moves forwards into the living chamber. They consist of mother of pearl, and the point of contact with the inner wall of the shell is formed by so-called suture lines, which are most easily examined with the help of the fossilized centers. The shape of the sutures is an important characteristic for classification. In the most primitive representatives the sutures are round, while the more developed representatives have single, lobe-like curving sutures. More complicated folds, which are convex towards the opening of the mouth, are described as *saddles*. The lines which are convex, but in the other direction, are *lobes*. Approximately in the center of the septa there is an opening through which the siphon passes during the cephalopod's lifetime. This is a more or less integrated *siphuncle tube* coated with calcite (calcium carbonate). On the one hand, it consists of *septal sutures*, short, tube-like units which run along the siphuncle opening from the septa; on the other hand, of *connecting rings*, a membranous part of the siphon between the end of the septal suture and the siphuncle opening of the previous septum. Depending on the arrangement of septal sutures and connecting rings, shapes can be distinguished which are more or less identical in their external appearance and difficult to tell apart. Many Nautiloidea with a straight shell have secondary calcareous deposits in the chambers, which sometimes entirely fill the original hollow chambers. Their position is important for classification. Although there are usually only growth lines on the surface of the shells, the structure can also consist of transverse and lengthwise ribs, and may have tubercles and spines.

Nautiloidea developed during the Upper Cambrian, and reached their peak during the Ordovician and the Silurian. During the Upper Paleozoic, the number of species, which was largest at the start of the Mesozoic, suddenly declined. The species which exist today, are a small remainder of the once widespread group. The structure of the siphuncle tube and of the inner calcareous deposits are important for the classification of Nautiloidea with a straight or curved shell; they are examined with the help of polished models of the siphuncle tube. In helically coiled shells, particularly the more developed Mesozoic types, the shape of the sutures is most important. The study of the external morphology is only applied in the context of the lower categories in the classification. Recent research shows that the precise position of the subclass of Nautiloidea is not entirely clear.

Morphology of the shell of a nautiloid cephalod:
1 – living chamber, 2 – phragmocone, 3 – apertura of the shell, 4 – hyponomic sinus, 5 – transverse ribs, 6 – growth lines, 7 – muscle scar, 8 – septum , 9 – septal suture, 10 – connecting ring, 11 – calcareous deposits in the chambers, 12 – structures of the siphuncle tube filling up, 13 – protoconcha

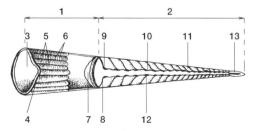

Bathmoceras complexum
Lower Ordovician, Prague-Šárka, Czech Republic

Michelinoceras michelini
Upper Silurian, Lochkov, Czech Republic

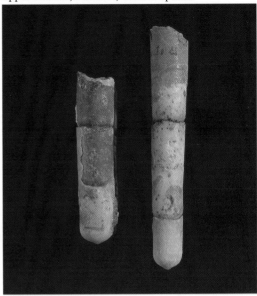

Order: Ellesmerocerida

UPPER CAMBRIAN – ORDOVICIAN

The slightly curved or straight conical shells of small dimensions are slightly compressed at the sides. The exocentrically positioned siphuncle tube is broad, the septa are close together. Ellesmerocerida are amongst the oldest nautiloid cephalopods.

Bathmoceras ∎

ORDOVICIAN

The shells of the nautiloid genus *Bathmoceras* are relatively large (40–50 cm/15³/₄–19¹/₂ in), straight and conical. The living chamber is large, and there are a large number of gas-filled chambers, one behind the other. The siphuncle tube is closer to the wall of the shell, the septa between the gas-filled chambers are virtually straight, and only extended into a conical shape near the siphuncle tube, which points to the mouth opening of the shell with the umbo. The genus *Bathmoceras* inhabited the relatively cool Ordovician seas in areas of present-day Central and Northern Europe, and representatives have also been recorded in areas of China and Australia. The incomplete fossilized center of the specimen shown here, *Bathmoceras complexum*, is 14.5 cm (5³/₄ in) long.

Order: Orthocerida

ORDOVICIAN – TRIASSIC

The shells are generally long, orthoceraconical, occasionally slightly curved with a rounded or oval cross section. The narrow siphuncle tube runs subcentrally, and there are relatively few septa which have short, straight, or slightly curved siphuncle tubes at the edges. The connecting rings are thin and cylindrical. There may be secondary calcareous deposits in the chambers of the siphuncle tube. On the surface the shells can be smooth or sculpted.

Michelinoceras ∎

SILURIAN – TRIASSIC

The genus *Michelinoceras* has a large, long, slender conical shell (up to one meter long), rounded in cross section. The narrow siphuncle tube runs exactly through the middle of the shell or in a very slight exocentric position. The connecting rings are long and narrow. In view of the length of the shell, the chambers are relatively long. The surface on the outside of the shell is completely smooth or just has fine transverse grooves. This is an important genus that is particularly common in Silurian strata. More than twenty species have been recorded in Europe, Asia and North America. The incomplete shell of the specimens shown here, which belong to the species *Michelinoceras michelini* shown here, is 4.5–7 cm (1³/₄–2³/₄ in) long.

Kionoceras doricum
Upper Silurian, Mořina, Czech Republic

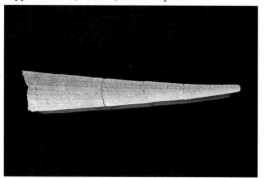

Dawsonoceras annulatum
Upper Silurian, Dudley, Great Britain

Kionoceras ∎

MIDDLE ORDOVICIAN – LOWER PERMIAN

The genus *Kionoceras* is characterized by a medium-sized, slender conical shell which is round in cross section. The surface sculpture of the shell consists of fine transverse ribs; striking ribs alternate with less striking ribs. The siphuncle tube is in a more or less subcentral position. Representatives of the genus *Kionoceras* lived from the Middle Ordovician to the Lower Permian, and more than twenty species have been recorded in Europe, Asia, North America and Australia. The specimen in the photograph belongs to the species *Kionoceras doricum,* and has a shell 15.5 cm (6 in) long.

Spyroceras ∎

ORDOVICIAN – DEVONIAN

The trochoceraconical shells of the genus *Spyroceras* are an average size, starting narrow and gradually becoming broader. The upper part of the shells can be cyrtoceraconical. The surface sculpture consists of a combination of thicker diagonal rings and fine

Spyroceras pseudocalamiteum
Lower Devonian, Koněprusy, Czech Republic

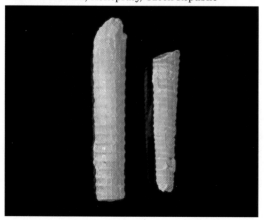

transverse grooves and ribs. Representatives of the genus *Spyroceras* have been recorded in Ordovician to Devonian strata in Europe, Asia and North America. The specimens shown here belong to the species *Spyroceras pseudocalamiteum,* and fragments of the shell varying in length from 5.5–6.8 cm (2–2$^1/_2$ in) are shown here.

Dawsonoceras ∎

SILURIAN

The relatively large shells of the genus *Dawsonoceras* (up to 75 cm/29$^1/_2$ in long) are in the shape of slender cones which only become wider very gradually. There are no septal sutures, and the connecting rings are cylindrical at the free ends. The characteristic surface sculpture of this genus consists of a combination of thick, transverse rings and fine, wavy or straight growth lines. More than fifteen species have been recorded of the Silurian genus *Dawsonoceras* in areas of Europe and North America. The species *Dawsonoceras annulatum* in the illustration is typical because of the striking transverse rings and the clearly undulating growth lines. The fragment of the shell is 13 cm (5 in) long.

Order: Oncocerida

ORDOVICIAN – CARBONIFEROUS

The shells are orthoceraconical or cyrtoceraconical, short, usually conical or barrel-shaped, and rarely helically coiled. The narrow mouth opening often has a complicated construction. During the juvenile stages, the siphuncle tube has narrow curves and there are cylindrical siphuncle rings along the whole length of the chambers. The older stages have short septal sutures and long connecting rings, curving towards the walls of the shell. In some representatives, siphuncle deposits have developed in the form of vertical, transverse lamellae.

Oonoceras sp.
Upper Silurian, Lochkov, Czech Republic

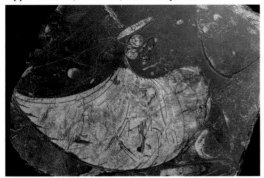

Octamerella callistomoides
Upper Silurian, Prague-Podolí, Czech Republic

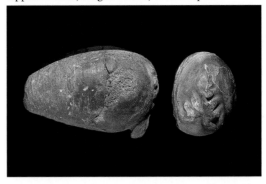

Oonoceras ■

SILURIAN

The genus *Oonoceras* is characterized by cyrtocera-conical shells which are average in size (10–15 cm//4–6 in), getting narrower towards the top. The side of the shell is slightly compressed. The ventral side is less rounded than the dorsal side. The siphuncle tube is closer to the ventral side of the shell. The shells are virtually smooth, or the surface sculpture consists of indistinct, fine, transverse ribs. Approximately twenty species of the genus *Oonoceras* have been recorded in Silurian sediments in Central Europe (Barrandien).

Octamerella ■

SILURIAN

The average-sized shells of the genus *Octamerella* are virtually orthoceraconical and an elongated oval shape. In the posterior part of the phragmocone the ventral and dorsal sides are concave, at the front and in the area of the living chamber the walls are convex. The mouth opening of mature specimens is strikingly narrower on the ventral side, and there are four pairs of lateral lobes on the sides. The surface sculpture of the shell consists of indistinct lengthwise ribs. There are approximately ten species of the genus *Octamerella* (this genus is sometimes considered to be synonymous with the genus *Conradoceras*) in the Silurian strata of Central Europe (Barrandien) and North America. The specimen shown here belongs to the species *Octamerella callistomoides*, and has a shell 8 cm (3$^1/_4$ in) long. The mouth opening is 5 cm (2 in) high.

Ptenoceras ■

LOWER DEVONIAN

The small to average-sized shells of the genus *Ptenoceras* are gyroceraconical, freely coiled, with regularly repeated lateral extremities from the mouth opening.

The shell becomes slightly broader towards the mouth opening, which has developed a slightly wavy back with a fold, which used to contain the hyponome. There are also two pairs of long, wing-shaped growths by or near the mouth opening, probably preventing rapid movements when swimming. The siphuncle tube is segmented, and the individual bobbin-shaped segments are slightly convex. The surface sculpture consists of fine growth lines. Up to now only a few species have been described from areas of Europe and North America. The specimen shown here belongs to the species *Ptenoceras alatum* and has a shell measuring 4 cm (1$^1/_2$ in).

Ptenoceras alatum
Lower Devonian, Koněprusy, Czech Republic

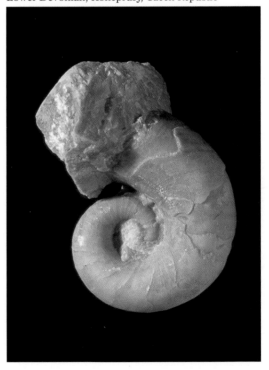

Cenoceras (Metacenoceras) moutierense
Middle Jurassic, Caen, France

Eutrephoceras bellerophon
Lower Palaeocene, Vigny-en-Vexin, France

Order: Nautilida

DEVONIAN – RECENT TIMES

The shells are nautiliconical, and in some cases gyroceraconical. The surface sculpture consists only of growth lines. The sutures may be simple, but can also be more complicated, clearly divided into saddles and lobes. The narrow siphuncle tube is in a subcentral position and the septal sutures are short and straight or slightly curved. The connecting rings are usually cylindrical. There are no secondary calcareous deposits.

Cenoceras ∎

UPPER-TRIASSIC – CRETACEOUS

The genus *Cenoceras* has a clearly involute shell with a flat outside. In cross section the whorl is trapezium-shaped and the ventral and lateral sides are slightly convex. The siphuncle tube is near the center. The sutures on the walls of the whorls are fairly wavy in the ventral and lateral lobes, with a large fold pointing backwards. The surface of the shell sometimes has a fine net-like sculpture, though the shells are often completely smooth. A large number of species of the genus *Cenoceras* have been recorded in Upper Triassic to Cretaceous sediments all over the world. The shell of the specimen shown here belongs to the species *Cenoceras (Metacenoceras) moutierense* and measures 6.5 cm (2¹/₂ in). The smaller shell belongs to a representative of the recent species, *Nautilus pompilius*.

Eutrephoceras ∎

MIDDLE JURASSIC – MIOCENE

The genus *Eutrephoceras* is characterized by an involute or pseudo-involute smooth shell with whorls which are extremely oval in cross section, horseshoe-shaped and rounded on the ventral side. The position of the siphuncle tube varies: it is always subcentral and never at the edge of the shell. The suture is virtually straight. A large number of species of the genus *Eutrephoceras* have been recorded all over the world, dating from the Middle Jurassic to the Miocene. The center of the specimen shown here, which belongs to the species *Eutrephoceras bellerophon*, is 6 cm (2¹/₄ in) long.

Pseudaganides ∎

JURASSIC

The shell of the genus *Pseudaganides* is characterized by a trapezium shape in cross section, flattened on the ventral side and also flattened on the lateral sides.
The siphuncle tube is closer behind the center than the ventral side of the shell. The lines of the sutures

Pseudaganides aganiticus franconicus
Upper Jurassic, Gräfenberg, Germany

Hercoglosa danica
Lower Paleocene, Vigny-en-Vexin, France

are characterized by a shallow, broad ventral lobe and a deep, rounded lateral lobe. Several dozens of species have been described in Jurassic sediments in Europe and Asia. The specimen shown here belongs to the subspecies *Pseudaganides aganiticus franconicus* and has a shell measuring approximately 7 cm (2³/₄ in).

Hercoglossa ∎

UPPER CRETACEOUS – EOCENE

The involute round shell of the genus *Hercoglossa* is smooth, the whorl is semi-oval in cross section, and the height of the whorls is greater than the width. The outside and the sides are symmetrically convex and the siphuncle tube is closer to the center of the shell. The suture has developed three lobes altogether, a broad, deep lateral lobe, a fistula lobe and a dorsal lobe. The ventral saddle suture is large and flattened or slightly concave at the top. The genus *Hercoglossa* has been recorded from the beginning of the Upper Cretaceous to the Eocene. Dozens of species have been described from all over the world. In the specimen shown here, which belongs to the species *Hercoglossa danica*, the center has survived containing four chambers, as well as the cavity which was the living chamber. The septal sutures are very striking. The fragment of the center shown here measures 8 cm (3¹/₄ in).

Permodomatoceras ∎

PERMIAN

The genus *Permodomatoceras* is considered by some palaeontologists as a synonym for the genus *Domatoceras*. The shells are evolute and smooth, and the whorls are almost as broad as they are high, with a straight or only very slightly curved ventral edge.
In cross section the whorls are trapezoid. Towards the mouth opening of the shell, the diameter of the

inside of the whorls gradually becomes bigger. The umbilicus is relatively wide, and in the middle there is a striking opening like a fistula. The ventral lobe of the suture is very well developed. Up to now, only a very few species of this genus dating from the Permian have been recorded in Europe and Asia. The specimen shown here belongs to the species *Permodomatoceras trapezoidale* and has a shell measuring 7.5 cm (3 in).

Permodomatoceras trapezoidale
Lower Permian, Urals, Russia

145

Hercoceras mirum
Lower Devonian, Prague-Hlubočepy, Czech Republic

Germanonautilus bidorsatus
Middle Triassic, Germany

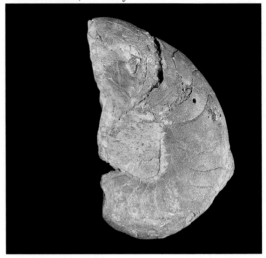

Hercoceras ◼

DEVONIAN

The relatively large shells of the genus are gyrocera-conical or trochoceraconical with evolute whorls. In cross section the whorls are broad and oval or almost trapezoid. On the outside there are tubercles arranged in regularly repeated spirals. These represent the edges of the area around the mouth opening, and could be mistaken for spines. The siphuncle tube is close to the ventral edge of the shell. The virtually straight suture consists of only small lobes and saddles. Representatives of the genus *Hercoceras* have been recorded in Devonian strata in Europe. The fossilized center of the specimen shown here belongs to the species *Hercoceras mirum* and measures 12 cm ($4^3/_4$ in).

Liroceras gavendi
Upper Carboniferous, Ostrava-Poruba, Czech Republic

Liroceras ◼

CARBONIFEROUS – PERM

The average-sized, almost round shell of the genus *Liroceras* is nautiliconical, usually involute and less often convolute. The whorls rapidly increase in height and width and are kidney-shaped in cross section. The sutures are straight, with only a very small dorsal lobe, while the siphuncle tube lies between the middle and the ventral side of the whorls. This tube is thin, with short, straight, narrow siphuncle lines and cylindrical connecting rings. A fairly large number of species of the genus *Liroceras* has been recorded dating from the Carboniferous and the Permian, in areas of Europe. A smaller number have been found in Asia and North America. The illustration shows the 7 cm ($2^3/_4$ in) long fossilized center of a specimen of the species *Liroceras gavendi* .

Germanonautilus ◼

TRIASSIC

The genus *Germanonautilus* is characterized by an average-sized, clearly coiled shell with whorls which rapidly increase in size. In cross section the whorls are trapezoid or a square shape. The ventral wall of the whorls is flattened. The siphuncle tube is in a central position and compressed like a chain. The suture has developed a shallow ventral lobe, while the lateral lobe is broader and deeper. The convex connecting rings are characteristic, but only visible on a polished specimen. On the surface on the outside of the shell, it is often only possible to see transverse growth lines. Sometimes these lines cross lengthwise grooves. About ten species of the genus *Germanonautilus* have been recorded in Triassic sediments in Europe, Africa, Asia and North America.

A fragment of the fossilized center of a specimen of the species *Germanonautilus bidorsatus* is shown here, measuring 6.5 cm (2¹/₂ in). It has been deformed as a result of pressure.

Aturia ◼

PALEOCENE – MIOCENE

Representatives of the genus *Aturia* are characterized by a disc-shaped, nautiliconical shell, 2–20 cm (³/₄–7³/₄ in) in diameter, coiled in an involute manner. The laterally flattened whorls are semi-oval or semi-elliptical in cross section. The siphuncle tube is closer to the dorsal side. On the suture there is a broad, almost angular ventral saddle, on the sides a narrow, asymmetrical narrow lobe and a broad rounded saddle. On the outside the surface is completely smooth. In the Tertiary, the genus *Aturia* was widespread all over the world. The genus *Aturia* is the most common representative of the Nautiloidea, which existed from the Palaeocene to the Miocene. About fifty species have been described, which have been found in areas of Europe, Africa, Asia, North and South America and Australia.

The specimen of the species *Aturia (Aturoidea) parkinsoni* shown here has a shell measuring 17 cm (6¹/₂ in).

Order: Discosorida

ORDOVICIAN – DEVONIAN

The representatives of this order are usually characterized by a cyrtoceraconical type of shell. The mouth opening is narrow. The siphuncle tube is in an exocentric position, and is broad with very short siphuncle lines curving against the walls of the shell, and long connecting rings. The inside of the siphuncle tube is often filled with conical, calcareous structures, so-called *endoconuses*.

Phragmoceras ◼

SILURIAN

The genus *Phragmoceras* is characterized by a broad conical shell which is slightly coiled or only curved. The whorls rapidly broaden out and are elongated or oval in cross section, and the septa are close together. The siphuncle tube has secondary calcareous deposits. The mouth opening of mature specimens is narrower in the middle, and can sometimes be in the shape of a capital T. The surface structure of the shell consists of fine transverse and lengthwise ribs.

There are dozens of species of the genus *Phragmoceras* in Silurian marine deposits in Europe and North America. The specimen shown here belongs to the species *Phragmoceras broderipi* and has a shell measuring 14 cm (5¹/₂ in).

Aturia (Aturoidea) parkinsoni
Lower Eocene, St. Pankraz, Austria

Phragmoceras broderipi
Upper Silurian, Beroun – Dlouhá Hora,
Czech Republic

147

Lituites lituus
Lower/Middle Ordovician, Öland, Sweden

Order: Barrandeocerida

ORDOVICIAN – DEVONIAN

This genus comprises cephalopods with a cyrtoceraconical shell, which is nautiliconical in terms of shape, as well as cephalopods with a shell that developed secondarily.

The siphuncle tube is thin with simple connecting rings, and runs through the middle of the shell or closer to its ventral edge.

Lituites ∎

ORDOVICIAN – SILURIAN

The shell of the genus *Lituites* is characteristic because only the first whorls are plano-spirally coiled, and the majority of the shell develops as a straight slender cone. The living chamber is characterized by a slit-shaped mouth opening which broadens into a spout. This siphuncle tube is in an exocentric position and moved to the ventral side of the shell. The sculpture of the surface on the outside consists of fine growth lines. The genus *Lituites* includes some of the first cephalopods which could actively swim. It is found in Ordovician and Silurian strata in Europe and Asia. The larger of the two specimens of the species *Lituites lituus* illustrated here has a shell approximately 12 cm (4³/₄ in) long.

Peismoceras ∎

SILURIAN

The genus *Peismoceras* is characterized by an average-sized trochoceraconical shell. The whorls are rounded in cross section. The oldest whorls are coiled in the shape of long protruding spirals, while the last free whorl is erect. The sculpture consists of striking transverse ribs which run on the ventral side towards the oldest whorls. These ribs partly disappear on the walls of the living chamber. Up to now only a few species have been recorded in Silurian marine deposits in Central Europe (Barrandien). The shell of the specimen shown here, which belongs to the species *Peismoceras pulchrum*, measures 6.8 cm (2¹/₂ in).

Peismoceras pulchrum
Upper Silurian, Prague – Butovice, Czech Republic

Eushantungoceras pseudoimbricatum
Lower Silurian, Gotland, Sweden

Sactoceras pellucidum
Upper Silurian, Beroun – Kosov, Czech Republic

Loxoceras breynii
Lower Carboniferous, Moscow area, Russia

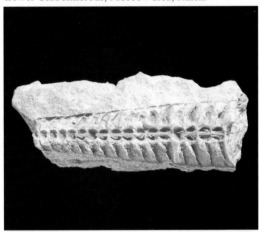

Subclass: Actinoceratoidea – Actinoceratoidea

ORDOVICIAN – CARBONIFEROUS

The actinoceratoidea include the relatively large Paleozoic cephalopods, with a straight or curved shell. The siphuncle tube is ex-centric and has a complicated construction. It is broad with short, curved siphuncle lines and long connecting rings. In the siphuncle tube there is a system of radial canals, radiating outwards and ending in a round canal called the *perispatium*. In the siphuncle tube and the chambers there are often secondary calcareous deposits. There is now only one subclass which belongs to this order, the Actinocerida.

Eushantungoceras ■

SILURIAN

The representatives of the genus *Eushantungoceras* are characterized by an orthoceraconical shell which is oblong and fairly large. The gas-filled chambers are very short and close together. The suture points towards the ventral side. The broad siphuncle tube is very close to the ventral edge of the shell. The connecting rings are very short and thicker, pressing against the septa. The deposits in the siphuncle tube are strongly developed on the ventral side. They either do not penetrate to the dorsal side, or only just penetrate. Several species of the genus *Eushantungoceras* have been recorded in Silurian strata in Europe and Asia. The illustration shows a shiny specimen of a 6.3 cm (2$^1/_2$ in) long incomplete phragmocone of the species *Eushantungoceras pseudoimbricatum*.

Sactoceras ■

SILURIAN

The shell of the genus *Sactoceras* is orthoceraconical or slightly cyrtoceraconical. It is rounded or oval in cross section. The surface of the outside is completely smooth or has only a fine sculpture so that it is very similar to other Nautiloidea. The original color of the shell can only be determined in very few species for the genus *Sactoceras*. The suture is slightly wavy. The siphuncle tube is relatively narrow, and usually in an exocentric position, but sometimes runs through the middle of the shell. Dozens of species have been recorded of the genus *Sactoceras* in Silurian strata in areas of Europe, Asia and North America. The shell of the specimen shown here belongs to the species *Sactoceras pellucidum*. It is 18 cm (7 in) long, has dark transverse stripes, and there are very rare traces of the original colors.

Loxoceras ■

CARBONIFEROUS

The genus *Loxoceras* is characterized by an orthoceraconical type of shell that is dorsoventrally compressed. The shell becomes increasingly broad towards the mouth opening. The suture inclines towards the ventral side, thus forming a ventral lobe. The siphuncle tube is in an exocentric position near the ventral edge of the shell. The connecting rings are convex or elliptical in cross section. The genus *Loxoceras* is one of the last representatives of the western, northern and eastern areas of Europe. The incomplete fossilized center shown here belongs to a specimen of the species *Loxoceras breynii* and is 8 cm (3$^1/_4$ in) long. The deposits which have survived are unusual, and the original shell has disappeared.

Dideroceras sp.
Ordovician, Kinnekulle, Sweden

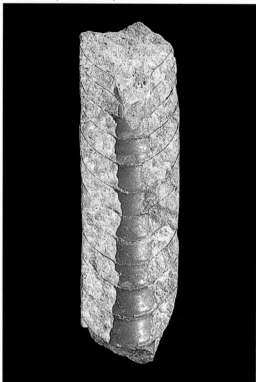

Subclass: Endoceratoidea

ORDOVICIAN – SILURIAN

The large or gigantic shells of the Endoceratoidea (3–4 m/10–13 ft long, or occasionally even 10 m//33 ft long) are usually orthoceraconical. The broad siphuncle tubes which run along the venter often take up one or two thirds of the length of the shell. In general, the siphuncle lines are very long, and in this case the siphuncle tube is filled with calcareous deposits in the shape of thin horns, one inside the other, known as *endocones*. If the siphuncle lines are shorter, connecting rings may have developed. The Endoceratoidea are amongst the most important groups of cephalopods in the Ordovician.

Dideroceras ∎

LOWER ORDOVICIAN – MIDDLE ORDOVICIAN

The shells of the genus *Dideroceras* grow to an average sized (20–30 cm/7³/₄–12 in) and are orthoceraconical. The siphuncle tube is broad on the venter of the shells. The endoconuses are well developed and their umbos are close to the transverse axis of the siphuncle. The siphuncle lines are unusually long, extending beyond the two gas-filled chambers. Representatives of the genus *Dideroceras* have been

found in Lower and Middle Ordovician strata, mainly in areas of Scandinavia, but also in areas of Northeast Europe and South America. The polished fragment of the shell of the specimen in the illustration belongs to the genus *Dideroceras* and is 8 cm (3¹/₄ in) long.

Suecoceras ∎

ORDOVICIAN

The shells of the genus *Suecoceras* are slender, almost cylindrical and rounded in cross section. At the apical angle of the shell there is a thicker fold which is convex on the dorsal side. The whole of the rest of the shell is straight up to the mouth opening. The septal suture lines run the whole length of a chamber towards the umbo. They are so long that they penetrate the mouth opening of the next septal suture.

The gas-filled chambers have an average length and start at the umbo. The broad siphuncle tube is in an exocentric position. Several species of the genus *Suecoceras* have been recorded in Ordovician strata in Europe and North America. The illustration

Suecoceras cf. *barrandei*
Middle Ordovician, Öland, Sweden

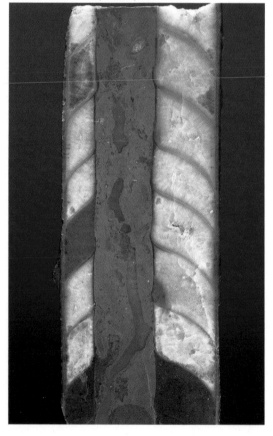

shows an 8 cm (3¹/₄ in) long cross section of a specimen belonging to the species *Suecoceras* cf. *barrandei*, with clearly visible septa and a broad siphuncle tube filled with calcareous deposits.

Cameroceras

MIDDLE ORDOVICIAN – UPPER ORDOVICIAN

Some palaeontologists equate the genus *Cameroceras* with the genus *Endoceras*. Like most other Endoceratoidea, it has a smooth shell of the trochoceraconical type. The ventral side of the shell is slightly flattened. The siphuncle tube is placed on the venter of the shell. The septal sutures are long and run from the umbo along the whole length of a chamber. The endocones are short, closer to the venter of the shell. The sutures are virtually straight. Only about ten species have been described. The genus *Cameroceras* was widespread in areas of Europe, Asia and North America during the Middle and Upper Ordovician. The cross section of the incomplete fossilized center of the specimen shown here, belongs to the species *Cameroceras peregrinum* and has a diameter of 8 cm (3¹/₄ in).

Cameroceras peregrinum
Middle Ordovician, Mýto, Czech Republic

Lobocyclendoceras sp.
Lower Ordovician, Estonia

Lobocyclendoceras

LOWER ORDOVICIAN

Some palaeontologists consider the genus *Lobocyclendoceras* to be equivalent to the genus *Anthoceras*. It has a fairly large trochoceraconical shell, which is rounded or slightly flattened in cross section. The broad siphuncle tube is right next to the shell. In earlier stages of development, the gas-filled chambers are longer, and later on they become increasingly short. The surface on the outside of the shell is smooth. One important characteristic is a deep sutural lobe, which is on the side near the siphuncle tube. Representatives of the genus *Lobocyclendoceras*, which lived in the Lower Ordovician, are very common in regions of Northern and Eastern Europe. The specimen shown is part of a fossilized center, 9.5 cm (3³/₄ in) long.

Subclass: Ammonoidea – ammonoids

DEVONIAN – CRETACEOUS

Ammonoids in the broadest sense of the word represent a large group of more than ten thousand species of extinct cephalopods with four gills and an external shell. The internal position of the soft tissue of the ammonoids is determined on the basis of the anatomical information available about present-day Nautiloidea. In some ammonoids there is a striking dimorphism between the sexes, and female shells are larger than male shells. The shape of the mouth opening of male shells is often complicated.

The structure of ammonoid shells is like that of the Nautiloidea: every shell starts with a small, round or barrel-shaped embryonic chamber (0.3–0.8 mm/ /0.01–0.03 in), a so-called *protoconch*, and the first whorl develops from this. The living chamber covers a half to two whorls. The shells are normally planospiral and may be evolute with a broad umbilicus, convolute or involute with a narrow, often reduced umbilicus. The shells are irregularly coiled, and are characterized as being *aberrant* or *heteromorphous*. The mouth opening of the shell is simple or compound. Only in primitive ammonoids is there a hyponomic sinus. The higher species of ammonoids have developed a saddle there, or a beak-like extremity known as a *rostrum*. Concave structures may develop on either side of the mouth opening (sinuses), as well as all sorts of convex structures (*apophyses*). The strongly curved *septa* divide the *phragmocone* into numerous small chambers which were filled with gas during the ammonoid's lifetime. The *sutures* always comprise lobes and saddles which are sometimes very complicated and are therefore of enormous significance for the classification of ammonoids. In general, the sutures can be classified into three fundamental types: 1 – the simple *goniatitic* type, characterized by smooth saddles and lobes, in which the paired lobes later become pointed and a secondary saddle develops in the outer lobes; 2 – the *ceratitic* type with smooth, rounded saddles and wavy or serrated lobes; 3 – the *ammonitic* type with fine, sometimes extremely complicated segmented saddles and lobes. As in the Nautiloidea, there was a fleshy siphuncle which ran through an opening in the septa when the ammonoids were alive. The thin, simple siphuncle tube is almost always on the outside of the whorls (the circumference) in ammonoids, except in some species dating from the Devonian. The septal sutures of species dating from the Paleozoic run towards the embryonic chambers (the *retrosiphonate* type), though they run towards the mouth opening in higher species (the *prosiphonate* type). Although the shells of the ammonoids can be smooth and only contain growth lines some shells are sculpted, usually with transverse ribs. These can be straight or curved towards the mouth opening or to the back. Sometimes there are S-shaped or sickle-shaped curved ribs. The ribs can be simple or with many branches and different patterns of branches. The ribs branching off the basic ribs (the *primary* ribs) are known as *secondary* ribs. The ribs which do not connect with the basic ribs are usually shorter, and are known as indented ribs. Apart from ribs, there may also be other transverse elements on the shells of ammonoids, usually tubercles at the place where the ribs divide. The lengthwise structures are usually represented by spiraling ribs. In the sediments where the ammonoids are found, there are often calcite specimens consisting of two shells which resemble the shells of bivalves, so-called *aptychi*. On the other hand, single specimens are called *anaptychi*. These originally consisted of chitin. Both structures referred to in the literature in the past as ammonoid lids, correspond to the lower jaw of the chewing mechanism. The aptychi are referred to by the family name, and an artificial classification has been developed in relation to them.

The classification of ammonoids is based particularly on the structure of the suture at an early stage. The position and the function of the siphuncle tube are also of fundamental importance. The lower units of classification are classified on the basis of the morphology of their shell. The most primitive group was probably the Bactritoidea, which lived from the Ordovician to the Permian, and were seen in the past as an independent subclass. Nowadays some palaeontologists see them as a transitional group from the

Diagram of an ammonoid shell (seen from the side):
1 – wall of the living chamber, 2 – growth line,
3 – mouth opening, 4 – wall of the phragmocone,
5 – gas-filled chamber, 6 – sutures (septa), 7 – fossilized center, 8 – size of the shell

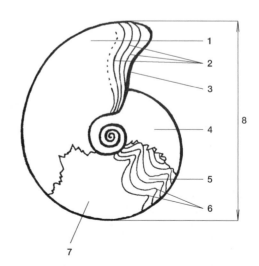

Gyroceratites gracilis
Lower Devonian, Prague – Hlubočepy, Czech Republic

Anetoceras hunsrueckianum
Lower Devonian, Germany

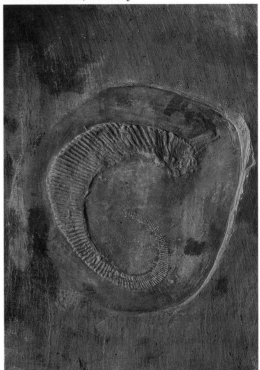

orthoceraconical Nautiloids and the subclasses of Ammonoidea and Coleoidea.

Order: Anarcestida

LOWER DEVONIAN – UPPER DEVONIAN

These are primitive ammonoids with a lens-shaped or slender disc-shaped shell, in which the retrosiphuncle tube lies on the ventral side of the shell. The suture is always of goniatitic type, and in the most primitive representatives only three lobes have developed. More developed types can have compound and segmented sutures.

Gyroceratites ■

LOWER DEVONIAN

The relatively small shell of the genus *Gyroceratites* is thin and disc-shaped, coiled in an evolute manner. The outer whorls are sometimes ventrally compressed with pairs of corners or keels on the ventrolateral edges of the whorls. In cross section the whorls are elliptical. In the large umbilicus in the axis of the whorls there is a small, fistula-like aperture, and often there is also the convex start of a chamber. There is no striking sculpture on the surface on the outside of the shell, but in some cases there are radial ribs, quite far apart, and growth lines closer

together. The genus *Gyroceratites* represents one of the most important fossil guides for the later part of the Lower Devonian and it probably developed from representatives of the related *Teicherticeras* family. It was widespread in areas of present-day Western Europe, Asia, North Africa and North America. The illustration shows the fossilized center of an unusually large specimen of the species *Gyroceratites gracilis* (5.6 cm/$2^1/_4$ in), next to a specimen with a partly preserved shell measuring 2.7 cm (1 in).

Anetoceras ■

LOWER DEVONIAN

The genus *Anetoceras* has a fairly modest shell, with whorls freely coiled in a spiral, which is characteristic of the oldest forms of ammonoids. The shell gradually broadens out towards the mouth opening. The surface sculpture consists of radial ribs. At the front of the shell the ribs incline towards the mouth opening on the inner edges of the whorls. Representatives of the primitive genus *Anetoceras* have been recorded in Lower Devonian strata in Europe, North Africa, Asia and North America. The deformed shell of the specimen illustrated here belongs to the species *Anetoceras hunsrueckianum* and measures 7.5 cm (3 in).

153

Teicherticeras discordans
Lower Devonian, Choteč, Czech Republic

Teicherticeras ■

LOWER DEVONIAN

The shell of the genus *Teicherticeras* is fairly small and evolute. The individual whorls touch each other and gradually become larger towards the mouth opening. During the last stages of growth the whorl was not complete, resulting in a broad fistula-like opening. The sutures have a striking dorsal lobe. The

Agoniatites cf. *bicanaliculatus*
Middle Devonian, Ougarta, Morocco

surface sculpture consists of radial ribs, alternating with thicker ribs further apart, and thinner ribs closer together. Several species of the genus *Teicherticeras* dating from the Lower Devonian have been recorded in Europe, Asia, Australia and probably also North America. The specimen shown here belongs to the species *Teicherticeras discordans* and has a slightly deformed shell measuring 3 cm (1¼ in).

Agoniatites ■

LOWER DEVONIAN – MIDDLE DEVONIAN

The genus *Agoniatites* is characterized by a disc-shaped, involute shell with a narrow umbilicus without any perforations. In most cases, growth lines can be clearly distinguished on the surface of the shell. The suture has developed a small, narrow ventral lobe and the lateral lobe is broad, like the rounded dorsal lobe. A large number of species of the genus *Agoniatites* have been recorded in Lower and Middle Devonian strata in Europe, Asia, Africa, North America and Australia. The specimen shown here belongs to the species *Agoniatites* cf. *bicanaliculatus* and has a shell measuring 3.5 cm (1¼ in).

Mimagoniatites ■

LOWER DEVONIAN

The genus *Mimagoniatites* is characterized by a relatively large, disc-shaped shell (up to approximately 25 cm/9¾ in), entirely coiled in an evolute manner. The whorls touch or barely cover each other. Their diameter gradually increases, and the last whorl of the living chamber is strikingly high with a rounded, trapezoid cross section. The outside of the whorls is flattened. The umbilicus is open in the middle. There are three lobes on the suture – a small ventral lobe, a broad dorsal lobe, and a lateral lobe. The surface sculpture consists of growth lines which are close together and extend to the ventral edge. Representatives of the genus *Mimagoniatites* have been recorded in a number of different marine sediments dating from the Lower Devonian in areas of Europe, North Africa and Asia. The illustration shows a splendid specimen of the species *Mimagoniatites fecundus*, with a shell measuring 4.7 cm (1¾ in).

Pinacites ■

MIDDLE DEVONIAN

The shell of the genus *Pinacites* is of an average size, lens-shaped and clearly coiled in an involute manner. The whorls are compressed on the sides, and quickly increase in size. The ventral part of the last whorl is narrow, like a keel. The umbilicus is broad, without an opening in the middle. The wavy suture consists of six lobes. As the shell is slender and has a smooth surface, we know that these animals were

Mimagoniatites fecundus
Lower Devonian, Bubovice, Czech Republic

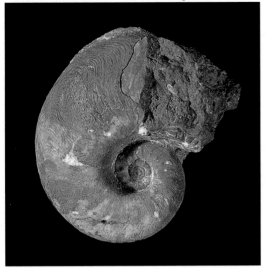

Pinacites jugleri
Middle Devonian, Prague – Hlubočepy, Czech Republic

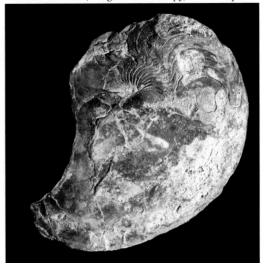

active swimmers. Representatives of the genus *Pinacites* have been recorded in the earliest strata of the Middle Devonian, particularly in areas of Germany and the Czech Republic. Specimens of this genus have also been found in North Africa, Asia and North America. The specimen shown here belongs to the species *Pinacites jugleri* and has a shell measuring 11.2 cm (4¹/₂ in).

Order: Clymeniida

UPPER DEVONIAN

The Clymeniida usually develop evolute shells which are disc-shaped or triangular. Unlike all the other ammonoids, the retrosiphuncle tube is positioned on the dorsal side of the whorls. The goniatitic sutures of the oldest representatives have three basic lobes. Subsequently this number increases in more developed species, though it may also be reduced in some of the branches that have developed.

Wocklumeria ■

UPPER DEVONIAN

The genus *Wocklumeria* is characterized by a small, disc-shaped or convex shell, more or less coiled in an involute manner, with broad whorls and a broad umbilicus. In juvenile specimens the shell has a triangular appearance, while the circumference of mature animals is round. The suture consists of six pointed lobes. Representatives of the genus *Wocklumeria*, which is very important from the stratigraphic point of view, have been recorded in areas of Europe and North Africa. The fossilized center of the species *Wocklumeria spheroids* shown in the illustration measures 3.2 cm (1¹/₄ in).

Wocklumeria sphaeroides
Upper Devonian, Oberrödinghausen, Germany

Genuclymenia frechi
Upper Devonian, Enkeberg, Germany

Protornoceras planidorsatum
Upper Devonian, Saoura, Morocco

Genuclymenia ■

UPPER DEVONIAN

The genus *Genuclymenia* has a characteristic, not very large shell, more or less coiled in an involute manner, with whorls only gradually increasing in size. The last whorl is a rounded trapezium shape in cross section. The umbilicus is broad, without an aperture in the middle. The surface sculpture consists S-shaped curved ribs which are very close together. Representatives of the genus *Genuclymenia* are very primitive from an evolutionary perspective, and specimens have been recorded in Upper Devonian strata in Europe (Germany). The specimen illustrated here

Clymenia laevigata
Upper Devonian, Koestenberg, Germany

belongs to the species *Genuclymenia frechi* and measures 3.2 cm (1¹/₄ in).

Clymenia ■

UPPER DEVONIAN

The shell of the genus *Clymenia* is not large, but flat and disc-shaped. It consists of rounded, only slightly involute whorls, forming a strikingly broad umbilicus. In cross section the whorls are oval. The surface on the outside of the shell is smooth, except for the very weak, almost straight growth lines, and there are no visible ribs. The ventral part of the whorl is rounded, but can also be pointed. Representatives of the genus *Clymenia*, which are just one branch in the development of the Clymeniida, are stratigraphically important for the Upper Devonian period for determining the age. They have mainly been recorded in areas of Europe, and although there are some doubts, in Australia. The fossilized center of the specimen shown here belongs to the species *Clymenia laevigata* and measures 5.2 cm (2 in).

Order: Goniatitida – goniatites

MIDDLE DEVONIAN – UPPER PERMIAN

Goniatites have a flattened shell which can be coiled in different ways. The siphuncle tube of the prosiphonate type runs along the ventral edge of the shell. The sutures of the goniatitic type have developed four lobes in the most primitive species. In more developed species there are more lobes, and the sutures may even be of the ammonoid type.

Protornoceras ■

UPPER DEVONIAN

The shell of the genus *Protornoceras* is coiled in a convolute manner and has a broad umbilicus. In

Nomismoceras germanicum
Lower Carboniferous, Velká Střelná, Czech Republic

Sporadoceras biferum
Upper Devonian, Marhouma, Morocco

cross section the whorls are in the form of an elongated horseshoe and the ventral side of the shell is broad and rounded, while the lateral sides are flatter. The suture comprises six lobes. The first lobe on the outside and on the side is more developed than the umbilical lobe. The surface of the shell has indistinct growth lines. A small number of species of the genus *Protornoceras* have been recorded in Upper Devonian strata in Europe and Asia. The specimen of the species *Protornoceras planidorsatum* illustrated here has a fine shell, measuring only 1.5 cm ($^1/_2$ in).

Nomismoceras ■

LOWER CARBONIFEROUS

The genus *Nomismoceras* has a flat, lens-shaped shell which is evolute in young specimens and gradually becomes involute in older specimens. The umbilicus is relatively broad. The ventral side of the whorl is like a keel. The whorls are regular at every stage of growth. There is a characteristic ventral lobe on the suture. The surface sculpture consists of a number of transverse growth lines. Only a few species of the genus *Nomismoceras* have been recorded in Carboniferous sediments in Europe.

Sporadoceras ■

UPPER DEVONIAN

Representatives of the genus *Sporadoceras* are characterized by a lens-shaped, strongly involute shell, rounded on the circumference. The umbilicus is very small. The suture consists of six sharp lobes. The genus *Sporadoceras*, which comprises many species, is characteristic of the Upper Devonian and specimens have been found in Europe, Asia, Africa, North America and Australia. The fossilized center of the specimen shown here belong to the species *Sporadoceras biferum* and measures 5 cm (2 in).

Goniatites ■

LOWER CARBONIFEROUS

The shell of the genus *Goniatites* is broad, disc-shaped or almost round. The whorls are involute. The umbilicus is narrow and shallow. The suture is typically goniatitic and comprises eight lobes. The last lobe is very narrow. The surface sculpture consists of slightly curving growth lines. In a few species there are fine spiraling lines or ribs. The genus *Goniatites* dates back to the Lower Carboniferous and a large number of species have been recorded all over the world, particularly in different marine sediments throughout the northern hemisphere. The larger of the two fossilized specimens of the species *Goniatites crenistria* shown here measures 4 cm ($1^1/_2$ in).

Goniatites crenistria
Lower Carboniferous, Blackburn, Great Britain

Gastrioceras carbonarium
Upper Carboniferous, Leek, Great Britain

Ceratites nodosus
Middle Triassic, Würzburg, Germany

Gastrioceras ■

UPPER CARBONIFEROUS

The genus *Gastrioceras* has a round shell composed of broad, flat whorls, rounded on the edges and slightly overlapping. The whorls are broader than they are high. The umbilicus varies from an average size to very broad and deep. The suture consists of eight lobes. The surface sculpture consists of a number of tubercles or short radial ribs around the umbilicus. The massive structure of the shell reveals that the representatives of the genus *Gastrioceras* were not fast swimmers. During the Carboniferous this genus, which did not include many species, inhabited shallow coastal areas all over the world (up to a depth of approximately 200 m/656 ft). The shell of the species shown here, *Gastrioceras carbonarium,* measures 2.5 cm (1 in).

Order: Ceratitina – ceratites

UPPER PERMIAN – LOWER JURASSIC

The plano-spiral shells of the ceratites can have different shapes and the sculpture is generally elaborate. The siphuncle tube runs along the ventral side of the shell, and in young specimens it can also have a central position. Primitive ceratites had sutures of the goniatitic type, and in the more developed species the sutures were of the ammonoid type.

Ceratites ■

MIDDLE TRIASSIC

The shell of the genus *Ceratites* is relatively large, only moderately involute and usually with a broad, shallow umbilicus. The whorls are not very high and have a flat lateral and ventral edge. The sculpture of

the shell consists of thick transverse ribs, often with striking coarse tubercles. The sculpture disappears on the ventral edge of the shell. The suture is of the ceratitic type. The first representatives of the genus *Ceratites* recorded in Asia were mainly found in Middle Triassic strata in Central and Southern Europe. They were particularly common in the so-called Germanic period when there were accumulations of shells in the shallow waters of the epicontinental sea. The species *Ceratites nodosus* illustrated here has a shell which is 11.5 cm (4¹/₂ in) long.

Trachyceras ■

MIDDLE TRIASSIC – UPPER TRIASSIC

The genus *Trachyceras* is characterized by a strong convolute shell, while the ventral edge of the whorls is rounded. In the middle of the ventral edge of the whorls there is a groove with rows of tubercles on either side. In cross section the whorls have a more or less trapezoid shape. The suture is of the ammonoid type and has two lobes. The surface sculpture consists of clearly curved ribs on the sides

Trachyceras aon
Upper Triassic, Hallstatt, Austria

of the whorls. The ribs can be single or forked. On the ribs there are tubercles arranged in spirals. Representatives of the genus *Trachyceras* were widespread all over the world during the Middle and Upper Triassic. The shell of the specimen shown here belongs to the species *Trachyceras aon* and measures 7.5 cm (3 in).

Cladiscites ■

UPPER TRIASSIC

The shell is of an average size (approximately 10 cm/4 in), involute, robust, and has broad whorls and a narrow umbilicus. In cross section the whorls are a more or less trapezoid shape. On the surface there is a thin, spiraling sculpture. The suture is of the ammonoid type, with clearly distinct lobes and saddles. The tops of the saddles are in a straight line and have two or four branches. The genus *Cladiscites* is found all over the world in Upper Triassic strata in Europe, Asia and Africa, and in Upper Triassic sediments in New Zealand.

Arcestes ■

MIDDLE TRIASSIC – UPPER TRIASSIC

The shell of the genus *Arcestes* is small or average-sized, broad, disc-shaped or oval, and consists of numerous low whorls coiled in an extremely involute manner. For this reason the umbilicus is completely closed. The living chamber is extremely long. The shape of the area around the mouth opening varies. The suture is of the ammonoid type, the lobes and saddles are strikingly segmented and have a triangular end.

The surface on the outside is smooth. The large number of species of the genus *Arcestes,* which is widespread all over the world, have been found in

Cladiscites sp.
Upper Triassic, Alps, Germany

Arcestes intuslabiatus
Upper Triassic, Hallstatt, Austria

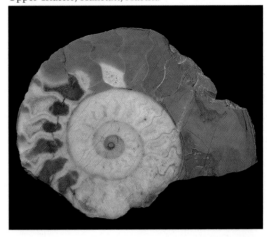

Middle and Upper Triassic strata. The illustration shows the species *Arcestes binacostomus* (4.5 cm/ $1^3/_4$ in), with a striking, two-lobed mouth opening. The species *Arcestes intuslabiatus* shows the polished cross section of the shell with a long living chamber.

Arcestes binacostomus
Upper Triassic, Hallstatt, Austria

159

Flexoptychites gibbus
Middle Triassic, Bosnia-Hercegovina

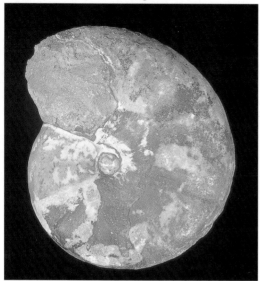

Monophyllites simonii
Upper Triassic, Hallstatt, Austria

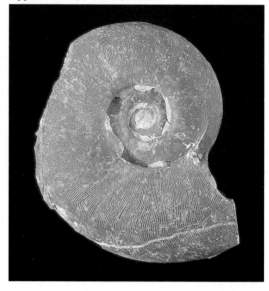

Flexoptychites ■

MIDDLE TRIASSIC

The average-sized shell of the genus *Flexoptychites* is greatly compressed and clearly involute with a small umbilicus. The suture is of the ammonoid type. The surface sculpture on the sides of the whorls consists of curving S-shaped folds which resemble ribs and are far apart. About fifteen species have been described in Middle Triassic strata in many areas in the Alps and the Himalayas. The fossilized

Pinacoceras metternichi
Upper Triassic, Hallstatt, Austria

center of the specimen shown here, which belongs to the species *Flexoptychites gibbus,* measures 9 cm (3$^1/_2$ in).

Pinacoceras ■

UPPER TRIASSIC

The genus *Pinacoceras* is characterized by a large or even gigantic shell (representatives of the species *Pinacoceras metternichi* have a shell which can grow to approximately 1.5 m/5 ft). The shell is very slender, flat and disc-shaped and consists of narrow, strongly involute whorls, which are sharp on the ventral side. The mouth opening is high up and narrow. The suture is of the ammonoid type and is characterized by a very complicated segmentation. The surface on the outside is smooth. The genus *Pinacoceras* includes the largest ammonoids dating from the Triassic; approximately twenty species have been found in many areas of Europe and Asia.

Order: Phylloceratida

LOWER TRIASSIC – UPPER CRETACEOUS

The shells of these conservative representatives are involute, smooth and with a simple surface sculpture. In juvenile specimens the siphuncle tube is in a central position, and in mature specimens it is close to the ventral edge of the shell. The sutures have leaf-shaped saddle tops. Young specimens have a well-developed primary suture with five lobes; in mature specimens the suture is more segmented.

Monophyllites ■

MIDDLE TRIASSIC – UPPER TRIASSIC

The genus *Monophyllites* is characterized by an average-sized, disc-shaped, slightly involute shell. The whorls are rounded in cross section. The umbilicus is broad and shallow. The suture can comprise four or more saddles, ending in a single leaf shape. The surface sculpture consists of fine growth lines curving in an "S" shape. The thin-walled shells indicate that the representatives of this genus were adapted to a quiet marine environment, and inhabited greater depths than most ammonoids (400–500 m/ 1,312–1,640 ft). About ten species have been recorded in Middle and Upper Triassic strata in Europe and Asia. The specimen shown here belongs to the species *Monophyllites simonii* and has a shell measuring 10.2 cm (4 in).

Phylloceras ■

LOWER JURASSIC – LOWER CRETACEOUS

The shell of the genus *Phylloceras* is disc-shaped, involute, and rounded on the ventral side, with a narrow umbilicus. In cross section the whorls are an extended oval shape. The surface sculpture consists of fine radial lines or indistinct wavy lines close together, although the surface of the shell is usually completely smooth. The suture is fairly complicated and the saddles end in a threefold leaf shape. A large number of very similar species have been described, particularly in deep sea sediments (representatives of the Phylloceratida lived at depths of about 600 m/ 1,968 ft). The genus *Phylloceras* lived from the Lower Jurassic to the Lower Cretaceous and was widespread throughout the world during this period, except in the cold seas of the Arctic regions.

Phylloceras heterophyllum
Lower Jurassic, Great Britain

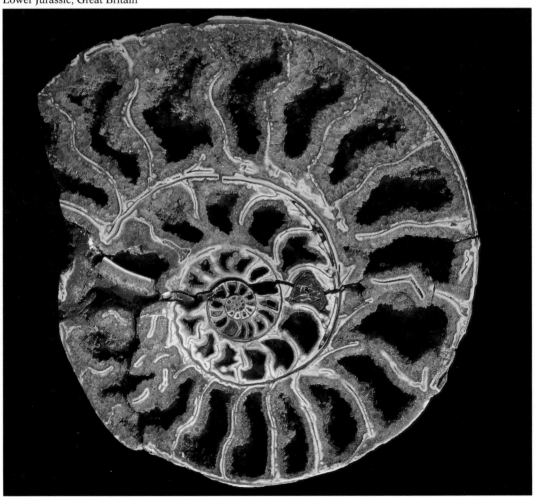

Holcophylloceras calypso
Lower Jurassic, Causse de Mende, France

Hamites attenuatus
Lower Cretaceous, Wissant, France

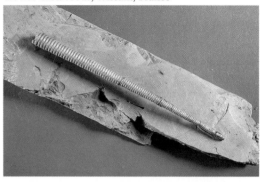

Holcophylloceras ■

MIDDLE JURASSIC – UPPER JURASSIC

The genus *Holcophylloceras* has a smooth, involute, disc-shaped compressed shell with a rounded ventral edge. The presence of distinct structures like tongue-shaped ears (so-called *constrictions)*, which can occur on the center and the surface of the outside of the shell, is a characteristic feature. The outer saddle of the suture ends in two small lobes, while the first saddle on the side has three lobes. The genus *Holcophylloceras* was represented by a smaller number of species from the Middle to the Upper Jurassic, and was widespread all over the world. The specimens of the species *Holcophylloceras calypso* shown in the photograph measure 4.5 cm (1³/₄ in).

Order: Lytoceratida

TRIASSIC (?), LOWER JURASSIC – UPPER CRETACEOUS

The thin-walled shells of the Lytoceratida are evolute, and have a broad umbilicus. The whorls are rounded in cross section. The shells are smooth or have growth lines or simple ribs, which can sometimes be wavy. The primary suture has five or six lobes. Mature

Lytoceras cornucopiae
Lower Jurassic, Causse de Mende, France

specimens have sutures of the ammonoid type with a lower number of pairs of lobes and saddles.

Lytoceras ■

The genus *Lytoceras* comprises representatives of ammonoids with disc-shaped, strongly evolute shells, a broad and shallow umbilicus, and whorls which are rounded or slightly square in cross section. The mouth opening is simple. The sculpture consists of a large number of fine transverse ribs and wrinkles. Sometimes there are also repeated thick ribs, and occasionally there are fine transverse ribs. The suture has two lateral lobes, a ventral lobe and a dorsal lobe. The genus *Lytoceras* has spread all over the world. The specimen of the species *Lytoceras cornucopiae* shown here measures approximately 10.5 cm (4¹/₄ in) large, though this species can grow to 20 cm (7³/₄ in).

Order: Ancyloceratida

UPPER JURASSIC – UPPER CRETACEOUS

The shells are aberrant and have developed in different ways. Sometimes they are straight; sometimes they are helically coiled. In some freely coiled species the development of the shells has resulted in tightly plano-spiraling coils. There are only four lobes on the primary suture (the first suture line from the ontogenetic point of view).

Hamites ■

LOWER CRETACEOUS

The genus *Hamites* is a typical representative of aberrant ammonoids. It is characterized by a complicated shell consisting of three more or less parallel ribs which do not touch.
The short, straight part of the shell is curved in a hook, ending in a short, straight piece, again curving in a hook. The last rib is also curved back at 180°

Baculites compressus
Upper Cretaceous, South Dakota, United States

despread all over the world. The part of the fossilized center shown here reveals the right part of the phragmocone and a clearly visible suture. It belongs to the species *Baculites compressus* and measures 6 cm (2¹/₄ in).

Macroscaphites ■

LOWER CRETACEOUS

The first stage in the development of the fairly small ammonoid shell of the genus *Macroscaphites* is coiled in an evolute spiral. The last whorl is erect and bends back in a hook. The whorls are oval in cross section, with a broad, shallow umbilicus. The surface sculpture consists of striking transverse ribs. In the spiraling part of the shell they are closer together and arranged in a radial pattern. In the straight part of the shell the ribs are arranged at an angle in relation to the axis. Sometimes there are small tubercles at the ends of the ribs. A number of species of the genus *Macroscaphites* have been recorded in Lower Cretaceous strata in different areas of Europe, North Africa and Asia. The specimen of the species *Macroscaphites yvani* shown here measures 13 cm (5¹/₄ in).

Macroscaphites yvani
Lower Cretaceous, Angles, France

in the shape of a hook. The shell is round or oval in cross section. The sculpture on the surface consists of numerous ring-shaped, straight radial ribs without tubercles, curving to the front on the sides. The suture has developed a small third lateral saddle. The genus *Hamites* has been recorded in Lower Cretaceous deposits in Europe, Africa, Asia and North America. The fragment of the specimen shown here, which belongs to the species *Hamites attenuatus*, measures 9.5 cm (3³/₄ in). Only the right part of the phragmocone has survived.

Baculites ■

LOWER CRETACEOUS – UPPER CRETACEOUS

The shells of the genus *Baculites* are large (up to 2 m/6 ft 6 in), and have developed in a secondary stage. They are mainly straight. In cross section they are more or less oval with a highly rounded or sharp ventral side. The living chamber is long. Occasionally the first part of the shell has also survived. This contains two small, normally spiraling whorls. The suture was simplified at a secondary stage. The surface of the shell is flat on the outside, but more often the sculpture consists of S-shaped ribs that are close together. The genus *Baculites*, which developed in a secondary stage, lived throughout the Cretaceous and during the Upper Cretaceous it was even wi-

Deshayesites forbesi
Lower Cretaceous, Varfy, France

Douvilleiceras mammilatum
Lower Cretaceous, Troyes, France

Deshayesites ■

LOWER CRETACEOUS

The shell of the genus *Deshayesites* is flat, slightly involute, and with a rounded or slightly flattened ventral side of the whorl. In cross section the whorls are a rounded or square oval shape. The umbilicus is fairly broad and deep. The mouth opening is relatively high. The clear ribs branch out and form forks, but longer ribs can also alternate with shorter ones. On the ventral side the ribs clearly curve towards the mouth opening. During the juvenile stages of development, tubercles are visible along the edges. More than thirty species have been recorded in Europe, North Africa, Asia, America, Australia and Antarctica. The specimen shown here belongs to the species *Deshayesites forbesi*, and has a shell measuring 2.5 cm (1 in).

Douvilleiceras ■

LOWER CRETACEOUS

The broad, disc-shaped evolute shell consisting of whorls which are round in cross section, are characteristic of the genus *Douvilleiceras*. The umbilicus is broad and deep. The surface sculpture consists of thick radial ribs at regular intervals. The ribs are straight and continue to the ventral side of the shell without interruption. There are tubercles on the ribs, at first only in the area of the fistula and on the ventrolateral edge of the ribs, and then spread out along the entire length of the ribs. They eventually disappear near the mouth opening.
Representatives of the genus *Douvilleiceras* first appeared at the end of the Lower Cretaceous and spread all over the world. The shell of the species *Douvilleiceras mammilatum* shown here measures 9 cm (3¹/₂ in).

Order: Ammonitida

LOWER JURASSIC– UPPER CRETACEOUS

The shells of the ammonoids in the narrower sense of the word are usually plano-spirally coiled with a different degree of overlap of the whorls. They can be smooth or sculptured, and in some cases keels are visible. The ribs vary and are both simple and branching, sometimes with tubercles. The mouth opening can be simple or compound. In young specimens the siphuncle tube is in a central position; in mature ammonoids, it is closer to the ventral edge. The segmentation of the sutures of ammonoids increases in stages in species which are more recent in terms of development. Many genera and species of the order of Ammonitida are extremely important from the biostratigraphic point of view.

Hoplites ■

LOWER CRETACEOUS

The species *Hoplites* is characterized by an evolute, disc-shaped shell with an open umbilicus. The whorls are square or oval in cross section. The sculpture consists of thick ribs close together, starting with the tubercles on the edge of the umbilicus. The ribs branch out, curving forwards on the outside and ending there. They are interrupted on the ventral

Hoplites dentatus
Lower Cretaceous, Troyes, France

Leioceras opalinum
Middle Jurassic, cliffs, Slovakia

side. The genus *Hoplites* is characteristic of the end of the Lower Cretaceous and has mainly been found in Europe, Asia and North America. The specimen shown here belongs to the species *Hoplites dentatus* and has a shell measuring 8 cm ($3^1/_4$ in).

Leioceras ■

MIDDLE JURASSIC

The shell is virtually involute with a narrow umbilicus. The flat sides of the whorls merge into a sharp ventral side with a clear keel. The mouth opening has clearly visible apophyses. The surface of the shell of the genus *Leioceras* is either smooth or finely sculpted with curved ribs like sinuses. The living chamber takes up about half of the length of the last whorl. Nowadays a large number have been recorded and described in Middle Jurassic sediments in Europe, North Africa, the Caucasians and Iran.

Hildoceras ■

LOWER JURASSIC

The shell of the genus *Hildoceras* is broad, oval and slightly involute. The umbilicus is broad and deep. The whorls of the shell have a rounded square shape in cross section. The venter is flat and has three smooth keels which are separated by two narrow grooves.
These are mainly visible on the centers. The lateral walls of the whorls are flat. There is a shallow, spiraling groove through the middle of the whorl, which divides the smooth surface of the whorl on the inside from the outside. The sculpture on the outside con-

sists of concave, simple curving ribs. The living chamber takes up three quarters of the length of the whorl. The genus *Hildoceras* has been found in Lower Jurassic strata in Europe, Asia and Africa. The three larger specimens shown here, which were replaced by pyrite, belong to the species *Hildoceras lusitanicum*, while the smaller ones belong to the species *Hildoceras bifrons*. The largest specimen measures 6.5 cm ($2^1/_2$ in).

Hildoceras lusitanicum, Hildoceras bifrons
Lower Jurassic, Grands Causses, France

Harpoceras subplanatum
Lower Jurassic, Causse de Mende, France

Pseudogrammoceras fallaciosum
Lower Jurassic, Causse de Mende, France

Harpoceras ■

LOWER JURASSIC

The genus *Harpoceras* is characterized by a thin, disc-shaped shell with slightly involute whorls, and a narrower, deep umbilicus with sharp edges. The last whorl is sharp with flat, lateral edges, becoming broader towards the circumference. Along the central edges of the shell there is a striking keel, the sides of which have grooves which are very difficult to distinguish. In cross section the whorls are oval, when seen vertically. On the outside a simple sharp keel has developed along the edge. On the sides the sculpture consists of thin, sickle-shaped curved ribs close together, which have developed more clearly on the outside than on the inside of the whorls. The genus *Harpoceras* is found virtually all over the world.

Grammoceras thouarsense
Lower Jurassic, Causse de Mende, France

The smaller of the two specimens shown here, which belong to the species *Harpoceras subplanatum*, measures 6 cm (2¹/₄ in).

Grammoceras ■

LOWER JURASSIC

The genus *Grammoceras* has an evolute, more or less oval shell, with whorls which are elongated upwards, so that each subsequent whorl covers more than half of the previous one. The umbilicus is rather broad and shallow. There is a hollow keel in the middle of the convex ventral edge of the shell. The ribs are large, simple, and curved in a slight sickle shape. The ribs are closer together, around the rounded umbilical depression. They bend forwards in the top quarter of the sides of the shell, so that they are interrupted by grooves on the edge of the venter. The genus *Grammoceras* has been recorded in Lower Jurassic strata in Europe, Africa, Asia and South America. The larger of the two specimens of the species *Grammoceras thouarsense* shown here, measures 5 cm (2 in).

Pseudogrammoceras ■

LOWER JURASSIC

In contrast with the previous genus, the shells of the genus *Pseudogrammoceras* have higher, flatter whorls. There is an even transition from the lateral to the ventral sides. The surface structure consists of numerous ribs, which are more strongly curved and narrower than in the genus *Grammoceras*. The keel on the venter of the shell is high. The suture consists of slightly broader lobes and saddles. Only a few species have been recorded of the genus *Pseudogrammoceras*, in Jurassic strata in Europe and Asia. The largest specimen of the species *Pseudogrammoceras fallociosum* shown here measures 4.3 cm (1¹/₂ in).

Polyplectus discoides
Lower Jurassic, Causse de Mende, France

Haugia variabilis
Lower Jurassic, Airvault, France

Polyplectus ■

LOWER JURASSIC

The genus *Polyplectus* has developed narrow, disc-shaped, involute shells with whorls which are thick and elongated in cross section. The lateral edges of the whorls are more or less flat, and merge evenly with the sharp ventral edge of the shell. The ventral keel is not very striking. The umbilicus is very narrow and rather deep. The surface sculpture of the shell consists of sickle-shaped curved ribs which are close together. Only a few species have been recorded in Lower Jurassic sediments in Europe and Asia. The illustration shows some of the stages of development of the species *Polyplectus discoides*. The largest specimen has a shell which is 5.8 cm (2$^1/_4$ in) long.

Haugia ■

LOWER JURASSIC

A laterally flattened, slightly involute shell with a broad umbilicus is characteristic of the genus *Haugia*. The whorls become increasingly tall towards the living chamber. The surface sculpture consists of two or three large ribs which slope to the front of the venter from the tubercles on the edge of the umbilicus. The ribs on the older parts of the shell are extremely striking, becoming gradually less so towards the mouth opening. A large number of species of the genus *Haugia*, which lived at the end of the Lower Jurassic, have been recorded, mainly in Europe and South America. The fossilized center of the specimen shown here, which belongs to the species *Haugia variabilis*, measures 9 cm (3$^1/_2$ in).

Labeceras ■

LOWER CRETACEOUS

The spiraling part of the genus *Labeceras* consists of fairly modest whorls, which are clearly open. The surface sculpture consists of clear, relatively thick ribs and rows of tubercles. The suture has developed just two lobes on the side. Representatives of the genus *Labeceras* dating from the Lower Cretaceous have been found in the southern hemisphere and have been recorded in Africa and Australia. The larger of the two specimens of the species *Labeceras bryani* shown here measures 8 cm (3$^1/_4$ in).

Labeceras bryani
Lower Cretaceous, Walsh River, Queensland, Australia

Didymoceras stevensoni
Upper Cretaceous, Westan County, Wyoming, USA

Scaphites sp.
Upper Cretaceous, Fall River, South Dakota, USA

Didymoceras ∎

UPPER CRETACEOUS

The genus *Didymoceras* belongs to the so-called aberrant type of ammonoids, in which there is a secondary whorl of the shell. *Didymoceras* is characterized by sinistrally helically coiled shells, though the whorls are not close together. The oldest part of the shell is only coiled in a hook shape, while the part with the living chamber is also coiled in an irregular way. The shells are more or less round in diameter. The surface has very striking transverse ribs. Representatives of the genus *Didymoceras* have been recorded in Upper Cretaceous strata, particularly in areas of North America. Complete specimens of this genus are relatively rare. This illustration shows two excellently preserved shells of specimens of the species *Didymoceras stevensoni* measuring 23.2 cm (9^1/$_4$ in).

Scaphites ∎

LOWER CRETACEOUS – UPPER CRETACEOUS

The oldest part of the shell of this genus is more or less involute, plano-spirally coiled and compressed. The youngest part is much shorter, erect and bends back like a hook. The sculpture consists of transverse branching ribs with tubercles on the venter. The genus *Scaphites* has been recorded from the end of the Lower Cretaceous to the end of the Upper Cretaceous in areas throughout the northern hemisphere, although representatives have also been found on Madagascar. The specimens of the genus *Scaphites* shown here have a shell measuring 5.2 cm (2 in).

Hoploscaphites ∎

UPPER CRETACEOUS

The shell of the genus *Hoploscaphites* is more or less involute, with a narrow, deep umbilicus. Initially it is tightly coiled, but it ends in a hook-shaped rib which curves backwards with a living chamber. The surface sculpture consists of striking transverse ribs, and in the ventrolateral area there may be distinct tubercles. There are also numerous fine indented ribs, which are straight and only slightly wavy in the older parts of the shell. The genus *Hoploscaphites* has been recorded in Upper Cretaceous strata in many areas of the northern hemisphere. The smaller of the two specimens of the species *Hoploscaphites nodosus* shown here has a shell measuring 10 cm (4 in).

Amaltheus gibbosus, Amaltheus margaritatus
Lower Jurassic, Causse de Mende, France

Hoploscaphites nodosus
Upper Cretaceous, Meathe County, South Dakota, USA

Amaltheus ■

LOWER JURASSIC

The genus *Amaltheus* is characterized by a slender, disc-shaped, slightly involute shell with a narrow umbilicus. The venter of the shell is sharp with a striking, finely notched keel along its entire length. The surface sculpture consists of transverse, sickle-shaped, curved ribs. In some species there are sometimes also lengthwise grooves and lateral tubercles on the surface of the shell. The genus *Amaltheus* lived in the Lower Jurassic in Europe, Asia and North Africa. The picture shows two specimens which have turned into pyrite of the species *Amaltheus gibbosus* on the left, while a specimen of the species *Amaltheus margaritatus* is shown on the right. The largest specimen measures 5.5 cm (2¼ in).

Pseudoamaltheus engelhardti
Lower Jurassic, Lixhausen, France

Pseudoamaltheus ■

LOWER JURASSIC

The average-sized to very large shell of the genus *Pseudoamaltheus* is narrow and disc-shaped. The laterally compressed whorls are coiled in an involute manner, and the umbilicus is narrow and relatively deep. The mouth opening is narrow and high. The surface sculpture consists of fine, spiraling lines. There are only a small number of species in the genus *Pseudoamaltheus,* mainly found in Lower Jurassic sediments, particularly in Europe. The shell of the species *Pseudoamaltheus engelhardti* measures 27 cm (10½ in).

Pleuroceras spinatum
Lower Jurassic, Unterstürmig, Germany

Peronoceras vorticellum
Lower Jurassic, Causse de Mende, France

Pleuroceras ■

LOWER JURASSIC

The shell of the genus *Pleuroceras* is evolute and has a relatively broad umbilicus. The whorls are almost square in cross section, with only slightly convex lateral edges. The surface sculpture consists of thick radial ribs which are not very close together, ending in tubercles on the edge of the umbilicus and on the ventrolateral edge. The ribs are curved slightly forwards near the outer edge of the shell. On the ventral edge of the shell there is a clear, fibrous medial keel, with shallow grooves on the sides. The genus *Pleuroceras* lived in the Lower Jurassic in Europe and North Africa. The specimen shown here belongs to the species *Pleuroceras spinatum* and has a shell measuring 5.5 cm (2¹/₄ in), with clearly visible septa.

Peronoceras ■

LOWER JURASSIC

The shell of the genus *Peronoceras* is strongly evolute. In cross section the whorls are round, though their walls are only slightly convex. The surface sculpture of the shell consists of numerous ribs placed closely together. Individual ribs alternate with pairs of ribs, which end in long spines on the vent-

rolateral edge of the shell. In the space between these ends, there are usually one or two simple ribs without spines. Only a few species have been recorded of the genus *Peronoceras*, dating form the Jurassic in Europe and Asia. The specimen shown here belongs to the species *Peronoceras vorticellum* and measures 5.5 cm (2¹/₄ in).

Dactylioceras ■

LOWER JURASSIC

The genus *Dactylioceras* has a strongly involute shell, with whorls which are round or a vertical oval shape in cross section. The ribs, which are close together, are very striking. They are either simple, or forked near to the outer edges of the whorls, dividing into two or three branches. Where they branch, there are sometimes protuberances, though these do not resemble clearly separate tubercles. On the ventral edge, these ribs either become straight lines or curve slightly forwards. The genus *Dactylioceras* was widespread all over the world during the Lower Jurassic.

Dactylioceras commune
Lower Jurassic, Holzmaden, Germany

Stephanoceras ■

MIDDLE JURASSIC

The genus has a broad, oval shell coiled in an evolute manner, with a broad, deep umbilicus. The whorls are low, and broader than they are high. The venter of the whorls is moderately compressed, and in cross section they are almost elliptical.

Stephanoceras curvicosta
Middle Jurassic, Echingen, Germany

The surface sculpture consists of thicker primary ribs, which have only developed in the fistula part of the whorls. From approximately the middle of the side of the whorls the thickest ribs divide into clear, fine, sharp secondary ribs, which continue to the ventral side of the whorls without interruption. Clearly visible tubercles have developed where the ribs branch, forming a spiraling line. Representatives of the genus *Stephanoceras* were common during the Middle Jurassic, when they were found all over the world.

Macrocephalites ■

MIDDLE JURASSIC

A broad disc-shaped, involute shell developed in the genus *Macrocephalites,* with a narrow, strikingly deep umbilicus. The venter of the shell is rounded in a regular fashion, and the whorls are horseshoe-shaped in cross section. The surface sculpture consists of distinct, narrow ribs at regular intervals, which divide approximately in the middle of the whorls to continue across the venter. A number of species of the genus *Macrocephalites* were widespread virtually all over the world during the Middle Jurassic. The specimen shown here belongs to the species *Macrocephalites compressus* and measures 12.5 cm (5 in).

Macrocephalites compressus
Middle Jurassic, Anwil, Switzerland

Bullatimorphites bullatus
Middle Jurassic, Pamproux, France

Quenstedtoceras carinatum
Upper Jurassic, Luków, Poland

Bullatimorphites ■

MIDDLE JURASSIC

The shells of the genus *Bullatimorphites* are strongly convex with a deep, funnel-shaped umbilicus. The last whorl is higher, but also slightly narrower. The side walls of the whorls are shorter, in the shape of an angular fold between the venter and the walls of the umbilicus. The umbilical ribs developed on the oldest whorls, but are replaced later on by tubercles. Representatives of the genus *Bullatimorphites* lived in the Middle Jurassic and have mainly been recorded in Western Europe.

Quenstedtoceras ■

UPPER JURASSIC

The shell of the genus *Quenstedtoceras* is disc-shaped and slightly involute, with a deep, narrow umbilicus. In cross section the whorls are round, slightly oval or even more or less triangular.

Indosphinctes (Elatimes) cf. *prehecquensis*
Middle Jurassic, Pamproux, France

The venter is rounded in a regular fashion, though it can also be relatively sharp. The surface sculpture of the shell consists of a moderate number of thick primary ribs, slightly curving to the front, and branching into two or three secondary ribs. They touch each other without interruption, forming a sharp corner on the venter. The ribs gradually disappear on the youngest parts of the shell, so that the surface of the living chamber is completely smooth. The genus *Quenstedtoceras* was widespread during the Upper Jurassic in Europe, Asia and North America.

Indosphinctes ■

MIDDLE JURASSIC

The genus *Indosphinctes* has an evolute shell with a broad, shallow umbilicus. The ribs are indistinct on the lower half of the oldest whorls, and are often reduced to blunt tubercles on the edge of the umbilicus. The sculpture disappears on the next whorls, and only reappears on the sides of the living chamber. The sculpture becomes clearer towards the ventral opening of the shell. Approximately twenty species have been described which lived in areas of Europe and Asia during the Middle Jurassic. The picture shows a male specimen measuring 4.5 cm ($1^3/_4$ in) of the species *Indosphinctes (Elatmites)* cf. *prehecquensis*.

Parkinsonia ■

MIDDLE JURASSIC

The genus *Parkinsonia* is characterized by a disc-shaped, slightly involute shell with a broad or otherwise narrow, deep umbilicus. The walls of the whorls are light and regularly convex, and the venter is rounded. In cross section the whorls are oval in a vertical direction. The surface sculpture consists of thick transverse ribs, slightly curving to the front, which

Parkinsonia depressa
Middle Jurassic, Sengenthal, Germany

Reineckeia anceps
Middle Jurassic, Pamproux, France

divide into a fork on the outside of the circumference of the shell, and are interrupted on the venter by a smooth, deep groove. Sometimes there are also lateral tubercles. The genus *Parkinsonia* has been recorded in Middle Jurassic strata in Europe, Asia and Africa. The complete specimen shown here belongs to the species *Parkinsonia depressa*. The mouth opening has survived and the shell measures 9.5 cm ($3^3/_4$ in).

Reineckeia ■

MIDDLE JURASSIC

The genus *Reineckeia* has developed a slightly involute shell with a broad umbilicus. The older whorls on the inside of the shell are broader than they are high, and the younger whorls become increasingly high. The surface sculpture consists of straight primary ribs ending in clear tubercles. The ribs divide into two or more secondary ribs close to the ventral edge of the shell. On the venter the ribs are separated by a smooth medial groove. More than twenty species have been described of the genus *Reineckeia*. During the Middle Jurassic it was widespread almost all over the world. The picture shows a specimen of the species *Reineckeia anceps*, with a shell measuring 21 cm ($8^1/_4$ in). The last air chambers are filled with calcite crystals.

Collotia ■

MIDDLE JURASSIC

The average-sized shells of the genus *Collotia* are clearly coiled in an evolute manner. The size of the whorls only gradually increases, and in cross section they are more or less oval or a rounded square shape. The umbilicus is very broad and shallow. The mouth opening of the shell is segmented in a relatively complicated way, with striking lateral spines that are thick

at the base. The surface sculpture consists of distinct ribs, which divide into forks towards the venter, about halfway up the whorls, and come together on the ventral edge of the whorls without interruptions. Representatives of the genus *Collotia* have mainly been recorded in Middle Jurassic marine sediments in areas of Western Europe. The male specimen of the species *Collotia oxyptycha* shown here measures 12 cm ($4^3/_4$ in).

Collotia oxyptycha
Middle Jurassic, St. Maixent l'École, France

Neolissoceras grasianum
Lower Cretaceous, Podbranč, Slovakia

Neolissoceras

LOWER CRETACEOUS

Neolissoceras is characterized by a semi-involute smooth shell, in which the sides of the whorls are flat, while the venter is broad and rounded. The narrow umbilicus is funnel-shaped. The genus *Neolissoceras* was very common in the Lower Cretaceous throughout the Mediterranean, as well as in the Western Carpathians. The fossilized center of the specimen shown, of the species *Neolissoceras grasianum*, measures 7 cm (2³/₄ in).

Teschenites

LOWER CRETACEOUS

Representatives of the genus *Teschenites* have an involute shell with tall, slender whorls and a relatively narrow umbilicus. On the inner whorls there are thin ribs, relatively close together, which become noticeably thicker and are further apart on the wall of the living chamber. They are usually in pairs, starting at the umbilical tubercles, and curving in an "S" shape, with the ventral side in the direction of the mouth opening. A few of the ribs divide, or ribs are inserted on the side of the whorls. The stratigraphically important genus *Teschenites* has been recorded in Lower Cretaceous strata, and most specimens are found in areas of Western Europe. The size of the shells reveal that the species *Teschenites flucticulus* shown here, is characterized by a clear sexual dimorphism; the male shells, so-called *microconches*, are smaller than the female *macroconches*. The specimen shown here belongs to the microconches and measures 4.7 cm (1³/₄ in).

Teschenites flucticulus
Lower Cretaceous, Podbranč, Slovakia

Abrytusites

LOWER CRETACEOUS

The genus *Abrytusites* is characterized by a semi-evolute shell with not very high, convex whorls and a relatively broad umbilicus. On the last whorls there are six strikingly thicker ribs, with numerous thinner ribs between them. They are curved, and the ventral edge curves towards the protoconch. Representatives of the genus *Abrytusites* have been found in Lower Cretaceous strata in Western Europe (France). The specimen shown here belongs to the species *Abrytusites julianyi*. It dates from the Lower Cretaceous, and comes from the cliffs of the western Carpathians. It measures 8.2 cm (3¹/₄ in).

Hecticoceras

MIDDLE JURASSIC – UPPER JURASSIC

The convolute shells of the genus *Hecticoceras* are relatively large and have a broad, shallow umbilicus. In cross section the whorls are oval of a rounded square shape. The shells have a low keel, and the surface sculpture consists of striking ribs, often with tubercles where they curve.

The tubercles may also be found on the inner edge of

Abrytusites julianyi
Lower Cretaceous, Podbranč, Slovakia

the shell. The suture consists of lobes and saddles, with a relatively coarse structure. There are dozens of species, classified in a number of subgenera, which inhabited areas of Europe, North Africa, Asia and South America during the Middle and Upper Jurassic. The fossilized center of the specimen shown here belongs to the species *Hecticoceras (Chanasia) bannense*, and measures 11 cm (4$^1/_4$ in).

Paralcidia ▪

MIDDLE JURASSIC

The genus *Paralcidia* has a fairly modest, broad, disc-shaped shell, elliptical in profile and clearly coiled in an involute manner. The whorls rapidly increase in size, and towards the mouth opening the body whorl increases strikingly in height. The umbilicus is very narrow and deep. The surface on the outside of the shell is smooth, with indistinct fine ribs only on the ventral edge of the whorls. The genus *Paralcidia* comprises a small group of species which have been recorded in Middle Jurassic sediments in areas of Western Europe.

Paralcidia mamertensis
Middle Jurassic, Pamproux, France

The fossilized center of the specimen shown here, which belongs to the species *Paralcidia mamertensis*, measures 8 cm (3$^1/_4$ in).

Schlotheimia ▪

LOWER JURASSIC

The genus *Schlotheimia* is characterized by a disc-shaped evolute shell with a broad, shallow umbilicus. In cross section the whorls are virtually vertically oval. The lateral edges are slightly convex, while the venter is flat. The surface structure usually consists of enormous transverse ribs which are close together and curve forwards, near to the outer edge of the whorls. On the ventral edge the ribs which are opposite each other meet at a sharp angle. However, they do not touch, because they are separated by a narrow band or smooth shallow groove which runs through the middle of the ventral edge of the shell. Representatives of the genus *Schlotheimia* have been found in Lower Jurassic marine sediments all over the northern hemisphere. The specimen shown here belongs to the species *Schlotheimia polyeides*, and has a shell measuring 6.5 cm (2$^1/_2$ in).

Schlotheimia polyeides
Lower Jurassic, Buer, Germany

Arietites ∎

LOWER JURASSIC

The shell of the genus *Arietites*, which can grow to a considerable size, is strongly evolute and has whorls which barely overlap. The umbilicus is broad and relatively shallow. In cross section the whorls are more or less square, or sometimes oblong. The venter is flat and has three low keels separated by narrow grooves. Large ribs have developed at regular intervals on the lateral sides of the whorls. These are straight on the inner whorls, but curve forwards on the outer whorls. The outer lobe of the suture is always longer than the lateral lobe. The genus *Arietites* includes a few dozen species which have been recorded in Lower Jurassic strata in many areas of Europe, Asia and America.

Coroniceras ∎

LOWER JURASSIC

The shell of the genus *Coroniceras* is evolute and has a broad umbilicus. In cross section the whorls are more or less square, but in the largest specimens the ventral edge of the whorls is broader. The surface sculpture consists of relatively strong, simple ribs, not very close together. The ribs sometimes end in moderately high tubercles close to the outer edge of the shell. There is a striking keel with indistinct grooves on the sides, running through the center of the outer edge of the shell. There are a few species of the genus *Coroniceras* which have been recorded in Lower

Jurassic strata in Europe and North and South America. The specimen shown here belongs to the genus *Coroniceras* and measures 5.5 cm ($2^{1}/_{4}$ in).

Aptychi

DEVONIAN – CRETACEOUS

Aptychi are calcareous species consisting of two shells, reminiscent of the shells of bivalves. Together with the anaptychi, they correspond to the lower jaw of the chewing mechanism of ammonoids. The aptychi are classified by family names and an artificial system has been developed for their classification.

Laevaptychus ∎

UPPER JURASSIC

The genus *Laevaptychus* is characterized by two thick, relatively broad calcareous plates with a more or less triangular shape. On the outside surface there are fine pores, while there are very thin growth lines on the inside. The aptychus shown here is probably a representative of the genus *Aspidoceras*. Representatives of the genus *Laevaptychus* have been recorded in Europe and North Africa. The picture shows a specimen that is 4.6 cm ($1^{3}/_{4}$ in) broad.

Lamellaptychus ∎

MIDDLE JURASSIC– LOWER CRETACEOUS

The genus *Lamellaptychus* consists of two narrow calcareous plates. These have clear ribs on the sur-

Arietites costatus
Lower Jurassic, Forchheim, Germany

Coroniceras sp.
Lower Jurassic, Frick, Switzerland

face on the outside, curved in different ways, but usually parallel to the edge. The aptychus probably belongs to the ammonoids of the genus *Oppelia*. The genus *Lamellaptychus* dates from the Middle Jurassic to the Lower Cretaceous and specimens have been found in Europe and North Africa. The specimen shown here is 1.1 cm ($^1/_4$–$^1/_2$ in) wide.

Subclass: Coleoidea – two-gilled cephalopods

LOWER DEVONIAN(?), CARBONIFEROUS – RECENT TIMES

These are exclusively marine cephalopods with an internal shell, which is partly or wholly reduced in recent representatives. They breathe through a pair of gills which have developed on the side of the body. On the other side, they protrude into the mantle cavity where they are surrounded by water. There are eight to ten tentacles around the mouth opening on the head. The genera with ten tentacles have two longer ones which broaden out at the distal end. On the inside of the tentacles there are suckers or chitinous hooks. The mouth opening usually has bony jaws and a serrated radula. The majority of these two-gilled cephalopods have an ink sac containing a black fluid. When it is in danger, the animal empties this through the hyponome, so that the water becomes cloudy. Two-gilled cephalopods are nowadays divided into nine to eleven orders, on the basis of the structure of the internal shell and the soft body. The order of Belemnitida mentioned below is of stratigraphic importance.

Order: Belemnitida – belemnites

LOWER CARBONIFEROUS – UPPER CRETACEOUS

These are extinct bivalve cephalopods, reminiscent of the modern squid. Impressions of the soft parts reveal that they probably had ten arms with hooks, large eyes, fins, an ink sac and horny jaws.

Belemnites usually have a straight internal shell consisting of three parts – the *plate*, the *phragmocone* and the *rostrum*. The plate which is rarely entirely preserved *(pro-ostracum)* is a very thin, arched plate, which extends from the phragmocone on the dorsal side. On the surface of the plate there are lengthwise grooves known as *asymptotes*, as well as growth lines. The *phragmocone* with an apical angle of 12°– 32° is the middle part of the shell of belemnites and is divided into small hydrostatic chambers by septa. A siphuncle tube runs from the venter through these septa, with septal suture lines running towards the embryonic chamber.

The thin wall of the phragmocone is known as the *conotheca*. The posterior end of the plate of belem-

Laevaptychus sp.
Upper Jurassic, Solnhofen, Germany

nites, the so-called guard *(rostrum)*, is usually bullet-shaped. It has a pointed posterior end, known as the *apex*. The deep conical cavity, the *alveolus,* is characteristic of the anterior section, where the front part of the shell, the phragmocone, fitted. The massive part of the rostrum behind the alveolus is the *postalveolar* section. In cross section there are radiating calcite fibers. The rostrum can have a smooth surface, but there are often many impressions of capillaries, grooves or grains, and their arrangement is important for the classification of the belemnite. For a precise classification, the lengthwise grooves are the most important. These are divided on the basis of their position into *ventral* grooves (on the ventral side of the rostrum), *apical* grooves (which only relate to the apical area), *dorsal* grooves (on the dorsal side), or pairs of grooves on the sides (lateral grooves, sometimes indicating the earlier impressions of cartilaginous bands where the lateral fins were attached). As only the rostrum is usually preserved in belemnites, the systematic classification is based on the morphological characteristics of this section, using the shape, length, cross section, apical angle, and pattern of grooves on the surface as a starting point. On the basis of earlier research, it is clear that belemnites to some extent survived the processes of extinction which took place at the transition from the Cretaceous to the Tertiary. However, recent studies suggest that representatives believed to date from the Tertiary (which have been recorded and have even been found to date from the Eocene) actually belong to other groups.

Lamellaptychus sp.
Upper Jurassic, Solnhofen, Germany

Passaloteuthis ■

LOWER JURASSIC

The genus *Passaloteuthis* is characterized by an ave-rage-sized, cylindrical rostrum, gradually ending in a spine. The rostrum sometimes becomes narrower, also near the alveoli. In cross section it is oval, and the rostrum is laterally compressed. At the posterior end of the rostrum there is a ventral groove. There are also a number of grooves on the spine. The most stri-king ones are two dorsolateral examples. The alveols extended approximately one fifth to two fifths along the length of the rostrum on the ventral side. There are several dozen species of the genus *Passalo-teuthis,* recorded in Lower Jurassic strata in Europe, Asia and South America. The rostrum shown here belongs to a belemnite of the genus *Passalotheutis* and is 11 cm (4¹/₄ in) long.

Salpingoteuthis ■

LOWER JURASSIC– MIDDLE JURASSIC

The fairly large genus *Salpingoteuthis* (measuring approximately 20–30 cm/7³/₄–12 in) is characterized by a long, cylindrical rostrum, rounded in cross section, and gradually becoming narrower towards the pointed end. There is a ventral groove, and two

Salpingoteuthis acuarius
Lower Jurassic, Holzmaden, Germany

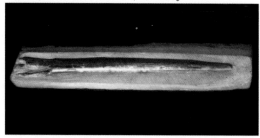

thin dorsolateral grooves at the top. The alveolus is short, and in some individuals, very long tubular extensions of the rostrum have been found (a so-cal-led *epirostrum*). Representatives of the genus *Sal-pingoteuthis* have been recorded in Lower and Middle Jurassic strata in Europe and Asia. The spe-cimen shown here belongs to the species *Salpin-goteuthis acuarius* and is 19 cm (7¹/₂ in) long.

Dactyloteuthis ■

LOWER JURASSIC

The rostrum of the species *Dactyloteuthis* is of an average size (approximately 10 cm/4 in), massive and fairly short, considering its width. It is widest towards the posterior end, and then rapidly becomes narro-wer towards the slightly rounded or completely blunt apex. The rostrum is round in cross section, or so-metimes oval, and compressed on the sides. The sur-face is smooth on the outside. There is a short groove on the ventral side at the top of the rostrum. The alveolus usually extends halfway along the rostrum.

Dactyloteuthis irregularis
Lower Jurassic, Meilenhofen, Germany

Megateuthis gigantea
Middle Jurassic, Sengenthal, Germany

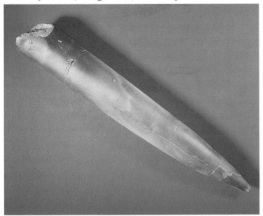

There are a few species in Europe. The specimen shown here belong to the species *Dactyloteuthis irregularis*, and are approximately 5.5 cm (2¹/₄ in) long.

Megateuthis ■

MIDDLE JURASSIC

The genus *Megateuthis* is characterized by a strikingly large rostrum up to 2.5 m (8 ft) in length, which narrows towards the end. It can be round in cross section, though it is usually oval, and clearly laterally compressed. At the top of the rostrum there are two pairs of striking, lengthwise, dorsolateral wrinkles and grooves. The ventrolateral grooves are usually less distinct. The alveolus takes up approximately a quarter of the length of the rostrum. Approximately ten species of the genus *Megateuthis* have been recorded in Middle Jurassic strata in Europe and Asia. The rostrum shown here belongs to a relatively young specimen of the species *Megateuthis gigantea* and is 26 cm (10¹/₄ in) long.

Belemnites panderi
Lower Jurassic, Russia

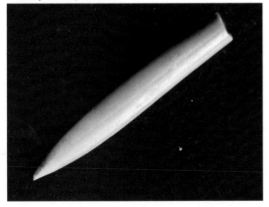

Belemnites ■

LOWER JURASSIC

The rostrum of the belemnites of the genus *Belemnites* is more or less cylindrical and ends in a point at the posterior end. The alveolus takes up approximately two fifths of the rostrum. There are dorsolateral grooves near the apex. The genus *Belemnites* was widespread in the Lower Jurassic, particularly in areas of Europe, Asia and South America.

Hibolites ■

MIDDLE JURASSIC – UPPER JURASSIC

The genus *Hibolites* is characterized by an average-sized, slender, torpedo-shaped rostrum (up to 20 cm/7³/₄ in), which is broadest towards the posterior end. From there the alveolus gradually narrows towards the spiny apex. The rostrum broadens out again from the start of the alveolus to the anterior end. In cross section the rostrum is rounded, and the alveolus is short, taking up barely one quarter of the rostrum. There is a striking ventral groove, which runs from the anterior edge about halfway up the rostrum, and occasionally virtually up to the spine. Representatives of the genus *Hibolites* have been recorded in Middle to Upper Jurassic strata in Europe, Asia, North America and Indonesia. The longest rostrum of the species *Hibolites semihastatus* shown in the illustration is 17 cm (6¹/₂ in) long.

Hibolites semihastatus
Middle Jurassic, Kandern, Austria

Neohibolites aptiensis ewaldisimilis
Lower Cretaceous, Carniol, France

Neohibolites ∎

LOWER CRETACEOUS – UPPER CRETACEOUS

The genus *Neohibolites* has a small, slender, torpedo-shaped rostrum (only a few cm long), which gradually narrows towards the apex and the posterior end of the alveolus. The rostrum is round in cross section. It has developed a short ventral groove, which extends to the anterior edge of the rostrum and about halfway up its length. The alveoli have survived only in rare specimens, because of the lack of calcification. The genus *Neohibolites* lived from the Lower to the Upper Cretaceous and was eventually widespread all over the world. The largest specimen of the subspecies *Neohibolites aptiensis ewaldisimilis* in the illustration is 4 cm (1^1/$_2$ in) long.

Suebibelus pressulus
Upper Jurassic, Sengenthal, Germany

Suebibelus ∎

UPPER JURASSIC

Representatives of the genus *Suebibelus* are amongst the smallest belemnites known in the world. The short rostrum clearly becomes broader towards the posterior end, and then immediately narrows again to a short, relatively blunt point. The genus has mainly been found in Upper Jurassic strata in Western Europe. The longest rostrum of the species shown here, *Suebibelus pressulus*, is only 9 mm (^{3}/$_4$ in) long.

Duvalia ■

MIDDLE JURASSIC – LOWER CRETACEOUS

The rostrum of the genus *Duvalia* grows to an average size, and differs significantly in shape from most other belemnites. It is much narrower laterally, but broadens out dorsoventrally towards the posterior end with a much more convex ventral side. The apex is extremely rounded. The rostrum is oval in cross section. There is a striking short groove from the edge of the fairly short alveolus, to the back of the rostrum, via the dorsal side. There is no ventral groove. Representatives of the genus *Duvalia* lived from the Middle Jurassic to the Lower Cretaceous and have been found in Europe, Africa, Asia and Indonesia. The rostrum of the belemnite shown here belongs to the species *Duvalia dilatata* and is 7 cm (2³/₄ in) long.

Actinocamax ■

UPPER CRETACEOUS

The genus *Actinocamax* has an average-sized rostrum with a cylindrical or slight bobbin shape, in which the vertical side is usually flatter than the convex dorsal side. In cross section the rostrum is round. There are slight dorsolateral grooves on the edge of the alveolus, and short alveolar slit on the ventral side. The short alveolus is not very deep and it can be assumed that its walls were not entirely calcified. For this reason, the alveolar walls disappeared, forming a characteristic, blunt, conical anterior end. Most of the representatives of the genus *Actinocamax* are amongst the most important fossils of the Upper Cretaceous; they have been found in Europe, Asia and North America. The specimens of the species

Duvalia dilatata
Lower Cretaceous, Castellane, France

Actinocamax plenus Upper Cretaceous, Kostelec nad Labem and Nová Ves, Czech Republic

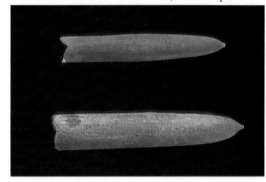

Actinocamax plenus shown here are 8.3 and 6.7 cm (3¹/₄ and 2¹/₂ in) long.

Gonioteuthis ■

UPPER CRETACEOUS

Belemnites of the genus *Gonioteuthis* grow to a length of approximately 10 cm (4 in) and are very similar to the genus *Actinocamax*. They differ from the genus *Actinocamax* by having a slightly longer alveolus, which can take up approximately one tenth to one quarter of the length of the rostrum. The rounded apex ends in a short extension. On the surface of the outside there are vascular impressions and lengthwise grooves, and usually a clearly visible grainy structure. Only a few species have been recorded of the genus *Gonioteuthis,* in Upper Cretaceous strata in Europe. The picture shows a specimen of the species *Gonioteuthis quadrata,* which is approximately 8.5 cm (3¹/₄ in) long.

Gonioteuthis quadrata
Upper Cretaceous, Höver, Germany

5. Bryozoans and brachiopods

Phylum: Bryozoans

ORDOVICIAN – RECENT TIMES

Moss animals include sessile, aquatic and colonial animals which leave moss-like fibers on all sorts of objects, mainly the sea bed. Colonies of moss animals of different shapes and sizes are created by creatures known as *zooids*. Zooids of moss animals which live in saltwater and freshwater environments differ from the morphological point of view. Moss animals which live in the sea form zooids with different appearances, and are therefore polymorphous. A distinction can be made between so-called *autozooids* and specialized *heterozooids*. On the body of the autozooids it is possible to distinguish a posterior section protected by a cuticula, which contains the digestive system and reproductive organs, the so-called *cystid*, and the anterior section, where there are tentacles surrounding the mouth – the so-called *polypid*. The cells of the ectoderm secrete the cuticulum of the zooids, the so-called *zooecium*. This is the protective cover for the soft organs, which is often reinforced in marine animals by chitin or calcium carbonate. In zooecia with a different shape (cylindrical, cup-shaped, prism-shaped, pear-shaped) and cross section, every chamber also has a different shaped mouth (round, oval, star-shaped or polygonal). Sometimes a connected or sickle-shaped wall in the shape of a lid develops round the mouth, which can completely cover the mouth in some species. In general, the zooecia are entirely divided by septa, but sometimes these are incomplete. The individual zooecia join together to form an exoskeleton of a group of moss animals, the so-called *zooarium*, that can exist in many different shapes (as a chain, a fan, branching etc.) and sizes (in exceptional cases, up to 50 cm/ $19^{1}/_{2}$ in). Heterozooids are adapted to different biological functions. They usually have a protective function, and the solid case, known as the *heterozooecium*, differs from normal zooecia from the morphological point of view. In terms of shape, they can be reminiscent of a bird's head (*avicularia*), and the so-called *vibracules* consist of small polypids ending in a long fiber, while the *ovicells* create sac-like organs which serve to protect the center.

Fossilized moss animals are subdivided nowadays into three categories on the basis of their ontogenisis and the general morphology of the colony. The Stenolaemata and Gymnolaemata are the most common classes.

Left: *Utropora nobilis*
Lower Devonian, Koněprusy, Czech Republic

Class: Stenolaemata

ORDOVICIAN – RECENT TIMES

This class comprises marine polymorphous moss animals with cylindrical, calcified zooecia, which can contain partitions or *diaphragms*. Of the five orders, the following three are the most important for paleontology: Cyclostomata, Cryptostomata and Trepostomata.

Order: Cyclostomata

ORDOVICIAN – RECENT TIMES

In general, moss animals of the genus Cyclostomata form tubular, or more rarely, prismatic zooecia with a ring-shaped, lidless mouth, and the zooecia are interconnected by pores. The heterozooecia are often represented by ovicells which can differ in shape and are often important for the systematic classification of these animals. The moss animals of the genus Cyclostomata have a simple structure, and therefore it is possible to classify them without polished specimens.

Diagram showing the construction of an autozooid:
1 – antenna, 2 – digestive tract, 3 – avicularia,
4 – zooecium, 5 – contracting muscle, 6 – mouth,
7 – anal opening, 8 – intestine, 9 – gut, 10 – reproductive organs.

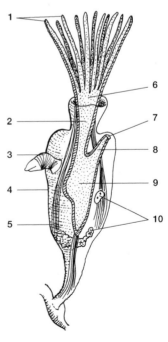

183

Hornera reteporacea
Middle Miocene, Chanay-sur-Lathan, France

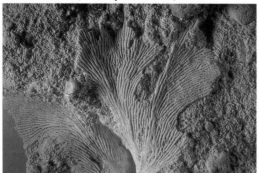

Hornera

EOCENE – RECENT TIMES

The zooaria of the genus *Hornera* are bifurcated and erect. The mouth of the calcareous, thick-walled zooecia is only on the front of the zooarium. The ovicells are like large blisters. Representatives of the genus *Hornera*, which has survived up to the present, were first discovered in Eocene strata in Europe. Nowadays, this genus lives in the Atlantic Ocean and the Mediterranean. The fragment of the zooarium of the specimen shown here belongs to the species *Hornera reteporacea* and measures 6 cm (2¹/₄ in).

'Ceriopora'

TRIASSIC – MIOCENE

The zooaria of the moss animals of the genus *'Ceriopora'* look like long, branching stalks. On the surface there are mouth openings of cylindrical or prismatic zooecia, arranged in an irregular pattern. Representatives of the genus *'Ceriopora'* have been found in Triassic to Miocene sediments in Europe, Asia and North America. The fragment of the zooarium shown here belongs to the species *'Ceriopora' angulosa* and measures 2.5 cm (1 in).

'Ceriopora' angulosa
Upper Jurassic, Schnaitheim, Germany

Berenicea

TRIASSIC – RECENT TIMES

The genus *Berenicea* is characterized by flat, thin, fan-shaped or leaf-shaped zooaria consisting of one layer. In many cases there are also radially arranged branches from the starting point of the colony, in which case the zooarium is ring-shaped. The zooecia are simple and tubular. Fossilized representatives of genus *Berenicea*, which lived from the Triassic to the present day, have been found mainly in Europe and North America. The zooarium of the genus *Berenicea* shown here measures 1.1 cm (¹/₂ in) and is on an echinoderm of the genus *Apiocrinus*.

Entalophora

JURASSIC – RECENT TIMES

The zooaria of the genus *Entalophora* look like straight, branching stalks, like the genus *'Ceriopora'*. The difference is that the mouth of the zooecia protrudes significantly above the surface of the colony. The genus *Entalophora* has been recorded in Jurassic sediments, and fossilized representatives of this genus have been found in Europe and North America. Nowadays the genus *Entalophora* lives in almost all the seas, except in arctic waters. The largest fragments of zooaria shown here belong to the species *Entalophora heros* and measure 1 centimeter.

Osculipora

UPPER CRETACEOUS

The genus *Osculipora* is characterized by small branching zooaria. They are long, tubular and erect, ending with the mouths at the end of the lateral branches. The genus *Osculipora*, which dates from the Upper Cretaceous, has only been recorded in Europe. The largest of the two fragments of zooaria of the species *Osculipora plebeia* shown in the photograph, measures 1.6 cm (¹/₂ in).

Berenicea sp.
Middle Jurassic, Bradford-on-Avon, Great Britain

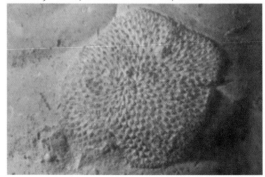

Entalophora heros
Upper Cretaceous, Kutná Hora, Czech Republic

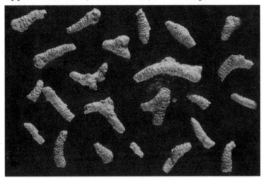

Corymbopora sp.
Upper Cretaceous, France

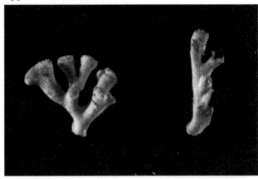

Corymbopora ■

CRETACEOUS – RECENT TIMES

The zooaria of the genus *Corymbopora* are bifurcated. Towards the distal end the branches are broader, while the ends are flat or convex. Around the zooarium there may be a large number of pores on the branches which were left by the older zooecia. The genus *Corymbopora* has been recorded in Cretaceous strata, and has survived up to the present day. The larger of the two fragments shown here belong to the genus *Corymbopora* and measures 9 mm ($^3/_8$ in).

Order: Cryptostomata

LOWER ORDOVICIAN – TRIASSIC

The moss animals of the genus Cryptostomata formed net-like colonies, in rarer cases with a bush-like shape in two layers or spiraling in a coil. The net-like or bush-like species consist of straight, rod-like branches connected by septa or *dissepimenta*. They can also consist of wavy branches, which grow together where they touch. The empty frames of the structure created in this way are known as *fenestrule*.

On the branches there are usually low pear-shaped chambers in two or more rows, in which the upper tubular part is known as the *vestibulum*. In the vestibulum there are two septa – an upper and a lower septum. At the top, the chambers open with a round mouth, which is closed by a lid in many species. A spiny keel usually develops on the branches. These moss animals first appeared in the Ordovician and reached a peak in the Upper Paleozoic era. They became extinct towards the Mesozoic.

Fenestella ■

ORDOVICIAN – PERMIAN

The genus *Fenestella* has fan-shaped or funnel-shaped, hollowed-out zooaria, consisting of thin, more or less parallel branches. There are two rows of zooecia on the branches, which are interconnected with smooth septa, creating a net-like structure. There is sometimes a smooth keel or a keel with tubercles across the middle of the branches. The genus *Fenestella* was widespread all over the world. The fragment of the zooarium shown here belongs to the species *Fenestella exsilis* and measures 4.5 cm ($1^3/_4$ in).

Osculipora plebeia
Upper Cretaceous, Kamajka near Čáslav, Czech Republic

Fenestella exsilis
Lower Devonian, Prague-Zlíchov, Czech Republic

Hemitrypa tenella
Lower Devonian, Prague-Zlíchov, Czech Republic

Isotrypa acris
Lower Devonian, Koněprusy, Czech Republic

Hemitrypa ■

SILURIAN-PERMIAN

Hemitrypa are characterized by a funnel-shaped, two-layered zooarium. The construction of the lower layer is similar to that of the genus *Fenestella*. The mouth openings of the zooecium point towards the outside of the branches. The upper covering layer forms a net which is supported by pillars growing from the keels of the lower layer at regular intervals. *Hemitrypa* has been recorded from the Silurian to the Permian and is widespread. The specimen shown is of *Hemitrypa tenella* and has a fragmentary zooarium measuring 3 cm (1¹/₄ in).

Isotrypa ■

DEVONIAN

The zooarium of *Isotrypa* is funnel-shaped, and consists of two layers composed of branches interconnected by septa. The mouth openings of the zooecium are found on the outside of the branches in two rows. The outside is only attached to the lower layer by keels which are on the branches of the lower layer. No keels have developed on the septa. Representatives of the genus *Isotrypa* have been recorded in Devonian strata in Europe, Asia and North America. The incomplete zooarium of *Isotrypa acris*, shown, measures 7 cm (2³/₄ in).

Cyclopelta ■

SILURIAN – LOWER CARBONIFEROUS

The genus *Cyclopelta* has funnel-shaped zooaria. The branches have two rows of zooecia and are interconnected by broad septa. The mouth openings of the zooecia point towards the outside of the branches. They are separated from each other by high keels which become broader further up. The genus

Cyclopelta has been recorded in Silurian to Lower Carboniferous strata and spread all over the world during its development. The incomplete zooarium of the species *Cyclopelta sacculus* in the picture measures 4 cm (1¹/₂ in).

Polypora ■

ORDOVICIAN – LOWER TRIASSIC

The zooaria of the genus *Polypora* are funnel-shaped and to some extent resemble the zooaria of the genus *Fenestella*. However, they are more massive and have strong branches with more than two rows of zooecia. There are no middle keels and the tubercles between the rows of zooecia are far apart. The genus *Polypora* dates from the Ordovician to the Lower Triassic. During the period when the order of Cryptostomata became extinct on a large scale towards the end of the Paleozoic era, this genus, which lived all over the world, was still very common. The specimen shown here belongs to the species *Polypora ehrenbergi* and has a zooarium measuring 1.2 cm (¹/₂ in).

Cyclopelta sacculus
Lower Devonian, Koněprusy, Czech Republic

186

Polypora ehrenbergi
Upper Permian, Pössneck, Germany

Monotrypa kettneri
Middle Ordovician, Prague-Řeporyje, Czech Republic

Acanthocladia ■

LOWER CARBONIFEROUS – PERMIAN

Acanthocladia is characterized by a branching zo-oarium. There are short side branches on the central branch. The zooecia are found in several rows on the branches. During the period from the Upper Carboniferous to the Permian *Acanthocladia* was widespread almost all over the world, and is often found in limestone rocks. The partly preserved zoo-arium of the species *Acanthocladia anceps* in the picture measures 1.2 cm ($^1/_2$ in).

Acanthocladia anceps
Upper Permian, Pössneck, Germany

Order: Trepostomata

LOWER ORDOVICIAN – UPPER TRIASSIC

These moss animals reached the peak of their development during the Ordovician. They are fairly massive, spherical, branching or sometimes plate-like colonies. No communication pores have developed between the individual zooecia. One of the characteristics of the zooaria of the order of Trepostomata is the differing thickness of the walls of the shells in the central area and on the edge. The middle part of the colony, the so-called immature area, comprises younger specimens with thin-walled zooecia. This means that the mature area has developed on the circumference and that the curved, thick-walled zooaria on the surface have more septa. Hetero-zooecia are represented as well as the normal zoo-ecia. Polished specimens are most suitable for studying these moss animals.

Monotrypa ■

ORDOVICIAN – PERMIAN

The zooaria of these primitive representatives of moss animals in the order of Trepostomata are spherical, semi-spherical or disc-shaped, or they have an irregular shape. The zooecia are narrow and prism-shaped, and there is only one type, without too many septa, and in some cases with no septa at all. The walls of the zooecia are thin and spherical, and the mouth opening is polygonal in cross section. Moss animals of the genus *Mono-trypa* are often found on the shells of marine bivalves, with which they lived in a symbiotic relationship. Representatives of this genus have been recorded in Europe, Asia and North America. The cross section of the zooarium of the species *Mono-trypa kettneri* shown here is 6.7 cm ($2^1/_2$ in) across.

Polyteichus novaki, Polyteichus sp.
Middle Ordovician, Prague-Michle, Czech Republic

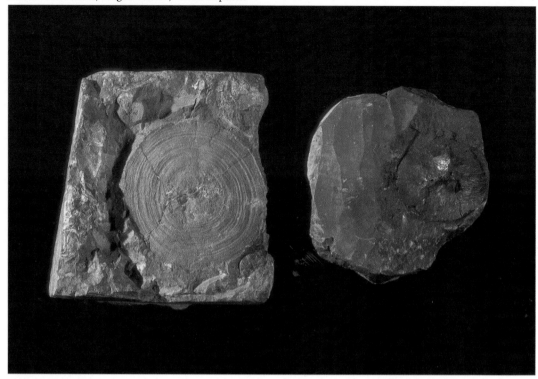

Polyteichus ∎

ORDOVICIAN

The zooaria of the genus *Polyteichus* are flat and lens-shaped or disc-shaped and very striking. On the upper side there is an edge in the shape of a three, or occasionally a five-pointed star, which is formed by two rows of zooecia. The zooecia are narrow prisms with only occasional septa. In areas of Central Europe (Barrandien), moss animals of the genus *Polyteichus* dating from the Ordovician can be so important that they form their own layer within an accumulation of layers which were in shallow sea water. The larger of the two specimens shown here has a zooarium measuring 3.1 cm (1¼ in).

Class: Gymnolaemata

LOWER ORDOVICIAN – RECENT TIMES

The zooids of these moss animals are generally box-shaped, bag- shaped or in the shape of a short cylinder. The zooecia are fibrous or chitinous, and are often not completely calcified. They include most of the fossilized and living animals.

Order: Cheilostomata

UPPER JURASSIC – RECENT TIMES

The zooecia are calcified, flexible or rigid. In addition to autozooecia and ovicells, there can also be heterozooecia which vary in terms of shape, and have a protective function. The mouth of the zooecia can be closed with a lid. The characteristics which allow for the classification include the shape of the mouth, the ovicells and the heterozooecia.

Lunulites goldfussi
Upper Cretaceous, Rügen, Germany

Lunulites ■

CRETACEOUS – EOCENE

Lunulites has a disc-shaped or broad dish-shaped, curving zooarium, with radiating zooecia. This genus, like the other Cheilostomata, lived freely on the substratum. *Lunulites* included a fairly large number of species, and lived in Europe and North America from the Cretaceous to the Eocene. The largest zooarium of *Lunulites goldfussi*, shown, measures 4 mm ($^5/_{32}$ in) (side view from below).

Discoporella ■

MIOCENE – RECENT TIMES

The zooarium of the *Discoporella* is in the shape of a dish and is very similar to *Lunulites*. The zooecia have numerous pores. Fossils of *Discoporella*, which lived from the Miocene, have been recorded in many areas of Europe. Nowadays it is found in the Mediterranean Sea and the Atlantic Ocean. The largest zooarium in the picture measures 9 cm ($3^1/_2$ in).

Retepora ■

EOCENE – RECENT TIMES

Retepora is characterized by a net-like zooarium, with branches growing from a broader base. The zooecia have a round mouth opening, below which there is a small, slit-shaped hole. *Retepora* lived from the Eocene and is still found today. Fossils have been found mainly in Europe and North America. The fragment of the zooarium shown in the picture measures 1 cm ($^3/_8$ in).

Phylum: Brachiopoda – brachiopods

LOWER CAMBRIAN – RECENT TIMES

Brachiopods include marine, solitary and benthic animals. They have a separate mouth and anal opening. Linnaeus originally classified them under bivalves, because their shell also consists of two valves of calcium carbonate, or sometimes of chitin and calcium phosphate. However, in contrast with the bivalves, the axis of symmetry runs through the umbos and the middle of the anterior edge of the shell, and not between the valves. Two valves of different sizes, one on the ventral side (the ventral valve) and one on the dorsal side (the dorsal valve) protect the soft body. The first is generally larger and more convex. The vertical symmetrical plane runs through the valves, dividing them into a right and left half. In less developed groups the shells are only connected by a system of muscles, while more developed groups have muscles and a hinge socket. The muscles open and shut the valves. At the surface on the inside of the shell on the ventral side,

Discoporella umbellata
Miocene, Beeringen, the Netherlands

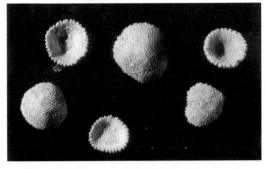

muscle scars are clearly visible where the muscles are attached. The hinge plate consists of two teeth protruding from the shell on the ventral side and in the sockets of the shell on the dorsal side.

The soft body of the brachiopods is formed by a *mantle* (which secretes the shell), a *visceral tract*, a *lophophore* and a stalk. The cavity in the shell is divided into two unequal parts by a membranous septum. The smaller part is taken up by the visceral tract. In the front part there is a cavity with a spinal system– the *lophophore (brachidium)*. This carries a nutritious flow of water to the mouth with vibrating filaments or cilia. The lophophore is strengthened with a skeleton (the *brachidial skeleton)*. A massive *stalk or pedicle* develops from the extension of the body wall, protruding from the valves at the back of the body. The stalk can be several millimeters or centimeters long. It usually serves to temporarily attach the animal to substratum, and occasionally is used for digging. Brachiopods live on the sea bed of mainly shallow seas. During the Paleozoic they represented the majority of benthic animals and inhabited oxygen-rich waters of coastal areas. Brachiopods are classified in three subphyla on the basis of the material of which the shells are composed, and on the basis of the presence or absence of a hinge socket.

Retepora sp.
Miocene, Italy

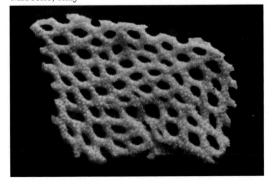

189

Subphylum: Linguliformea

LOWER CAMBRIAN – RECENT TIMES

This group includes the primitive brachiopods with a chitino-phosphatic shell. The valves are only connected by a complex system of muscles. The lophophore is not strengthened by a calcareous skeleton. In general, the stalk passes through the valves. The valves of Linguliformea consist of calcium phosphate, alternating with an organic mass in thin layers, which runs parallel to the surface of the valves. The valves on the dorsal and ventral side are usually similar, with unobtrusive umbos. They can be distinguished on the basis of oval muscle scars, or on the basis of the opening in front of the stalk in the shell on the ventral side. The subphylum of Linguliformea is divided into two classes on the basis of their ontogenetic development. The class of Lingulata is more important from the palaeontological point of view.

Class: Lingulata

LOWER CAMBRIAN – RECENT TIMES

This is a Linguliforma in which the primary (larval) shell is smooth or contains cavities. The body of the larva has long brushes on the sides, forming connected rows along the edge of the mantle. The digestive system is curved and the functional anal opening is moved to the front. Representatives of the important order Lingulida are listed below.

Illustration of the system of tentacles of brachiopods: A – view of the shell from the dorsal side, B – view of the shell from the ventral side

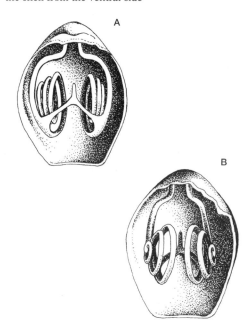

Obolus lamellosus
Lower Ordovician, Libečkov, Czech Republic

Order: Lingulida

LOWER CAMBRIAN – RECENT TIMES

The chitino-phosphatic shell is round, tongue-shaped or oblong. The valves are virtually the same size and are slightly convex. Concentric lines may appear on the smooth surface. The stalk passes through the valves, often via a groove on the ventral side.

Obolus ■

MIDDLE CAMBRIAN – LOWER ORDOVICIAN

The genus *Obolus* is characterized by flat, chitinous or calcified round shells. On the surface, there may be a sculpture of concentric circles which are close together, and may be crossed by fine, radiating ribs. The genus *Obolus* was widespread all over the world from the Middle Cambrian to the Lower Ordovician. The specimens of the species *Obolus lamellosus* shown here measure approximately 1 cm ($^3/_8$ in).

Linguila ■

ORDOVICIAN – RECENT TIMES

The thin-walled, chitinous shell of the genus *Linguila* is oval, with an elongated tongue-like shape. It is completely smooth on the surface or has fine concentric growth lines. The genus *Linguila* already existed during the Ordovician and spread all over the world. The specimens shown here have shells approximately 1.5 cm ($^1/_2$ in) long.

Pachyglosella ■

ORDOVICIAN

The genus *Pachyglosella* is characterized by a thin-walled shell which is oval lengthwise, and resembles that of *Linguila* to a certain extent. The surface sculpture consists only of fine concentric growth lines. Representatives of the genus *Pachyglosella* have been recorded in Ordovician sediments in North America. The specimen of the species *Pachyglosella biconvexa* shown in the picture has a shell measuring 1.3 cm ($^1/_2$ in).

Orbiculoidea ■

ORDOVICIAN – PERMIAN

The genus *Orbiculoidea* has a thin-walled, chitino-phosphatic shell with an umbo which has been moved approximately to the middle of the low, co-nical valve. A slit in the stalk is visible behind the umbo, and this can reach to the edge of the vale. The surface structure consists of fine concentric growth rings. The genus *Orbiculoidea* was widespread virtually throughout the world from the Ordovician to the Permian. The specimen shown here belongs to the species *Orbiculoidea intermedia* and has a valve measuring 7 mm ($^1/_4$ in).

Pachyglosella biconvexa
Ordovician, Criner Hills, Oklahoma, United States

Subphylum: Craniiformea

LOWER (?), MIDDLE CAMBRIAN – RECENT TIMES

This subphylum includes brachiopods with a calcareous shell. Like the subphylum of Linguiformea, though unlike the more developed brachiopods, the valve is not connected by hinges and a hinge socket on the ventral and dorsal sides. Only the class of Craniata has survived up to the present day with corresponding characteristics.

Order: Craniida

LOWER ORDOVICIAN – RECENT TIMES

These brachiopods are characterized by calcareous, porous shells which have not developed an opening for the stalk. They lived with the shell attached to the substratum on the ventral side, or were completely free-swimming.

Lingula sp.
Upper Cretaceous, Langenau, Germany

Orbiculoidea intermedia
Lower Devonian, Kosoř, Czech Republic

Crania ∎

UPPER CRETACEOUS – RECENT TIMES

The calcareous, thick-walled shell of the genus *Crania* is more or less round. The valve on the ventral side is more convex than the valve on the dorsal side. The surface structure consists of thick, radiating ribs. The flat ventral valve of the representatives of the genus *Crania* was attached to the substratum. The genus *Crania* has survived up to the present day, and dates back to the Upper Cretaceous, eventually spreading all over the world. The shell of the specimen shown here belongs to the species *Crania abnormis* and measures 1.8 cm ($^3/_4$ in). On the inside of the shell it is possible to see a thick edge with two pairs of deep muscle scars.

Isocrania ∎

CRETACEOUS

To some extent the shells of the genus *Isocrania* resemble those of the genus *Crania*, though the perimeter is square. Although both valves have a broad conical shape, the valve on the ventral side is not usually as convex as the valve on the dorsal side. The surface structure of the shell consists of striking radial ribs. These brachiopods were only attached to the substratum with a small part of their surface, and at later stages of development they were entirely free swimming. The genus *Isocrania* has only been recorded in Cretaceous strata in Europe, Asia and Africa. The ventral valves of the species *Isocrania costata* in the picture are 7 mm ($^1/_4$ in) across.

Subphylum: Rhynchonelliformea

LOWER CAMBRIAN – RECENT TIMES

The brachiopods of the subphylum Rhynchonelliformea are characterized by calcareous shells and valves which are connected by a hinge socket and a simple muscle system. In addition to the muscles which close the valves (the *aductor* muscles) and open the valves (the *deductor* muscles), there are also muscles for the stalk. The lophophore is usually supported by a calcareous system. The opening for the stalk is often under the umbo of the valve on the ventral side. The ventral valve of the Rhynchonelliformea is larger and more complex and also has a more striking umbo. A supporting system of tentacles is connected to the inside of the less strongly convex valve on the dorsal side. The whole shape of the shells is rather variable. They can be rounded and triangular, and the lateral edges can also end in wings. The curve of the valves can also differ – shells with the same curve are described as being *biconvex*; if the dorsal valve is more curved

Crania abnormis
Lower Pliocene, Aguilas, Spain

than the ventral, they are *dorsibiconvex* valves; if the dorsal valve is flat and the ventral valve is convex, they are *plan-convex* valves; if the valve on the dorsal side is concave and the ventral side is convex, it is referred to as a *concave-convex* valve, and conversely, convex valves are *convex-concave*. The line of junction between the two valves is formed differently around the front and is described by the term *commissure*. It can be straight (*rectimarginal*), or there may be an anterior fold which is convex in the valve on the ventral side (*sulcate*), or a reverse fold develops which is convex on the dorsal side (*plicate*). Under the umbo of the valves there is usually a triangular area, known as the *cardinal area*. In the middle there is usually an opening for the stalk by the ventral valve. If the opening for the stalk is triangular, it is called a *deltyrium*. The deltyrium may be covered with one or two calcareous plates known as the *deltidium*, so that the opening for the stalk can be completely closed. The surface of the shell is smooth in exceptional cases, but usually there are growth lines, radial lines or concentric or radiating ribs. Sometimes tubercles develop, as well as various long, spiny ends. The walls of the shells are covered with a thin organic layer. Underneath there are two layers of calcite, which can contain pores in the fossilized species. The subphylum is divided into five classes, including representatives of the classes Kutorginata, Strophomenata and Rhynchonellata.

Class: Kutorginata

LOWER CAMBRIAN – MIDDLE CAMBRIAN

This class of brachiopods is characterized by fibrous shells without pores. The valve on the ventral side is slightly more convex than the valve on the dorsal side. There is only one order of Kutorginida, with characteristics which correspond to the characteristics of the class.

Pompeckium ■

MIDDLE CAMBRIAN

The genus *Pompeckium* is characterized by a shell which is elliptical in cross section, in which the valve on the ventral side is slightly more convex than that on the dorsal side. The surface usually has simple, sometimes branching radial ribs. The concentric growth lines are usually not very distinct. Representatives of the genus *Pompeckium* inhabited shallow seas during the Middle Cambrian and were widespread all over the world.

Class: Strophomenata

MIDDLE CAMBRIAN – UPPER TRIASSIC

The Rhynchonelliformea can have shells of different shapes. They are usually flat, plan-convex or slightly concave-convex. The surface often has radial ribs, but there may also be concentric ribs. Nowadays there are four orders.

Isocrania costata
Upper Cretaceous, Ciply, Belgium

Pompeckium kuthani
Middle Cambrian, Lohovice, Czech Republic

193

Leptaena depressa
Lower Silurian, Gotland, Sweden

Strophonella bohemica
Lower Devonian, Koněprusy, Czech Republic

Order: Strophomenida

LOWER ORDOVICIAN – UPPER CARBONIFEROUS

Representatives of this order are characterized by valves with a hinge socket which is long and straight. The cardinal area is on both valves or only on the valve on the ventral side. The valves are usually biconvex, plan-convex or concave-convex.

Leptaena ■

LOWER ORDOVICIAN – LOWER CARBONIFEROUS

The shells of this genus are flat and concave-convex at the beginning, but during later stages of development the two valves curve back dorsally. The outside surface has fine radial ribs, as well very striking concentric walls. The hinge teeth are strongly developed. The genus *Leptaena* existed from the Lower Ordovician to the Lower Carboniferous and was widespread all over the world. The specimen shown here belongs to the species *Leptaena depressa* and measures approximately 2 cm ($^3/_4$ in).

Strophonella ■

LOWER SILURIAN – LOWER DEVONIAN

The dorsal valve of the genus *Strophonella* is concave in younger specimens and the ventral valve is convex. However, during later developmental stages this curved is reversed, and the shell clearly grows ventrally at the anterior edge and on the sides. Representatives of the genus *Strophonella* lived freely on the sea bed. They were widespread all over the worlds from the Lower Silurian to the Lower Devonian. The ventral valve of the specimen shown here belongs to the species *Strophonella bohemica* and measures 6 cm ($2^1/_4$ in).

Cymostrophia

UPPER-SILURIAN – MIDDLE/UPPER DEVONIAN

The genus *Cymostrophia* is characterized by a large broad shell, which curves high up dorsally during the later developmental stages. The surface of the outside of the valves has fine radial ribs, and in some species there may also be concentric ribs on the flat part of the valves. The genus *Cymostrophia* has been found in Upper Silurian to Middle and Upper Devonian strata in Europe, Asia and North America. The specimen shown here belongs to the species *Cymostrophia stephani* and has a ventral valve which is 5.2 cm (2 in) across.

Cymostrophia stephani
Lower Devonian, Koněprusy, Czech Republic

194

Order: Productida

LOWER DEVONIAN – UPPER PERMIAN,
TRIASSIC(?)

This order includes brachiopods with a concave-convex to plan-convex shell with a straight hinge socket. Teeth may have developed, but may also be absent. The surface sculpture is radial of concentric on the surface of both valves or hollow spines may have developed only on the ventral valve. In some representatives the shell can grow to a considerable size.

Parachonetes ■

LOWER DEVONIAN – MIDDLE DEVONIAN

The shell of the genus *Parachonetes* consists of a convex ventral and a concave dorsal valve. On the posterior edge of the shell there are slanting, laterally-oriented hollow spines, which probably served as a sensory organ. The surface on the outside has striking, blunt, radial ribs. It is quite possible that some representatives of the group, which includes the genus *Parachonetes,* were actually active swimmers. The genus *Parachonetes* existed from the Lower to the Middle Devonian, and there were representatives all over the world. The ventral valve of the species *Parachonetes verneuili* shown here is 4.3 cm (1$^1/_2$ in) across.

Dictyoclostus ■

LOWER CARBONIFEROUS

The shells of the genus *Dictyoclostus* are large, with a clear convex ventral valve and a concave dorsal valve. The genus is characterized by radial ribs close together, which are sometimes irregular. The surface of the two valves also contained groups of fine spines. The genus *Dictyoclostus* lived in areas of Europe in the Lower Carboniferous. The specimen

Dictyoclostus semireticulatus
Lower Carboniferous, Dublin, Ireland

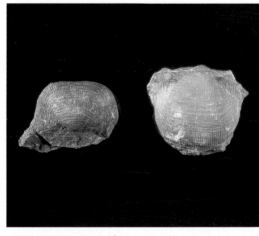

shown here belongs to the species *Dictyoclostus semireticulatus* and has a valve 6 cm (2$^1/_4$ in) across.

Horridonia ■

PERMIAN

The average-sized or large shell of the genus *Horridonia* has a strongly convex ventral valve and a moderately concave dorsal valve. The surface on the outside of the shell has concentric growth lines and long spines may have survived along the edge of the hinge socket, and on the flat posterolateral sides. The genus *Horridonia* is characteristic of the Permian and representatives have been recorded in Europe, the Arctic, Asia and Australia.

Parachonetes verneuili
Lower Devonian, Koněprusy, Czech Republic

Horridonia horrida
Upper Permian, Gera, Germany

Xystostrophia umbraculum
Middle Devonian, Mühlemosald, Germany

Clitambonites squamata
Middle Ordovician, Kohtla-Järva, Estonia

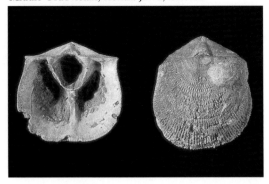

Order: Orthotetida

LOWER ORDOVICIAN – UPPER PERMIAN

Mature specimens of this order are characterized by concave-convex shells, although both valves may also be convex. The ventral valve has a high area which may be absent in the dorsal valve.

Xystostrophia ■

MIDDLE DEVONIAN

The genus *Xystostrophia* is characterized by large valves. The ventral valve is fairly convex around the umbo, becoming moderately concave towards the anterior edge. The dorsal valve is convex. An area has developed on both valves between the umbo and the hinge socket, while the opening of the stalk is closed off. There are narrow radial ribs on the surface on the outside. Representatives of this genus mostly lived freely on the sea bed, with their flat ventral valve turned down, but were also capable of swimming actively. The genus *Xystostrophia* dates from the Middle Devonian in Europe. The shell of the species *Xystostrophia umbraculum* in the picture is 4.4 cm (1³/₄ in) across.

Order: Billingsellida

MIDDLE CAMBRIAN – UPPER ORDOVICIAN

These are primitive brachiopods with a biconvex or plan-convex shell and a well-developed hinge socket.

Clitambonites ■

LOWER ORDOVICIAN – MIDDLE ORDOVICIAN

The shell of the genus *Clitambonites* has only a moderately convex dorsal valve. The strongly convex ventral valve is curved at the short part of the umbo. Between the umbo and the line of the hinge socket on the ventral valve, there is a triangular area. The deltyrium is narrow, leaving only a small opening for the stalk. The surface structure consists of numerous overlapping lamellae. The genus *Clitambonites* lived in the course of the Lower and Middle Ordovician in Europe and Asia. The largest of the specimens shown here, which belong to the species *Clitambonites squamata*, has a shell measuring 2.7 cm (1 in).

Class: Rhynchonellata

LOWER CAMBRIAN – RECENT TIMES

This includes a varied group of brachiopods, with shells which are usually biconvex and can differ considerably in terms of shape. The teeth in the ventral valve and those in the dorsal valve may develop to a different extent, and the *brachiophores* (calcareous extremities which served to support the lophophore) are usually clearly visible. Nowadays there are ten orders altogether, and the majority of the representatives are mentioned below.

Order: Orthida

LOWER CAMBRIAN – UPPER PERMIAN

The shell of these brachiopods, which lived exclusively in the Paleozoic, is usually biconvex and occasionally plan-convex or concave-convex. The surface has radial ribs. The walls of the shells are uninterrupted. The edge of the hinge socket is usually straight and sometimes fairly long. The deltyrium is usually open and there is no deltidium. The teeth sockets are surrounded by brachiophores on the inside (extremities which support the system of tentacles).

196

Plaesiomys ■

MIDDLE ORDOVICIAN – UPPER ORDOVICIAN

The genus *Plaesiomys* is characterized by relatively flat shells with a more or less semicircular perimeter. The surface sculpture is composed of numerous fine, radial ribs. The arrangement of the internal structures, particularly of the muscle scars, is important for the accurate classification of this genus. Representatives of the genus *Plaesiomys* have been recorded in Middle and Upper Ordovician strata in Europe and North America. The specimen of the species *Plaesiomys subquadrata* shown in the picture has a shell 2 cm ($^3/_4$ in) across.

Euorthisina ■

LOWER ORDOVICIAN

The shells of the genus *Euorthisina* are similar and biconvex, slightly broadening out. The surface sculpture of the shells consists of thick, rounded radial ribs. High teeth plates have developed in the ventral valve. Representatives of the genus *Euorthisina* have been recorded in Lower Ordovician strata in Europe, North Africa and South America.

Order: Pentamerida

MIDDLE CAMBRIAN – UPPER DEVONIAN

This group is exclusively limited to the oldest Paleozoic. The smooth or radiating ribbed shells with uninterrupted walls are strongly biconvex, and an elongated oval shape. The larger ventral valve has a distinct umbo. The commissure is lobe-shaped. The edge of the hinge socket is short, and the open deltyrium has a triangular shape. The hinge teeth of the ventral valve are supported by calcareous plates which touch in the middle. In this way they form a characteristic additional skeletal element in this group, known as the *spondylium*. The spondylium can extend to the anterior half of the shell.

Porambonites aequirostris
Middle Ordovician, Kohtla-Järve, Estonia

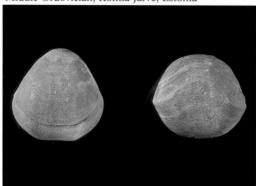

Conchidium

UPPER ORDOVICIAN – LOWER DEVONIAN

The genus Conchidium is characterized by strongly biconvex shells, approximately 10 cm (4 in) across. The umbo of the ventral valve extends far behind the umbo of the dorsal valve. The hinge socket is very short, and the commissure is only slightly wavy. The surface on the outside has radial ribs that are close together. Representatives of the genus *Conchidium* are amongst the best-known fossilized brachiopods and were probably described by Linnaeus. This genus lived in many parts of the world from the Upper Ordovician to the Lower Devonian. The largest specimen of the group shown here, which belongs to the genus *Conchidium*, measures 5 cm (2 in).

Porambonites

LOWER ORDOVICIAN – LOWER SILURIAN

The genus *Porambonites* is characterized by a shell which can be biconvex, but may also have a flat ventral valve. During the growth of the shell a groove develops in the middle of the ventral valve which becomes more distinct in the anterior section, so that the front commissure curves dorsally. There may be fine radial ribs on the surface of the valves, sometimes with fine hollows in the grooves between them. The genus *Porambonites* lived from the Lower Ordovician to the Lower Silurian and spread all over the world. The largest of the specimens shown here, which belong to the species *Porambonites aequirostris*, measures 2.6 cm (1 in).

Gypidula

LOWER SILURIAN – UPPER DEVONIAN

The shell of the genus *Gypidula* is strongly biconvex, and the umbo of the helmet-shaped ventral valve is strongly curved. There is a shallow groove which runs through the middle of the dorsal valve. The anterior commissure is moderately curved towards the ventral valve. The surface on the outside is smooth, though there may be lengthwise ribs. Representatives of the genus *Gypidula* lived in shallow seas from the Lower Silurian to the Upper Devonian and were widespread all over the world. The shell of the largest specimen shown here, which belongs to the species *Gypidula galeata*, measures 2.5 cm (1 in).

Conchidium sp.
Upper Silurian, Great Britain

Gypidula galeata
Lower Silurian, Gotland, Sweden

Homoeorhynchia acuta
Lower Jurassic, Lixhausen, France

Order: Rhynchonellida

LOWER ORDOVICIAN – RECENT TIMES

This order includes brachiopods with relatively small, often biconvex shells with a rounded or convex triangular perimeter. The very short hinge socket is curved. There is a strongly reduced area below the large curving umbo. The deltyrium is often hidden, but the opening for the stalk is usually preserved. On the shells, the saddle and a groove are usually well developed.

Torquirhynchia ■

UPPER JURASSIC

The most characteristic feature of the genus *Torquirhynchia* is the bilateral asymmetry. The left and right halves of the shell are not in the same plane at the front. The valves are relatively large, with the appearance of a broad triangle, and the surface sculpture consists of numerous sharp, radial ribs. The genus *Torquirhynchia* was widespread in Europe during the Upper Jurassic. The picture shows a specimen of the species *Torquirhynchia speciosa* with a valve 7 cm ($2^3/_4$ in) across.

Torquirhynchia speciosa
Lower Jurassic, Saal, Germany

Homoeorhynchia ■

LOWER JURASSIC

The shells of the genus *Homoeorhynchia* are triangular with a flat dorsal and a convex ventral valve. There is a high wall on the dorsal valve and a deep groove on the ventral valve. The commissure curves towards the dorsal valve. Most of the surface of the shell is smooth, and there may be ribs close to the anterior edge of the valves. Representatives of the genus *Homoeorhynchia* have been found in Lower Jurassic strata in Europe and Asia. The specimen shown here belongs to the species *Homoeorhynchia acuta* and has a shell 2 cm ($^3/_4$ in) long.

Burmirhynchia ■

MIDDLE JURASSIC

The genus *Burmirhynchia* has moderately lobe-shaped shells, with a strong convex dorsal and ventral valve and a strongly curved umbo. The opening for the stalk is elliptical; the deltidium is narrow. The commissure is dorsally curved. The surface sculpture consists of clear radial ribs that are close together. Representatives of the genus *Burmirhynchia* have been found in Middle Jurassic strata in Europe and Asia. The largest specimen of the subspecies *Burmirhynchia decorata decorata* shown in the picture measures 4.2 cm ($1^1/_2$ in). The photograph shows the original ontogenetic stages.

Burmirhynchia decorata decorata
Middle Jurassic, Poix-Terron, France

Lacunose arolica
Upper Jurassic, Holderbank, Switzerland

Cyclothyris compressa
Upper Cretaceous, Kent, Great Britain

Lacunosella ■

UPPER JURASSIC – LOWER CRETACEOUS (?)

The shells of the genus *Lacunosella* are very variable in terms of shape and size. Indistinct, often bifurcated, branching ribs may appear on the inside surface, particularly on the anterior parts of both valves. The cardinal area is not very striking. The genus *Lacunosella* was extremely common from the Upper Jurassic to (?) the Lower Cretaceous in parts of Europe and Asia. The larger of the two specimens shown here, which belong to the species *Lacunosella arolica*, has a shell measuring 3 cm (1¹⁄₄ in).

Cyclothyris ■

CRETACEOUS

The genus *Cyclothyris* is characterized by average-sized oval shells which are slightly broadened out. The ventral valve has a striking umbo. The anterior commissure curves towards the dorsal valve. The surface structure consists of numerous radiating ribs. Representatives of the genus *Cyclothyris* have been found in Cretaceous strata, and a large number of species have been described in Europe. The specimen shown here belongs to the important genus *Cyclothyris compressa*, and has a shell which measures 4.5 cm (1³⁄₄ in).

Kutchirhynchia ■

MIDDLE JURASSIC

The shells of the genus *Kutchirhynchia* are biconvex with a more or less round circumference. The ventral valve is less convex than the dorsal valve. The umbo of the ventral valve is strongly curved, with a striking round opening for the stalk. The saddle is clearly visible on the anterior part of the dorsal valve, while the ventral valve has developed a broad groove. The surface structure consists of thick radial ribs. The genus *Kutchirhynchia* was

widespread in Europe during the Middle Jurassic. The largest specimen shown here, which belongs to the species *Kutchirhynchia moreirei*, measures 2.7 cm (1 in).

Order: Atrypida

LOWER ORDOVICIAN – UPPER DEVONIAN

The shells are dorsi-biconvex and rounded, and the walls of the valves are uninterrupted. On the surface of the shells the sculpture usually consists of different sorts of ribs. The edge of the hinge socket is short and curved, or occasionally straight. The cardinal area on the ventral valve is small with a triangular deltyrium. There is no cardinal area on the dorsal valve.

Kutchirhynchia moreirei
Middle-Jurassic, Luc-sur-Mer, Wouistreham, France

Dayia ■

UPPER SILURIAN – LOWER DEVONIAN

The small shells of the genus *Dayia* are asymmetrically biconvex, with a very high, helmet-shaped ventral valve and a much flatter dorsal valve. There is a shallow groove running through the middle of the dorsal valve. The surface on the outside of the shell is smooth. Representatives of the genus *Dayia* have been found in Upper Silurian to Lower Devonian strata in Europe, Asia and North Africa. The shells shown here belong to the species *Dayia bohemica* and measure approximately 1 cm ($^3/_8$ in).

Spinatrypa ■

DEVONIAN

The genus *Spinatrypa* is characterized by more or less round shells, and the ventral valve has only a small umbo. The surface structure consists of thick radial ribs and striking concentric growth lines. While these brachiopods were alive, long hollow spines appeared on the surface of the shell. A large number of species have been recorded in Devonian sediments in Europe, Asia and North America. The specimens shown here belong to the subspecies *Spinatrypa aspera aspera*, and have a shell measuring approximately 1.5 cm ($^1/_2$ in).

Order: Athyridida

UPPER ORDOVICIAN – LOWER CRETACEOUS

Representatives of this order have smooth valves with a round circumference, porous walls and a distinct umbo. The external structure resembles that of the Atrypida, but the brachidium has a more complicated structure. It is probable that they actually developed from representatives of the order of Atrypida. However, it is also possible that they developed directly from representatives of the order of Rhynchonellida.

Spinatrypa aspera
Middle Devonian, Schwirzheim, Germany

Meristina ■

LOWER SILURIAN – UPPER DEVONIAN

The large shells of the genus *Meristina* are strongly biconvex. The anterior commissure is curved towards the dorsal valve. There are no teeth in the ventral valve, while the muscle scars are deep. The umbo of the ventral valve is strongly curved. The opening for the stalk can only be seen in younger specimens, and in older specimens the opening is closed. The surface on the outside of the shell is smooth. Mature specimens of the genus *Meristina* partly dug themselves into the sea bed of shallow seas. Species have been described from every part of the world. The largest specimen of the species *Meristina tumida* shown here has a shell measuring 4.5 cm ($1^3/_4$ in).

Dayia bohemica
Upper Silurian, Prague-Řeporyje, Czech Republic

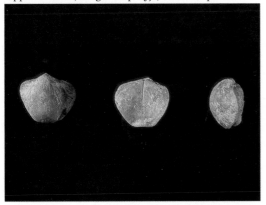

Meristina tumida
Lower Silurian, Dudley, Great Britain

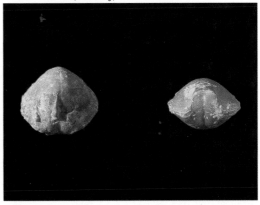

Paraspirifer bownockeri
Middle Devonian, Sylvania, Ohio, United States

Cyrtospirifer verneuili
Upper Devonian, Barvaux, Belgium

Order: Spiriferida

LOWER SILURIAN – LOWER JURASSIC

This group is mainly limited to the Paleozoic. The shells are mainly biconvex, and usually strongly laterally elongated, so that they are broader than they are long. The surface of the shells has radiating ribs, and the walls are usually uninterrupted. The cardinal area has usually developed in both valves, and in the ventral valve it is broad with a triangular deltyrium. There is a small round opening, but other than that the deltyrium under the umbo is completely closed.

Paraspirifer ■

LOWER DEVONIAN – MIDDLE DEVONIAN

The case is broad and has a long hinge plate. The sinus on the dorsal valve and the saddle on the ventral valve are distinct, without ribs. On the edges of the sides of the vales there are rounded ribs, as well as fine concentric growth lines. The genus *Paraspirifer* lived from the Lower to the Upper Devonian and a small number of species from Europe and North America have been described. The specimen shown here belongs to the species *Paraspirifer bownockeri* and measures 5 cm (2 in).

Brachyspirifer ■

LOWER DEVONIAN – MIDDLE DEVONIAN

The genus *Brachyspirifer* is characterized by biconvex valves with a clear groove on the ventral valve and a distinct saddle on the dorsal valve. The anterior edge of the commissure forms a striking dorsal fold in the medial section. The surface sculpture consists of radial ribs which are close together, and striking growth lines. The genus *Brachyspirifer* probably attached itself to the larger valves of other invertebrates or corals etc. with a thick stalk. This genus lived mainly in Europe and North America from the Lower Devonian to the Middle Devonian. The specimen of the species *Brachyspirifer audaculus* shown here grows to a size of 3.5 cm (1¼ in).

Cyrtospirifer ■

UPPER DEVONIAN

The shells of the genus *Cyrtospirifer* are elongated, as seen from the side, while the convex ventral valve ends in a massive apex and the dorsal valve is flatter. The latter has a striking saddle, and there is a broad groove which runs through the middle of the ventral valve. There is a triangular cardinal area below the apex. There are radiating ribs close together on the surface of the outside. A large number of

Brachyspirifer audaculus
Middle Devonian, Sylvania, Ohio, United States

Spinocyrtia ostiolata
Middle Devonian, Gondelsheim, Germany

Spirifer ventricosa
Upper Devonian, Eifel, Germany

species which belong to the genus *Cyrtospirifer* have been described. They date from Upper Devonian and have been found all over the world. The specimen shown here belongs to the species *Cyrtospirifer verneuili* and has a shell which is 7 cm (2³/₄ in) across.

Spinocyrtia ■

MIDDLE DEVONIAN – UPPER DEVONIAN

The genus *Spinocyrtia* is characterized by large biconvex shells with a round circumference and low radial ribs that are close together. There is a striking rib that runs through the middle of the dorsal valve, and a broad groove on the ventral valve. A small number of species have been described of the genus *Spinocyrtia*. They have been recorded in Middle and Upper Devonian strata in Europe, Asia and North America. The picture shows a series of specimens of the species *Spinocyrtia ostiolata* at different stages of their ontological development. The largest is 3.7 cm (1¹/₂ in) across.

Spirifer ■

UPPER SILURIAN – PERMIAN

The shell of the genus *Spirifer* is more or less round or semi-elliptical, and strongly laterally elongated. The valves are regularly biconvex with a straight

hinge socket. The umbos are low. The saddle on the dorsal valve and the groove on the ventral valve are very striking. The ventral cardinal area is narrow, and the anterior edge of the commissure forms a dorsally curving fold. Distinct radial ribs can be seen on the surface of the outside of the shell. The genus *Spirifer* existed from the Upper Silurian to the Permian and reached the peak of its development during the Carboniferous, when it was common all over the world. The specimen shown here belongs to the species *Spirifer ventricosa* and measures 3 cm (1¹/₄ in).

Cyrtia ■

SILURIAN – DEVONIAN

The genus *Cyrtia* is characterized by a rounded triangular shell, and the ventral valve ends in a high, pointed umbo. Below this, there is a large cardinal area with a narrow deltyrium. The dorsal valve is only slightly convex. The saddle of the dorsal valve is low, and the groove on the ventral valve is shallow. The surface on the outside of the shell has very fine radial ribs. Representatives of the genus *Cyrtia* have been found all over the world. The largest specimen of the species *Cyrtia exporrecta* shown here is 2.6 cm (1 in) across.

Uncites ■

MIDDLE DEVONIAN

The genus *Uncites* has an elongated, oval or triangular shell with unequal, biconvex valves. The ventral valve is much more convex and has a clearly beak-like curving umbo. The spine of the dorsal valve penetrates the deltyrium of the ventral valve. The concave deltidium has only a small, round opening for the stalk. The hinge socket is short and curves outwards. The surface structure consists of radial ribs at regular intervals. Representatives of the genus *Uncites* have been found in Europe and Asia. The specimen of the species *Uncites gryphus* shown here measures 5 cm (2 in).

Cyrtia exporrecta
Lower Silurian, Dudley, Great Britain

Uncites gryphus
Middle Devonian, Bergisch Gladbach, Germany

Spiriferina rostrata
Lower Jurassic, Neuvy-Saint-Sepulcre, France

Stringocephalus sp.
Middle Devonian, Schlade, Germany

Order: Spiriferinida

LOWER DEVONIAN – LOWER JURASSIC

The walls of the shell of these brachiopods are porous and often have distinct growth lines. The surface of the shells sometimes also has tubercle-like extremities or spines.

Spiriferina ■

TRIASSIC – LOWER JURASSIC

The shell of the genus *Spiriferina* is characterized by unequal, biconvex valves with a more or less round circumference. The ventral valve may have a large curving umbo with a short, triangular cardinal area with rounded outer edges. The anterior commissure forms a distinct fold curving towards the dorsal valve in the middle, with smaller ventral folds on the edges. There is a low saddle with grooves on the edges of the dorsal valve, and shallow grooves on the ventral valve. The surface sculpture consists of blunt radial ribs that are far apart, and may also be absent, as well as clearly visible growth lines. The genus *Spiriferina* lived from the Triassic to the Lower Jurassic, when it was common all over the world.

Thecidea papillata
Upper Cretaceous, Maastricht, the Netherlands

Order: Thecideida

UPPER TRIASSIC – RECENT TIMES

The oval to rounded triangular shells of the representatives of this order are partly attached to the substratum by the ventral valve. The cardinal area is on this ventral valve and has developed a deltidium. There are clear tentacle scars on the dorsal valve.

Thecidea ■

CRETACEOUS

The genus *Thecidea* is characterized by an oval or rounded triangular shell which has developed a ventral cardinal area and a closed deltyrium. There is a striking calcareous mechanism on the surface on the inside of the ventral valve for attaching the lophophore, the axis of which ran through a deep groove. The genus *Thecidea* lived in shallow waters and was common in areas of Western Europe during the Cretaceous. The complete shells and individual valves of the species *Thecidea papillata* shown here measure 6–7 mm ($^1/_4$ in).

Order: Terebratulida

LOWER DEVONIAN – RECENT TIMES

These brachiopods reached their peak mainly during the Mesozoic era. The shells are biconvex, with a round or elongated oval circumference. The hinge socket is usually short and curved. The walls of the shells are porous. In the ventral valve there is a small cardinal area with a deltyrium which is closed by two plates. The umbo of the ventral valve protrudes strikingly and there is a clear opening for the stalk below the umbo.

Stringocephalus ■

MIDDLE DEVONIAN

The shells of the genus *Stringocephalus* are large and round, strongly biconvex, and the anterior commissure is completely straight. The ventral valve ends in a clear, beak-shaped, curving umbo. The broad opening for the stalk is below this. The surface on the outside is smooth, with only fine growth lines. Representatives of the genus *Stringocephalus* lived almost all over the world during the Middle Devonian and are amongst the most important leading fossils. The specimen shown here, which belongs to the genus *Stringocephalus,* measures 10 cm (4 in).

Terebratula ■

EOCENE – PLIOCENE

The genus *Terebratula* is characteristic because of its biconvex shells with an elongated oval shape. The ventral valve has a distinctive umbo, and below this there is a striking round opening for the stalk. The hinge socket is short and curved. The surface on the outside of the shell is smooth with only fine growth lines. Representatives of the genus *Terebratula* lived in Europe and North America from the Eocene to the Pliocene. The specimen shown here belongs to the species *Terebratula grandis* and measures 5.5 cm (2¹/₄ in).

Terebratula grandis
Lower Pliocene, Weinheim, Germany

Nucleata nucleata
Upper Jurassic, Kirchheim, Germany

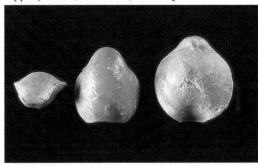

Nucleata ■

UPPER JURASSIC

The shells of the genus *Nucleata* are semicircular or round. There is a distinct groove in the anterior part of the dorsal valve. The anterior commissure is ventrally developed into a distinct, broad curve. The umbo of the ventral valve is unmistakably curved. The surface on the outside of the shell is smooth or has fine radial ribs. The genus *Nucleata* lived in Europe during the Upper Jurassic. The largest of the specimens shown here, which belong to the species *Nucleata nucleata,* has a shell measuring 1.5 cm (¹/₂ in).

Gibbithyris ■

UPPER CRETACEOUS

The shell of the genus *Gibbithyris* is biconvex and the strongly curving umbo of the ventral valve has a small round opening for the stalk. The anterior commissure of the valves is curved towards the dorsal valve. The surface on the outside of the valves is smooth, with only some fine concentric growth lines. The genus *Gibbithyris* was recorded during the Upper Cretaceous in Europe. The largest of the two valves shown here, which belong to the species *Gibbithyris semiglobosa* is 3.1 cm (1¹/₄ in)across.

Gibbithyris semiglobosa
Upper Cretaceous, Dover, Great Britain

Terebratulina ■

JURASSIC– RECENT TIMES

The genus *Terebratulina* has a small, moderately bi-convex to plan-convex shell, which is round or tear-shaped. The hinge socket is straight. The surface of the outside has thin, radial, branching ribs. Fossilized representatives of many different species of the *Terebratulina*, which still exists today, have been recorded in Jurassic strata in Europe, Asia and Africa. Nowadays, the genus is found in the Atlantic Ocean and near the coast of New Zealand. The largest of the specimens shown here, which belongs to the species *Terebratulina chrysalis*, measures 1.9 cm ($^3/_4$ in).

Cheirothyris ■

UPPER JURASSIC

The shells of the genus *Cheirothyris* are characterized by four, high, radially arranged ribs on each valve. On the anterior edge of the valves the ribs

Cheirothyris fleuriausa
Upper Jurassic, Nattheim, Germany

protrude like fingers, so that the shells look like the webbed feet of birds from above. Several species have been recorded in Jurassic strata in Europe. The largest of the specimens belonging to the species *Cheirothyris fleuriausa* in the picture measures 3 cm ($1^1/_4$ in).

Trigonellina ■

UPPER JURASSIC

The genus *Trigonellina* is a small brachiopod, with a shell that is normally round or a broad tear shape, with a protruding umbo on the ventral valve. The dorsal valve has a medial saddle, and in the middle of the ventral valve there is a clear groove. The surface structure consists of a network of ten distinct radial ribs, which sometimes end in short spines on the edges, and of less distinct growth lines. The genus *Trigonellina* lived in Europe during the Upper Jurassic. The largest of the specimens shown here, which belong to the species *Trigonellina pectuncula*, measures 1.1 cm ($^1/_2$ in).

Trigonosemus ■

UPPER CRETACEOUS

The genus *Trigonosemus* is characterized by thick-walled shells, with a ventral valve which is more strongly convex than the less convex or completely flat dorsal valve. The umbo is clearly curved and the opening for the stalk is large and round. The middle section of the anterior commissure is curved towards the ventral valve. The surface sculpture consists of fine ribs, close together. Representatives of the genus *Trigonosemus* date from the Upper Cretaceous in Europe and Asia. The largest of the two shells shown here, which belongs to the species *Trigonosemus elegans*, measures 3 cm ($1^1/_4$ in).

Coenothyris ■

MIDDLE TRIASSIC

The genus *Coenothyris* has strongly biconvex shells with an almost perfect spherical shape. The ventral valve is more strongly convex and ends in a short, broad umbo with a broad, round opening for the stalk below it. The surface on the outside is smooth with fine growth lines. The commissure is moderately convex on the front towards the dorsal valve. Representatives of the genus *Coenothyris* have been recorded in Middle Triassic strata in Europe and North America. The largest of the specimens shown here, which belongs to the species *Coenothyris cycloides*, measures 1.5 cm ($^1/_2$ in).

Juralina ■

UPPER JURASSIC

The shells of the genus *Juralina* are more or less tear-shaped, or may be in the shape of a rounded pentagon, with a large round opening for the stalk in the umbo of the ventral valve. The dorsal valve contains only an indistinct, broad medial groove. Concentric growth lines may be visible on the surface of the outside of the shell. Representatives of the genus *Juralina* have been found in Upper Ju-

Trigonosemus elegans
Upper Cretaceous, Ciply, Belgium

rassic strata in Europe. The largest specimen of the species *Juralina insignis* shown here, measures 4 cm ($1^1/_2$ in).

Coenothyris cycloides
Middle Triassic, vicinity of Kronach, Germany

Juralina insignis
Upper Jurassic, Saal, Germany

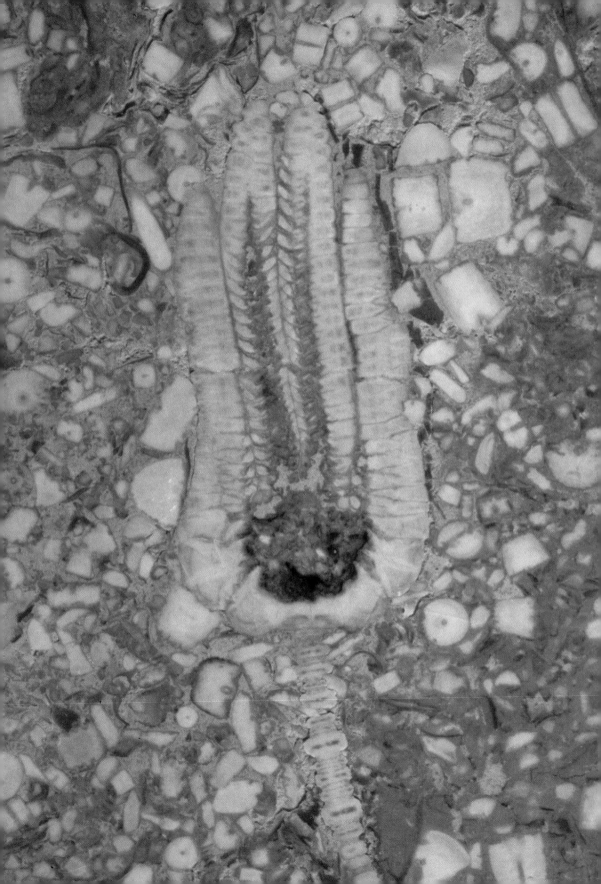

6. Echinoderms and Hemichordates

Phylum: Echinodermata – echinoderms

PROTEROZOIC(?), CAMBRIAN – RECENT TIMES

Echinoderms are an old phylum, the oldest specimens of which have been found in sediments in Southern Australia. These are marine, solitary and usually benthic animals. From the early Paleozoic there was a colorful diversity of shapes in this phylum, usually with a radiating symmetry based on the five most important axes. A study of the bilaterally symmetrical larvae of recent echinoderms and the oldest representatives of this phylum reveals that this symmetry is a secondary result of the transition to a lifestyle with very little movement.

Echinoderms are characterized by the presence of an *ambulacral system*, comprising the organ for obtaining food, the vascular system, the respiratory system, as well as organs for locomotion. Water which circulates through the ambulacral system not only provides the organism with oxygen, but moves microscopic particles of food towards the mouth. The system starts at the surface with an opening known as the *hydropore*, or with a perforated calcareous *madrepore plate*. Water penetrates this to the water vascular system, gradually passing into the *radial canal* to be taken to every part of the body. There are fine extremities along the sides of the radial canals. These usually have suckers at the ends, which reach the surface of the body via small openings in the skeleton. These extremities, described as organs of locomotion, helped the animals to move, or served as feelers.

Echinoderms developed an internal calcareous skeleton, the so-called *theca*, which consists of fixed plates or plates of $CaCO_3$ connected by joints. The connection of the body with the individual radial ambulacral canals is achieved by the *ambulacral plates* (all the ambulacra together form the so-called *ambulacrum*), and the *interambulacra* are between these. The name of this entire phylum is based on the fact that there are usually numerous spines sticking through the skin, which covers the calcareous skeleton to appear on the surface.

Living representatives of the echinoderms are subdivided into five classes. The systematic classification is more complicated for fossilized representatives and is constantly changing. Some of the representatives dating from the Cambrian, classified up to now in the subphylum Homalozoa, could probably also be classified in the phylum of chordates (Chordata).

Left: *Encrinus liliiformis*
Triassic, Neidenfels, Germany

There are five subphyla altogether, and of these the subphyla Blastozoa, Crinozoa and Echinozoa are particularly important for paleontology.

Subphylum: Homalozoa

MIDDLE CAMBRIAN –UPPER CARBONIFEROUS

In contrast with most other animals characterized by pentamerous symmetry, these echinoderms have developed a bilateral symmetry, or the symmetry has disappeared altogether. There is usually a tentacle-like extremity covered with plates, at the end of the flattened body. The function of this is not clear, but perhaps it served for obtaining food. It is sometimes said that it is rather like the stem of the genus Antedon, as in the primitive Chordata.

Class: Homostelea

MIDDLE CAMBRIAN

The skeleton of this class consists of thecae and an unsegmented stem. The theca is flat, and moderately asymmetrical, consisting of a large number of plates. The large plates on the edge surround the small one in the middle. There is a small oral opening at the anterior end of the body, and food was taken in through one or two clearly visible grooves.

Trochocystites ∎

MIDDLE CAMBRIAN

The genus *Trochocystites* has a flat theca with an oval or round shape. At the edges of the theca, there are two edge plates and a small central plate with an irregular shape. The oral opening is at the front, while the stem becomes narrower towards the distalend. Representatives of the genus *Trochocystites* have been recorded in Middle Cambrian strata in Central and Western Europe.

Trochocystites bohemicus
Middle Cambrian, Skryje, Czech Republic

209

Dendrocystites baredgeei
Middle-Ordovician, Zahořany, Czech Republic

Class: Homoiostelea

UPPER CAMBRIAN – LOWER DEVONIAN

In addition to a theca and a stem, the skeleton of the representatives of this class also developed a tentacle, with which these echinoderms obtained food. The theca is almost bilaterally symmetrical and consists of a large number of plates of different sizes. The plates on the edge do not differ from the inner plate, and the anal opening is to the side of the theca. The stem, which narrows towards the distal end, is already segmented.

Dendrocystites ■

MIDDLE ORDOVICIAN

The genus *Dendrocystites* is characterized by a rounded triangular theca, the end of which has a long arm consisting of two rows of plates. There is a pyramid consisting of plates around the anal opening. The stem is long, narrowing towards the distal end. The genus *Dendrocystites* lived on the sandy sea bed in areas of Central Europe during the Middle Ordovician.

Subphylum: Blastozoa

CAMBRIAN – RECENT TIMES

These are sessile echinoderms, with a skeleton which usually consists of a calyx, a stem and arms. The largest calyx, characterized by its pentamerous symmetry, is usually in the form of a bag, dish or ball, and consists of calcareous plates of a regular or irregular shape. The *oral opening* is in the middle

of the upper part. On the oral side there are also ambulacral grooves leading to the oral opening and often ending either in simple arm-like extremities (*brachioles*) or in long, usually complex segmented arms. With a few exceptions, the Blastozoa attach themselves to the substratum with a segmented stem, or directly with the base of the calyx. The plates of the calyx grow in a horizontal direction, while the stem and the arms grow vertically. The subphylum of Blastozoa consists of five classes, in which only the classes of Eocrinoidea, Diploporita and Rhombifera of the superclass of Cystoidea and Blastoidea are common.

Class: Eocrinoidea

CAMBRIAN – SILURIAN

This ancient group includes the primitive representatives of the subphylum of Blastozoa. The theca consists of a calyx with brachioles and a short stem. The vase-shaped calyx can consist of a smaller number of plates that are horizontally arranged, or a larger number of irregular plates. Five, sometimes branching, brachioles developed around the oral side of the calyx. The anal opening is on the side of the calyx. In older representatives, the stem is covered with plates. In younger representatives it is segmented, becoming narrower towards the distal end. Although some of the characteristics (e.g., the thecal plates of crystalline limestone) of the Eocrinoidea are similar to chordates, recent research has revealed that the Eocrinoidea are closest to the members of the blastoids, and could even be their ancestors.

Akadocrinus nuntius
Middle Cambrian, Jince, Czech Republic

Akadocrinus ■

MIDDLE CAMBRIAN

The Eocrinoidea of the genus *Akadocrinus* are characterized by a bottle-shaped calyx which is flat at the top end, with a larger number or brachioles on the upper edge. The calyx is narrower at the base and is attached with a long stem with a broad covering plate. The stem served to attach the animal to the substratum. Representatives of the genus *Akadocrinus* inhabited shallow sandy sea beds during the Middle Cambrian period. They were found in areas of Central Europe. The theca of the larger of the two specimens shown here, which belong to the species *Akadocrinus nuntius,* measures 1.2 cm ($^1/_2$ in).

Lichenoides ■

MIDDLE CAMBRIAN

The genus *Lichenoides* is characterized by a calyx which consists of three rings, large polygonal plates and long, thin brachioles. In the sutures between the plates there are numerous pores in the grooves which are arranged at regular intervals. There is no stem. During the earliest stages, the animal probably attached itself to the substratum with the thick base of the calyx, and mature animals were able to move freely. Representatives of the genus *Lichenoides* have been recorded in Middle Cambrian strata in Central Europe (Barrandien). The specimen shown here, which belongs to the species *Lichenoides priscus,* has a theca measuring 1.3 cm ($^1/_2$ in).

Macrocystella ■

UPPER CAMBRIAN – MIDDLE ORDOVICIAN

The theca of the genus *Macrocystella* is very similar to that of the representatives of the class of Rhombifera, and there is also a close phylogenetic relationship between the Cystoidea and the Eocrinoidea. The thin polygonal plates with a cylindrical calyx are strikingly ribbed, the brachioles are long, and the long stem broadens towards the calyx. Representatives of the genus *Macrocystella* have been found in Upper Cambrian to Middle Ordovician strata in Europe. The impression of the fragment of the theca shown here belongs to a specimen of the species *Macrocystella bohemica* and measures 1.7 cm ($^1/_2$ in).

Lichenoides priscus
Middle Cambrian, Jince, Czech Republic

Macrocystella bohemica
Middle Ordovician, Trubská, Czech Republic

Aristocystites bohemicus
Middle Ordovician, Zahořany, Czech Republic

Superclass: Cystoidea

ORDOVICIAN – DEVONIAN

These primitive echinoderms do not yet reveal any radial symmetry. Their skeleton consists of a calyx, usually a short stem, though this is sometimes absent, and tentacles (*brachioles*). The calyx is usually bag-shaped, round or in the shape of a calyx, and consists of irregular plates, which can vary greatly in number (from thirteen to several hundred). The thecae, which consist of a small number of hexagonal plates, have a striking surface sculpture, usually in the form of walls and ribs. The tentacles, which are close to the oral opening, have only survived in exceptional cases. The small anal opening, which is covered with five triangular plates, forms the so-called *anal pyramid*. Between the mouth and the anal opening there is an exit for the genital

Codiacystis bohemica
Middle Ordovician, Zahořany, Czech Republic

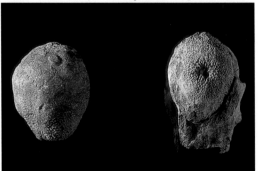

glands and hydropores. The stem of the Cystoidea, which gradually becomes narrower towards the calyx, consists of segments which stack together. There is a broad canal in the stem. The group of Cystoidea is divided into two classes – the Diploporita and the Rhombifera.

Class: Diploporita

MIDDLE ORDOVICIAN – MIDDLE DEVONIAN

The theca of this group is usually bag-shaped and consists of numerous small bony plates. In the plates there are usually double rows of pores, arranged in an irregular pattern, known as *diplopores*. The internal part of the body of the Cystoidea communicated with the outside environment through these, and in this way the animal was able to compensate for the osmotic pressure in the body. The stem only developed to a limited extent and is entirely absent in some representatives. The calyx is directly attached to the substratum. Five ambulacra have developed in every case.

Aristocystites ■

MIDDLE ORDOVICIAN

The genus *Aristocystites* has a bag-shaped or pear-shaped theca, with a narrow end with which the animal was attached to the substratum. The oral opening at the top is bobbin-shaped, and two strong, long tentacles developed on either side of the mouth. There is a hexagonal anal opening, consisting of plates, below the low pyramid. The diplopores are well developed. Representatives of the genus *Aristocystites* have been recorded in Middle Ordovician strata in Europe and Asia.

Codiacystis ■

MIDDLE ORDOVICIAN – UPPER ORDOVICIAN

The round or oval theca of the genus *Codiacystis* consists of numerous thick-walled plates, and the base is unusually thick. The animals dig themselves into the sea bed with this base, and because of their low center of gravity, they did not fall over, even in a strong current. There was an oval oral opening at the top of the theca, from which there were five short ambulacral grooves. At the ends of these there were areas with numerous fine tentacles. Representatives of the genus *Codiacystis* lived from the Middle to the Upper Ordovician in areas of Europe. The specimens shown here belong to the species *Codiacystis bohemica* and measure 3.2 and 3 cm (1¹/₄ in).

Class: Rhombifera

MIDDLE ORDOVICIAN – UPPER DEVONIAN

There are a small number of plates which form the theca of this group. They are large, and to compensate for the osmotic pressure in the body they contain so-called *route pores*, or pores connected in twos, on the adjacent plates. Together they form a more or less diamond shape, and the longest forms a diagonal suture between the two adjacent plates. The stem is always well developed. The representatives of this class usually have three or five ambulacra.

Echinosphaerites ■

MIDDLE ORDOVICIAN – UPPER ORDOVICIAN

The theca of the genus *Echinosphaerites* is round or oval and consists of numerous polygonal plates; the stem is short. The oral opening is on a small central platform on the theca, while the anal opening is ex-centric, below the pyramid of plates. There are three long brachioles, consisting of two rows of plates around the oral opening. Representatives of the genus *Echinosphaerites* have been recorded in Middle and Upper Ordovician sediments in Europe, Asia and North America and were so numerous that they were even important for rock formation. The specimen shown here, which belongs to the species *Echinosphaerites aurantium,* measures 4 cm (1^1/$_2$ in).

Orocystites ■

MIDDLE ORDOVICIAN – LOWER SILURIAN

The genus *Orocystites* has thecal plates, decorated with striking radial ribs, across the sutures between the plates. The oval theca on the crown ends in two short tubes and the oral and anal openings are at the ends of these. The brachioles were very short and have not usually survived. Representatives of the genus *Orocystites* have been recorded in sediments in the shallow waters of the Middle Ordovician to

Echinosphaerites aurantium
Middle Ordovician, Öland, Sweden

Orocystites helmhackeri
Middle Ordovician, Chrustenice, Czech Republic

the Lower Silurian in Europe and Asia. The specimen shown here belongs to the species *Orocystites helmhackeri* and measures 2.5 cm (1 in).

Arachnocystites ■

MIDDLE ORDOVICIAN

As regards their shape, the genus *Arachnocystites* is most similar to the genus *Echinosphaerites*. The thecal plates are not arranged in a very regular pattern, the oral opening does not face the top and the long brachioles around the oral opening do not branch. There is a fairly strong stem. Representatives of the genus *Arachnocystites* inhabited the sandy bed of cold shallow seas in Europe, Southern Asia and North Africa during the Ordovician. The specimen of the species *Arachnocystites infaustus* shown in the picture has a theca measuring 3 cm (1^1/$_4$ in).

Arachnocystites infaustus
Middle Ordovician, Zahořany, Czech Republic

Class: Blastoidea – blastoids

CAMBRIAN (?) – SILURIAN-PERMIAN

The blastoids are an extinct Paleozoic group, of which approximately a hundred orders have been described up to now. They are characterized by a clearly visible pentamerous symmetry, and a body consisting of a calyx, tentacles and a stem. The calyx is usually preserved in its entirety, and is round, oval or pear-shaped, and reminiscent of a flower bud as regards its appearance. It consists of thirteen interconnected plates, arranged in three rings, one above the other. The grooved ambulacra are some way from the oral opening along the sides of the theca. The fragile tentacles (*brachioles*) are very close to the oral opening. The segmented stem of the blastoids is fairly long. The most important development of the blastoids took place during the Upper Paleozoic, mainly in areas of North America.

Pentremites ■

LOWER CARBONIFEROUS

The genus *Pentremites* is characterized by an oval or pear-shaped pentagonal theca, which is elongated towards the lower edge and narrows towards the top in a flat crown. The broad ambulacra are leaf-shaped and extend to the area around the base of

Pentremites godoni
Lower Carboniferous, Floraville, Illinois, United States

Cordyloblastus cf. *eifelensis*
Middle Devonian, Gerolstein, Germany

the calyx. Representatives of the genus *Pentremites* have been recorded in Lower Carboniferous strata in North America. The picture shows specimens of the species *Pentremites godoni* seen from above (the largest specimen measures 1 cm/³/₈ in).

Cordyloblastus ■

MIDDLE DEVONIAN

Representatives of the genus *Cordyloblastus* are characterized by short ambulacra, which are limited to the top part of the calyx. In cross section the slender, high calyx is star-shaped. The genus *Cordyloblastus* has been recorded in Middle Devonian strata in Europe. The specimens shown belong to the species *Cordyloblastus* cf. *eifelensis*, and measure 6 mm (¹/₄ in) (viewed from the top) and 1.7 cm (¹/₂ in) (viewed from the side).

Cryptoschisma ■

DEVONIAN

Like the other blastoids, the theca of the genus *Cryptoschisma* is characterized by its pentamerous symmetry. The ambulacra are broad. Representatives of the genus *Cryptoschisma* have been found in Devonian sediments in Southern Europe. The specimens shown here, which belong to the species *Cryptoschisma schultzii*, measure 1.1 cm/³/₈ in (viewed from the side) and 7 mm (¹/₄ in) (viewed from the top).

Subphylum: Crinozoa

CAMBRIAN – RECENT TIMES

The subphylum of Crinozoa includes two classes, of which the class of Crinoidea (sea lilies) is of stratigraphic importance.

Cryptoschisma schultzii
Middle Devonian, Leon, Spain

Class: Crinoidea
– sea lilies

MIDDLE CAMBRIAN – RECENT TIMES

As the only class in the subphylum of Crinozoa, sea lilies have survived up to the present (approximately six hundred species are extant). At the same time they are one of the largest classes, and more than a thousand genera have been described. The body of sea lilies consists of a calyx, which has grown in size during the course of evolution, tentacles and a stem. The oral opening is at the top of the calyx, while the anal opening opens at the back of the interambulacrum. There are five tentacles growing from the calyx, which are normally branched, and form the *crown* together with the calyx. The actual calyx is usually in the shape of a beaker, bell, cone or sphere. There may be calcareous plates in two (*radial* or *basal*) of three (*radial, basal and infrabasal*) rings, one above the other. Each ring consists of five plates. Apart from the basal plates, there may also be an *anal* plate. In some species of sea lilies the lowest tentacle plates (*brachial* plates), *interradial* and *interbrachial* plates are also part the calyx. The tentacles are connected with the calyx by the *radial* plates. More developed sea lilies have bifurcating tentacles. Sometimes there is a flexible segmented stem which can be several metres long, attached to the base of the calyx by the central plate. The segments can vary in appearance. In some species the stem was shorter or disappeared. These attach themselves to the substratum with the base of the calyx, or with short extremities called *cirri*. An axial canal of different diameters runs through the stem. The stem is attached to the sea bed or to objects under water with root-like or anchor-like extremities. Some Paleozoic sea lilies have developed special spherical entities called *lobolites*, which serve to anchor or float the sea lily.

The classification of sea lilies is based mainly on the morphology of the calyx and the arrangement of its plates, the construction of the tentacles and the stem. They are subdivided into five subclasses, of which the representatives of the Camerata, Inathinata and Articulata are the most important from the stratigraphic point of view. Complete fossils of sea lilies are very rare, and therefore an artificial system has been developed for a few of the individual elements of the skeleton, e.g., for segments of the stem.

Subclass: Camerata

LOWER ORDOVICIAN – UPPER PERMIAN

The calyx of these sea lilies consists of numerous massive plates arranged in two or three rings; all the plates have fused together. The tentacles consist of one or two rows of plates, and branch at least once. Short segmented side branches developed on these, known as *pinnules*. In some species there are lobolites.

Scyphocrinites ■

UPPER SILURIAN – LOWER DEVONIAN

These are the large representatives of camerate sea lilies, with a crown more than half a meter long and a stem which can reach one meter. The monocyclic calyx is pear-shaped, becoming narrower at the bottom and consisting of small plates sculpted with a number of radial ribs. The basal plates (in the bottom part of the calyx) and radial plates are less numerous, although there are many interradial and interbrachial plates. Ten bifurcating tentacles are connected to the edge of the calyx with joints, and only the ends of these tentacles are free. The five-pointed canal in the rounded segments of the stem is also characteristic. The root ends in large spherical floating bodies or lobolites (up to 18 cm/7 in in diameter) divided into chambers by dissepimenta. The genus *Scyphocrinites*, which is important from the stratigraphic point of view, lived in the last part of the Upper Silurian and the Lower Devonian in Europe, Asia, North Africa and North America.

Scyphocrinites elegans
Lower Devonian, Prague-Podolí, Czech Republic

Platycrinites hemisphericus
Lower Carboniferous, Crawfordsville, Indiana, USA

Eucalyptocrinites rosaceus
Middle Devonian, Eifel, Germany

Platycrinites ■

DEVONIAN – UPPER PERMIAN

The genus *Platycrinites* is characterized by a low broad calyx with three unequal large, broad basal plates which are often fused together, and five larger radial plates connected to five segmented tentacles. Representatives of the genus *Platycrinites* lived in areas of North America from the Devonian to the Upper Permian. The complete crown of the specimen shown here, which belongs to the species *Platycrinites hemisphericus*, is 6 cm (2¹/₄ in) across.

Eucalyptocrinites ■

SILURIAN – MIDDLE DEVONIAN

The calyx of the genus *Eucalyptocrinites* is massive and low, in the shape of a broad dish, with a broad, tall roof in the middle. At the base, the calyx is flat with four basal plates. The radial plates are large. On the interradial plates there are two others, forming deep grooves at the place of contact, in which the tentacles can be hidden. The genus *Eucalyptocrinites* lived from the Silurian to the Middle Devonian and was widespread all over the world. The specimen of the species *Eucalyptocrinites rosaceus* shown here is 2.5 cm (1 in) across.

Thylacocrinus vannioti
Lower Devonian, St. Germain le Guillaume, France

216

Thylacocrinus ■

LOWER DEVONIAN

The genus *Thylacocrinus* is characterized by a large, broad, conical or disc-shaped shell, with plates arranged in three rings. The crown of the calyx is low. It is connected to 20 to 24 unbranched free tentacles, consisting of two rows of plates. The genus *Thylacocrinus* is found in Lower Devonian sediments in many areas all over the world. The fragment of the crown of the species *Thylacocrinus vannioti* shown here is 10 cm (4 in) across.

Agariocrinus ■

LOWER CARBONIFEROUS

The calyx of the genus *Agariocrinus* is low, and the base may be reinforced with three basal plates. The crown of the calyx is highly convex, almost pyramid-shaped. The tentacles consist of two rows of plates and are connected to the proximal end with thick semi-spherical plates. Representatives of the genus *Agariocrinus* have been recorded in Lower Carboniferous strata in North America. The crown of the specimen shown here, which belongs to the species *Agariocrinus bullatus*, measures 6 cm (2¼ in).

Hexacrinites ■

UPPER SILURIAN – LOWER DEVONIAN

The calyx of the sea lily of the genus *Hexacrinites* is simple, and consists of three basal and five high radial plates. Between these, there is the first plate of the anal opening, near the middle or on the edge of the convex crown of the calyx. The free parts of the tentacles are formed by only one row of plates, and there are two simple or branching tentacles in every arm. The genus *Hexacrinites* lived in Europe, Asia and North America from the Upper Silurian to the Upper Devonian. The specimen of the species *Hexacrinites anaglypticus* shown here has a calyx measuring 3.7 cm (1½ in).

Subclass: Inathinata

LOWER ORDOVICIAN – UPPER PERMIAN

Like the camerate sea lilies, these sea lilies also have plates arranged in a calyx consisting of two or three rings. The plates of the calyx have fused together. The tentacles are usually free. These sea lilies reached their peak during the Carboniferous and became extinct during the Permian.

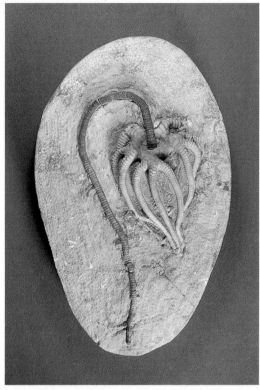

Agariocrinus bullatus
Lower Carboniferous, Crawfordsville, Indiana, USA

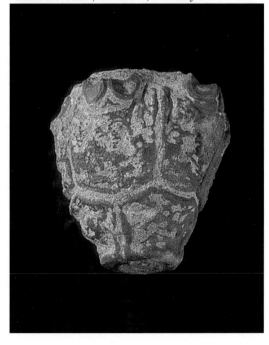

Hexacrinites anaglypticus
Middle Devonian, Gerolstein, Germany

Cupressocrinites hieroglyphus
Middle Devonian, Gerolstein, Germany

Cupressocrinites ■

MIDDLE DEVONIAN

The genus *Cupressocrinites* is characterized by a broad and low dish-shaped calyx. Five broad, simple, unbranched tentacles grow from the broad radial plates. There are short side branches on the sides of the tentacles, similar to pinnules. The stem is square in cross section. Representatives of the genus *Cupressocrinites* lived in the seas of the Middle Devonian in areas of Europe. The crown of

Codiacrinus schulzei
Middle Devonian, Bundenbach, Germany

the specimen shown here, which belongs to the species *Cupressocrinites hieroglyphus*, measures 7 cm (2³/₄ in).

Codiacrinus ■

LOWER DEVONIAN – MIDDLE DEVONIAN

The calyx of the sea lily of the genus *Codiacrinus* is large and dish-shaped, with slender branching tentacles, consisting of a row of plates. The stem is rounded in cross section. Representatives of the genus *Codiacrinus* lived in areas of Europe from the Lower to the Middle Devonian. The specimen shown belongs to the species *Codiacrinus schulzei* and measures approximately 20 cm (7³/₄ in).

Caleidocrinus ■

ORDOVICIAN

The fine calyx consisting of basal and radial plates connected to many branching tentacles, is characteristic of the genus *Caleidocrinus*. The stem is long, and consists of low segments which are round in cross section. Representatives of the genus *Caleidocrinus* have been found in Ordovician sediments in Europe and North America. The specimen of the species *Caleidocrinus multiramus* in the illustration has a crown 1.5 cm (¹/₂ in) tall.

Crotalocrinites ■

SILURIAN

The calyx of the genus *Crotalocrinites* is semi-spherical or round and consists of plates arranged in three rings. There is an anal plate joined to one of the basal plates. The roof of the calyx consists of five unequal fused oral plates, while the anal cone is low. The tentacles are bifurcated, and those lying next to each other have fused together on the side. The genus *Crotalocrinites* has been recorded in Silurian strata and became widespread all over the world during its period of development. The specimen shown here belongs to the species *Crotalocrinites rugosus* and has a calyx 3.5 cm (1¹/₄ in) high.

Gissocrinus ■

UPPER SILURIAN – LOWER DEVONIAN

The genus *Gissocrinus* is characterized by a small, conical or dish-shaped calyx and strong tentacles consisting of powerful segments, bifurcating several times. Representatives of the genus *Gissocrinus* have been recorded in Upper Silurian to Lower Devonian strata in areas of Europe and North America. The specimen shown here belongs to the species *Gissocrinus involutus* and has a crown 4 cm (1¹/₂ in) tall, with tentacles coiled inwards.

Caleidocrinus multiramus
Upper Ordovician, Zahořany, Czech Republic

Gissocrinus involutus
Upper Silurian, Mořina, Czech Republic

Subclass: Flexibilia

MIDDLE ORDOVICIAN – UPPER PERMIAN

The calyx with plates arranged in three rings is characteristic of this subclass of sea lilies. It consists of three infrabasal, and five basal and radial plates. In addition, the calyx consists of an anal and an interbrachial plate, attached to the lower part of the tentacles. The plates of the calyx are fused by a springy material so that they can move. The tentacles consist of a row of plates, and do not have any pinnules. The stem is composed of rounded segments with no cirri.

Pycnosaccus ■

SILURIAN – DEVONIAN

The crown of the genus *Pycnosaccus* is spherical. It has a massive calyx consisting of three rows of plates and clearly separated from the base of the tentacles. The radial plates are smooth. Sometimes there may be distinct ribs running from the middle of the plates perpendicular to the edges. The tentacles are broad and short, and their distal ends coil inwards, so that they cover the roof of the calyx. The genus *Pycnosaccus* has been recorded in Silurian and Devonian strata in Europe and North America. The specimen of the species *Pycnosaccus scrobiculatus* shown here has a crown 4 cm (1¹/₂ in) tall.

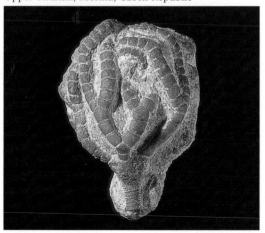

Crotalocrinites rugosus
Upper Silurian, Mořina, Czech Republic

Pycnosaccus scrobiculatus
Upper Silurian, Mořina, Czech Republic

Taxocrinus colleti
Lower Carboniferous, Crawfordsville, United States

Encrinus liliiformis
Middle Triassic, Kirchberg an der Jagst, Germany

Taxocrinus ∎

MIDDLE DEVONIAN – PERMIAN

The genus *Taxocrinus* has a large conical calyx, consisting of a large number of plates. In addition, it consists of infrabasal, basal and radial plates, as well as brachial, interbrachial, and anal plates respectively. The tentacles are visibly bifurcated. Representatives of the genus *Taxocrinus* have been recorded in Middle Devonian to Permian strata in areas of Europe and North America. The specimen shown here belongs to the species *Taxocrinus colletti* and has a crown 5 cm (2 in) tall.

Subclass: Articulata

TRIASSIC – RECENT TIMES

This is the only diverse group of sea lilies which has survived up to the present day. They are characterized by a very complicated structure of the calyx, which consists of two or three rings of plates. The growth of the basal plates may be retarded, or they can fuse together, so that it is sometimes possible to distinguish only two rings. The tentacles consist of a row of plates, and in rare cases there are two rows, often strongly branching. Pinnules often develop in the Articulata. The juvenile specimens always have stems, but mature specimens usually lose these.

Encrinus ∎

TRIASSIC

The calyx of the genus *Encrinus* is low and pan-shaped. It is very strong and consists of small brachial plates. The tentacles are robust, consisting of a row of plates at the base and two rows at the top. The tentacles are connected to the calyx and curve inwards in the middle. The stem has rounded segments, usually alternating with smaller segments. The genus *Encrinus* was an important genus in Europe during the Triassic. The name was first used by G. Agricola in the 16th century. The illustrations

show a complete crown and a cross section. The specimens shown here are 5 cm (2in) across.

Eugeniacrinites ∎

UPPER JURASSIC– LOWER CRETACEOUS

The genus is characterized by strongly developed, protruding brachial plates, which form a space for the protection of the tentacles when they close. The stem is short and consists of a few cylindrical segments, narrowing towards the calyx. The tentacles consist of a row of plates, and are forked with short pinnules. Representatives of the genus *Eugeniacrinites* have been recorded in Upper Jurassic to Lower Cretaceous strata in areas of Europe. The calyxes and part of the stem in the illustration belong to sea lilies of the species *Eugeniacrinites caryophyllites*, with a stem 2 cm ($^3/_4$ in) long.

Eugeniacrinites caryophyllites
Upper Jurassic, Sengenthal, Germany

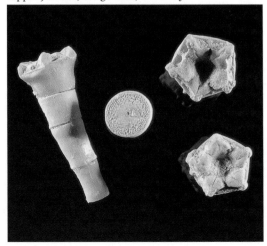

Pterocoma pennata
Upper Jurassic, Eichstätt, Germany

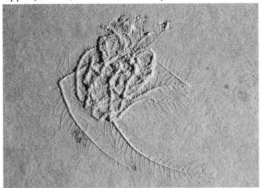

Pterocoma █

UPPER JURASSIC– LOWER CRETACEOUS

The calyx of the genus *Pterocoma* is small with cirri growing at the base. Tentacles which branch once grow in a circle round the calyx, so that there are ten in all. Because of the long pinnules, they are reminiscent of a bird's feathers. Representatives of the genus *Pterocoma* probably floated freely in the sea water. They lived in areas of Europe from the Upper Jurassic to the Upper Cretaceous. The specimen

Millericrinus munsterianus
Upper Jurassic, Liesberg, Switzerland

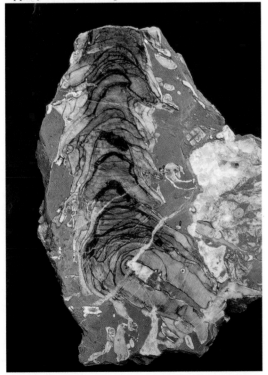

shown here belongs to the species *Pterocoma pennata* and measures 9 cm (3¹/₂ in).

Millericrinus █

MIDDLE JURASSIC – UPPER JURASSIC

The genus *Millericrinus* is characterized by a large calyx, consisting of five thick basal and five radial plates. The calyx is broad and low, with five points. Species with a reduced stem were directly attached to the substratum. Representatives of the genus *Millericrinus* have been recorded in Middle Jurassic to Upper Jurassic strata in areas of Europe. The illustration shows the cross section of a stem 16 cm (6¹/₄ in) across of a sea lily belonging to the species *Millericrinus munsterianus*.

Seirocrinus █

LOWER JURASSIC

The calyx of the species *Seirocrinus* is small, and the tentacles with pinnula are long and irregularly branched several times. The crown of some specimens could grow to a width of 80 cm (31¹/₂ in). The stem is very long and could grow to a length of 18 m (59 ft). Young specimens of the genus *Seirocrinus* attached themselves to floating pieces of wood (they were planktonic). Mature specimens usually attached themselves to the sea bed. The genus *Seirocrinus* has been recorded in Lower Jurassic strata in Europe. The crown of the specimen shown here belongs to the species *Seirocrinus subangularis* and is 12 cm (4³/₄ in) tall.

Seirocrinus subangularis
Lower Jurassic, Holzmaden, Germany

Saccocoma pectinata
Upper Jurassic, Solnhofen, Germany

Saccocoma ■

UPPER JURASSIC – LOWER CRETACEOUS

The genus *Saccocoma* is characterized by a small, spherical calyx with ten tentacles ending in small branches. In fossilized specimens it is possible to see the coiled spiraling tentacles. In the basal part of the tentacles there are broader, leaf-shaped elements on the sides, which probably served to help the organism to float freely in the water. There is no stalk. The genus *Saccocoma* lived from the Upper Jurassic to the Lower Cretaceous and large numbers have been found in the limestone rocks dating from the Upper Jurassic in Solnhofen. Representatives of this genus have been recorded from North America to Cuba, as well as in Europe.

Uintacrinus ■

UPPER CRETACEOUS

The calyx of the genus *Uintacrinus* is spherical. It consists of a large number of small plates, mainly brachial and interbrachial plates. The basal and radial plates are small. Ten thin tentacles consisting of one row of plates, and up to 1 meter long, grow from the calyx. Short pinnules grow on the sides of the tentacles. There is no stalk.

The genus *Uintacrinus* has been recorded in Upper

Cretaceous sediments in Europe and North America.

Marsupites ■

UPPER CRETACEOUS

The genus *Marsupites* is spherical and consists of five large infrabasal plates, five large basal and five large radial plates. The tentacles grow from the calyx and branch profusely. There is no stalk. The genus *Marsupites* was a free-swimming crinoid which

Uintacrinus socialis
Upper Cretaceous, Kansas, United States

222

inhabited the seas of the Upper Cretaceous. Representatives have been found in many areas all over the world. The species *Marsupites testudinarius* in the illustration has a calyx measuring 3.3 cm (1¼ in).

Subclass: Echinozoa

LOWER CAMBRIAN – RECENT TIMES

This subphylum usually comprises free-swimming echinoderms with a disc-shaped, spherical or cylindrical body. The tentacles have not developed any extremities. The body is often radially symmetrical, growing in a diamond shape. The original pentamerous symmetry of the ambulacra changed in some species into a bilateral symmetry. The subclass of Echinozoa now includes six classes, but only the class of Echinoidea is stratigraphically important.

Class: Edrioasteroidea

LOWER CAMBRIAN – LOWER CARBONIFEROUS

The Edrioasteroidea include the very oldest echinoderms. Some paleontologists place the start of the development of the Edrioasteroidea as far back as the Upper Proterozoic. At first sight, the Edrioasteroidea are reminiscent of starfish, but they do not have pentamerous symmetry. There is usually no stem, and when it has developed, it is strong and short and usually covered with plates. The theca may be spherical, disc-shaped or sac-shaped. It consists of numerous polygonal or round plates, which often overlap. The oral opening is in the middle of the upper part and five straight or spiraling curved *ambulacral grooves* lead away from it. The *interambulacra* are between these grooves. There is sometimes a *hydropore* between the oral opening and the ex-centrically placed anal opening, so that water can enter the ambulacral system. Ambulacral or tube *feet* passed through small pores in the plates of the ambulacral grooves and were used to take food to the mouth.

Stromatocystites ■

LOWER CAMBRIAN – MIDDLE CAMBRIAN

The theca of the genus *Stromatocystites* is flat and pentagonal. It consists of polygonal plates, and there are five ambulacral grooves leading from the oral opening to the edge of the theca. The anal pyramid is not very striking. Representatives of the genus *Stromatocystites* have been recorded in Lower and Middle Cambrian strata in Europe and North America. The specimen shown here belongs to the species *Stromatocystites pentagularis* and measures 1.8 cm (¾ in).

Marsupites testudinarius
Upper Cretaceous, Lüneburg, Germany

Stromatocystites pentagularis
Middle Cambrian, Týřovice, Czech Republic

Class: Echinoidea
– sea urchins

ORDOVICIAN – RECENT TIMES

Sea urchins represent the second biggest class of echinoderms, with more than 760 recorded species. These include moving echinoderms with a disc-shaped, semi-spherical, conical or heart-shaped calcareous skeleton surrounding the inner organs. The size of sea urchins varies from 1 to 15 cm (6 in). The skeleton is covered by a thin, soft skin. The mouth, which may have a chewing mechanism, is at the bottom (*oral side*) in the middle of the oral area – the *peristome*. The chewing mechanism is known as *Aristotles' lantern* and is attached to the margin of the peristome with the help of muscles on the calcareous framework. The anal opening is either opposite the oval opening at the top of the upper (*aboral*) end in the so-called anal area (the *periproct*) or on the side. The ambulacral system starts with the madreporite, as in the case of the other echinoderms. Numerous tube feet reach the surface through the ambulacral plates. These are both organs for locomotion and sensory organs. The skeleton of sea urchins consists of a composite shell made up of calcite plates, subdivided into four basic areas: the area of the peristome, the periproct, the area of the ambulacra and interambulacra, which together form the so-called *crown*, and the aboral area. The plates of the interambulacra are larger than those of the ambulacra and there are semicircular bosses on the surface *(protuberances, tubercles)* from which the spines grew during the sea urchin's lifetime. On the aboral side, each interambulacrum had a so-called *genital* plate with an opening for the genital glands. One of these plates is porous and serves as a *madreporite*. Every ambulacrum consists of a so-called *ocular* plate with an opening, through which a light-sensitive feeler protruded when the sea urchin was alive. The ocular and genital plates together form a ring of plates – the *oculogenital system.*

The crown plates of more primitively developed sea urchins were free and overlapped like scales. Higher groups have plates which have fused together. Sea urchins are divided into two main groups on the basis of the position of the mouth and anal openings: regular and irregular echinoids. Regular echinoids have a mouth in the middle of the oral side and the anal opening in the middle of the aboral side. In irregular echinoids, the anal opening is moved further back, and their original radial symmetry has changed to a bilateral symmetry.

In regular echinoids, the ambulacra are uninterrupted from the anal opening to the mouth. In irregular echinoids, the ambulacra arranged in pairs are reduced to the aboral (dorsal) side of the crown. The pores on the edges of the ambulacra may be arranged in one row (*uniserial* pores), two rows (*biserial* pores) or in several rows (*polyserial* pores). The ambulacral plates sometimes have spines or bosses. The spines of sea urchins are articulated to the bosses or tubercles on the interambulacra. At the top of the primary bosses there is a hollow, which contained the tissue for holding the spine. Sometimes the spines are microscopically small; sometimes they reach a length of several feet. They also differ in shape; they can be cylindrical, spiky or club-like. Some of the spines have changed into special stalks

The morphology of a sea urchin: A – aboral view, B – oral view, 1 – primary spine, 2 – periproct, 3 – boss, 4 – areole, 5 – ocular plate, 6 – interambulacrum, 7 – ambulacrum, 8 – genital plate, 9 – anal opening, 10 – mouth, 11 – peristome, 12 – secondary spines

A

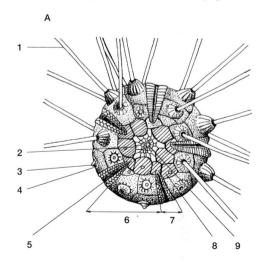

B

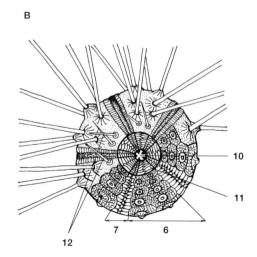

Plegiocidaris coronata
Upper Jurassic, Friesener Warte, Germany

known as *pedicles*, which may have a poisonous gland. Some irregular echinoids have relatively smooth lines on the crown known as *fascioles,* which were covered with fine cilia during the sea urchin's lifetime. These were used to stir the water to clean the sea urchin's body.

Paleozoic sea urchins lived in relatively quiet waters, as revealed by their thin skeleton. They become more numerous from the Devonian to the Carboniferous, but almost became extinct during the Permian (only six species of sea urchin are known to date from the Permian). They have been relatively common from the Jurassic to the present day. Sea urchins can be divided into two subclasses: Perischoechinoidea and Euechinoidea.

Subclass: Perischoechinoidea

ORDOVICIAN – RECENT TIMES

This subclass includes all the Paleozoic sea urchins, but only a small proportion of more recent sea urchins. The ambulacrum consists of two to twenty rows of plates, the interambulacrum of one to fourteen rows. The oculogenital system consists of one or two rings of plates, and the anal opening is placed in the middle of this system. The most important order of the four orders of these sea urchins is the order of Cidaroida.

Order: Cidaroida

LOWER DEVONIAN – RECENT TIMES

The sea urchins of this order have spherical skeletons, with more or less flat upper and lower ends. They usually consist of fused plates, while the plates of the Paleozoic representatives were free. The in-

terambulacra comprised two, or occasionally four to eight rows of large plates. The openings for the attachment of the spines are striking: there are large bosses around these openings, with many more, smaller bosses around them. The narrow ambulacra consist of two to four rows of plates. The spines of these sea urchins were extremely strong, and were often thicker at the distal end.

Plegiocidaris ■

UPPER TRIASSIC – UPPER JURASSIC

The genus *Plegiocidaris* is characterized by a dorsoventrally compressed shell with simple, narrow ambulacra consisting of two rows of plates with pores. The interambulacral plates are large with perforated tubercles, surrounded by a margin. The large primary club-shaped spines have developed sizable thin knobby ribs. Representatives of the genus *Plegiocidaris* have been recorded in Upper Triassic to Upper Jurassic strata in Europe. The illustrations show a complete shell of the sea urchin of the species *Plegiocidaris coronata* which measures 5 cm (2 in), as well as the spines of a sea urchin of the species *Plegiocidaris propinqua* which measures approximately 2 cm ($^3/_4$ in).

Plegiocidaris propinqua
Upper Jurassic, Nollhof, Germany

'Cidaris' forchhammeri
Paleocene, Vigny-en-Vexin, France

Rhabdocidaris mayri
Upper Jurassic, Solnhofen, Germany

'Cidaris' ■

TRIASSIC – RECENT TIMES

The strong shell of the genus *'Cidaris'* is usually spherical and can be significantly dorsoventrally compressed. The ambulacra are narrow, slightly wavy and biserial, and have perforated plates. The broad interambulacra consist of several larger plates, grouped together in two alternating columns. There is a large boss on the surface of every plate. The peristome is large and rounded. The body of the massive spines is sculpted. Representatives of the genus *'Cidaris'*, which have survived up to the present day, have been recorded in Triassic strata. Nowadays, this genus is considered only as a source of information, which probably comprised a number of different genera. Fossilized representatives have been found in areas of Europe, Asia and America. The specimen of the species *'Cidaris' forchhammeri* shown here has a shell which is 8 cm (3¼ in) across.

Rhabdocidaris ■

UPPER JURASSIC – EOCENE

The genus *Rhabdocidaris* has a shell with more or less wavy ambulacra. The primary bosses have openings and notches on the edges. The primary spines are often thorny, extremely long, and sometimes very broad at the distal end. Representatives of the genus *Rhabdocidaris* have been recorded in Upper Jurassic to Eocene strata in areas of Europe.

Tylocidaris ■

UPPER CRETACEOUS

The shells of the genus *Tylocidaris* are spherical, with strongly developed primary bosses. There are no openings in the bosses, or serrated edges around them. The primary spines are club-shaped, and on the surface there are numerous fine knobby ribs. Representatives of the genus *Tylocidaris* have been recorded in Upper Cretaceous strata in Europe and North America. The specimen illustrated here belongs to the species *Tylocidaris clavigera* and has a shell which is 2.6 cm (1 in) across. It has several spines.

Subclass: Euechinoidea

UPPER TRIASSIC – RECENT TIMES

This subclass comprises both regular and irregular echinoids. The ambulacra and interambulacra consist of two rows of plates. A chewing mechanism has developed in some sea urchins. The subclass of Euechinoidea, which comprises a large number of orders, is usually subdivided into three superorders: Diadematacea, Gnathostomata and Atelostomata.

Tylocidaris clavigera
Upper Cretaceous, Charlton, Great Britain

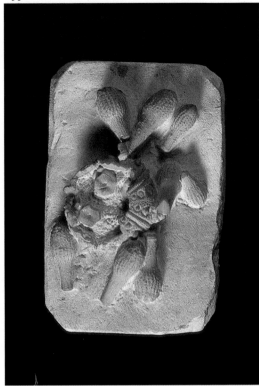

Hemicidaris crenularis
Upper Jurassic, Novion Porcien, France

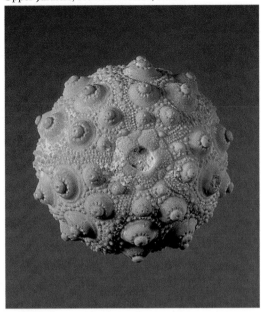

Salenia ■

UPPER JURASSIC – RECENT TIMES

The spherical shell with narrow, straight or curved ambulacra is characteristic of the genus *Salenia.* The ambulacral plates are biserial, like the pattern of their pores. The primary bosses are semicircular and often serrated on the edges. The primary spines are round, but can broaden out in a shovel shape towards the distal end. The oculogenital plates are the same size. The anal opening is in the middle of the periproct. The genus *Salenia* has been recorded in the Upper Jurassic; fossilized representatives have been found in Europe, Asia, Africa and North America. The largest of the specimens shown here, which belong to the species *Salenia petalifera*, has a shell which measures 2 cm ($^3/_4$ in).

Superorder: Diadematacea

UPPER TRIASSIC – RECENT TIMES

These regular echinoids are similar to the representatives of the order of Cidaroida. The shells are more or less radially symmetrical. The chewing mechanism is well developed. The long thin spines are hollow along the axis, and consist of a few radiating calcite lamellae. The spine is set directly on the head of the radiating tubercle.

Hemicidaris ■

MIDDLE JURASSIC – UPPER CRETACEOUS

The shell of the genus *Hemicidaris* is spherical, but flattened at the bottom. Each interambulacral plate has large, high bosses which are perforated and serrated. The ambulacra consist of large plates. The lower plates have high, perforated bosses. In the upper part, the ambulacra are narrower and the large bosses are missing. The genus *Hemicidaris* lived from the Middle Jurassic to the Upper Cretaceous and spread all over the world. The specimen of the species *Hemicidaris crenularis* shown here has a shell which is 3 cm ($1^1/_4$ in) across.

Salenia petalifera
Lower Cretaceous, province of Castellón, Spain

227

Tetragramma sp.
Upper Jurassic, Painten, Germany

Acrocidiaris nobilis
Upper Jurassic, La Rochelle, France

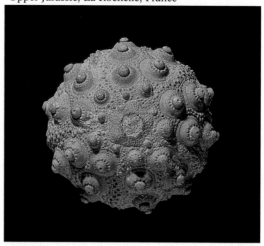

Tetragramma ■

UPPER JURASSIC – UPPER CRETACEOUS

The shell of the genus *Tetragramma* is dorsoventrally compressed, and the ambulacra are narrower than the interambulacra. The four large bosses on each interambulacrum are characteristic. Representatives of the genus *Tetragramma* lived from the Upper Jurassic to the Upper Cretaceous and have been found in Europe, Asia and North America. The illustration shows a specimen of the genus *Tetragramma* which measures 9.5 cm (3³/₄ in). In addition to the numerous spines, the chewing mechanism is also clearly visible.

Schizechinus serialis
Lower Pliocene, province of Almeria, Spain

Schizechinus ■

MIOCENE – PLIOCENE

The genus *Schizechinus* is characterized by slightly higher, semi-spherical shells with no ornamentation. There are only some large, smooth secondary bosses which have developed up to the upper plates. Representatives of the genus *Schizechinus* lived in the warm seas of Mediterranean areas from the Miocene to the Pliocene. The best specimens have been found in Spain. The specimen of the species *Schizechinus serialis* shown here measures 3.3 cm (1¹/₄ in).

Acrocidaris ■

MIDDLE JURASSIC – UPPER CRETACEOUS

Sea urchins of the genus *Acrocidaris* have a low wavy shell, flattened at the bottom and with relatively broad ambulacra. One of the characteristics is the striking boss on every genital plate. The spines can have all sorts of different shapes; the large serrated bosses have long, thick spines, while the spines of the upper bosses are short. Representatives of the genus *Acrocidaris* have been found in Europe and North America. The specimen of the species *Acrocidaris nobilis* in the illustration has a shell measuring 3.5 cm (1¹/₄ in).

Stomechinus ■

LOWER JURASSIC – LOWER CRETACEOUS

The genus *Stomechinus* has a semi-spherical shell with a flattened base. The ambulacra consist of three primary plates, which are perforated with two or three rows of pores. On the surface of the plates there are bosses which are not serrated and have no perforations. They are the same size as the bosses on the interambulacra. The genus *Stomechinus* lived from the Lower Jurassic to the Lower Cretaceous in areas of Europe, Africa and Asia (Turkey). The largest of the specimens shown here, which belong to the species *Stomechinus bigranularis*, has a shell measuring 3.5 cm (1¼ in).

Glypticus ■

MIDDLE JURASSIC – UPPER JURASSIC

The shell of the genus *Glypticus* is regular, flattened at the bottom and strikingly convex at the top. The ambulacra consist of large plates, of which three are primary plates. In the area of the peristome, the number of these plates was greater (four to five). The bosses, which are not serrated or perforated, are not easy to distinguish on the plates. The surface on the outside consists of a pattern of bosses consisting of skeletal material. Representatives of the genus *Glypticus* have been recorded in Middle to Upper Jurassic strata in Europe, North Africa and Asia Minor. The largest of the specimens of the species *Glypticus sulcatus* shown here has a shell measuring 1.2 cm (½ in).

Stomechinus bigranularis
Middle Jurassic, Dorset, Great Britain

Glypticus sulcatus
Upper Jurassic, Engelhardtsberg, Germany

Conoclypeus vilanovae
Lower Eocene, province of Alicante, Spain

Conoclypeus vilanovae
Lower Eocene, province of Alicante, Spain

Superorder: Gnathostomata

LOWER JURASSIC – RECENT TIMES

These irregular echinoids have fixed plates. The anal opening is not in the area of the oculogenital system. Keel-shaped teeth have developed for the chewing mechanism. The spines are hollow.

Conoclypeus

LOWER EOCENE – MIOCENE

The genus *Conoclypeus* has a large, elongated oval shell, with a flat oral side. The pores of the ambulacra are arranged in such a way that the rows radiated away from the periproct. They come together on the dorsal side, but do not join together, so that the ambulacrum remains open. The outer pores are larger than the inner pores, and the adjacent pores are connected by a groove. The peristome is in the middle of the oral side, while the periproct is close to the ventral edge. It has developed a chewing mechanism. Representatives of the genus *Conoclypeus* lived from the Lower Eocene to the Miocene in Europe, Asia and Africa. The largest of the two specimens shown here, which belong to the species *Conoclypeus vilanovae,* measures 6 cm (2¼ in). The specimen which belongs to the species *Conoclypeus conoideus* has a shell which measures 13.5 cm (5¼ in).

Echinocyamus

UPPER JURASSIC – RECENT TIMES

This is one of the smallest sea urchins that exists today, with a shell which is oval in shape and usually long. The oral side is often flat and sometimes slightly concave. The ocular and genital plates have fused together. The periproct is small and located on the bottom, fairly far from the ventral edge. On the ambulacra, the double rows of pores form an indistinct rosette. The ambulacrum on the dorsal side is closed. The genus *Echinocyamus,* which has survived up to the present day, first appeared in the Upper Jurassic, and then spread all over the world. The largest of the specimens shown here, which belong to the species *Echinocyamus luciani,* measures 1.2 cm (½ in).

Sismondia

EOCENE – MIOCENE

The elliptical or rounded pentagonal shell, in which the ventral side is concave, is characteristic of the genus *Sismondia.* The rosette, consisting of pores on the ambulacra, remains open. Representatives of the genus *Sismondia* lived from the Eocene to the

Conoclypeus conoideus
Middle Eocene, St. Pankraz, Austria

Echinocyamus luciani
Upper Eocene, Syrt Basin, Libya

Sismondia saemanni
Middle Eocene, Syrt Basin, Libya

Clypeaster sp.
Miocene, Slatinky, Czech Republic

Miocene and were spread all over the world. The largest of the specimens shown here, which belong to the species *Sismondia saemanni,* measures 1.2 cm ($^1/_2$ in).

Galerites ■

UPPER CRETACEOUS

The shell of the genus is semi-spherical. The narrow ambulacra are arranged in a regular pattern and consist of simple plates. The pores on the plates are arranged in one row. They are only spread in an irregular fashion around the simple peristome, which has no chewing mechanism. The periproct is on the side near the ventral edge of the shell. Representatives of the genus *Galerites* have been recorded in Upper Cretaceous strata in Europe, Asia and North Africa. The larger of the two specimens shown here of the genus *Galerites* measures 3.5 cm ($^1/_4$ in).

Clypeaster ■

EOCENE – RECENT TIMES

The largest known sea urchins belong to the genus *Clypeaster.* The genus is characterized by a low, disc-shaped, rounded, pentagonal skeleton of different sizes. The aboral side of the skeleton is usually highly convex with either a rounded or a sharp edge. The oral side is flat or concave. The rows of pores on the ambulacra touch each other at the top. The periproct is at the bottom of the skeleton and is occasionally moved to the side. The peristome is in a central position and has a funnel-shaped oral opening of different depths. The chewing mechanism is strongly developed. The primary bosses have pores with an edge on the circumference. The spines are

simple and short. The genus *Clypeaster* lived from the Eocene and fossil representatives, of which several hundred have been recorded, have been found in Europe, Asia and North and South America. Nowadays this genus inhabits tropical seas.

Galerites sp.
Upper Cretaceous, Rügen, Germany

Scutella faujasi
Middle Miocene, Doué-la-Fontaine, France

Echinocorys humilis
Upper Cretaceous, Coesfeld, Germany

in a small extremity. The genus *Echinocorys* comprises many species, and lived from the Upper Cretaceous to the Lower Paleocene. Representatives have been found in Europe, Asia, Africa and North America. The specimen of the species *Echinocorys humilis* has a shell which measures 5.5 cm (2¹/₄ in).

Scutella ∎

PALEOGENE – RECENT TIMES

The shell of the genus *Scutella* is flat and disc-shaped, with a round circumference, a moderately convex aboral side and a flat oral side. The pores are arranged in a rosette which closes on the dorsal side. In the middle of the aboral side, there is an apical system with four genital pores. The periproct is on the orale side; the peristome is central. The genus *Scutella* dates back to the Paleocene and fossilized representatives have been found in Europe and North America. The specimen of the species *Scutella faujasi,* shown on the extreme right in the illustration, has a shell that measures 6 cm (2¹/₄ in) across.

Superorder: Atelostomata

LOWER JURASSIC – RECENT TIMES

These are irregular sea urchins, in which the crown consists of fixed plates. There is no chewing mechanism. The ambulacral plates are always narrower than the interambulacral plates.

Echinocorys ∎

UPPER CRETACEOUS – LOWER PALEOCENE

The shell of the genus *Echinocorys* is often strikingly convex, with an almost conical shape. The ambulacra are identical and the pores almost touch at the surface. The periproct is on the flat bottom of the shell near the posterior edge, which often ends

Hemipneustes ∎

UPPER CRETACEOUS

The genus *Hemipneustes*, which is amongst the largest Cretaceous sea urchins, has an extremely convex shell that can be distinguished from the genus *Echinocorys* because it has developed a deep groove on the anterior ambulacrum. The pores vir-

Hemipneustes striatoradiatus
Upper Cretaceous, Valkenburg, the Netherlands

Nucleolites scutatus
Upper Jurassic, Trouville, France

Echinolampas canteranensis
Lower/Upper Eocene, Lesparre-Médoc, France

tually touch each other on the surface. The peristome is curved forwards. The genus *Hemipneustes* lived in the Upper Cretaceous period in Europe, Asia and Africa. The specimen of the species *Hemipneustes striatoradiatus* shown in the illustration has a shell which is 8.5 cm (3¹/₄ in) across.

Nucleolites ■

MIDDLE JURASSIC – UPPER CRETACEOUS

The shell of the genus *Nucleolites* has a rounded, trapezium-shaped circumference and relatively high edges. The ambulacra on the dorsal side are relatively broad, and the pores do not touch. The peristome is slightly moved to the front, while the periproct is in a deep groove on the dorsal side of the shell. The genus *Nucleolites* lived from the Middle Jurassic to the Upper Cretaceous, and representatives have been found in Europe and Africa. The largest of the specimens shown here, which belongs to the species *Nucleolites scutatus*, is 4 cm (1¹/₂ in) across.

Echinolampas ■

EOCENE – RECENT TIMES

The genus *Echinolampas* is characterized by a disc-shaped shell with a broad, oval circumference. The pores of the ambulacra virtually touch on the dorsal side. The pentagonal or round peristome is very close to the middle of the oral side. There is no chewing mechanism in mature specimens. The spines are thin, with a simple construction. Representatives of the genus *Echinolampas*, which has survived up to the present day and comprises many species (approximately 300) first appeared in the Eocene, but the majority became extinct at the end of the Miocene. Fossilized representatives have been found in many areas all over the world. The shell of the specimens shown here, which belong to the species *Echinolampas canteranensis*, measures 4.2 cm (1¹/₂ in).

Toxaster ■

LOWER CRETACEOUS – UPPER CRETACEOUS

The shell of the genus *Toxaster* is heart-shaped. The anterior ambulacrum is in the deep groove which runs from the top to the anterior edge, where it partly extends as far as the oral side. The ambulacra are narrow, and the rows of pores almost touch on the aboral side of the shell. No fasciola have developed. The countless small tubercles are perforated and serrated on the circumference. Representatives of the genus *Toxaster* in Europe and North and South America from the Lower to the Upper Cretaceous. The largest of the specimens of the species *Toxaster amplus* shown here measures 3 cm (1¹/₄ in).

Toxaster amplus
Lower Cretaceous, Trigance, France

233

Spatangus purpureus
Lower Pliocene, province of Almería, Spain

Schizaster meslei
Upper Cretaceous, Libya

Spatangus ■

EOCENE – RECENT TIMES

The genus *Spatangus* has a large heart-shaped shell, with a moderately convex aboral side. The oral side is flat. The anterior ambulacrum is in a broad frontal groove, and the rows of pores of the ambulacra touch on the dorsal side. The peristome is in a depression towards the anterior edge. Representatives of the genus *Spatangus*, which still exists today, first appeared during the Eocene and fossilized specimens have been found in Europe and North America. The specimen of the species *Spatangus purpureus* shown here has a shell which measures 8 cm ($3^1/_4$ in).

Schizaster ■

UPPER CRETACEOUS – RECENT TIMES

Sea urchins of the genus *Schizaster* vary from heart-shaped to broad, oval specimens with a broad groove containing the anterior ambulacrum. The series of pores of the individual ambulacra touch dorsally. The two posterior ambulacra are shorter than the anterior ambulacrum. The peristome is in a depression towards the anterior edge. Representatives of the genus *Schizaster*, which still exists today, first appeared during the Upper Cretaceous and spread all over the world during the course of their development.

Micraster ■

UPPER CRETACEOUS – RECENT TIMES

The genus *Micraster* is characterized by relatively large, heart-shaped shells. The aboral side is convex, the oral side is flat. The anterior ambulacrum is in a deep groove, while the other four ambulacra are in shallow grooves. The rows of pores do not touch dorsally. The peristome lies towards the anterior edge of the shell. Representatives of the genus *Micraster*, which still exists today, first appeared in the Upper Cretaceous, and fossilized specimens have been found in Europe, North Africa, Madagascar and Cuba. The larger of the two specimens of the species *Micraster coranguinum* shown here measures 6 cm ($2^1/_4$ in).

Clypeus ■

MIDDLE JURASSIC – UPPER JURASSIC

The shell of the genus *Clypeus* is large, disc-shaped, only moderately convex, and has a flat oral side. The ambulacra are clearly visible and extend to the periphery of the shell, and the rows of openings touch dorsally. The periproct is placed ex-centrically in a deep groove, which extends to the posterior edge of the shell. The peristome is pentagonal. There are small perforated bosses on the surface. Representatives of the genus *Clypeus* lived from the Middle to the Upper Jurassic and spread all over the world. The specimen of the species *Clypeus ploti* shown in this illustration measures 10 cm (4 in).

Subphylum: Asterozoa

LOWER ORDOVICIAN – RECENT TIMES

These are free-living echinoderms with a radially symmetrical body, usually star-shaped and dorso-ventrally compressed. The central section consists of a disc, with four or five tentacles. The mouth is on the ventral side and faces downwards. Complete specimens are rarely found. More frequently, individual discs or parts of tentacles are found. The subphylum Asterozoa comprises the classes of Stelleroidea and Ophiuroidea, which are seen as an independent class in some systems of classification.

Micraster coranguinum
Upper Cretaceous, St. Rémy-du-Bois, France

Subclass: Asteroidea – starfish

LOWER ORDOVICIAN – RECENT TIMES

This is a group which has developed very slowly, and therefore recent representatives are very similar to ancestors which are millions of years old. The number of tentacles varies a great deal. Usually there are between five and fifteen, but they can also have more than forty. The curiously-shaped *oral* plates surround the mouth. Like the whole of the body, the tentacles are also covered with calcareous plates which also have a protective function. The outer edge of the tentacles is formed by peripheral or *marginal* plates. The largest specimens can grow to a length of more than one meter. Starfish move over the surface of the sea with the help of numerous small feet, actively looking for prey. They live in both warm and cold seas. They are highly predatory, and live mainly on mollusks and shellfish, or infrequently on small fish.

Clypeus ploti
Middle Jurassic, Bourton on the Water, Great Britain

Pentasteria longispina
Upper Jurassic, Weissenstein, Switzerland

Lophidiaster ornatus
Miocene, Southern Australia

Pentasteria ◼

LOWER JURASSIC – EOCENE

The genus *Pentasteria* is characterized by a low theca and large, extremely long, slender tentacles, which are clearly separated from the rest of the body. The marginal plates are broad. The genus *Pentasteria* existed in areas of Europe from the Lower Jurassic to the Eocene. The specimen of the species *Pentasteria longispina* shown here measures 19 cm (7$^1/_2$ in).

Lophidiaster ◼

LOWER CRETACEOUS – MIOCENE

The theca of this starfish has five tentacles with small, virtually triangular marginal plates. On the oral side, there is a striking ambulacral groove in each tentacle. The spines do not develop from bosses. Representatives of the genus *Lophidiaster* existed from the Upper Cretaceous to the Miocene and were spread all over the world. The specimen of the species *Lophidiaster ornatus* shown here measures 2.5 cm (1 in).

Urasterella ■

The genus *Urasterella* is characterized by long, narrow tentacles, which grow from the very small disc of the body. The tentacles are round in cross section, and there are spines growing on the surface. The main function of these was to clean the surface around the respiratory openings. Representatives of the genus *Urasterella* lived in Europe from the Upper Ordovician to the Permian. The largest specimen shown here measures 7 cm ($2^3/_4$ in).

Calliderma ■

UPPER CRETACEOUS – OLIGOCENE

The pentagonal theca of the genus *Calliderma* is a typical average-sized disc with short tentacles and broad marginal plates. The plates of the theca are covered with small grainy spines. Representatives of the genus *Calliderma* lived in areas of Europe from the Upper Cretaceous to the Oligocene.

Subclass: Ophiuroidea – Brittle stars

LOWER ORDOVICIAN – RECENT TIMES

Brittle stars are freely moving members of the starfish family, with a body which consists of a disc and five tentacles. However, in contrast to starfish, their tentacles are long and thin, simple and branching, and clearly separated from the disc of the body. They can measure up to 60 cm ($23^1/_2$ in), and curve sinuously. The ambulacral system is limited to the disc of the body. There is no anal opening. Brittle stars are the most freely moving echinoderms, and they move only with the help of tentacles. They are found both in coastal waters and at depths of up to

Calliderma schulzei
Upper Cretaceous, Hejšina, Czech Republic

500 m (1,640 ft). They live on plant matter, seaweed and protozoa.

Encrinaster ■

UPPER ORDOVICIAN – LOWER CARBONIFEROUS

The genus *Encrinaster* has a star-shaped theca. The long tentacles are reminiscent of the backbone of vertebrates; the vertebrae of the right and left half of the tentacles alternate. The edge of the disc of the body has a clear margin. The genus *Encrinaster* lived in Europe and North America from the Upper Ordovician to the Lower Carboniferous. The largest of the two specimens of the species *Encrinaster tischbeinianum* grew to a size 8 cm ($3^1/_4$ in).

Urasterella asperula
Lower Devonian, Bundenbach, Germany

Encrinaster tischbeinianum
Lower Devonian, Bundenbach, Germany

Geocoma carinata
Upper Jurassic, Zandt, Germany

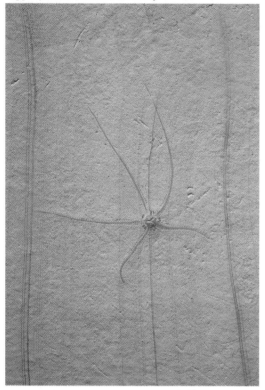

Geocoma ■

JURASSIC – RECENT TIMES

The theca of the genus *Geocoma* shows how the bases of the individual tentacles are attached to the large plates. Together these form a striking ring which extends almost to the middle of the body disc. The individual plates of the tentacles are cylindrical and they are placed in two (non-alternating) rows next to each other in every tentacle. Representatives of the genus *Geocoma* lived in the Jurassic and have survived up to the present day. They are most often found in Upper Jurassic sediments in Europe. The specimen of the species *Geocoma carinata* shown here is 6 cm (2¹/₄ in) across.

Phylum: Hemichordata – hemichordates

MIDDLE CAMBRIAN – RECENT TIMES

The phylum of Hemichordata includes curious creatures with different shapes. Their common characteristics are mainly found during the period of embryonic development. The soft body of hemichordates consists of three parts – the *prosoma*, the *mezosoma* and the *metasoma*. The most important characteristic of the hemichordates is an extremity in the prosoma usually called the Hemichorda, which is similar to the nerve cord of chordates. The similarity between hemichordates and chordates is emphasized by the presence of gill which perforate the pharynx. The animal can breathe through the pharynx through the peribranchial cavity. Hemichordates are nowadays normally divided into three classes – the Enteropneusta, the Pterobrachnia, and the Graptolithina. Only the last class is of stratigraphic importance.

Class: Graptolithina – graptolites

MIDDLE CAMBRIAN – UPPER CARBONIFEROUS

Graptolites represent small marine animals which lived in colonies and are now extinct. Their organic skeleton, which served for support and protection, usually formed branches (stipes), and is known as the *rhabdosome*. The wall of the rhabdosome has two layers consisting of semicircular rings, placed parallel along a wavy thread on the ventral and dorsal sides. The dark outer layer consists of lamellae. The whole colony developed from chambers, the so-called *sicula*, which consisted of two parts differing in shape – the oldest *prosicula* and the oldest *metasicula*. In the top of the spiraling siculae, there is a long, strong, hollow fiber, the *nema*. The mouth is at the open end of a metasicula, and it has spiny ends. The individual organisms (*zooids*) lived in small cup-shaped *thecae*, which were usually placed in one or two rows along the branches (stipes). In some graptolites all the thecae were of the same type, but in others the shape varied. All the individuals in a colony were interconnected by a separate cord or *stolon*, which budded from the embryonic zooid. Graptolites were sessile planktonic orga-

Detail rabdosomu dendroidního graptolita:
1 - téky, 2 - disepimentum

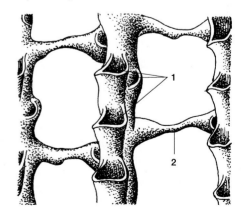

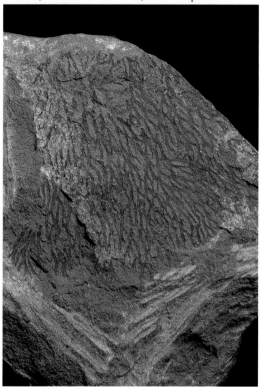

nisms which reproduced sexually and asexually (the branches developed by budding). Nowadays, six to eight orders are distinguished on the basis of some of the characteristics regarding the development of colonies, the shape and arrangement of thecae and the presence or absence of a stolon. Only the orders of Dendroidea and Graptoloidea are of stratigraphic importance.

Order: Dendroidea – dendroid graptolites

MIDDLE CAMBRIAN – UPPER CARBONIFEROUS

This primitive group of hemichordates develops branching, conical, net-like or bushy rhabdosomes. The rhabdosomes are usually erect and attached with the top of the siculae. In some, a thick extremity has developed at the base of the rhabdosome in the shape of a so-called *basal disc* to attach the graptolite. In addition, irregular, root-like extremities served to attach it. The individual branches are interconnected by crossbars or *dissepimenta*, or they are intertwined. The stolons of dendroid graptolites have been preserved because of their chitinous tube. The thecae can be distinguished on the basis of three different shapes, containing male and

female specimens, and they are arranged in regular triads along the individual branches. In dendroid graptolites these thecae can only rarely be studied, as they were inside the bush and submerged in the sediment.

Callograptus ∎

ORDOVICIAN – LOWER CARBONIFEROUS

The rhabdosome of the genus *Callograptus* is usually funnel-shaped or fan-shaped, with thick, more or less parallel branches, only connected by dissepimenta once. The genus *Callograptus* lived from the Ordovician to the Lower Carboniferous and was widespread all over the world. The fragment of shale shown here, containing the specimen of the genus *Callograptus*, measures 8 x 6 cm ($3^{1}/_{4}$ x $2^{1}/_{4}$ in).

Dictyonema ∎

UPPER CAMBRIAN – LOWER CARBONIFEROUS

The genus *Dictyonema* has a funnel-shaped or almost cylindrical rhabdosome, usually attached by a thicker base. Occasionally the rhabdosome was suspended by a nema. The rhabdosome consists of virtually parallel, forking branches connected by dissepimenta. The stratigraphically important genus of *Dictyonema* lived from the Upper Cambrian to the Lower Carboniferous and spread all over the world. The fragment of the rhabdosome shown here belongs to a specimen of the species *Dictyonema elongatum* which measures 7.5 cm (3 in).

Dictyonema elongatum
Lower Devonian, Lejškov, Czech Republic

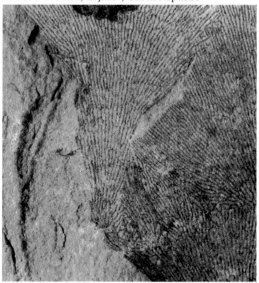

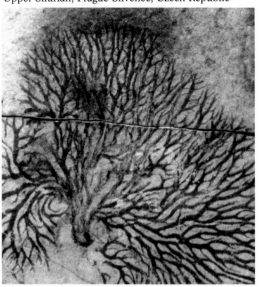

Coremagraptus ■

UPPER ORDOVICIAN – LOWER DEVONIAN

The rhabdosome of the genus *Coremagraptus* is bushy or funnel-shaped, with thick, irregularly intertwined branches. Representatives of the genus *Coremagraptus* lived in Europe from the Upper Ordovician to the Lower Devonian. The specimen of the species *Coremagraptus thallograptoides* shown here has a rhabdosome which measures 5.5 cm ($2^{1}/_{4}$ in).

Monograptus becki, Rastrites linnae, Petalolgraptus palmeus
Lower Silurian, Weinberg, Germany

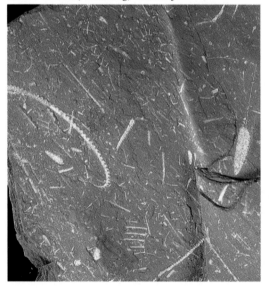

Order: Graptoloidea

LOWER ORDOVICIAN – LOWER DEVONIAN

This order comprises graptolites which are reminiscent of simpler forms of dendroids. Usually they have straight or curved rhabsodomes, sometimes rotated in a spiral. They usually consist of a small number of branches, though these are never connected by dissepimenta. The thecae vary as regards shape, but there is always only one type of theca. They are arranged at an angle to the axis of the individual branches in rows on one side (uniserial), two sides (biserial) or four sides. As a rule, every theca is partly covered by the preceding theca. The stolon did not have a fixed mantle, and therefore these have not been fossilized. The rhabdosomes are rounded or elliptical in cross section and developed from the siculae, which are turned with the mouth pointing downwards, in contrast with the dendroids. The more developed species of graptoloidea developed a so-called *virgula*, which served as the supporting axis of the rhabdosome.

Monograptus ■

LOWER SILURIAN – UPPER SILURIAN

The genus *Monograptus* has straight, or occasionally a curved, and very occasionally a spiraling rhabdosome. The thecae on the bottom touch each other on the sides. They are free at the ends and then curve back. The genus *Monograptus* lived throughout the Silurian period and spread all over the world. The actual size of the fragment of shale shown here is approximately 6 cm ($2^{1}/_{4}$ in).

Spirograptus spiralis
Lower Silurian, Gotland, Sweden

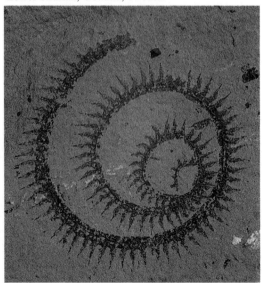

Cyrtograptus murchisoni bohemicus, Spirograptus spiralis
Lower Silurian, Velká Chuchle, Czech Republic

Testograptus testis
Lower Silurian, Králův Dvůr, Czech Republic

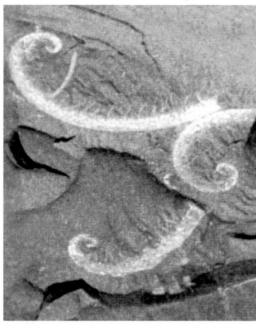

Spirograptus ■

LOWER SILURIAN

The rhabdosome of the genus *Spirograptus* is coiled in a spiral and the thecae have developed a roof over the mouth, which ends in sharp points or spines on the sides. Representatives of the genus *Spirograptus* have been recorded in Lower Silurian strata in Europe, North America, Asia and Australia.

Rastrites ■

LOWER SILURIAN

The rhabdosome of the genus *Rastrites* is straight, thin, curved or bent double. The long, entirely free thecae, which are virtually at right angles to the main branch, appear at various intervals. The genus *Rastrites* has been found in Lower Devonian sediments in Europe, Asia, North America and Australia.

Cyrtograptus ■

LOWER SILURIAN

The genus *Cyrtograptus* is characterized by thecae with tops which are always curved back towards the proximal part of the rhabdosome. Representatives of the genus *Cyrtograptus* lived in Europe, Asia and North America in the Lower Silurian.

Testograptus ■

LOWER SILURIAN

The rhabdosome of the genus *Testograptus* is broad, forming a strong spiral. There may be long spines by the mouths of the thecae. Representatives of the genus *Testograptus* lived in Europe, Asia and North Africa towards the end of the Lower Silurian. The fragment of clay shown here with graptolites of the species *Testograptus testis* measures 5.5 cm (2¹/₄ in).

Petalolgraptus ■

LOWER SILURIAN

The genus *Petalolgraptus* has a rhabdosome which is long or a short leaf shape. The thecae are long and narrow, and the axis clearly protrudes above the rhabdosome. Representatives of the genus *Petalolgraptus* lived throughout the world in the Lower Silurian.

7. Chordates

The most striking characteristic of the phylum of Chordata is the simultaneous presence of a nerve cord on the dorsal side (chorda dorsalis), the notochord (cartaliginous rod), and gill slits. In most chordates the nerves on the dorsal side are developed only during the embryonic stage. In mature organisms it is replaced by an ossified spinal column, consisting of a larger number of vertebrae. In lower organized groups – tunicates (Urochordata), chordates with no skull (Acraniata) and fish – the nerve cord survives on the dorsal side throughout the animal's lifetime. The central nervous system is above this, and the digestive tract is below. In the lower organized groups of chordates, the wall of the anterior section of the digestive tract is permanently perforated by gill slits. In the higher groups these are only indicated in the embryonic stage. In the tunicates and chordates with no skull the gill slits serve for the filtration of food from the water, in fish and in juvenile amphibians they are used for the exchange of oxygen between water and blood. In mature amphibians, reptiles, birds and mammals, the front gill slit becomes the Eustachian tube and the middle ear cavity. The other gill slits disappear after glands and lymphatic tissue have developed in the area of the gullet during the embryonic development. The heart, lies below the digestive tract. The digestive tract starts at the front end of the body with the mouth and ends towards the back, with the anal opening.

The oldest fossilized chordates belong to the genus *Pikaia* (probably an Acrania), found in the well-known strata dating from the Middle Cambrian of Burgess in areas of British Columbia (Canada). There is an even older creature very similar to chordates identified as the species *Yunnanozoon lividum* (Acrania). This was found a few years ago in Lower Cambrian deposits in China, and is 525 million years old. Therefore it seems that chordates developed at a very early stage, probably even during the Precambrian era, and that the true vertebrates probably evolved from ancestors without a skull. The current view is that chordates first lived in the sea because their presumed ancestors, semichordates (Hemichordata) – have only been found in marine sediments. The role of the oxygen content in the atmosphere played an extremely important part in the primary development of chordates. Life in surface waters allowed for an atmosphere which consisted of approximately one per cent oxygen, and this was already the case approximately 1,600 million years ago. The colonization of the coastal areas by organisms only took place when the oxygen content increased and these organisms lived on

phytoplankton. Subsequently the coastal areas were inhabited by sessile or semi-sessile organisms. Some of these started to secrete calcium and phosphorous in their body. They developed skeletons which served to protect their soft bodies, as well as a storage place for the elements that were vital to life.

The oldest vertebrates date back to the Upper Cambrian. They were almost certainly aquatic organisms, though for some key fossils, we are not sure whether they originate from marine or fresh water strata. Some paleontologists are inclined to think that the transition of chordates from saltwater to freshwater environments was essential for the evolution of vertebrates. Certainly a phylum of vertebrates colonized freshwater and saltwater environments at an early stage. Subsequently, they also colonized terrestrial areas during the Devonian. In the Mesozoic, they conquered the air.

Subphylum: Vertebrata – Vertebrates

UPPER CAMBRIAN – RECENT TIMES

Vertebrates are the most highly organized, and at the same time, an extremely diverse group of chordates, comprising both primitive lampreys and man. With the exception of the marine lamprey, they have all developed a skull. The presence of a spinal column is particularly characteristic. Although the majority of vertebrates alive today have jaws, most vertebrates in the Lower Silurian and the Lower Devonian did not have any. The large-scale evolution of animals with jaws started during the Devonian, approximately 380 million years ago. Vertebrates are characterized by their active search for food. They often cover large distances, moving from one place to another.

The body of vertebrates is bilaterally symmetrical. They have a well-developed head containing the *brain*. This is the most important part of the nervous system. It is followed by the body and a more or less developed caudal tail. One of the characteristics of vertebrates is *pairs of limbs* or *fins*, though in fish there may also be *unpaired fins*. The *internal skeleton* is extremely strong, and consists of the cranium or bone. The cartilaginous skeleton usually develops during the embryonic stage and exceptionally survives in mature animals. The skeleton of vertebrates can be distinguished as an axial skeleton, skull, limbs, and torso.

The basis for classifying vertebrates is the presence or absence of jaws. Therefore vertebrates are divided in those without jaws (Agnatha) and those with jaws (Gnathostomata).

Left: *Urodela*, Lower Miocene, Spain

Drepanaspis gemuendensis
Lower Devonian, Gemünden, Germany

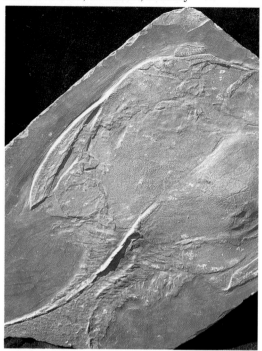

Superclass: Agnatha
– jawless vertebrates

UPPER CAMBRIAN – RECENT TIMES

Agnathans are reminiscent of fish because of their lifestyle and the shape of their body, but as they are not fish, we call them primitive vertebrates. The body of agnathans, dating from the Paleozoic, was enclosed by a strong bony shield which covered the head and the front part of the rest of the body. In some genera, the skeletal part of the head was also ossified, but there are no fossils of ossified spinal columns. The mouth was at the bottom of the head and had no jaws, operating only with a sucking function. At this spot, there were also small apertures leading to the gill cavities. The eyes were placed on the *top of the shield* with the start of a *pineal eye* between them. Below this, there was usually a small nasal opening. The sides of the head shield consisted of small polygonal plates. These may have formed part of a sensory system with the same function as the lateral line of present-day fish. In so far as there were any paired limbs, they only had *pectoral fins*. For the rest, fins were entirely lacking, and only folds developed in the skin which often consisted of strong scales. The *caudal fin* was well developed, as well as a few types of *dorsal fins*. The majority of agnathans lived in the Paleozoic. Only the lampreys and hagfish have survived up to the present day. The

first representatives of agnathans probably date back to the Upper Cambrian. Fossils have been identified in marine Middle Ordovician sediments. The greatest radiation (growth of diversity) of agnathans took place during the Silurian and the Lower Devonian. More than two hundred genera have been recorded. Agnathans are usually divided into two classes, Pteraspidomorphi and Cephalaspidomorphi.

Class: Pteraspidomorphi

CAMBRIAN – DEVONIAN

The Pteraspidomorphi include the oldest known fossils of vertebrates, e.g., the genera *Drepanaspis, Astraspis, Pteraspis, Anglaspis* and *Psammolepis*. They have a spool-shaped body, a flattened head and are compressed on either side at the back. They could grow to a length of 20–30 cm (7³/₄–12 in), and in exceptional cases even to 1.5 m (5 ft). They had no fins other than a caudal fin. The massive head shield at the front of the body consisted of a varying number of bony plates. A bony spine had developed on the so-called dorsal plate. The mouth opening was on the ventral side (lower mouth opening) or dorsal side (terminal mouth). The very first Pteraspidomorphi were usually small species 15–20 cm (6–7³/₄ in) long, with a narrow, rounded rostrum (*Pteraspis*). Later species reached lengths of about 50 cm (19¹/₂ in) and developed a blunt or elongated rostrum. The changes in the shape of the rostrum were related to the changing methods of obtaining food. The body was covered with numerous small diamond-shaped scales. The majority of Pteraspidomorphi were animals which fed on the sea bed by sucking up organic waste. Some species could move about a great deal because of the shape of their body. They used their tail as a rudder. The fins replaced elongated keel-shaped shields – hence the name Pteraspidomorphi ("shield fins").

Drepanaspis ■

LOWER DEVONIAN

The genus *Drepanaspis* is one of the characteristic representatives of fish-like agnathans. The head and thoras are large, oval in shape and dorsoventrally compressed. The large central dorsal plate is surrounded by a mosaic of small plates. The caudal part of the body is compressed on the sides and covered with thick scales like roof slates. These also form a striking comb on the dorsal side of the body. The upper lobe of the caudal fin is clearly smaller than the lower lobe. The orbits are at the front of the head and relatively far apart. The mouth is in the usual place (terminal). The genus *Drepanaspis* grew to a remarkable size: the body could be up to a maximum of 1 m (39 in) long. The genus has been found in Devonian sediments in Europe.

Class: Cephalaspidomorphi

LOWER SILURIAN – RECENT TIMES

In addition to Paleozoic representatives (Osteostraci, Anaspida), this class also comprises two living groups (Petromyzonida and Myxinoidea). They have a fish-like body shape and could grow up to a length of 60 cm (23$^1/_2$ in). Cephalaspidomorphi usually had paired pectoral fins, one or two dorsal fins and a differentiated caudal fin. The best-known subclass is the Osteostraci. These included, for example, the genera *Cephalaspis, Tremataspis,* and *Hemicyclaspis.* The body is completely enclosed in an armor of bony plates and scales. The broad flat head ended in a higher body which was flat on the ventral side. Both sides of the body were bordered with rows of scales which together formed a lengthwise edge. A bony shield covered the head. In primitive genera, striking extremities or horns grew from the sides of the bony shield for the head. The orbits were placed on the dorsal side on the head with a pineal opening between them. The small jawless mouth was at the bottom of the head and was used to filter the water. There were ten to twenty pairs of gill slits on the bottom and sides of the head. Behind the eyes and along the borders of the shield for the head there were "sensory areas", small hidden polygonal planes. The shield for the head was not segmented, and reached to the front part of the body, the rest of which was covered with bony plates. In some genera the shield extended to the anal opening.

The Osteostraci had two lobe-like pectoral fins covered with scales. When there were no scales, their function was taken over by an edge of skin. There were no pelvic fins, one or two dorsal fins, and the caudal fin consisted of two parts with a large lobe on the dorsal side.

Cephalaspis □

UPPER SILURIAN – UPPER DEVONIAN

The jawless *Cephalaspis* had a body enclosed in a case of bony plates and scales. The head was broad and flattened, the body was higher, triangular in cross section and with a flat ventral side. The interrelated row of scales covering the body formed a clearly visible keel on the sides. The head was protected by a strong interrelated shield, which ended in spiny extremities on the sides at the back. The orbits were close together and placed on the dorsal side. There was a pineal opening between them. The jawless mouth was at the bottom and was used to suck waste material up and to filter the water. There were also gill slits at the bottom of the head. *Cephalaspis* had two pectoral fins covered with scales. The dorsal fin was placed at the back of the body. This genus could grow to a length of 20 cm (7$^3/_4$ in), and was widespread from the Upper

Cephalaspis lyelli
Lower Devonian, Great Britain

Silurian to the Upper Devonian in Europe, Spitsbergen, Eastern Asia and North America.

Superclass: Gnathostomata – jawed fish

SILURIAN – RECENT TIMES

One of the most important stages in the evolution of vertebrates was the development of *jaws,* which allowed for the development of a predatory lifestyle. Gnathostomata comprise lower and higher vertebrates – fish-like organisms, fish, amphibians, reptiles, birds and mammals. They are characterized by a pair or well-developed jaws, probably developed from the third ribs. The upper jaw is connected to the skull, while the lower jaw can move. The oldest jawed fish have been found in Lower Silurian sediments.

Class: Placodermi – placoderms

LOWER DEVONIAN – CARBONIFEROUS

Placoderms are amongst the oldest and most common groups of fish-like Gnathostomata in the Paleozoic. The head and bones of the pectoral fin were concealed by a strong armor consisting of bony plates, which covered the head and front part of the body. The head was joined to the body with joints. Behind the armor, the head became narrower, ending in a fin consisting of two parts. This posterior part was covered with diamond-shaped scales or was completely bare. In contrast with agnathans, the Placoderms developed *pairs of fins*. The vertebrae were already partly ossified. There was a strong jaw function. The first placoderms have been recorded in salt and fresh waters, mainly in Devonian sediments all over the world. Some genera, like *Dunkleosteus*, could grow more than 2 m (6 ft 6 in) long, and were therefore the largest marine predators during the Devonian. For the purposes of classification, placoderms have been classified in nine orders.

Asterolepis

MIDDLE DEVONIAN – UPPER DEVONIAN

Placoderms of the genus *Asterolepis* are characterized by a short broad skull with orbits which are close together. The part of the armor covering the body is much better developed and has a striking

comb which runs across the dorsal section. The pairs of limbs extended to the middle of the body. *Asterolepis* had one dorsal fin placed in the caudal part of the body. These fish grew to relatively large sizes (60–70 cm/$19^1/_2$–$27^1/_2$ in). Their fossilized remains have been found in Devonian strata in Europe, North America, Greenland, Spitsbergen, Eastern Asia and Australia.

Bothriolepis

MIDDLE DEVONIAN – UPPER DEVONIAN

Bothriolepis is one of the most widespread genera of placoderms. It is characterized by a short, broad head shield. The shield covering the body has an oval shape characteristic of this genus. The pairs of pectoral limbs are very long, extending beyond the pectoral shield. The ventral fin is more or less in the middle of the body below the start of the first dorsal fin. The second dorsal fin reaches almost to the start of the first caudal fin. The body of the fish gradually narrows towards the back, ending in a narrow caudal part with a differentiated caudal fin in two parts, with a smaller upper lobe and a larger lower lobe. The orbits face forwards and are close together. The mouth is relatively small. Representatives of the genus *Bothriolepis* grew to a maximum length of 40–50 cm ($15^3/_4$–$19^1/_2$ in). They have been found in Devonian sediments in Europe, North America, Greenland, Asia and Australia.

Pterichthyodes

LOWER DEVONIAN – MIDDLE DEVONIAN

The shield for the head is short and broad. The orbits are placed close together and point to the front. Together with the nasal opening between them, they form the orbito-nasal opening. The lower part of the skull does not have armoring. There is a broad mouth and jaws with teeth. The long pairs of limbs, also covered with thick leathery plates, extend two thirds along the armor of the

Bothriolepis canadensis
Upper Devonian, Canada

Pterichtyodes productus
Devonian, Scotland

body. The dorsal fin is on the second half of the body, which is covered with scales. Representatives of the genus *Pterichtyodes* grew to fairly small sizes, and reached a maximum length of 30 cm (12 in). They were widespread in Europe and Australia during the Devonian.

Coccosteus

MIDDLE DEVONIAN

Coccosteus is a typical representative of the order of Arthrodiriformes and has a broad skull. The part of the armor covering the head was connected to the body by a pair of joints. The orbits are of an average size and are on the sides of the head, with a double pineal opening between them. The head was covered with a regular number of bony plates. There were small nasal openings at the front of the armor covering the head. The ventral fins were placed approximately in the middle of the body. There were two dorsal fins, the first in front of the middle of the body and the second at the back of the body. The anal dorsal fin was below the end of the second dorsal fin. The armor covering the body was strong and broad. The body itself was long and slender, ending in a narrow tail. This genus could grow to a length of 40 cm (15³/₄ in). Fossilized remains have been found in Devonian sediments in Europe.

Coccosteus, The Orkneys, Great Britain

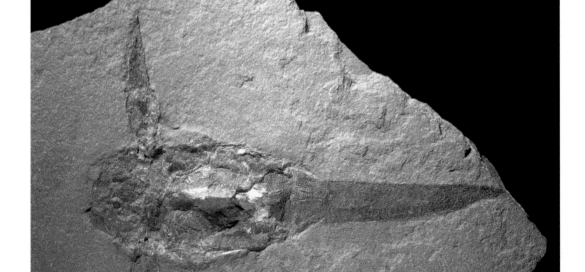

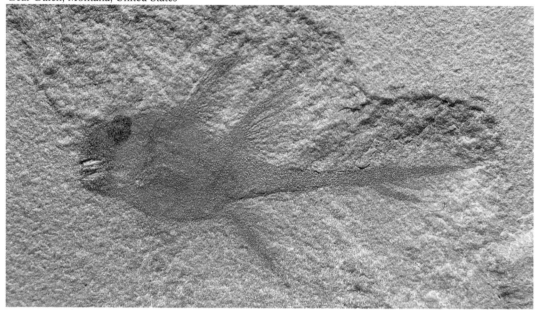

Echinochimaera meltoni
Bear Gulch, Montana, United States

Class: Chondrichthyes – chondrichthyans

UPPER SILURIAN – RECENT TIMES

The most characteristic feature of chondrichthyans is their *cartilaginous skeleton*, which may be reinforced with calcium carbonate. The bodies of vertebrates develop along the thin group of nerves on the dorsal side. In addition, calcareous layers grow on these in the form of concentric or radiating lamellae (*tectispondial* and *asterospondial* vertebrae). The external skeleton consists of *placoid* scales which can have different shapes, often with curved denticles made of dentine. In the area of the head and fins, these can develop into spines on the head or fins and sometimes also form larger plates. The fins which are not in pairs, and the ends of the pairs of fins, are strengthened with horny ends known as ceratotrichia. Chondrichthyans have five to seven pairs of gill slits directly linked to the external environment. In chimaerids, they are only covered by a lid *(operculum)*. The majority of chondrichthyans have a snout ending in a *rostrum*. The mouth and nasal openings are therefore on the ventral side. The teeth, consisting of strong dentine, are gradually replaced. They develop on a so-called dental plate, which constantly moves forwards during the course of life. Chondrichthyans do not have a swimbladder or lungs. There are species which lay eggs and species which bear live young, which is interesting in view of their primitive origins. They are sometimes referred to as living fossils because their develop-

ment is not characterized by any striking changes. The oldest known fossils are fragments dating from the Upper Silurian, but the most important diversification only took place in the Devonian. The majority of important groups became extinct at the end of the Paleozoic. There was another development of modern groups of chondrichthyans during the Mesozoic, the Jurassic and the Cretaceous. Nowadays, this group comprises approximately 165 genera and almost a thousand species of sharks, chimaerids and rays. Only the teeth have been found of most fossilized species; their cartilaginous skeleton only survived in rare cases. Chondrichthyans evolved along two lines: Holocephali – chimaerids, and the more extensive Elasmobranchii, which also include sharks and rays.

Subclass: Holocephali – chimaerids

DEVONIAN – RECENT TIMES

Chimaerids are active swimmers with a long whiplike tail. They differ from sharks in the structure of the skull. The gills are covered with a bag of skin, forming a so-called operculum, while the gill slits of sharks are completely open externally. In many cases there is a long rostrum, and there is usually a long spine in front of the dorsal fin. The jaws are short and broad with two types of teeth. The teeth are like those of sharks. However, there may also be tooth plates forming a system to crush the shells of invertebrates. The chimaerids reached a peak in the

Carboniferous, when they were amongst the most important groups of marine chondrichthyans.

Echinochimaera ■

LOWER CARBONIFEROUS

The genus *Echinochimaera* is one of the representatives of fossilized chimaerids. The front part of the body is barrel-shaped. The body narrows fairly quickly towards the back, ending in a slender tail with a symmetrical fin. The head is very short with large orbits and a mouth low down on the head. Like every chimaerid, this genus also has two dorsal fins, the first of which is erect with a short base ending in an erect spine. On the other hand, the second dorsal fin is low with a broad base. The dorsal part of the body is covered with a number of spines which also continue on the tail. *Echinochimaera* have been found only in Lower Carboniferous sediments in North America.

Subclass: Elasmobranchii

MIDDLE DEVONIAN – RECENT TIMES

Elasmobranchii are a very important and widespread group, comprising sharks and rays. Their archaic appearance is the result of the sickle-shaped, often asymmetrical caudal fin, the striking dorsal fin and the mouth, which is low down on the ventral side of the head. Because of the cartilaginous skeleton it is mainly the teeth and placoid scales that have survived.

Most Elasmobranchii have very sharp teeth which are regularly changed during their lifetime. Tooth plates develop on the inside. The rows of teeth move towards the edge of the jaw during growth, like a rolling carpet, to replace the previous row. The teeth of rays are tile-shaped and adapted to crushing the hard plates, for example, of mollusks. There is a great variety of sharks' teeth, revealing a high level of dependence on different types of food. Some sharks have extremely sharp pointed teeth (*Odon-*

Terminology of sharks' teeth: A – labial side,
B – lingual side, – C – mesial side

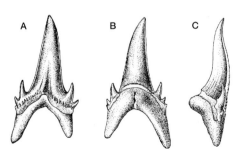

Orthocanthus gigas
Carboniferous, Nýřany, Czech Republic

taspis), which served to tear up their prey. Dog sharks (*Scyliorhinus*) have teeth which are adapted to grabbing and holding onto their prey. Flat teeth with a serrated edge can cut up the prey very easily (*Galeocerdo*). The second major problem for the identification of fossilized teeth is the so-called *heterodont dentition*, which means that the teeth are very different in one jaw, or in the upper and lower jaw. For the description of the tooth, a distinction is made between the internal side (*lingual side*) and the external side (*labial side*). As regards the position of the tooth in the jaw, there is the *mesial side* towards the middle of the jaw, and the *distal side*, pointing towards the back of the jaw. A thorough knowledge of the teeth of modern sharks is a precondition for the identification of fossilized sharks' teeth. It is only in this way that it is possible to prevent an excessive number of descriptions of teeth of new species. Elasmobranchii usually divided into thirteen orders, some of which are already extinct, such as the order of Xenacanthiformes.

Orthiacanthus □

CARBONIFEROUS – UPPER TRIASSIC

Orthacanthus belongs to a group of extinct freshwater sharks of the order of Xenacanthiformes. They were slender animals with a laterally compressed naked body, with the mouth at the bottom. One of the characteristic features of this shark is the presence of a long, sharp spine behind the head. This genus has teeth in which the crown has bifid (split) points, which are clearly separate and move slightly away from each other. The lingual and labial sides of the crown are curved in a convex shape. The biting edges are sharp. The root of the tooth is high and relatively massive with a heart-shaped perimeter. The basal side is perpendicular to the point of the crown. This genus is very common in Paleozoic sediments in Europe and North America. The latest fossils to be found date from the Triassic.

Heptranchias sp.
Oligocene, Bystřice nad Olší, Czech Republic

Heptranchias ■

EOCENE – RECENT TIMES

The shark of the genus *Heptranchias* has extremely interesting teeth. In the upper jaw they are long with narrow points, suitable for tearing their prey apart. The lower jaw has flattened serrated teeth used to cut the prey. The illustration shows a serrated tooth in the lower jaw. This shark has only been found in fossilized form in a few locations: in North America (Eocene), Venezuela (Oligocene) and Italy (Miocene). In modern seas there

Isurus hastalis
Middle Miocene, Mikulov, Czech Republic

is only one species, the *Heptranchias perlo* – a shark with seven gills. It has a long slender body with a narrow head and pointed snout. One of its characteristics is that it only has a dorsal fin. Nowadays, it is widespread in warm parts of the oceans up to depths of 800 m (2,624 ft).

Isurus ■

UPPER PALEOCENE – RECENT TIMES

The genus *Isurus* belongs to the important order of Lamniformes. Its teeth are the same in both jaws, very slender and pointed with a smooth edge, and without lateral teeth at the bases. They are mainly suitable for tearing up their prey. The body can grow to a length of 3 m (10 ft), and is elongated and bobbin-shaped with a long pointed head and a snout with a pointed conical shape. It has a dark blue back and a white belly, and is one of the sharks which have a virtually symmetrical arched caudal fin. It is one of the fastest sharks in existence, and is extremely dangerous, attacking ships and people. This shark spread all over the world. The teeth of the shark *Isurus* are found in Upper Paleocene sediments of Europe, Africa, South and North America and Australia.

Cetorhinus ■

EOCENE – RECENT TIMES

The shark of the genus *Cetorhinus* has been found in a fossilized state because of the frequent discoveries of parts of ribs, *branchiospines*. The base is compressed at the sides and is in the shape of a blade ending in a long slender, flattened spine. This covered the insides of the ribs. With this special mechanism, the shark filters plankton in the same way as some whales. The brachiospines are renewed every year, and it therefore not surprising that they are often found as fossils. The shark of the genus *Cetorhinus* was widespread from the Eocene up to the present day and fossilized remains have been found in Europe, North America and Japan. Nowadays, it can grow to extremely large sizes, up to a length of 15 m (49 ft) and a weight of four tons. The branchiospines of the shark *Cetorhinus parvus* shown here measure 4 cm ($1^{1}/_{2}$ in).

Squalicorax ■

LOWER CRETACEOUS – UPPER CRETACEOUS

The teeth of this extinct shark have a triangular crown. The front teeth are straight, while the lateral teeth curve backwards. The top of the crown can be sharp or blunt. The sharp biting edges are serrated along their entire length in a very striking way. The mesial edge is long and strikingly convex, while the distal edge is short, also convex at the base and then more or less straight. The root is strong and

Cetorhinus parvus
Oligocene, Litenčice, Czech Republic

Squalicorax pristodontus
Upper Cretaceous, Maastricht, The Netherlands

high. The teeth grow to a maximum length of 3 cm (1¹/₄ in). This genus was widespread all over the world during the Cretaceous. It has been found in Mesozoic sediments in Europe, Russia, North and South America, Western India, North and West Africa, the Near East, Japan and Australia.

Carcharocles ◼

MIDDLE EOCENE – PLIOCENE

The teeth of the shark of the genus *Carcharocles* are extremely large and can grow to a length of 15 cm (6 in). The tall crown has a triangular shape and a slightly convex labial side, also covering the labial side of the root to some extent. The lingual side of the crown clearly covers the root. One of the typical characteristics is the serrated cutting side of the teeth. The base of the crown is broad and massive, indented in a more or less regular way, forming two lobes *Carcharocles*, the ancestor of the modern man-eating shark, estimated to grow to a maximum of 20 m (65 ft), was without any doubt the biggest predator in the seas of the Tertiary all over the world. The tooth shown here is 9 cm (3¹/₂ in) long.

Carcharocles megalodon
Middle Miocene, Mikulov, Czech Republic

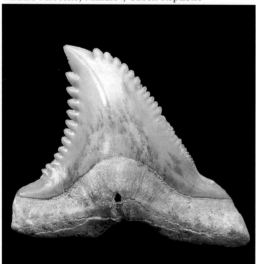

Hemipristis ■

MIDDLE EOCENE – RECENT TIMES

The shark of the genus *Hemipristis* in the order of Carcharhiniformes was first described on the basis of fossilized teeth. The teeth of the upper jaw have a high triangular crown, curving towards the back part of the jaw. The tooth shown here comes from the lateral side of the upper jaw. The mesial edge of the tooth (approximately in the middle of the jaw) is slightly curved, concave from the jaw and then with a clear convex curve up to the top of the tooth. The whole edge is finely serrated. The distal edge (further removed from the middle of the jaw) is clearly concave and also has a smaller number of larger teeth. The root is long with a striking lingual extremity and a groove with an opening in the middle. The tooth shown here is 2.5 cm (1 in) long. Teeth of the genus *Hemipristis* are found in Tertiary sediments from the Middle Eocene to the Pleistocene in

Galeocerdo aduncus
Middle Miocene, Mikulov, Czech Republic

Europe, North and South America, North and West Africa, India and Indonesia. The modern shark *Hemipristis elongata* grows to a length of approximately 2.4 m (8 ft). It lives in the shallow waters of the Northern Indian Ocean.

Galeocerdo ■

LOWER EOCENE – RECENT TIMES

The genus *Galeocerdo* is represented here by lateral teeth (on the side) with a characteristic triangular shape, a long root and a relatively high crown which curves towards the back of the jaw. The front teeth are obviously more erect in general. The mesial side of the edge of the tooth is convex and long, slightly serrated along its whole length. The distal edge is short on the other side, and there are larger teeth. The labial side of the crown is flat, while the lingual side and the root are more convex. There is also a lingual extremity with a short groove. The length of the teeth of the specimen shown here is approximately 1.5 cm ($^{1}/_{2}$ in). Fossilized remains have been recorded in Lower Eocene sediments in Europe, North and South America, Northern, Western and Southern Africa, India and Japan. The only species which still lives in modern seas is the feared tiger shark (*Galeocerdo cuvieri*).

Squatina ■

UPPER JURASSIC – RECENT TIMES

The genus *Squatina* is the only representative of the monotypical order of Squatinformes. It is a shark which resembles rays with a dorsoventrally flattened body and broad pectoral fins. Behind these there are also broad ventral fins. The dorsal fins have been completely moved to the posterior part of the back onto the thin tail. The caudal fin itself is barely developed and there is no anal fin. The head is round with only a short rostrum hiding the mouth. The teeth of the genus *Squatina* are broader than they are long. Whole skeletons of the genus *Squatina* have been identified, particularly in Upper Jurassic strata in Germany. Individual teeth have been found in many places dating from the Mesozoic to the Quaternary.

Class: Acanthodii

SILURIAN – PERMIAN

Acanthodii are an extinct group of fish. They are characterized by a long conical body in the shape of a fish, covered by an armor consisting of small square scales. They had well-developed fins, which were either in pairs or unpaired. In some cases there were two dorsal fins. The caudal fin is heterocercal. All the fins, with the exception of the caudal fin, were supported at the front by a spine made of dentine, (hence the name Acanthodii). The more primi-

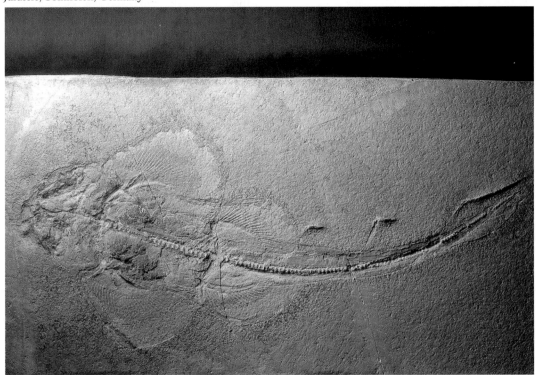

tive species also developed additional pairs of fins with spines between the pectoral and ventral fin. Well-preserved skeletons have been found dating from the Lower Devonian, though their fin spines only date from the Lower Silurian. Acanthodii superficially resemble sharks, but their internal skeleton already contained ossified elements. The majority of Acanthodii have been found in marine sediments, while most species dating from the Devonian inhabited freshwater environments. This group comprises almost 70 species and was very widespread geographically. Fossils have even been discovered in Antarctica.

Acanthodes

UPPER CARBONIFEROUS – LOWER PERMIAN

The Acanthodii of the genus *Acanthodes* have a long but strong body with a dorsal fin moved to the posterior end of the body. The anal fin is just in front of the dorsal fin. The pectoral fins are located on the ventral side of the body, followed by the ventral fins. All the fins are strengthened by a spine with a surface consisting of dentine. In this genus no other ventral spines developed between the fins. The caudal fin is heterocercal. The head has relatively large orbits and is blunted at the front. The mouth is slightly subterminal, placed at the bottom

of the head, and no teeth have developed in the jaws. The species shown here, *Acanthodes* sp., is 15 cm (6 in) long. The genus *Acanthodes* has been found in Upper Carboniferous to Lower Permian sediments in Europe, North America, Australia, South Africa and Asia.

Acanthodes sp.
Permian, Malá Lhota, Czech Republic

Class: Osteichthyes – bony fish

SILURIAN(?), DEVONIAN – RECENT TIMES

Osteichthyans represent a very extensive group of aquatic vertebrates which are jointly referred to as "fish".

The skeleton consists of bony tissue, though in some groups this was reduced to cartilage at a secondary stage (Chondrostei). Bones have developed in the skull which are found in all groups in this class with small variations. They are also found in the skulls of all quadrupeds. The skeleton has two origins. It consists of bones used as cover, for example, the operculum which protect the gills. These developed as a result of the enlargement of scales. The second type of bone, the reserve bones, developed through the ossification of embryonic cartilage. These two types are combined in the skull, jaws and shoulder blades. On the one hand, bony fish have pairs of fins (pectoral and ventral fins); on the other hand, the fins are unpaired (dorsal, anal and caudal fins). The caudal fin can be *heterocercal* with a larger lobe at the top, and the end of the spinal column projects into this, or it can be *difficercal*, so that the internal symmetry is retained. A fin with an internal symmetry is *homocercal*, and in a *hypocercal* fin, the end of the spinal column projects into the lower lobe (see illustration). The body of the oldest bony fish was covered with thick diamond-shaped *ganoid* or *cosmoid* scales (on the basis of the presence of the substances, ganoin and cosmine). Higher bony fish developed thin *elasmoīd* scales and there is no cosmoid or ganoid layer. In addition, these scales are divided into *ctenoid and cycloid* scales (see illustration). Most bony fish have a swim bladder, as long as this was not reduced at a secondary stage.

The class is divided into three very different subclasses: Actinopterygii, Dipnoi and Crossopterygii.

Types of caudal fins of sharks and fish: A heterocercal, B – homocercal, C – difficercal, D – hypocercal

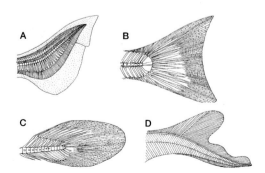

Examples of scales in sharks and fish: A – placoid, B – ganoid, C – ctenoid, D – cycloid

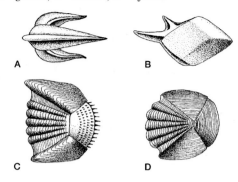

The Actinopterygii are distinct from the other groups because they have a different type of fins, there are no internal nasal openings and because of the character of their scales.

Subclass: Actinopterygii

LOWER DEVONIAN – RECENT TIMES

Like other Ostheichtyans, the Actinopterygii probably developed in the Paleozoic in fresh waters, and their numbers reached a peak at the end of the Triassic. The Actinopterygii, which include the most well-known fish, can be distinguished from the other two groups by a different type of fin. Their pairs of fins consist of radially arranged rays attached directly to the bone of the limbs. The primitive types have only one dorsal fin, and some groups also have a so- called adipose fin. The scales are either ganoid, or elasmoid, in contrast with the cosmoid scales of the Dipnoi and the Crossopterygii. They have no internal nasal openings, and a lateral line serves as a sensory canal. One of the characteristic features is the small number of so-called sclerotal plates in the orbits. The Actinopterygii are divided into three subclasses: the Chondrostei, Holostei and Teleostei.

Superclass: Chondrostei

MIDDLE DEVONIAN – RECENT TIMES

The subclass of Chondrostei includes the most primitive representatives of the Actinopterygii. The bony tissue of recent representatives consists largely of cartilage. These also include the present-day sturgeon with reduced ossification. However, Palaeozoic specimens had a skeleton which was more ossified, and their body was covered with ganoid scales. The common characteristic of all Chondrostei is the connection between the maxila (the bone in the upper jaw), the preoperculum (the bone covering the gill) and the bones of the palate. The maxila is not free and movable as in the Holostei, and the Teleostei. The sclerotal plates form a ring around the orbit. All the representatives have a heterocercal fin. The Chondrostei mainly include primitive Palaeozoic and Triassic types of Actinopterygii.

Order: Paleonisciformes

MIDDLE DEVONIAN – LOWER CRETACEOUS

The Paleonisciformes represent the oldest Actinopterygii and are the largest extinct group of the subclass of Chondrostei. They had a cigar-shaped or elongated tear-shaped body. The dorsal and anal fins formed a characteristic triangle. The heterocircle fin had a striking dorsal lobe covered with ganoid scales and was deeply indented. The pectoral fins were just behind the head, slightly closer to the ventral side of the body. The ventral fins were not very striking. The whole body was covered with shiny diamond-shaped scales of ganoid type. Keel-shaped scales developed along the front edges of the unpaired fins in the form of a V (*fulcra*). In the Paleonisciformes the nerve cord remained along the back throughout the fish's life. Non-ossified ribs also developed. The large eyes, surrounded by sclerotal bones, were moved forwards to a considerable extent. The jaws of the relatively large mouth had narrow sharp teeth. The Paleonisciformes emerged in Middle Devonian freshwater sediments, together with the Crossopterygii and the Dipnoi. They include one of the oldest genera, *Cheirolepis.* One of the best-known genera, *Palaeoniscus,* also appeared during the Carboniferous and the Permian. In addition, some species of the genus *Palaeoniscus* started to live in the sea. There was a significant decline in numbers during the Triassic, and by the Lower Cretaceous only an insignificant number of this species had survived.

Bourbonella ☐

LOWER PERMIAN

The genus *Bourbonella* is amongst the average-sized paleoniscid fish. It has a relatively broad head and rounded profile and strikingly large orbits. The caudal fin is relatively long and pointed and lies in the second part of the body. The broad ventral fin starts in front of the first rays of the dorsal fin, while the sharp anal fin is situated below its end. The heterocercal dorsal fin itself is well-developed. The body is covered with square scales arranged in diagonal wheels. The genus *Bourbonella* has been recorded in Permian sediments in Europe.

Bourbonella guiloti
Lower Permian, Bourbon L'Archambault, France

Amblympterus reussi
Lower Permian, Košťálov, Czech Republic

Guildayichtys carnegiei
Lower Carboniferous, Bear Gulch, Montana

Amblympterus □

LOWER PERMIAN – UPPER PERMIAN

The genus *Amblympterus* is another representative of paleoniscid fish. The body is relatively strong and it has a large head and orbits. The front part of the head ends in a blunt snout. The dorsal fin is relatively large, pointed and triangular, and is in the second half of the body. Diagonally opposite this there is an anal fin which is also well-developed. The pectoral and ventral fins are broad. The body, which ends in a heterocercal fin, is covered with square scales. The specimen shown here measures 19 cm ($7^1/_2$ in). The genus *Amblympterus* has been recorded in Permian sediments in Europe and North America.

Guildayichtys ■

LOWER CARBONIFEROUS

Guildayichtys is a small, oval, paleoniscid fish with a high back. The head has large orbits and is higher than it is long; the snout is pointed at the front. The relatively large dorsal fin starts after the end of the body. The ventral fin is below this, followed by a long anal fin. The caudal fin is rounded. The body

Gyrodus hexagonus
Upper Jurassic, Solnhofen, Germany

is covered with diamond-shaped scales. The genus only grows to a length of about 6 cm ($2^1/_4$ in). It has been recorded in Lower Carboniferous sediments in North America.

Gyrodus ■

MIDDLE JURASSIC – UPPER CRETACEOUS

The genus *Gyrodus* is characterized by a round or high oval body. The head is short and high with a blunt profile. The orbits are large and placed at the front end of the head. The jaws have round oval teeth which are pointed in juvenile specimens. The dorsal and anal fins are opposite each other in the second half of the body. The ribs are long, reaching to the ventral profile of the body. The caudal fin is deeply indented. The genus *Gyrodus* was widespread from the Middle Jurassic to the Upper Cretaceous and has been found in Europe, Africa and Cuba.

Acipenser □

UPPER CRETACEOUS – RECENT TIMES

The genus *Acipenser* is one of the few Chondrostei that belong to the order of Acipenseriformes. These fish reveal an extreme reduction of the skeleton: in the sturgeon there was only a slight ossification of the internal skeleton. The body has retained an archaic shape, resulting above all from the presence of the heterocercal caudal fin. The dorsal fin is right

Acipenser sp.
Oligocene, Cereste, France

at the back, like the ventral and anal fin. The head is elongated to the rostrum and the orbits are small. One of the characteristics of sturgeons is the strongly ossified, tall plates, which form a row on the dorsal and ventral sides. Sturgeons have been found in a fossilized state in the Upper Cretaceous layers in Europe and North America.

Superorder: Holostei

UPPER PERMIAN – RECENT TIMES

The Holostei are included amongst the most primitive Chondrostei and the higher Teleostei. The upper jaw is no longer connected to the preoperculum, and the slit of the mouth is short compared to that of the Chondrostei. The scales have a diamond shape, or they are rounded and no cosmoid layer has developed. The caudal fin is still heterocercal. Holostei are widespread in Mesozoic sediments.

Urocles ■

UPPER JURASSIC

The genus Urocles comprises average-sized fish with a greatly elongated body. The oblong head is rounded, and the slit of the mouth is relatively deep. The teeth in the jaws are pointed. The dorsal fin has a reasonably broad base, and starts approximately in the middle of the body. The ventral fin is placed slightly above the dorsal fin, and the anal fin is below the end of that fin. The pectoral fins are fan--like and relatively well developed. The caudal fin is rounded. The specimen shown here is 26 cm (10^{1}/$_{4}$ in) long. The genus *Urocles* has been found in Jurassic sediments in Europe.

Caturus ■

LOWER JURASSIC – LOWER CRETACEOUS

Caturus is an average-sized fish with a slender salmon-like shape. The spinal column is not completely ossified. The head is relatively large with a small eye, but with long jaws with strong teeth. The dorsal fin is small and pointed, starting in the middle of

Caturus furcatus
Upper Jurassic, Solnhofen, Germany

the body. The anal fin has been moved to the end of the body. The very large, deeply indented caudal fin is striking. The body is covered with scales. The genus *Caturus* grows to a length of up to 30 cm (12 in). It has been found in Jurassic and Cretaceous sediments in Europe and West Africa.

Pachycormus ■

UPPER JURASSIC

The genus *Pachycormus* has a relatively large broad head, which is pointed at the front. The slit of the mouth is fairly long and the jaws have pointed teeth. The orbits are small. The small dorsal fin is triangular and starts only after the middle of the body. The anal fin is fairly far back along the body and is not very striking. On the other hand, the pectoral fins are very long. The caudal fin is powerfully developed, broad and deeply indented. The genus *Pachycormus* has been found in Upper Jurassic sediments in Europe.

Urocles elegantissimus
Upper Jurassic, Solnhofen, Germany

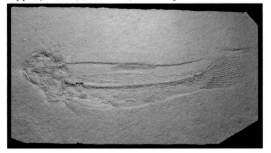

Pachycormus
Upper Jurassic, Ste-Colombe Yonne, France

Eurycormus speciosus
Upper Jurassic, Solnhofen, Germany

Tharis dubius
Upper Jurassic, Eichstätt, Germany

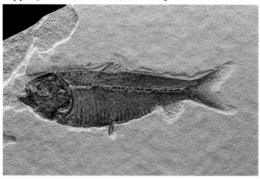

Eurycormus ■

UPPER JURASSIC

The genus *Eurycormus* is an average-sized fish with a relatively strong body. The head is relatively large, more or less as long as it is high, and the front part of the snout is slightly pointed. The slit for the mouth is of an average length. The large orbits are placed in the upper part of the head. The small caudal fin is in the second half of the body, and the anal fin is below the end of the dorsal fin. The caudal fin is very large and deeply indented. The specimen shown here is 22 cm (8$^1/_2$ in) long. The genus *Eurycormus* has been found in Upper Jurassic sediments in Europe.

Superorder: Teleleostei

TRIASSIC – RECENT TIMES

In terms of development, the Teleostei represent the highest group of Actinopterigii. Their skeleton is almost entirely ossified. In these fish there was some reduction and a change in the function of some of the bones in the jaws, and several new bones appeared in the head (postparietal). The layer of scales covering the body and the individual scales are reduced. The scales are cycloid or ctenoid, and have an elasmoid structure. With more than 22,000 living species, the Teleostei are the largest group of vertebrates. They are divided into 35 orders, and approximately 100 families, of which almost 70 are already extinct. They represent the most important prevailing groups of fish since the Cretaceous.

Glossanodon musceli
Oligocene, Mouchnice, Czech Republic

Tharis dubius
Upper Jurassic, Eichstätt, Germany

Tharis ■

UPPER JURASSIC

The genus *Tharis* was a representative of the primitive Teleostei in the order of Leptolepiformes. It was a long, slender fish with an oval profile. The relatively short head is pointed at the front. The orbits are large. The dorsal fin is behind the middle of the body, with the small, narrow ventral fins opposite them. The anal fin lies behind the end of the dorsal fin. The pectoral fin is directly behind the head on the ventral side. The caudal fin is deeply indented. The genus *Tharis* has been found in Upper Jurassic sediments in Europe.

Knightia □

EOCENE

The genus *Knightia* is a representative of herring-like fish in the order of Clupeiformes – "boneless" fish. In this genus the body is highest behind the head and then becomes gradually narrower. The head is relatively short with an average-sized mouth. The orbits are close together at the front of the head. The triangular dorsal fin is in the middle of the body opposite the ventral fins. The anal fin is between the end of the ventral fin and the first rays of the caudal fin, which is deeply indented. The body is covered with cycloid scales, which develop into thick keels on the ventral side. *Knightia* grows to a length of approximately 15 cm (6 in). The genus has been found in Eocene freshwater sediments in South and North America.

Glossanodon ■

OLIGOCENE – RECENT TIMES

A small, long, silver-colored fish with a large, elongated head and large orbits. The dorsal and ventral fins begin approximately in the middle of the body, while the anal fin is a long way towards the back. The fish is often fossilized in a coiled position. The body of the specimen shown here is 5.5 cm ($2^1/_4$ in)

Scopeloides glarisianus, luminescent organs
Oligocene, Litenčice, Czech Republic

long. The genus *Glossanodon* has been found in Oligocene sediments in Europe and the Caucasians. These fish are very common in present-day seas at great depths in the Northern Atlantic Ocean.

Scopeloides ■

OLIGOCENE

The genus *Scopeloides* is represented by a very interesting order of luminescent fish, Stomiiformes. The dorsal fin is approximately in the middle of the body and the anal fin is further back. The ventral fin lies between the pectoral and anal fin. The fish is approximately 20 cm ($7^3/_4$ in) long. The luminescent organs are arranged in two rows and can be clearly seen on the fossils as bituminous points (see photograph). In the jaws, small teeth alternate with large incisors, as in the related dangerous-looking tooth bream. The genus *Scopeloides* has been found in Oligocene sediments in Europe and Iran.

Scopeloides glarisianus
Oligocene Litenčice, Czech Republic

Scopeloides glarisanus, lower jaw
Oligocene, Litenčice, Czech Republic

Argyropelecus cosmovicii,
Oligocene, Bystřice nad Olší, Czech Republic

Argyropelecus cosmovicii, luminescent organs
Oligocene, Bystřice nad Olší, Czech Republic

Argyropelecus ∎

OLIGOCENE – RECENT TIMES

The genus *Argyropelecus*, which also belongs to the order of Stomiiformes, is represented by a very curious fish with a high and strongly compressed body and a deeply indented caudal fin. The eyes are large and rotated upwards (telescopic). The luminescent organs are connected with special scales and arranged in groups, particularly on the ventral side of the body. The fish camouflage this side by emitting light. They imitate the pale light which comes from the surface and in this way become invisible. The specimen shown here is 2 cm ($^{3}/_{4}$ in) long. The genus *Argyropelecus* has been found in Tertiary sediments in Europe, the Caucasians and North America.

Diaphus ∎

OLIGOCENE – RECENT TIMES

The genus *Diaphus* represents the order of *Myctophiformes*, which mainly comprises deep-sea fish, whose most characteristic feature is the presence of luminescent organs. Their shape is in no way unusual. The dorsal fin is placed in the middle of the body and the anal fin starts on the vertical last ray of the dorsal fin. The ventral fin is in middle between the pectoral fins and the anal fin. The large eye and long mouth are striking. The luminescent organs are connected to special scales and are mainly placed on the ventral side of the body. This can also be clearly seen in the fossils. The fossilized representatives from the Carpathians, where the specimen of *Diaphus meniliticus* shown here was also found, are amongst the oldest known examples of these fish. The genus *Diaphus* has been found in Tertiary sediments in Europe. The specimens shown here are 7 cm ($2^{3}/_{4}$ in) long.

Leuciscus ☐

OLIGOCENE – RECENT TIMES

The genus *Leuciscus* is one of the well-known freshwater rock-bass, and is a representative of the order of Cypriniformes, carp. It is a small, slender fish, slightly longer than it is high. The highest point lies behind the head. The mouth is fairly long. The dorsal fin is approximately in the middle of the body and a little way behind the smallest ventral fin. The anal fin has a slightly longer base and lies below the end of the dorsal fin. The caudal fin is long and moderately indented. The ribs are strong and extend to the ventral edge of the body. The body is covered with cycloid scales. This fish can grow up to 10 cm (4 in) long. It has been found in Oligocene freshwater sediments in Europe.

Diaphus meniliticus,
Oligocene, Litenčice, Czech Republic

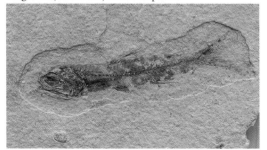

Diaphus meniliticus, luminescent organs
Oligocene, Litenčice, Czech Republic

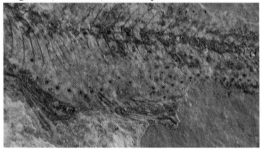

Leuciscus sp.
Miocene, Ardèche, France

Capros radobojanus
Oligocene, Vážany nad Litavou, Czech Republic

Berybolcensis ∎

MIDDLE EOCENE

The genus *Berybolcensis* represents small fish with a diameter which is largest just behind the head. The head is relatively large, and approximately as high as it is long. The orbits are large, and the long slit of the mouth extends to below the middle of the body. There are two dorsal fins: the first starts immediately behind the head and consists of hard rays. The second, which starts after the middle of the body, consists of soft rays. The anal fin starts below the second dorsal fin. The ventral fin lies below the pectoral fin. The genus *Berybolcensis* can grow to lengths of approximately 12 cm (4³/₄ in). It has been found in Middle Eocene sediments in Europe.

Berybolcensis leptacanthus
Middle Eocene, Monte Bolca, Italy

Capros ∎

OLIGOCENE – RECENT TIMES

The genus *Capros* is a representative of the order of Zeiformes. It has a high, round, greatly flattened body on the sides, with a large head and strikingly large orbits. The head is concave at the top, ending in a pouting mouth which points diagonally downwards. The dorsal fin consists of two parts; the first part is formed by hard rays in which the third is the longest ray, while the second part consists of soft short rays. The first rays of the ventral and anal fins are also hard. Representatives of the genus *Capros* have been found in Oligocene strata in Europe and North Africa. The specimen of the species *Capros radobojanus* is 2.2 cm (³/₄ in) long.

Zenopsis clarus
Oligocene, Litenčice, Czech Republic

Priscacara liops
Eocene, Wyoming, United States

Zenopsis ■

OLIGOCENE – RECENT TIMES

At first sight, the genus *Zenopsis* is similar to the genus *Capros*. The body is also high and greatly flattened on the sides. However, the posterior end of the body is symmetrically convex, ending in a narrow tail with a brush-like caudal fin. The head is relatively large. There is a striking first dorsal fin just behind the head, in which the hard rays are longest (in contrast with the genus *Caprus*). The anal fin is relatively far back and also starts with hard rays. The profile of the ventral side is bordered with small but strongly ossified plates. The body of the specimen shown here is 2 cm (³⁄₄ in) long. The genus *Zenopsis* has been found in Tertiary sediments in Europe and the Caucasians.

Sphyraena bolcensis
Eocene, Monte Bolca, Italy

Sphyraena ■

EOCENE – RECENT TIMES

The genus *Sphyraena*, the barracuda, comprises long, slender fish with a narrow head. The small orbits are placed in the upper part. The long jaws are elongated, ending in a small rostrum and with very strong teeth. The first dorsal fin consists of hard rays and starts in front of the middle of the body. The second dorsal fin is on the third part of the body opposite the anal fin. The pectoral and ventral fins are small. The caudal fin is large and deeply indented. The genus *Sphyraena* has been recorded in Eocene strata and has survived up to the present day. It is found in marine sediments in Europe, Africa, India, Asia and North America.

Priscara ☐

EOCENE

The genus *Priscara* includes small to average-sized fish with sharp fins. The body is compressed on the sides and is highest at the point where the dorsal fin begins. The head is just as high as it is broad, with an average-sized mouth and relatively large orbits. The first dorsal fin consists of hard rays, the second only starts behind the middle of the body and consists of soft rays. The anal fin is strengthened with hard rays at the front. The slightly rounded caudal fin is not indented. The genus *Priscara* has been found in Eocene freshwater sediments in North America.

Scatophagus frontalis
Eocene, Monte Bolca, Italy

Mene rhombea
Eocene, Monte Bolca, Italy

Scatophagus ■

EOCENE – RECENT TIMES

The genus *Scatophagus* comprises small, laterally compressed fish. Their body is highest just behind the head where the first dorsal fin starts. The head is high and triangular with large orbits. The dorsal fin consists of hard and soft rays like the anal fin, which only starts after the middle of the body. The pectoral and ventral fins are behind the head; the pectoral fin is round and the ventral fin is below this, also strengthened with hard rays. The body grows to a length of approximately 12 cm (4³/₄ in). The genus *Scatophagus* is found in marine and brackish water sediments in Europe.

Mene ■

PALEOCENE – RECENT TIMES

The genus *Mene* comprises average-sized, round or square fish which are strongly laterally compressed. The profile of the dorsal side is slightly convex while the appearance of the ventral side is strikingly elongated around the ventral fin. The dorsal fin starts approximately in the middle of the body. Its rays are greatly reduced towards the back and as in the anal fin they consist of thin ossified plates. The ventral fin is characteristic of this genus, with very long thread-like rays. The caudal fin is short and is not indented either. Specimens can grow to a length of about 30 cm (12 in). The genus *Mene* has been found in Tertiary marine sediments in Europe and North America.

Serranus ■

MIDDLE EOCENE – RECENT TIMES

The genus *Serranus* belongs to the group of sea bass in the order of Perciformes – the bass family. The head is approximately as long as it is high, with a diagonal mouth and large orbits. The dorsal fin consists of hard and soft rays, starting behind the head slightly further than the ventral fin opposite it. The anal fin is approximately in the middle of the body and starts with three hard rays. The body is covered with small ktenoid scales. The specimen shown here belongs to the genus *Serranus* and is 3.3 cm (1¹/₄ in) long. This genus has been found in marine sediments dating from the Eocene onwards, in Europe and North America.

Serranus budensis
Lower Oligocene, Mouchnice, Czech Republic

Bilinia uraschista
Middle Oligocene, Kučlín, Czech Republic

Lepidopus glarisianus
Lower Oligocene, Litenčice, Czech Republic

Bilinia ☐

OLIGOCENE

In contrast with the genus *Serranus*, the genus *Bilinia* is a freshwater representative of the family of Serranidae and has been found in Tertiary sediments in Central Europe. It can grow to a length of about 9 cm (3¹/₂ in).

Lepidopus ■

EOCENE – RECENT TIMES

The genus *Lepidopus* has a long ribbon-like body consisting of about 120 vertebrae. For this reason, entire skeletons are only found very rarely. The head is long and accounts for approximately one seventh of the length of the body. The jaws are large and strong with large teeth for tearing up prey, which are often found individually. The long dorsal fin, which extends as far as the caudal fin, starts behind the head. The anal fin is approximately in the middle of the body and, like the dorsal fin, extends to the end of the body. The pectoral and ventral fins are directly behind the head. The recent species *Lepidopus caudatus* is found along the whole east coast of the Atlantic Ocean and in the Mediterranean Sea, at depths up to 400m. The genus *Lepidopus* has been found in Tertiary sediments in Europe, Africa, India and North America. The section of the spinal column of the *Lepidopus glarisianus* shown here measures 7 cm (2³/₄ in).

Oligolactoris ■

OLIGOCENE

The fish of the Genus *Oligolactoris* belonged to the Tetraodontiformes – "fish with four teeth", because of the special dentition adapted to crunching up the hard shells of mollusks and corals. The *Oligolactoris* has a cigar-shaped body, typical of many related genera of the family of Tetrodontiformes. The most important organ for movement is the caudal fin, which can make rotating movements. The dorsal and anal fins are on the posterior part of the body. The pectoral fins are fairly high up behind the head. This genus has striking spines with lengthwise grooves, in front of the eyes and the anus. The body itself is enclosed in a hard case consisting of strong hexagonal scales which fit together with their finely serrated edges. The specimen shown here is 3.3 cm (1¹/₄ in) long. This genus is found in Oligocene sediments in the Western Carpathians.

Subclass: Dipnoi – lungfish

LOWER DEVONIAN – RECENT TIMES

Dipnoi represent a very conservative group of fish which have existed since the Lower Devonian and have survived up to the present day. There are two dorsal fins on the elongated, fish-like body. The first of these is usually reduced. The pairs of fins are elongated and symmetrical, of the archipterygian type. The body of the oldest lungfish was covered with strong cosmoid scales; these gradually became thinner and acquired the character of cycloid scales. The scales also cover the surface of the fins. Present-day representatives have difficercal fins, which means that they are symmetrical on the inside. These gradually develop from the original heterocercal fins when the anal and second dorsal fin fused together. In the oldest species, the skull was covered with thick dermal bones, which could even form a strong armor. One of the characteristic features of Dipnoi is the reduction of the bones of the upper jaw and some of the bones of the lower jaw. They developed separate toothplates. The skeleton was partly ossified, and partly consisted of cartilage. These fish are able to breathe oxygen in the air with a breathing organ (hence the name). However, it is assumed that they only developed this ability in the Tertiary. Originally, it was thought that lungfish were the ancestors of terrestrial vertebrates. They are divided into eight orders, two of which have survived up to the present day.

Oligolactoris bubiki
Lower Oligocene, Bystřice nad Olší, Czech Republic

Oligolactoria bubiki, scales
Lower Oligocene, Bystřice nad Olší, Czech Republic

Ceratodus

LOWER TRIASSIC – PALEOCENE

The genus *Ceratodus* is represented here by a dental plate, which is part of a special type of biting mechanism characteristic of lungfish. In the mouth cavity, extensions of the plates pointed outwards, while the spherical side opposite pointed to the middle of the palate. The dental plates were covered with a layer of dental enamel. The tooth-plates illustrated here measure 5 cm (2 in) across. Representatives of the genus *Ceratodus* were extremely common in the Triassic and the Jurassic in Europe.

Subclass: Crossopterygii – brush fins

LOWER DEVONIAN – RECENT TIMES

Unlike lungfish, brush fins are predators which move very quickly. Their name is derived from the pairs of fins with muscle tissue surrounding the inner skeleton of the fin. This, as well as their internal fin skeleton, shows that they are related to terrestrial vertebrates. They always had two dorsal fins, an anal fin and pairs of pectoral and ventral fins. The caudal fin is heterocercal or difficercal. The body is covered with diamond-shaped or round scales. Another important characteristic is the division of the skull (neurocrania) into the front

Ceratodus kaupi
Triassic, Hoheneck, Germany

part with an olfactory function and the auditory part at the back.

Like the lungfish, their head was covered with der-

Cardiosuctor populosum
Lower Carboniferous, Bear Gulch, Montana, United States

mal blocks of the cosmoid type, forming a strong armor. Brushfin fish are divided into two fundamental groups: the superorders of Rhipidistia and Actinista. The Rhipidistia are important from the point of view of evolution, because quadrupeds evolved from this group. They differ from the Actinista, amongst other things, by the presence of internal nasal openings and because of the arrangement and number of dermal bones on the head.

Superorder: Actinista

MIDDLE DEVONIAN – RECENT TIMES

This group comprises the present day *Latimeria chalumnae*, a typical example of a living fossil. Up to 1938, when this extraordinary fish was caught, the Crossopterygii were considered to have become extinct in the Mesozoic. Actinista could grow to a length of 40 cm ($15^3/_4$ in) to 1.5 m (5 ft). The strong body was covered with thin cycloid scales without cosmoid layers. The most characteristic feature is their three-pointed difficercal caudal fin. The fins are not in pairs and form brush-like structures. One of the other important characteristics is the calcified breathing organ. The Actinista originally lived in freshwater environments, and during the Triassic some adapted to a marine environment.

Cardiosuctor ◼

LOWER CARBONIFEROUS

The genus *Cardiosuctor* comprised slender, predatory fish with brush-like fins, which were small or average-sized. The head is round and has large orbits. The snout is slightly rounded with an average-sized mouth. The first dorsal fin is only approximately halfway along the body, while the second dorsal fin is in the lowest third part of the body. The ventral fins and the anal fins are relatively small and lie opposite the dorsal fin. The pectoral fins are round. The caudal fin is difficercal, elongated and has three lobes. The middle lobe ends in a brush. The genus *Cardiosuctor* grew to a length of approximately 20 cm ($7^3/_4$ in). It has been found in Upper Carboniferous strata in North America.

Macropoma ◼

CRETACEOUS

This is a brushfin fish with an elongated body. The relatively small head has a large mouth and is as long as it is high. The backbone is not entirely ossified, and only the arches of the vertebrae are visible. The calcified breathing organ takes up more than half of the length of the body. The specimen shown here, which is extremely well preserved, is 45 cm ($17^3/_4$ in) long. The genus *Macropoma* has been found in sediments of shallow waters dating from the Cretaceous in Central Europe.

267

Tetrapoda – quadrupeds

Quadrupeds include all vertebrates with four limbs, which serve primarily for moving over land. Subsequently, these limbs could develop to become wings or paddle-like shapes or they could disappear completely (reduction). The oldest quadrupeds, which include amphibians, reptiles, birds and mammals, appeared in the Upper Devonian. According to the traditional system of classification, quadrupeds are divided into classes (amphibians, reptiles, birds and mammals). However, in some of the more recent systems of classification they were classified as an independent class, the Tetrapoda, which includes the subclasses amphibians and Amniota.

Class: Amphibia – amphibians

Amphibians represent the transition between aquatic and terrestrial jawed animals. They are the oldest and most primitive quadrupeds. This class has the following characteristics: well-developed *pairs of limbs* (with some exceptions when the limbs are subsequently reduced); *changing body temperature* (they are cold blooded – *ectothermic);* no amnion develops in the egg during the development of the embryo (*Anamnia*); the eggs are mainly laid in water; the larvae develop in water and first breathe with gills (like fish); this first period of their life ends in a *metamorphosis*. During this process the body partly changes and the aquatic larva becomes an amphibian that is adapted to life on land (lungs).

Nowadays, amphibians usually grow to a size of several centimeters, and in exceptional cases may even grow to a length of one meter. However, some fossilized species reached lengths of up to 6 m (20 ft). The shape of the body depends on the environment the amphibians live in. The most frequent species are those similar to a salamanders (*Salamandra*), lizards (*Triturus*), frogs (*Rana*) and toads (*Bufo*). Fossilized amphibians include species which look like small crocodiles (*Mastodonsaurus*) or eels (*Ophiderpeton*). The body has a naked surface or is covered with horny scales or bony plates. A study of the teeth of fossilized amphibians reveals that the mature specimens were predators. In a few rare cases they were herbivorous (*Diadectes*). They inhabited freshwater, marshy environments and lakes, and sometimes hunted in shallow coastal waters.

The existence of the oldest amphibians has been proved on the basis of well-preserved traces found in deposits dating from the Lower Devonian in Southern Australia. The oldest fossils have been found in Eastern Greenland (Upper Devonian) and Russia (Upper Devonian). This reveals that they spread all over the world and moved onto land at the same time in many parts of the world. There is a great deal of discussion, which has continued up to the present day, regarding the reasons for the transition onto land. In fact, we cannot be sure whether amphibians colonized the mainland as a result of climate changes or whether new sources of food played a role. There is no doubt that in the course of time, many areas of the gigantic ancient continent known as Pangea were colonized. This gradually started to fall apart during the course of the Palaeozoic. Numerous discoveries of the oldest amphibians in Europe, Asia, North and South America, Greenland, Africa, Australia and Antarctica are evidence for the movement of the continents.

The oldest amphibians inhabited warm tropical or subtropical areas. A strong link with water was necessary because they reproduced in water, and because most amphibians found a permanent source of food there. During the course of the Carboniferous they became the dominant group of animals, and they are considered as the ancestors of

Tooth – cross section
Labyrinthodontia (magnified)

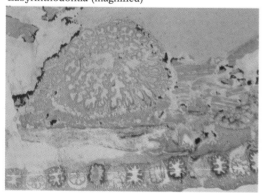

Acanthostega gunnari
Upper Devonian, Greenland

all other terrestrial vertebrates. The most primitive amphibians lived up to the beginning of the Cretaceous, and entirely new and modern species developed during the Jurassic – true frogs and primitive amphibians with a tail. Nowadays, they are an individual group of animals. They are considerably specialized, and in many respects they are far removed from their Palaeozoic ancestors. They are divided into three subclasses, of which representatives of the subclasses of Labyrinthodontia and Lissamphibia are described here.

Subclass: Labyrinthodontia

MIDDLE DEVONIAN – LOWER CRETACEOUS

This is a large group of extinct amphibians of which the most primitive forms resemble brush fins. The higher forms are very similar to primitive reptiles. The most characteristic feature is the curious structure of their teeth in which the dentine wrinkles up like a labyrinth around the central cavity, as seen in horizontal cross section. The teeth served only to grab hold of the prey, which was swallowed whole. Therefore the digestive organs were used to grind up and digest the prey. The vertebrae of all amphibians are ossified, as cartilage would not be able to carry the weight of their body, even if this was reduced by being in water. The limbs of the first amphibians are strong and well developed. Juvenile specimens lived in water, while mature animals probably moved onto land like present-day amphibians. However, they could return to the water. The Labyrinthodontia were a successful group and were the ancestors of modern amphibians and reptiles.

Order: Ichtyostegalia

UPPER DEVONIAN – LOWER CARBONIFEROUS

This large order comprises the largest known amphibians, which also includes the orders *Acanthostega* and *Icthyostega*.

Acanthostega □

UPPER DEVONIAN

Because of the discoveries of a number of specimens, the genus *Acanthostega* has become the best-known species of quadrupeds which moved into water at a later stage. The primitive spinal column, with a nerve cord which was retained in the mature animal, was able to tolerate some mechanical weight when the animal swam. On land it would not be able to carry this amphibian. The tail had fins which reached almost up to the head along the back.

Although there were oval protective plates on the ventral side, the short, thin ribs would not be able to protect any vital organs on land. The relatively

Ichthyostega stensioei
Upper Devonian, Greenland

long limbs with well-developed fingers were not able to carry the body weight on land. The internal gills are also a sign of an aquatic lifestyle. They are similar to those found in fish (external gills have developed in all other amphibians with gills). Although the genus *Acanthostega* had many of the characteristics of fish, the development of the limbs was more advanced than that of the fins. It now appears that the genus lived in shallow freshwater environments full of aquatic plants and pieces of wood. The genus *Acanthostega*, an amphibian approximately 60 cm (19$^1/_2$ in) long, has been found in Upper Devonian river sediments in Eastern Greenland.

Ichthyostega □ ●

UPPER DEVONIAN

Some of the primitive characteristics of fish which were more developed in some of the other oldest quadrupeds (e.g., the genus *Acanthostega* and *Ventastega*) can be found on the skull of the amphibians of the genus *Ichthyostega*. On the other hand, the bodies of specimens of the genus *Ichthyostega* had fewer characteristics of fish behind the head than was the case for the genus *Acanthostega*. As in fish, the nerve cord remained intact throughout the animal's life. The interesting characteristic of the axial part of the skeleton of the genus *Ichtyostega* was the long, thick, flattened ribs which crossed over. The limbs were able to carry part of the body and the hind limbs were used particularly for swimming. Another interesting aspect is the sharpened lower edge of the fins, which reveals that they moved over land. The *Ichthyostega* was a large predator, approximately 1 m (39 in) long, which hunted for fish in coastal waters. It has been found in Upper Devonian sediments in eastern Greenland.

Actinodon frossardi
Lower Permian, Autun, France

Archegosaurus decheni
Lower Permian, Lebach, Germany

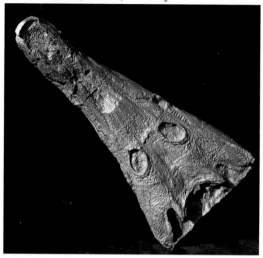

Actinodon □ ●

LOWER PERMIAN

The genus *Actinodon* has a skull which narrows at the front, with a blunt rostrum and orbits which have moved to the front part of the back half of the skull. The ventral armor consists of narrow oblong plates which are pointed at either end. The genus *Actinodon* dates back to the Lower Permian in Europe.

'Branchiosaurus' □ ●

UPPER CARBONIFEROUS – LOWER PERMIAN

This is a very primitive, small amphibian. The skull is short and the spinal column is only slightly ossified. Some of the other parts of the skeleton, e.g., the radial and tarsal bones, consist of cartilage, and have therefore not survived. Although a separate group was initially created for branchiosaurians, their position in the systematic classification was not entirely clear in the order. Some developed from larvae into mature specimens by means of metamorphosis. However, in some other, there was a process of neoteny, in which the characteristics of a lower stage of the specimen, i.e., the larva, remain unchanged up to the mature stage (in many fossils of the genus *'Branchiosaurus'* there are clear traces of external gills). Nowadays, it appears that branchiosauruians were closely related to the genus *Eryops*, another well- known and widespread genus of amphibians in the order of Temnospondyli. The genus *'Branchiosaurus'* lived in Europe and North America at the end of the Carboniferous and the start of the Permian. The specimens of the species *'Branchiosaurus' petrolei* shown here are approximately 3.5 cm (1¼ in) long.

Order: Temnospondyli

LOWER CARBONIFEROUS – LOWER CRETACEOUS

The body still resembles that of a fish, but in many species it is dorsoventrally flattened like the head. Species which adapted to life on land developed strong, short limbs. However, the majority of these primitive amphibians lived mainly in water, and their limbs were reduced.

'Branchiosaurus' petrolei
Lower Permian, Autun, France

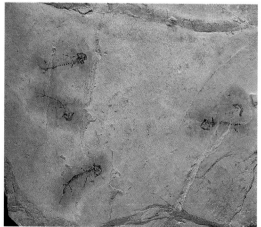

Archegosaurus □

LOWER PERMIAN

Juvenile specimens of the genus *Archegosaurus* are characterized by a triangular head, but in mature specimens the rostrum is considerably elongated. The orbits are small and the nasal openings are at the front edge of the snout. The ventral armor consists of small, overlapping, keel-shaped scales. The genus *Archegosaurus* was aquatic and fed on fish. It is found in Lower Permian deposits in Europe.

Parotosuchus □

TRIASSIC

Mature representatives of the genus *Parotosuchus* have an oblong triangular head with small orbits and small nasal openings which have been moved to the front edge of the skull. The changes in the proportions of the skull during their ontogenetic development can be clearly seen in the representatives of the genus. In juvenile specimens the skull has a parabolic circumference and a short rostrum, while the part in front of the orbits is elongated in mature specimens. Representatives of the genus *Parotosuchus* have been found in Triassic sediments in Europe, Asia, Africa, North America and Australia.

Wetlugasaurus □

LOWER TRIASSIC

This genus is not very large and is similar to the genus *Capitosaurus*. Representatives are characterized by a parabolic skull in which the section in front of the orbits is clearly elongated.

On the sides of the skull, the system of canals containing the sensitive sensory cells is clearly visible. The nasal openings are elongated and the frontal

Parotosuchus aliciae
Lower Triassic, Queensland, Australia

bone does not extend to the edges of the orbits. The spinal column and the bones of the limbs were not completely ossified. Representatives of the genus *Wetlugasaurus*, which lived in water, have been found in Lower Triassic sediments in Eastern Europe and Greenland.

Wetlugasaurus angustifrons, top view
Lower Triassic, Eastern Europe

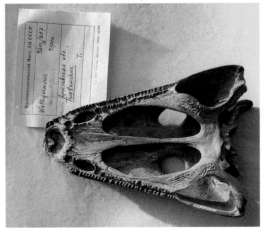

Wetlugasaurus angustifrons, bottom view
Lower Triassic, Eastern Europe

271

Order: Anthracosauria

UPPER DEVONIAN – UPPER PERMIAN

This order includes amphibians with a long body and short limbs. The oldest reptiles developed from this group. In the representatives of amphibians which lived in water at a later stage, the limbs are often reduced.

Greererpeton □

LOWER CARBONIFEROUS

The genus *Greererpeton* is the extremely primitive representative of the genus *Anthracosaurus*. It is characterized by an oblong body, a large number of vertebrae which cross over (approximately forty) and relatively short, weak limbs. The flattened skull with orbits placed far forwards is extremely primitive, and is reminiscent of the related genus *Ichthyostega*. The genus *Greererpeton* was one of the very first representatives of the transition to life on land, although it subsequently returned to the water. *Greererpeton*, which grew to an estimated length of 1.5 (5 ft), inhabited freshwater marshes in North America during the Lower Carboniferous period.

Discosauriscus □ ●

LOWER PERMIAN

Representatives of the genus *Discosauriscus* are very well-known amphibians in the suborder of Seymouriamorpha. In individual specimens the shape of the skull reveals a great deal of morphological diversity, which is partly caused by the process of fossilization. However, in the past, these amphibians were therefore subdivided into a number of genera and species.

However, recent studies have revealed that the number of these taxa is much smaller. The genus *Discosauriscus* could grow to a length of approximately 50 cm (19½ in), and had a flat triangular skull with clearly grooved bones covering the skull.

Greererpeton burkenmorani
Lower Carboniferous, Virginia, United States

Discosauriscus austriacus
Lower Permian, Kochov – Horka, Czech Republic

The long body was carried by limbs which were not very strong. The radial and tarsal bones probably consisted of cartilage, because they have not survived. The long strong tail had a striking line of fins, which were used for swimming. It is interesting that the majority of representatives that have been described are juvenile specimens. The most important of these were the representatives of the species *Discosauriscus austriacus* and *Discosauriscus pulcherrimus*, which were described and also studied in recent years in world-famous locations dating from the Lower Permian, the quarries of Boskovice in Moravia (Czech Republic). The skull of the species *Discosauriscus austriacus* shown here is 3 cm (1¼ in) long.

Subclass: Lissamphibia

LOWER TRIASSIC – RECENT TIMES

The subclass Lissamphibia comprises a large range of modern amphibians (more than 4000 species), which are divided into three orders. Representatives of the orders Salientia (Ecaudata) and Urodela (Caudata) are described here.

Discosauriscus austriacus
Lower Permian, Drválovice, Czech Republic

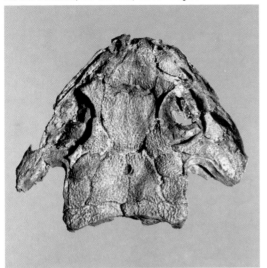

Triadobatrachus massinoti
Lower Triassic, Madagascar

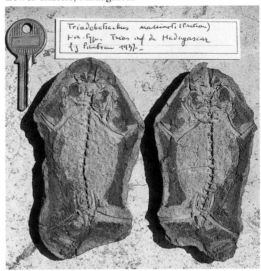

Order: Salientia (Ecaudata) – frogs and Toads

LOWER TRIASSIC – RECENT TIMES

This is a group of extremely organized amphibians whose uniform appearance is the result of their specific lifestyle. Salientia have a relatively short, thickset body, a semicircular or semi-elliptical flat head, large orbits, short front and long rear limbs, and a small number of vertebrae (sometimes only five). They first appeared at the beginning of the Triassic, approximately 225 million years ago, and this well-adapted group is still very widespread today.

Triadobatrachus ☐ ●

LOWER TRIASSIC

The genus *Triadobatrachus* could be distinguished by a characteristic frog skull with striking orbits. The frontal and occipital bones were fused together in a single element separated by a suture (*frontoparietal suture*). This distinguished *Triadobatrachus* from the amphibians of the subclass of Labyrinthodontia. The spinal column consisted of a total of 21 vertebrae. All the vertebrae, except for the last five (postsacral) vertebrae were connected to ribs. Neither the bones of the upper forelimb, nor those of the tibia, were fused, and in this way *Triadobatrachus* could be distinguished from true frogs. This indicates that the genus *Triadobatrachus* had both primitive characteristics (free ribs, bones in the upper limb and the tibia which were not fused), and specialized characteristics (the fused frontoparietal suture, the toothless bone of the lower jaw, the reduced number of uncrossed vertebrae (fourteen)).

Triadobatrachus was probably aquatic but was certainly also able to move over land. This is the oldest known representative of the order of Salientia, and has been found in Lower Triassic sediments of Madagascar.

Eodiscoglossus ☐

UPPER JURASSIC

The genus *Eodiscoglossus* comprises small frogs with eight vertebrae. They were not able to rotate the radial bones. The genus *Eodiscoglossus* comprises the oldest representatives of frogs in the family of Eodiscoglossidae, which have been found in fine-grained limestone in Spain. A specimen of the species *Eodiscoglossus santonjae* in the illustration measures approximately 2.8 cm (1 in).

Eodiscoglossus santonjae
Upper Jurassic, Montsech, Spain

273

Latonia seyfriedi
Middle Miocene, Öhningen, Germany

Palaeobatrachus grandipes
Upper Oligocene, Bechlejovice, Czech Republic

Latonia ●

OLIGOCENE – PLEISTOCENE

The genus *Latonia* comprises terrestrial turtles which could grow to a length of 20 cm (7³/₄ in). The surface of the bones covering the skull was clearly grooved, they had small shoulder blades and long hind limbs. Frogs of the genus *Latonia* lived in Europe from the Oligocene to the Pleistocene. The specimen of the species *Latonia seyfriedi* shown here is approximately 20 cm long (7³/₄ in).

Palaeobatrachus □

UPPER CRETACEOUS – PLIOCENE

The genus *Palaeobatrachus* has a frontoparietal bone consisting of one piece without any grooves. It has developed nine vertebrae. The bottom vertebrae have not fused with the urostyl. (This stick-like element is an extension of the spinal column and is the result of the fusion of the fifth and sixth vertebrae.) The fingers on the fore and hind limbs are very long. These frogs were exclusively aquatic and therefore fossilized representatives are often found. Larvae are also found very frequently. The genus *Palaeobatrachus* lived from the Upper Cretaceous to the Pliocene. Representatives have been found in Europe and North America.

Eopelobates ●

EOCENE – PLIOCENE

The large frogs of the genus *Eopelobates*, which grew to a size of approximately 12 cm (4³/₄ in), had a flat or dorsally convex skull. The frontoparietal bone is grooved, and the sculpture is more clearly visible towards the lateral sides of the bone. These were terrestrial frogs which only went into the water to mate and lay eggs. For this reason complete mature specimens are very rarely found, and it is more common to find the larvae. The genus *Eopelobates* lived in Europe from the Eocene to the Pliocene.

Bufo ●

MIDDLE PALAEOCENE – RECENT TIMES

Like other toads, the genus *Bufo* is characterized by a thick-set body with short limbs. The jaws do not have any teeth and there are at most eight vertebrae, though this number can fluctuate slightly when some vertebrae fuse together. There are no free ribs, as these have fused with the transverse extremities of the vertebrae. Possible ancestors or these toads have been found in Lower and Middle Jurassic sediments. It seems probable that the first real toads appeared at the end of the Cretaceous. After the break-up of Gondwana at the end of the Mesozoic, there were probably two centers where the toad family developed in areas of South

Eopelobates anthracinus
Upper Oligocene, Rott, Germany

Bufo sp.
Miocene, Ardèche, France

America and Africa. The oldest fossilized representatives of the genus *Bufo* have been found in stony deposits dating from the Middle Paleocene in Brazil, from where they gradually penetrated to Europe via North America and Asia. The South African representatives remained restricted to that continent. During the course of evolution, toads increasingly adapted to a terrestrial lifestyle. The specimen of the genus *Bufo* shown here measures 11.6 cm (4¹/₂ in).

Rana   □ ●

OLIGOCENE – RECENT TIMES

The genus *Rana* belongs to a group of frogs which is very well adapted to hopping. It is characterized by a slender body and long hind legs. The size of these frogs varies enormously. In addition to small and average-sized species, there are also large species. Some recent representatives reached sizes of up to 20 cm (7³/₄ in), without including the limbs. Frogs of the genus *Rana* are found in many biotopes. Some species are limited to aquatic environments and shores, while others are found in dryer areas. Up to now, approximately fifty fossilized species of the genus *Rana* have been recorded. The oldest date back from the Eocene. They are very frequently found in stony deposits dating from the Pliocene and the Pleistocene. The specimen shown here, which belongs to the species *Rana aquensis*, measures 3.5 cm (1¹/₄ in).

Rana aquensis
Oligocene, province of Cereste, France

275

Chelotriton ogygius
Upper Oligocene, Germany

Order: Urodela (Caudata) – Salamanders

MIDDLE JURASSIC – RECENT TIMES

This is a group of well-known amphibians, which includes representatives that have survived up to the present day, such as, e.g., the salamander and the cave salamander. The skull is usually flat, broad and relatively short. The eyes are large and covered with the whole lids, but may also be small and rudimentary, and are often covered with skin. The teeth are small, conical and pointed. The elongated body is naked and the tail can have different lengths. The limbs are weak, short, and in some cases, completely absent.

Chelotriton □

EOCENE – PLIOCENE

The genus *Chelotriton* represents an important genus of salamander-like amphibians. Until recently, it was known only on the basis of vertebrae, and the cranial bones, which were difficult to identify. A characteristic sculpture of bosses can be found on the cranial bones and the dorsal horizontal planes of the neural spines of the last vertebrae. The ribs are also characteristic, with one or more dorsal spines to support glands in the skin. Complete specimens that were found recently confirm the view that du-

ring the Neogene there were at least two species of this genus in Europe. The genus *Chelotriton* lived in areas of Europe from the Eocene to the Pliocene.

Amniota

UPPER CARBONIFEROUS – RECENT TIMES

The amniota, which include reptiles, birds and mammals, are defined on the basis of their embryonic development. One of the characteristics of these animals is the presence of three amnoitic membranes, which serve to protect the embryo from drying out. The embryo is usually enclosed in a calcareous or leathery egg together with the amniotic membranes.

Class: Reptilia – reptiles

UPPER CARBONIFEROUS – RECENT TIMES

Reptiles are amongst the largest terrestrial vertebrates. They can be distinguished from amphibians by many characteristics, both as regards their development and as regards ecology.

The following characteristics are typical of reptiles: most have a changing body temperature (they are cold-blooded, *ectothermic*), although some reptiles with mammalian characteristics, and probably also the dinosaurs, had a regular body temperature like birds and mammals (in other words, they were warm-blooded, *endothermic*); the body is covered with a dry skin with horny scales, plates or armor. However, the body of reptiles with mammalian characteristics was probably covered with a fleece. Only insignificant glands developed in the skin; the virtually entirely ossified skeleton has a spinal column with a clearly defined neck area. The skull is usually connected to the spinal column by only one joint (a few lines which evolved towards the mammals are an exception to this); the development is direct, without metamorphosis (reptiles never developed gills), the veins and arteries to the heart are better distributed than in amphibians; the eggs have a shell, and ·the embryo inside is protected by amniotic membranes which ensure that it does not dry out.

In comparison with the flat skull of amphibians, the skull of reptiles is higher and narrower. Important changes took place in the area of the temples, usually containing the striking openings behind the orbits. These probably developed as a result of the enlargement of the muscles used for chewing and the increase in the size of the skull. In places where the cranial bones (dermal bones) touch, there can be triangular slits and areas or *fontanels*. Because of the increase in size of the muscles used for chewing, the fontanel was not closed at the place of contact with three bones, resulting in a permanent opening there. The muscles used for chewing could be compressed in this space when the jaws shut or the muscles contracted. As these muscles increased in size, the opening became larger. This facilitated che-

the second largest groups of terrestrial vertebrates (approx. 6,000 species), but they are a long way from the success achieved during the Mesozoic era. Fossilized representatives of the oldest reptiles are very rare. The genus *Hylonomus*, one of the oldest reptiles, dates from the beginning of the Upper Carboniferous and has been found in North America. Fossils of larger specimens of the species Pelycosaurus dating from the Upper Carboniferous are more numerous. A representative of the well-known species *Edaphosaurus* has been found both in Zbyšov in Moravia and in the Plzeň basin. Nowadays, reptiles are divided into three subclasses. Representatives of the subclasses Anapsida and Diapsida are described here.

Subclass: Anapsida

UPPER CARBONIFEROUS – RECENT TIMES

This is a group of primitive reptiles characterized by the fact that there are no opening in the skull behind the orbits (*anapsid type*). Altogether it includes three classes in which the order of Chelonia (turtles) is the best known.

Order: Chelonia (Testudines) – turtles

UPPER TRIASSIC – RECENT TIMES

This is an old group of reptiles which have not evolved significantly. The short, flattened body is protected by a characteristic *bony armor*, into which the animal can withdraw with its head, neck, limbs and tail. The shell consists of a dorsal section (carapax) and a ventral section (*plastron*). It consists of a large number of plates made of bony tissue. The surface is covered with smaller horny plates. Turtles were originally terrestrial, but some have returned to the water. The first turtles appeared during the Upper Triassic and turtles are still fairly common today.

Trionyx ☐

CRETACEOUS – RECENT TIMES

The genus *Trionyx* belongs to the true turtles, a group of fairly large animals in which the shell can grow to a size of almost 1 m (39 in). The shell is flat and strongly reduced. In recent representatives it is flexible and covered with a leathery skin. The skull is considerably elongated with large orbits. The limbs have large claws. The genus *Trionyx*, which has survived up to the present day, already existed in the Cretaceous period in Europe, Asia, Africa and North America. This genus is no longer found in Europe today. The complete shell of the species *Trionyx* cf. *rostratus* shown here measures 16 cm (6¼ in).

wing and increased the pressure of the jaws. The shape of the openings and the position of the skull are related to the development of the muscles of the jaw, and can differ in different groups.

The teeth of most reptiles are conical, have no roots and are replaced by new teeth throughout life. In some fossils they are flat or knobby, and lizards (Sauria) and snakes (Serpents) also have teeth in the palate. Turtles have a horny beak instead of teeth. The partial differentiation of the teeth (a distinction based on function) can be seen in some of the higher reptiles with mammalian characteristics. Even in the order of Pelycosauria, some species developed one stronger tooth which separated the front incisors from the undifferentiated "cheek teeth" at the back. The development of reptiles, which are direct ancestors of birds and mammals, is clearly important. They first appeared during the Upper Carboniferous, but their unbelievable development took place during the Mesozoic. They were the dominant group of animals on earth for a period of more than 165 million years. During the transition from Mesozoic to Cenozoic there was a crisis in their development, probably as a result of enormous climate changes related to changes. It is probable that the collision of an asteroid during the transition from the Cretaceous to the Tertiary accelerated their rapid extinction. Although only a few species survived up to the Tertiary, there was a new expansion of species during that period. Nowadays, reptiles are

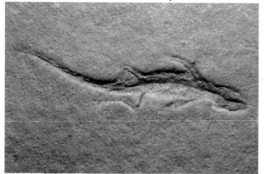

Subclass: Diapsida

UPPER CARBONIFEROUS – RECENT TIMES

This subclass is characterized by two openings behind the orbits. On the basis of the structure of the shell, the genus *Petrolacosaurus*, a reptile approximately 40 cm (15³/₄ in) long, dating from the Upper Carboniferous in North America, was considered as the most primitive representative of the subclass of Diapsida for a long time. However, the latest research shows that the oldest diapsids developed from a group of reptiles which have an anapsid type of skull, and were therefore mistakenly classified as representatives of the subclass Anapsida on the basis of this characteristic.

Infraclass: Lepidosauromorpha

UPPER PERMIAN – RECENT TIMES

This includes the genus *Sphenodon*, present-day lizards, snakes and their extinct representatives, including the two main groups of aquatic reptiles (the orders Nothosauria and Plesiosauria).

Superorder: Lepidosauria

UPPER PERMIAN – RECENT TIMES

The Lepidosauria are usually characterized by an elongated body covered with scales and a diapsid type of skull (with two openings behind the orbits). Other groups of reptiles, e.g., crocodiles, flying reptiles and dinosaurs, also have this type of skull. However, the Lepidosauria can mainly be distinguished by the presence of a large sternum. Their development started during the Permian and they are still extremely common today. According to the latest systems of classification, the Lepidosauria can be classified in three orders. Representatives of the orders of Sphenodonta and Squamata are described here.

Order: Sphenodonta

LOWER TRIASSIC – RECENT TIMES

These are average-sized reptiles which resemble lizards. However, they also have primitive characteristics, such as *amphicell vertebrae* (these vertebrae have hollows at the front and back), the presence of ventral ribs as a remnant of the ventral shield and a clearly visible *crown eye*. The teeth are *acrodont*, which means that they grow directly on the upper edge of the jaw. This group reached its peak during the Middle Triassic. From then on it became smaller, and nowadays there is only one species, a truly living fossil, the New Zealand tuatera.

Homoeosaurus ●

UPPER JURASSIC

The genus *Homoeosaurus* includes small terrestrial reptiles. They are related to the present day tuatera, which is characterized by an extremely long tail. Some specimens grew to a length of about 20 cm (7³/₄ in). Representatives of the genus *Homoeosaurus* lived in Europe during the Upper Jurassic. The specimen shown here belongs to the species *Homoeosaurus pulchellus* and is approximately 10 cm long.

Pleurosaurus ■

UPPER JURASSIC– LOWER CRETACEOUS

The genus *Pleurosaurus* represents primitive aquatic reptiles which have developed a long snake-like body with a large number of vertebrae and a strikingly long tail. The skull is elongated and the neck of the spinal column is short. The limbs, particularly the forelimbs are very short and unsuitable for moving over land. The genus *Pleurosaurus* lived in Europe from the Upper Jurassic to the Lower Cretaceous. The specimen shown here, which belongs to the genus *Pleurosaurus,* is approximately 73 cm (28³/₄ in) long.

Order: Squamata – scaly reptiles

UPPER PERMIAN – RECENT TIMES

One of the most important characteristics of this order is the kinetic skull, which means that a large number of bones in the skull are connected by joints or joint ligaments. This means that the skull is very elastic so that it is possible to devour relatively large prey. Snakes in particular have developed this sort of skull. Scaly reptiles constitute a diverse group with numerous species; together with turtles and crocodiles, they are the only reptiles to have survived up to the present day.

Eichstaettisaurus ●

UPPER JURASSIC

The small gecko of the genus *Eichstaettisaurus* is mainly characterized by a large head rounded at the front with large orbits close together. The jaws contained a large number of small teeth. The limbs were short and the soles of the fore and hind limbs were just as long as the shoulder and thigh bones. Like the present day gecko, the genus *Eichstaettisaurus* was also able to break off its tail in case of danger. Its lifestyle was probably also similar to that of present-day geckos. The large orbits reveal that it is active at night. It mainly fed on insects and spiders. The genus *Eichstaettisaurus* has been recorded in Upper Jurassic strata in Europe and is particularly common in the lithographic limestone of Solnhofen. The specimen shown here, which belongs to the genus *Eichstaettisaurus,* measures 19.5 cm (7¹/₂ in) long.

Eichstaettisaurus sp.
Upper Jurassic, Solnhofen, Germany

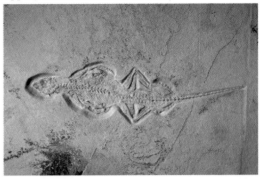

Mosasaurus ■

UPPER CRETACEOUS

The genus *Mosasaurus* is a representative of a group which is related to the Varanidae. It has adapted extremely successfully to marine life. The lizard-like body was approximately 12 m (39 ft) long, and the strong tail was the most important organ for locomotion. The pointed oblong skull was flattened dorsoventrally and the large orbits were far to the back. The spinal column consisted of a large number of vertebrae (up to 135), the limbs had changed into fins with a large number of joints in each digit. The Mosasaurus was one of the most feared predators in the seas of the Upper Cretaceous. The genus *Mosasaurus* lived in Europe, Africa and North America.

Mosasaurus sp.
Upper Cretaceous, Dolní Újezd, Czech Republic

Coluber sp.
Upper Miocene, Ardèche, France

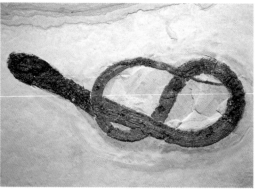

Viperidae gen. et sp. indet.
Miocene – recent, St. Bouzile, Ardèche, France

Coluber ●

LOWER MIOCENE – RECENT TIMES

Representatives of the genus *Coluber* belonged to the family of smooth snakes, one of the largest groups nowadays. The skull of the genus *Coluber* does not have any fangs, and the spinal column consists of numerous vertebrae which are convex at the front. In these snakes the limbs have been reduced. Smooth snakes are not only usually missing shoulder blades, but there is no trace either of any pelvic bones. Fossilized representatives of the smooth snake of the genus *Coluber,* like the majority of the representatives living today, were probably able to move around very easily and lived in hot, dry biotopes.

The oldest representatives of the genus *Coluber* to be identified with certainty were found in Lower Miocene sediments. Nowadays, this genus is found in Eurasia, Africa, North and Central America. The

specimen of the genus *Coluber* shown here is 18.6 cm (7¼ in) long.

Family Viperidae ●

LOWER MIOCENE – RECENT TIMES

Adders (Viperidae) are a very widespread group of poisonous or very poisonous snakes which are nowadays found in many different areas. They are usually characterized by a robust body with a short, broad head that it more or less triangular as seen from the top. The most characteristic feature of the head is the presence of large fangs in the upper jaw, which are part of a complete poison system. As in other snakes, the spinal column consists of a large number of vertebrae which are strongly compressed, as seen from the front. There is no sign of any limbs. The oldest adders appeared immediately after the start of the Miocene (like the other poisonous snakes, such as the cobras), and soon spread widely. Nowadays, adders are found in Europe (the species *Vipera berus* is even found near the Arctic Circle), Asia and Africa. The adder in the illustration is 13 cm (5¼ in) long.

Superorder: Sauropterygia

UPPER PERMIAN – UPPER CRETACEOUS

This class of reptiles is perfectly adapted to marine life. With this class, the adaptation of reptiles, which were originally terrestrial, reached its peak for life in an aquatic environment. The body was compressed and the tail often strongly reduced. Sauropterygia flourished in two periods: first in the Middle Triassic and subsequently in the Upper Cretaceous. Species in the Upper Cretaceous could grow to lengths of 12 m (39 ft) (*Elasmosaurus*). Nowadays, we distinguish three orders.

Placodus sp.
Middle Triassic, Germany

Keichousaurus hui
Middle Triassic, Ghuizou, China

Order: Placodontia

LOWER TRIASSIC – UPPER TRIASSIC

Placodontia are a special group of amphibian reptiles which looked for food in the seas and rested or laid their eggs on land. Their body was almost 2 m (6 ft 6 in) long, and they had a strong tail. The most interesting characteristic of the oldest Placodontia is the strong knobby teeth or plates covered with dentine. Placodontia specialized in catching marine mollusks and shellfish and their teeth served to crush the hard shells. Their position in the system of classification is not entirely clear.

Placodus ■ ●

MIDDLE-TRIASSIC – UPPER TRIASSIC

The genus *Placodus* is the best-known representative of the Placodontia. It could grow to a length of about 2 m (6ft 6 in), and hunted in the shallow coastal waters of the Middle to the Upper Triassic period in Europe.

Order: Nothosauria – nothosaurians

MIDDLE TRIASSIC – UPPER TRIASSIC

This order comprises marine reptiles 3.5 m (11 ft 6 in) long with an elongated body and a long, sinuously curved neck. The head was long, flat and narrow. There were long sharp teeth in the jaws. The limbs were short and strong with webbed membranes between the fingers and toes. The nothosaurians lived in shallow coastal waters, where they fed on fish.

Keichosaurus ■

MIDDLE TRIASSIC

The *Keichosaurus* could grow to a maximum length of 30 cm (12 in). It had a relatively short tri-

angular skull which was clearly broader in the area behind the orbits, and a pointed snout with undifferentiated teeth. The length of the forelimbs corresponded more or less with the length of the hind limbs or they were slightly longer. Fossilized specimens of the genus *Keichosaurus* have been found in Middle Triassic sediments in Europe (Germany) and Asia (China). The illustration shows a specimen of the species *Keichosaurus hui*, which is 24 cm (9¹/₂ in) long.

Pachypleurosaurus ■

MIDDLE TRIASSIC

The small skull and body with a neck and tail of average length are characteristic of the genus *Pachypleurosaurus*. The relatively slight extent of ossification of the limbs indicates that this genus lived in an aquatic environment. It moved along using its tail, which was flattened on either side. The *Pachypleurosaurus*, which could grow to a length of 1.2 m (4 ft), lived in Europe during the Middle Triassic period.

Pachypleurosaurus edwardei
Middle Triassic, Besano, Italy

Nothosaurus ∎

TRIASSIC

A long body with a long, S-shaped curved neck and a narrow, flat, long head are characteristic of the reptiles of the genus *Nothosaurus*. The long, sharp, notched teeth are well adapted to hunting fish. The limbs are short and strong, and the fingers and toes were webbed. Representatives of the genus *Nothosaurus* have been found in Triassic sediments in Europe, Southeast Asia and America. The illustration shows a tooth measuring 2.3 cm (1 in), which belongs to a specimen of the genus *Nothosaurus*.

Order: Plesiosauria – plesiosaurs

UPPER TRIASSIC – LOWER CRETACEOUS

This genus comprises healthy marine lizards that had adapted to marine life so successfully that their limbs changed into powerful paddles. The phenomenon of *hyperphalangia*, an increase in the number of joints in the digits, is characteristic of plesiosaurs. They reached a peak in the Cretaceous.

Plesiosaurus ∎

MIDDLE JURASSIC – UPPER JURASSIC

The genus *Plesiosaurus* comprises marine lizards with a long neck and small head. The limbs had changed into powerful paddles. The increased number of joints in the digits is characteristic of this genus. The *Plesiosaurus* fed on fish and existed in large numbers in Europe during the Middle and Upper Jurassic.

Infraclass: Archosauromorpha

UPPER PERMIAN – RECENT TIMES

This class comprises several different groups of diapsid reptiles. The most important and best known is the superclass of Archosauria. Their evolution during the course of the Triassic was essential for the later evolution of terrestrial vertebrates.

Superclass: Archosauria

UPPER PERMIAN – RECENT TIMES

This large group of reptiles, which was extremely widespread in the past, have a diapsid type of skull just like scaly reptiles. They also have progressive characteristics, such as a *thecondont* dentition (teeth are placed in sockets) – and only the most primitive genera have teeth in the palate. The method of locomotion usually uses two feet (i.e., these reptiles move on their two hind legs)

Order: Thecodontia

UPPER PERMIAN – LOWER JURASSIC

From the phylogenetic point of view, Thecodontia are a very important group of carnivorous or insectivorous reptiles which spread extensively in a relatively short time. They probably gave rise to other groups such as crocodiles pterosaurs and dinosaurs. The origin of Thecodontia is still not entirely certain. They appeared in the Upper Permian and reached the peak of their development during the Triassic.

Rutiodon sp.
Upper Triassic, Apache County, Arizona, United States

Longisquama insignis
Middle Triassic, Turkestan, Kazakhstan

Rutiodon □ ●

UPPER TRIASSIC

The genus *Rutiodon* belongs to a group of reptiles which closely resembled the later crocodiles because of the shape of their body and lifestyle, although these are not their direct ancestors. The nasal openings on the extremely long skull were placed far to the back, distinguishing the genus *Rutiodon* from crocodiles. The crocodile-like body was covered with strong, armor-like plates which often protected it entirely. The limbs were short, and the hind limbs were even shorter than the forelimbs. The genus *Rutiodon* lived in Europe, North America and probably also southern Asia during the Upper Triassic. The larger of the two teeth shown here, which belong to the genus *Rutiodon*, is 4 cm (1¹/₂ in) long.

Longisquama ●

MIDDLE TRIASSIC

The genus *Longisquama* is an unusual reptile, which belongs to the Thecodontia. The body was covered with overlapping scales that were keeled. The scales were extremely elongated on the back. It is still thought that these scales may have been a stage in the evolution of feathers, and this remains a subject of discussion. It is also possible that they served to break the creature's fall. The genus *Longisquama* lived in Asia during the Middle Triassic.

Sharovipteryx ●

UPPER TRIASSIC

The genus is a curious thecodontic reptile with wings on the hind limbs. An examination of the bones shows that *Sharovipteryx* was not an active flyer but actually glided through the air. The forelimbs were very small and according to some paleontologists they were not suited to climbing up trees very easily. It is possible that *Sharovipteryx* moved by making leaps and increased the length of its flights with the help of its wings, as in the case of present day flying squirrels. The genus *Sharovipteryx* lived in Asia during the Upper Triassic.

Sharovipteryx mirabilis
Upper Triassic, Kirgizistan, Russia

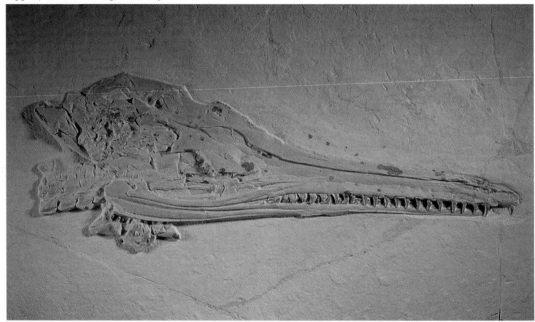

Order: Crocodilia – crocodiles

UPPER TRIASSIC – RECENT TIMES

Crocodiles are the only group of archosaurian reptiles that survived the crisis at the time of the transition from the Mesozoic to the Cenozoic era in Europe, North America, and probably also in South Asia. They probably developed from the Thecodontia at the end of the Triassic. They are a relatively conservative group, because recent representatives are not very different from fossilized specimens. The lifestyle of crocodiles is extremely similar to that of

Metriorhynchus superciliosus
Middle Jurassic, Villers-sur-Mer, France

their ecological predecessors –the fytosauruses, and they were usually amphibian. Modern reptiles have reached the peak as regards their physical organization.

Geosaurus ■

UPPER JURASSIC – LOWER CRETACEOUS

The genus *Geosaurus* is altogether very similar to the genus *Metriorhynchius*. The long skull was well adapted to catching fish, the jaws contained a large number of small pointed teeth. The forelimbs were very short. The genus *Geosaurus* lived from the Upper Jurassic to the Lower Cretaceous, and fossils have been found in Europe and South America. The skull of the species *Geosaurus* cf. *suevicus* shown here measures 35 cm (13³/₄ in).

Metriorhynchius ■

MIDDLE JURASSIC – UPPER JURASSIC

Like the genus Geosaurus, the genus *Metriorhynchus*, is a representative of so- called "marine crocodiles", which were perfectly adapted to marine life. *Metriorhynchus* had paddle-like limbs and it also had a tail which was similar to that of marine lizards. The genus *Metriorhynchus* could grow to a length of 2.5 m (8 ft 3 in), and lived in Europe and South America during the Middle to Upper Jurassic. The specimen illustrated here measures 7 cm (2³/₄ in).

Goniopholis □ ●

UPPER JURASSIC – LOWER CRETACEOUS

Crocodiles of the genus *Goniopholis* have a skull which is fairly similar to that of some of the specimens still found today. The skull is less elongated than in the specialized aquatic species. As in other crocodiles, the teeth are serrated lengthwise. The vertebrae have a primitive structure. The genus *Goniopholis* lived from the Upper Jurassic to the Lower Cretaceous in areas of Europe, Southeast Asia and probably also in North America. The largest of the teeth shown here, which belong to the genus *Goniopholis*, measures 1.3 cm ($^1/_2$ in).

Alligator □ ▣ ●

EOCENE – RECENT TIMES

The genus *Alligator* belongs to the crocodiles of the large subfamily Alligatorinae, which comprises 21 fossilized genera, and lived from the Upper Cretaceous to the present day. Alligators have a short, broad mouth. Characteristically they have a hollow on both sides of the upper edge of the skull. The fourth teeth of the lower jaw fit into this when the jaws close. In this way they cannot be seen when the mouth is closed, like the other teeth. Representatives of the genus *Alligator* which have survived up to the present day date back to the Eocene

Gonioholis sp.
Lower Cretaceous, Sehnde, Germany

and examples have been found in Europe, Asia and North and South America. The specimen shown here, which belongs to the genus *Alligator*, measures 79.5 cm ($31^1/_4$ in).

Alligator sp.
Eocene, Wyoming, United States

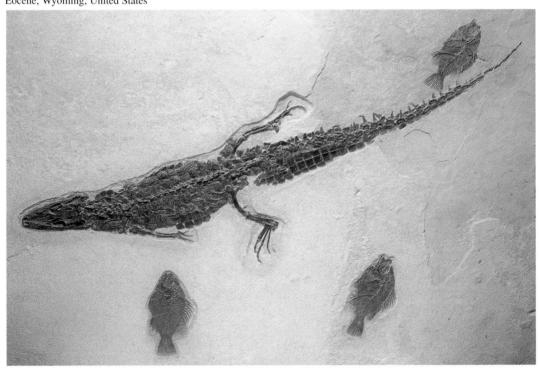

Order: Pterosauria – pterosaurs

UPPER TRIASSIC – UPPER CRETACEOUS

These diapsid reptiles had a body which was excellently adapted to flying. Like bats, they had membranous wings though this was only stretched between the body and the considerably elongated fourth finger. The short, thick body of these pterosaurs was covered with a woolly coat and it is possible that they were warm-blooded. The original small species dating from the Jurassic developed into the largest flying creatures of all time (*Quetzalcoatlus*, with a wingspan estimated at 11–12 m//36–39 ft).

Rhamphorhynchus ●

UPPER JURASSIC

The genus *Rhamphorhynchus* is one of the primitive representatives of pterosaurs which retained its long tail. The jaws of this genus have a large number of pointed teeth. The body was insulated by a woolly coat. The genus *Rhamphorhynchus* probably fed on fish, could grow to a length of 40–60 cm (15³/₄–23¹/₂ in) and had a wingspan of 1.8 m (6 ft). It lived in areas of Europe and East Africa during the Upper Jurassic. The specimen shown here belongs to the species *Rhamphorhynchus intermedius* and is approximately 30 cm (12 in) long.

Pterodactylus

UPPER JURASSIC

The genus *Pterodactylus* is a representative of one of the smaller pterosaurs in the Pterodactylidae family, in which the teeth were gradually replaced by a horny beak. A mature *Pterodactylus* was approximately the size of a thrush or a duck. There were teeth only in the upper part of the jaw, and the wings had a span of 25–50 cm (9³/₄–19¹/₂ in). In some specimens of the genus *Pterodactylus* the membranes of the wings and other soft tissues have survived, as well as the bones. The *Pterodactylus* was probably able to fly normally. Its small size and small teeth suggest that it hunted for prey that was not too large. The representatives which have been found of this genus include juvenile specimens no bigger than a human thumb. The first species of a pterosaur to be described was a *Pterodactylus* which was recorded in 1784. Fossils of pterodactyls have been found in Upper Jurassic sediments in Germany, as well as in France and in East Africa.

Pterodactylus longirostris
Upper Jurassic, Solnhofen, Germany

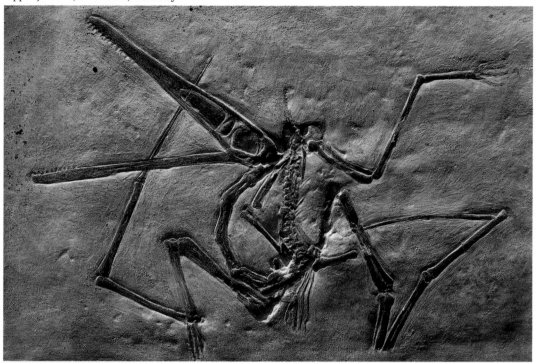

Order: Dinosauria – dinosaurs

MIDDLE TRIASSIC – UPPER CRETACEOUS

The dinosaurs are the very oldest group of fossilized vertebrates. They first appeared during the middle Triassic and were the dominant group of animals for a period of 165 million years. The first dinosaurs were average-sized carnivores with two feet (they walked on their hind limbs). Towards the end of the Triassic the first herbivorous dinosaurs developed which walked on four limbs. The majority of dinosaurs were characterized by their size.

Albertosaurus sp.
Upper Cretaceous, Bug Creek, Montana, United States

Although there are representatives of enormous sizes and weights (up to approximately 100 tons), species have also been found which were no bigger than a cockerel. Dinosaurs were divided into two large groups (suborders) on the basis of the structure of their pelvis – Saurischia (with a reptilian pelvis) and Ornithischia (with a bird-like pelvis). Representatives of Saurischia are described below which include both the largest carnivores and the largest terrestrial animals of all time (so-called sauropods).

Albertosaurus ●

UPPER CRETACEOUS

The genus *Albertosaurus* is included amongst the tyrannosaurs. It grew to approximately the same size as the best-known representative of this carnivorous dinosaur, the genus *Tyrannosaurus*. It was approximately 8 m (26 ft) long, moved on its powerful hind limbs and it had small, rudimentary forelimbs. The jaws of the large skull contained a large number of sharp serrated teeth. The genus *Albertosaurus* lived in areas of North America during the Upper Cretaceous. The tooth shown here belongs to a specimen of the genus *Albertosaurus* and measures 2.2 cm (³/₄ in).

Hypselosaurus ●

UPPER CRETACEOUS

The *Hypselosaurus* belonged to the large Saurischia in the family of Titanosauridae, and it is mainly its eggs which have been perfectly preserved. Fossilized bones of this genus had already been described in the 19th century. They were found in France, and fragments of the eggshells were found as well as bones. The paleontologist P. Matheron, who described the *Hypselosaurus* for the first time in 1869, was not sure whether the shell which had been found belonged to this saurian or to a larger bird unknown up to that time. It was only towards the end of the 1920s that it was possible to prove that the fragments really belonged to the genus *Hypselosaurus* by comparing the microstructure of these eggs with that of dinosaur eggs found in the Gobi desert. This sauropod could grow to a length

of 12 m (39 ft), and like the other titanosaurs, fed on vegetable matter. The larger species of carnivorous dinosaurs were a threat to it. The genus *Hypselosaurus* has been recorded dating from the Upper Cretaceous in Europe (France and Spain). The complete egg of the species *Hypselosaurus priscus* shown in the illustration measures 14.5 cm (5³/₄ in).

Infraclass: Ichthyopterygia – fin lizards

LOWER TRIASSIC – UPPER CRETACEOUS

This is an extremely specialized group of reptiles which is reminiscent of present-day dolphins because of the shape of their body and their lifestyle. They first appeared during the Triassic and were most widespread during the Jurassic. They became extinct before the end of the Cretaceous.

Hypselosaurus priscus
Upper Cretaceous, Aix-en-Provence, France

Stenopterygius sp.
Lower Jurassic, Holzmaden, Germany

Order: Ichthyosauria – fish lizards

LOWER TRIASSIC – UPPER CRETACEOUS

Ichthyosaurs are the only order of fish fins. These are reptiles which were excellently adapted to aquatic life and actively hunted their prey. They had a spool-shaped body without scales. The limbs were modified into fin-like organs. Like fish, these fish lizards also developed a dorsal fin and a strong vertical caudal fin and the spinal column extended into the ventral lobe. The average length of the body was 2–3 m (6 ft 6 in–10 ft).

Stenopterygius ■

LOWER JURASSIC

The fish lizards of the genus *Stenopterygius*, like other fish lizards, had a characteristic fish-like body shape. They had a very long skull, large orbits and many small teeth. The bones of the limbs are short. The large number of joints in the digits is characteristic and the limbs developed like paddles. These adapted organs meant that the animal could only move in water. The many discoveries of female specimens with unborn young reveal that the representatives of the genus *Stenopterygius*, like other fish lizards, bore live young. The genus *Stenopterygius* has been found in Lower Jurassic sediments in Europe. The illustration shows a vertebra of this genus measuring 7.5 cm (3 in).

Archaeopteryx lithographica
Upper Jurassic, Solnhofen, Germany

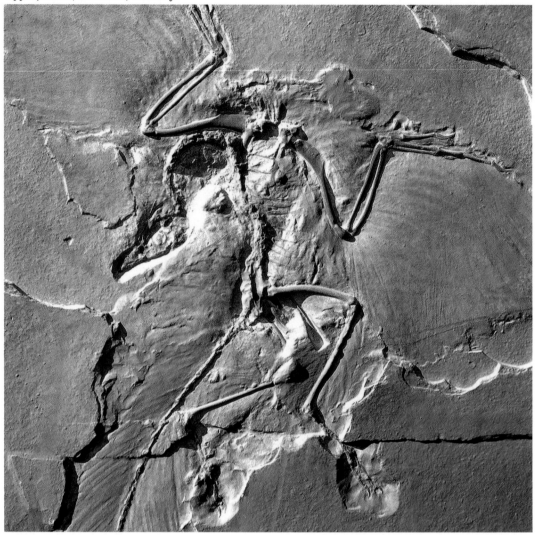

Class: Aves – birds

UPPER JURASSIC – RECENT TIMES

Birds are an interesting and highly specialized group of vertebrates which come in second place in the entire subclass in terms of their numbers. They are usually considered as a class in their own right, but because of the structure of their bones, they are closely related to some of the primitive dinosaurs in the subclass Theropoda. This similarity is particularly striking in primitive extinct species, represented by the genus *Archaeopteryx*. On this basis, some authors link the birds to the reptiles in a common taxon (class), Dinosauria.

However, compared to the ancestors of reptiles, birds had a few very specialized characteristics, the most important of which are: a very different structure of the forelimbs which were changed into wings; the presence of feathers; a functioning right arch of the aorta; a higher level of the central nervous system. For a long time the fact that they were warm-blooded was seen as one of the specific characteristics distinguishing birds from the ancestors of reptiles. This theory fails with regard to the new information that has been obtained about the fact that dinosaurs and Thecodontia were probably warm-blooded. The same applies for the presence of collarbones, which are fused in a specific way, forming a so-called *furcula*.

The *wings* are the original five-fingered forelimbs which are perfectly adapted to flying. In a few groups they were subsequently modified into organs for paddling, and in a group of so-called flightless birds, they were subsequently greatly reduced. There was a lot of reduction in several groups of birds, although flying remained the main method of movement. The development of specific strong muscles is related to flying as well as a considerable reduction in the weight of the body as a result of *air sacs, a high level of pneumaticity of the bones,* an aerodynamic body shape, a rapid metabolism and a high body temperature.

Feathers are a typical but by no means exclusive characteristic of birds. Feathers developed as a result of the modification of the reptile's scales, originally as insulation, to retain heat or probably as insulation against sunshine. The discovery of a reptile of the genus *Longisquama* in aquatic sediments dating from the Middle Triassic in Turkestan proved that feathers originally served a different function from the function of flight. This is also demonstrated by discoveries in Middle Triassic strata in Spain. In addition to feathers, the typical shape of the *furcula* is one of the most important characteristics of birds. For a long time it was mistakenly thought that this bone could only be found in birds. The furcula serves to provide an unusual degree of rigidity and springiness. This is necessary in view of the considerable mechanical efforts made by the forelimbs when birds are flying. In flightless birds, the furcula is often strongly reduced. In a more primitive form the furcula already existed in a few of the reptilian ancestors of birds, (e.g., the genera *Oviraptor, Velociraptor*). The first primitive birds can be traced back to the Upper Jurassic in Europe and Asia, and the first important radiation occurred during the Cretaceous.

Subclass: Sauriurae – primitive birds

UPPER JURASSIC – UPPER CRETACEOUS

This group comprises primitive birds dating back to the Upper Jurassic, which are reminiscent of small biped reptiles in the group of Theropoda. The similarity between these primitive birds and reptiles is so

Confuciusornis sanctus
Upper Jurassic/Lower Cretaceous Yixian, China

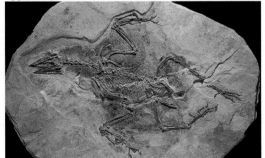

great that for a long time, some of the discoveries of primitive birds which were not accompanied by feathers were identified as reptiles.

Infraclass: Archaeornithes

UPPER JURASSIC – LOWER CRETACEOUS

Nowadays, this comprises two orders- the Archaeopterygiformes (Upper Jurassic) and Confucius ornithiformes (Lower Cretaceous), the representatives of which are described below.

Archaeopteryx ●

UPPER JURASSIC

Up to now, there have been a total of seven discoveries of the genus *Archaeopteryx*, all in lithographic limestone strata dating from the Upper Jurassic in Solnhofen. The limestone was created in a coastal environment where these primitive birds lived more than 150 million years ago. The birds developed during the Jurassic to become small carnivorous dinosaurs. The skeleton of the *Archaeopteryx* can be identified by a combination of characteristics which are generally found in reptiles, such as jaws with teeth, weak forelimbs with three claws, a long tail, and a head covered in scales. However, the body, wings and tail were covered in feathers similar to those of present-day birds. Like the bones of birds, the bones had a certain degree of pneumaticity (though this was limited). The clavicles were fused in a fork, and the thumbs of the hind limbs were rotated back. The pectoral muscles were not fixed and were therefore weak. *Archaeopteryx* could only flap its wings to a limited extent and was capable of making short flights. However, it was certainly not a good flyer, and probably usually moved about more or less horizontally between trees. *Archaeopteryx* fed on small animals. Nowadays, scientists suspect that *Archaeopteryx* represents only a branch in the evolution from reptiles to birds.

Confuciusornis ●

UPPER JURASSIC – LOWER CRETACEOUS

The genus *Confuciusornis* is the oldest known bird to have a beak. No teeth developed in the jaws. The wings had claws, as in *Archaeopteryx*, and the fingers were not connected. The *furcula* was almost identical to the furcula of the *Archaeopteryx*. The sternum was small. The tail of the genus *Confuciusornis* was shorter while the claws were stronger. The genus *Confuciusornis* has been found in sediments dating from the transitional period between the Upper Jurassic and the Lower Cretaceous in China. It is approximately 30 million years younger than *Archaeopteryx*. The specimen of *Confuciusornis sanctus* shown in the illustration measures 31.7 cm (12$^{1}/_{2}$ in).

Corvus sp.
Upper Oligocene, Cereste, France

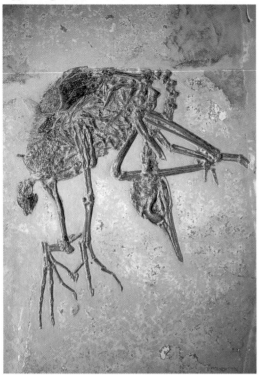

Subclass: Ornithurae – true birds

LOWER CRETACEOUS – RECENT TIMES

Unlike the previous species, representatives of this group have many characteristics which reveal the progress in their evolution, such as the considerably increased size of the brain cavity, the absence of real teeth in the jaws and the development of a horny beak. Horny examples which are reminiscent of teeth have only developed in a few groups. The spinal column of true birds is considerably shortened and the tail is reduced. In all flying birds there is a strong comb on the sternum, which serves for the attachment of the strong pectoral muscles. In the forelimbs there has been some reduction in the numbers of fingers and joints.

Infraclass: Neornhites

LOWER CRETACEOUS – RECENT TIMES

This includes all present-day birds. Only the representatives of the order of Passeriformes (songbirds), one of the most important orders of birds, are described here.

Order: Passeriformes – songbirds

LOWER EOCENE – RECENT TIMES

The most important development of this group of birds started during the earliest period of the Tertiary, and continues today. The oldest representatives date back to the Lower Eocene. From the osteological point of view this group is extremely uniform and therefore we do not know very much about their evolution.

Corvus

UPPER OLIGOCENE – RECENT TIMES

The genus *Corvus*, which includes the raven, the crow, the rook as well as the jackdaw, is included in the songbirds. It inhabits extensive areas of Europe, Asia and North Africa and some species have also penetrated North and South America. Fossilized representatives have also been found in New Zealand. Songbirds have existed since the Upper Oligocene, like the genus *Corvus*, which is found worldwide. *Corvus* inhabits forests with open spaces and the edges of forests, as well as cities. It lives on a mixed diet, ranging from insects to mammals. Some feed on carrion, seeds, grain and fruit. The specimen shown here measures 21.3 cm (8¼ in) long.

Class: Mammalia – mammals

UPPER TRIASSIC – RECENT TIMES

The first mammals probably appeared on earth towards the end of the Triassic, i.e. approximately 200 million years ago. They probably evolved from reptiles with mammalian characteristics during the Middle to Upper Triassic. Throughout the Mesozoic era they included small animals, with a body which was reminiscent of that of present-day insectivores (shrews, hedgehogs etc.). They were scarcely noticeable amongst the fauna at the time, and lived in the shadow of large numbers of enormous reptiles. For this reason, they sought refuge in a nocturnal lifestyle and probably lived in trees. Although mammals hardly changed during the Mesozoic from a morphological point of view, their internal organization was clearly perfected. We think that most still laid eggs. They were also slow to start caring for their young. At the end of Mesozoic there were important paleogeographical and climatological changes as a result of the peak in the formation of mountains in the Alps. This led to the mass extinction of reptiles which had been dominant up to that time. Mammals spread very quickly and extensively, and in a short time excellently adapted mammals had appeared in every possible environment and on every continent. Mammals have a large number of diagnostic characteristics, many of which cannot be determined in paleontology. Only the most important of these are mentioned here: mammals bear live young which feed on mother's milk (this characteristic of bearing live young probably developed gradually and only became dominant at the start of the Cenozoic. The body temperature is steady *(endothermic, homoiothermic)*; mammals have an exceptionally well-developed nervous system and the most developed brains of all animals; the heart consists of *two ventricles and two chambers* and only the left arch of the aorta has survived; the red blood cells do not have a nucleus; the surface of the body is covered with a *hairy skin*, with numerous *glands* including *lactic glands*; they have developed an external ear (with an internal auditory passage and an ear lobe); the skull is connected to the spinal column by two bony protuberances; a second palate developed at a subsequent stage; the middle ear contains three bones: the *stirrup, anvil and hammer;* the jawbone is *squamosodental* (consisting of the squamosum and dental bones); the lower jaw usually consists of one pair of dental bones; the dentition is *heterodont* and there are often two generations of teeth *(the milk set* and *the adult set);* the bones of the pelvis *(ilium ischium, pubis)* have fused into a single pelvic girdle. Mammals are an extremely varied group. The smallest are only a few cm long and weigh approximately 2 g, while the largest measure 30 m (98 ft) and weigh a maximum of 30 tons. They are probably the largest animals ever to live on our planet. One of the fundamental characteristics is locomotion on four limbs, but species which adapted to flying developed wings. Species which adapted to aquatic life have a perfect fish-shaped body. The oldest mammals date from the Upper Triassic, and lived in South and East Africa, Eastern Asia, Central and Southwest Europe, North America and Antarctica.

Subclass: Theria – viviparous animals

UPPER TRIASSIC – RECENT TIMES

Viviparous animals are an extremely diverse group of mammals. The skull does not reveal any traces of reptilian ancestors and the animals bear live young. The oldest viviparous animals date back to the Upper Triassic, but the earliest examples are often incomplete and very rare. Only the representatives of a few orders in this subclass are described below.

Infraclass: Placentalia – placental mammals

LOWER CRETACEOUS – RECENT TIMES

The most typical characteristic of placental mammals is the presence of a placenta which provides

Tadarida sp.
Upper Oligocene, Cereste, France

the food, nutrition and secretion of the embryo. The placenta also serves a protective function and means that the period of gestation can be extended.

Order: Chiroptera – flying mammals

LOWER EOCENE – RECENT TIMES

The Chiroptera are a very special group of mammals adapted to active flying. The shape of the body is more or less like that of a mouse. However, they have a characteristic membrane between the second and fifth finger of the forelimbs, the body, and often also the hind limbs and the tail. Chiroptera have been recorded in Lower Eocene strata, but they probably date back to the end of the Mesozoic, when they evolved from primitive insectivores which liked hot conditions and lived in trees. Nowadays, Chiroptera are the order of mammals with the most species (more than 1,000 species) which has evolved successfully from the Cenozoic and is still very large today.

Tadarida ●

UPPER OLIGOCENE – RECENT TIMES

This small bat species belongs to the family of Molossidae, fossils of which are also occasionally found in Europe. The genus *Tadarida* is part of the bat family characterized by a "free tail"; the tail extends beyond the membrane of the tail. Like many other bats, bats of the genus *Tadarida* also liked to hide in warm caves or caverns and fed on small insects at night. The colonies can be truly enormous, comprising several millions of bats. Nowadays the genus *Tadarida* is spread all over the world and is most common in Latin America. European fossilized specimens have been found in Upper Oligocene sediments in France. The specimen shown here, which belongs to the genus *Tadarida*, is 7.7 cm (3 in) long.

Hyaenodon horridus
Lower Oligocene, South Dakota, United States

Order: Creodonta – primitive predators

MIDDLE PALAEOCENE – UPPER MIOCENE

This is an extinct order of carnivorous bats, which evolved from primitive insectivores at the beginning of the Tertiary period. According to some specialists this order became extinct and was replaced by the order of Hyaenodonta, the representatives of which were originally also included in "primitive predators". Primitive predators are not directly related to present-day predators (order of Carnivora). They merely experienced a convergent development which is the result of a similar lifestyle.

Hyaenodon ●

UPPER EOCENE – LOWER MIOCENE

The genus *Hyaenodon* is reminiscent of the present-day hyena, but is larger and more aggressive. This carnivore had a massive skull with strong teeth and large canines, a slim body, and long strong limbs which probably had claws. It grew to a length of 1.6 m (5 ft), and was therefore able to hunt relatively large prey, such as plant-eating titanotheria. The genus *Hyaenodon* lived from the Upper Eocene to the Lower Miocene and species have been found in Europe and Asia, as well as North Africa and North America. The complete skull of the species *Hyaenodon horridus* shown in the illustration measures 27 cm.

Order: Carnivora – carnivores

MIDDLE PALAEOCENE – RECENT TIMES

This is an extremely extensive group of mammals adapted to hunting other animals. They are found on every continent except Antarctica. The animals are usually nocturnal or come out at night. They are terrestrial, and live both in trees and in water. Although they feed mostly on animals, many also eat vegetable matter (particularly bears and members of the weasel family, less so members of the cat family).

Crocuta ●

UPPER PLIOCENE – RECENT TIMES

The genus *Crocuta* is one of the two genera of hyenas, which still exist today. Hyenas evolved from civets and closely resemble canine predators. They have very strong teeth which are adapted to grinding the bones of large mammals. The forelimbs are longer than the hind limbs, and there has been some reduction of the thumb. Nails developed at the ends of the fingers, rather than claws. Fossilized representatives of the genus *Crocuta* which still exist today have been found dating from the Upper Pliocene in Europe, Asia and North Africa. Nowadays, the hyena of the genus *Crocuta* (spotted hyena) is found in South and Central Africa. The lower jaw of the species *Crocuta spelaea* shown in the illustration measures approximately 16 cm ($6^{1}/_{4}$ in).

Hoplophoneus ●

LOWER OLIGOCENE – UPPER OLIGOCENE

The genus *Hoplophoneus* is included amongst the predators of the cat family. The skull has long curving canine teeth which fit into a groove in the lower jaw. This characteristic has developed in many representatives of the so-called 'saber tooth cats', the general name for a group of cat-like predators which developed long canine teeth.

Crocuta spelaea
Upper Pleistocene, Moravian karst, Czech Republic

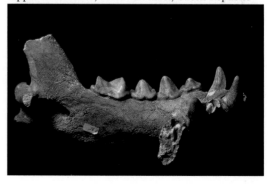

Hoplophoneus sp.
Lower Oligocene, Pennington, South Dakota, USA

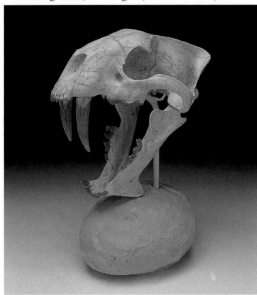

Hoplophoneus was a relatively small, cat-like predator with a skull approximately 15 cm (6 in) long. It could grow to the size of a lynx. The long canines appeared in various groups as they evolved and this is therefore a suitable example of the convergent development of other independent lines. The question arises why these teeth developed. They were certainly useful for hunting. Some paleontologists suspect that the predator used them to grab hold of the prey and keep hold of it, but this style of hunting would often have led to the canines breaking off. It is very rare to find fossilized teeth which broke off during the animal's lifetime. The current hypothesis which assumes that 'saber tooth' carnivores merely used their long canines to injure their prey in the neck or stomach and then waited for it to die at some distance seems more probable. The *Hoplophoneus* lived from the Lower to the Upper Oligocene and has been found in Asia and North America.

Ursus ●

LOWER PLIOCENE – RECENT TIMES

The cave bear (*Ursus spelaeus*), which was approximately one third larger than the present-day brown bear also had a skull with a cavity for the brain which was much higher and more convex at the front. A study of the teeth shows that the cave bear mainly fed on vegetable matter – the teeth are strongly ground down on all sides. The cave bear was very widespread by the end of the Lower Pleistocene. Representatives of the genus *Ursus*, which still exists today, already existed in the Lower Pleistocene and fossils have been discovered in Europe, Africa and North America. Nowadays, this genus is found all over the northern hemisphere.

Ursus spelaeus
Pleistocene, Drachenhöhle, Austria

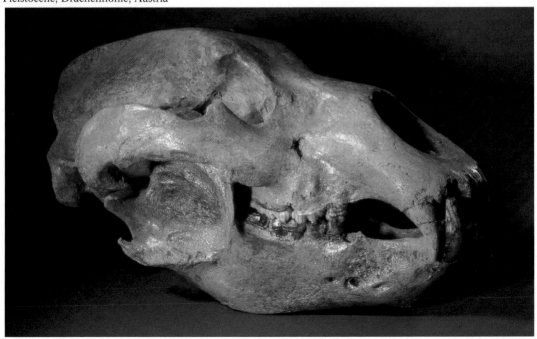

Bransatoglis cf. *micio*
Lower Oligocene, Valeč, Czech Republic

Order: Rodentia – rodents

UPPER PALEOCENE – RECENT TIMES

Rodents are the most widespread, and from the ecological point of view, the most successful group of mammals. They lived both in the tropics and in cold arctic regions, inhabit plains and mountains, deserts and water. Some live in trees and are even able to sail through the air. In most cases they are small herbivores, approximately 10 cm (4 in) long. Only very occasionally have species evolved the size of a bear. The most characteristic feature of rodents is their teeth, which consist of molars, as well as a single pair of upper and lower incisors. These strikingly long, chisel-like curved teeth do not have any roots and grow constantly as they wear out. There is a large space between the incisors and the molars- the *diastema*. The evolution of rodents is not entirely clear. It is probable that they are direct descendants of primitive insectivores.

Bransatoglis   ●

LOWER OLIGOCENE

The genus *Bransatoglis* from the Czech Valeč is represented by one of the best known fossils and has been studied by scientists since the first half of the 18ᶜ century. This fossil was already mentioned in a German edition of Linnaeus's work, *Systema Naturae,* dating from 1778, as well as in the work,

Les Ossements fossiles. It was kept in several different places, and was even lost for some time, until it was rediscovered by H. v. Meyer and again described in detail. For a long time, *Bransatoglis* was considered to be a representative of the squirrel family, until the Czech paleontologist classified

Glyptodont cf. *asper*
Pleistocene, province of Buenos Aires, Argentina

this fossil in the mouse family on the basis of a study of the teeth in the lower jaw. The genus *Bransatoglis* has been recorded in Lower Oligocene strata in Europe. The specimen of the species *Bransatoglis* cf. *micio* shown in the illustration is approximately 16 cm (6¹/₄ in) long.

Order: Edentata

PALAEOCENE – RECENT TIMES

The Edentata are primitive placental mammals which live in the tropics. The common characteristic is the strong reduction of the teeth. They evolved as a branch of insectivores and spread throughout South America. Nowadays they include the South American armadillos, sloths and anteaters.

Glyptodon ●

PLEISTOCENE

The armadillo of the genus *Glyptodon* was characterized by its large size: it was approximately 1.6 m (5 ft) long and 1 m (39 in) tall. Its strong, highly complex and complete carapace consisted of pentagonal or hexagonal plates with deep grooves. The skull, which was also protected by a small bony carapace at the top, was greatly reduced in the area in front of the orbits. Most of the vertebrae were fused and the tail was short and protected by rings of bony plates with spines. The representatives of the genus *Glyptodon* were herbivores. During the Pleistocene they lived in North and South America. The largest fragment of the carapace of the species *Glyptodon* cf. *asper* shown here measures 5.5 cm (2¹/₄ in).

Order: Perissodactyla – perissodactyls

UPPER PALAEOCENE – RECENT TIMES

From the palaeontological point of view, the perissodactyls are the best-known order of mammals. They evolved from the group of Condylartha (of the related order of *Tetraclaenodon*, which existed in the Middle Palaeocene in North America). The perissodactyls reached their peak during the Eocene. From that time their numbers reduced. Only a few species of tapirs, rhinoceroses and members of the horse family have survived up to the present day. The largest representatives, such as the gigantic Titanotheria, became extinct without any descendants. The perissodactyls were an extensive group of mammals with a characteristically long skull and usually long, slim limbs adapted to rapid movement.

Hyracodon nebraskensis
Oligocene, Dakota, United States

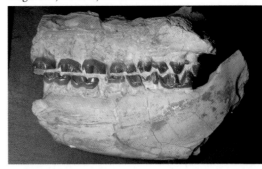

Hyracodon ●

LOWER OLIGOCENE – ONDER MIOCENE

The genus *Hyracodon* belongs to a group of very primitive rhinoceroses. It did not have any horns on its head and was relatively slender and able to run fast on its long, slim legs. The fore and hind limbs had only three toes. The genus *Hyracodon* lived in North America from the Lower Oligocene to the Lower Miocene. The fragment of the skull shown here belongs to the species *Hyracodon nebraskensis* and measures 14.2 cm (5¹/₂ in).

Teleoceras ●

MIDDLE MIOCENE – LOWER PLIOCENE

The genus *Teleoceras* belongs to the group of the 'true rhinoceroses', which evolved in North America towards the end of the Eocene. With its massive body and short limbs, it resembled the present-day hippopotamus. Like these animals, the *Teleoceras* spent most of the time in water. There was just one small – but strong – horn in the nasal area. Representatives of the genus *Teleoceras* existed in North America from the Middle Miocene to the Lower Pliocene. During the Pliocene they spread to eastern Asia. The larger of the two molars shown here, which belongs to the genus *Teleoceras*, measures 6 cm (2¹/₄ in).

Teleoceras sp.
Miocene, Florida, United States

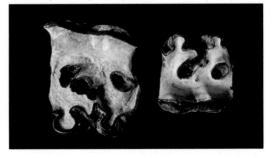

Coelodonta antiquitatis
Upper Pleistocene, Sutton Courtney, Great Britain

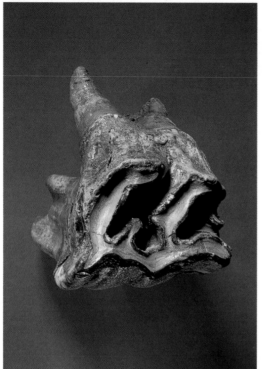

Dicerorhinus kirchbergensis
Upper Pleistocene, Prague, Czech Republic

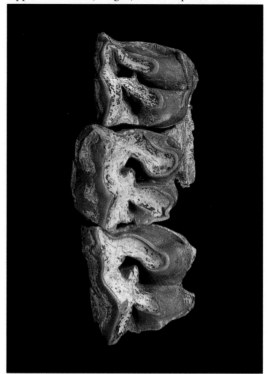

Coelodonta ●

LOWER MIOCENE – UPPER PLEISTOCENE

The genus *Coelodonta* is a very specialized rhinoceros, in which two horns developed, one behind the other. It was 3.5 m (11 ft 6 in) long and 1.6 m (5 ft) tall. The teeth of this rhinoceros, which adapted to the very cold climate of the arctic steppes, together with the mammoth, is completely adapted to eating the hard grasses of the steppes. The species *Coelodonta antiquitatis* originated in Northern Asia. Representatives of the genus *Coelodonta* have been recorded dating from the Lower Miocene to the Upper Pleistocene and have been found in Europe and Asia.

Dicerorhinus ●

OLIGOCENE – RECENT TIMES

One of the characteristics of the rhinoceros of the genus *Dicerorhinus* are the two horns placed one behind the other on the skull, the first of which is clearly larger than the second. This genus reached its peak during the warm periods of the Pleistocene (during the interglacial periods). Some species grew to a length of 2.5 m (8 ft 3 in) and were 1.5 m (5 ft) tall. Compared with later rhinoceroses (*Coelodonta*), they had relatively long limbs. *Dicerorhi-*

nus was hunted as prey by Palaeolithic hunters. Representatives of the genus *Dicerorhinus* first appeared during the Oligocene. Nowadays, this genus is only found in Indonesia. The illustration shows molars from the upper jaw of the species *Dicerorhinus kirchbergensis*, which form a row 16 cm (6$\frac{1}{4}$ in) long.

Lophiodon ●

LOWER EOCENE – UPPER EOCENE

The genus *Lophiodon* is one of the predecessors of the true tapirs. It is characterized by a long, narrow skull which is slightly concave on the dorsal side. The area in front of the orbits is usually cylindrical, and pointed on the oral side. The males develop striking upper canines, and the simple molars were separated from the canines by an empty space. The genus *Lophiodon* grew to a length of 2.8 m (9 ft) and a height of 1 m (39 in). It lived in Europe from the Lower to the Upper Eocene and fossilized remains have probably also been found in upper Eocene strata in Eastern Asia. The tooth shown here belongs to the species *Lophiodon rhinoceroides* and measures 6 cm (2$\frac{1}{4}$ in).

far more mineral salts. The enamel on the molars is curved much more than in present-day horses. The genus *Hipparion* lived from the Middle Miocene to the Middle Pleistocene and reached a peak at the end of the Miocene and in the Pliocene. Its remains have been found in Europe, North Africa, Asia and North America. The illustration shows a molar from the upper and lower jaws of the genus *Hipparion*. The largest molar measures 3 cm ($1^1/_4$ in).

Equus ●

MIDDLE PLIOCENE – RECENT TIMES

During the course of evolution there was a gradual reduction in the number of toes of the horse family. In the genus *Equus*, only the middle toe developed on the limbs and changed into a hoof. This perfected locomotion in a steppe environment. During the Pleistocene this important genus evolved a fairly large number of species, particularly in areas of Europe. It is divided into a number of subgenera, including zebras and donkeys. Representatives of the genus *Equus*, which is fairly widespread nowadays, lived from the Middle Pliocene. Fossilized remains have been found in Europe, Asia, Africa and North America. The molar shown here belongs to the genus *Equus* and measures 7 cm ($2^1/_4$ in).

Equus sp.
Pleistocene, Lathum, The Netherlands

Hipparion ●

MIDDLE MIOCENE – MIDDLE PLEISTOCENE

The genus *Hipparion* represents a well-known, small, three-toed horse, which was a side branch in the evolutionary line leading to modern horses. There has been a reduction in the number of fingers on the limbs to only three fingers. As a result of the transition from marshy jungle to steppes, the crown of the molars also became higher, and in this way *Hipparion* adapted to the change in the composition of its diet. It lived on the food of the steppes, which contained

Hipparion sp.
Miocene, Florida, United States

'Mastodon' americanus
Pleistocene, Palm Beach County, Florida, United States

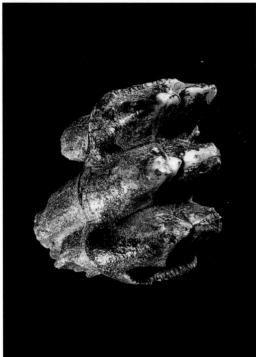

Order: Proboscidea

LOWER EOCENE – RECENT TIMES

The proboscidea are a well-known group of large mammals, which spread in large numbers during the Tertiary and the Quaternary in Africa, Eurasia and in North and South America. Nowadays, these animals are represented only by the African elephant (*Loxodonta africana*) and the Indian elephant (*Elephas maximus*). These large mammals are characterized by a strong skeleton, long columnar limbs, a moving trunk and enormous tusks, which developed as a result of a huge increase in the size of the canines. Proboscidea include the largest terrestrial mammals of all times. Their strong bones have also survived in the initially unfavorable period of fossilization and they are therefore found more often than bones of other animals. Proboscidea have been found on every continent except Australia and Antarctica.

'Mastodon' ●

MIOCENE – PLEISTOCENE, HOLOCENE (?)

The genus *'Mastodon'*, which includes a relatively large number of different genera, had tusks which sometimes grew to considerable lengths and were only slightly curved. Some representatives were hairy, because they gradually adapted to the changing climatological circumstances during the Quaternary. They grew to a length of 3.6 m (11 ft 10 in). Mastodons appeared in Africa at the beginning of the Miocene and penetrated throughout Eurasia, crossing over the Baring Straits to North and South America, where they survived the ice ages. They were probably hunted to extinction by the Indians (Mayas) before the Europeans arrived. The molar shown here belongs to the species *'Mastodon' americanus* and measures 10 cm (4 in).

Mammuthus ●

LOWER PLEISTOCENE – HOLOCENE

The genus *Mammuthus* is one of the most important extinct representatives of the elephant. The shape of the body was very similar to that of present-day elephants, but they were adapted to the extremely cold climates of the quaternary ice ages with a thick hairy coat. Some of the representatives of this genus grew to a height of 4.5m and they are amongst the largest known proboscidea. The tusks of some species reached lengths of up to approximately 5 m (16 ft), and the molars were up to 50 cm ($19^{1}/_{2}$ in) in height.
Because of the discoveries of the bodies of mam-

Mammuthus primigenus
Pleistocene, Lathum, The Netherlands

Archaeotherium sp.
Lower Oligocene, South Dakota, United States

moths which have remained intact in the permafrost of polar areas, it is possible to know exactly what their diet consisted of. An important proportion consisted of grasses and twigs of deciduous and coniferous trees. In winter, a period of scarcity, the mammoth ate the twigs of bushes, lichens and dry grass. The genus *Mammuthus* lived in the Lower Pleistocene. It became extinct towards the end of the Pleistocene in most of Europe, Asia and North America, although a few survived up the beginning of the Holocene. The molar of the mammoth of the species *Mammuthus primignus* in the illustration measures 30 cm (12 in).

Order: Artiodactyla – artiodactyls

LOWER EOCENE – RECENT TIMES

This is a large group of predominantly large herbivorous terrestrial animals with limbs that are generally adapted to running. It not only includes a large number of species which are still found today (e.g., the auroch, the hippopotamus, boar, cattle in general, deer), but also many fossilized representatives. The genus reached the peak of its development at the end of the Cenozoic, and this trend has continued up to the present day. One of the characteristic features of artiodactyls is the structure of their limbs. During the course of phylogenisis, there was a striking reduction in the number of toes. During the Oligocene, some species still had primitive limbs with five toes. With the loss of the first toe, there was a stage with four toes, which has continued up to the present time in the boar and the hippopotamus. As a result of a subsequent reduction, only the third and fourth toes remained on each limb. Although artiodactyls were still rare at the beginning of the Eocene, they accounted for a large proportion of the fauna by the end of this period.

Archaeotherium ●

LOWER OLIGOCENE – UPPER OLIGOCENE

The genus *Archaeotherium* belongs to the group of large artiodactyls known as entelodonts. The *Archaeotherium* could grow to a length of approximately 2.6 m (8 ft 6 in), and was characterized by a long skull with small orbits placed towards the back. There were striking protruding elements on the cheekbones and lower jaw, which could indicate the differences between the sexes. The structure of the teeth reveals that the *Archaeotherium* was herbivorous, though in certain cases also fed on animal matter. Representatives of this genus have been found dating from the Lower to the Upper Oligocene in North America and Eastern Asia. The skull shown here is 34.5 cm (13^1/$_2$ in) long.

Merycoidodon culbertsoni
Lower Oligocene, Douglas, Wyoming, United States

Merycoidodon ●

LOWER OLIGOCENE – UPPER OLIGOCENE

The primitive artiodactyl of the genus *Merycoidodon* was the size of the present-day sheep or pig. Its short, primitive limbs and a tail longer than that of a boar were characteristic features. The skull of the genus *Merycoidodon* was relatively short, and there was no space behind the front incisors and the first molars. The front upper incisors were reduced, while the first lower molar served as a canine. The *Merycoidodon* lived from the Lower to the Upper

Oligocene. It was a herbivore, with molars of the socalled solenodont type (with half-moon shaped lamellae on the chewing surfaces), which were suitable for chewing vegetable matter. The skull of the specimen shown here belongs to the species *Merycoidodon culbertsoni* and measures 21.3 cm (8$^{1}/_{4}$ in).

Poebrotherium ●

LOWER OLIGOCENE

The genus *Poebrotherium*, classified under camels (family of Camelidae), was much smaller than the present-day representative of camels. It grew to approximately the size of a deer. The skull had an elongated face and was carried on a long neck. It had a full set of teeth and the herbivorous diet was chewed by specially adapted teeth. The long limbs had two toes, the metacarpals and the tarsals (metapodia) were not fused together (as they are in present-day camels) although the ulna and the radius were fused. The genus *Poebrotherium* is seen as the direct ancestor of present day camels (Camelidae) and lived in North America during the Lower Oligocene period. The skull shown here measures 17.8 cm (7 in).

Poebrotherium sp.
Lower Oligocene, Wyoming, United States

302

Rangifer tarandus
Upper Pleistocene, Prague, Czech Republic

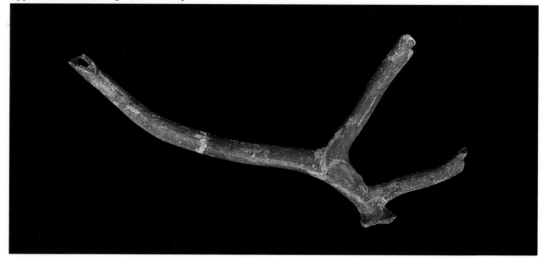

Rangifer ●

LOWER PLEISTOCENE – RECENT TIMES

The genus *Rangifer* (elk) belongs to the reindeer family. Both genera have antlers. Up to now, the precise way in which elk developed is not clear. They spread all over Europe during the Pleistocene. The genus *Rangifer* lived from the Lower Pleistocene and then spread across areas of Europe, Asia and North America, where they inhabited the tundra and taiga. Because of climatological changes at the beginning of the Holocene, the once extensive biotope extended further and further north, and nowadays this genus is restricted to northern parts of Eurasia and North America. The fragment of part of the antlers of the species *Rangifer tarandus* shown here measures 66 cm (26 in).

Order: Cetacea – whales

MIDDLE EOCENE – RECENT TIMES

Of all the placental mammals, whales are best adapted to life in water. This order probably includes the largest mammals of all times because they can grow to lengths of up to 33 m (108 ft) and weights of 150 tons. The ancestors of whales were probably closely related to the artiodactyls. Whales have a torpedo-shaped body. This fish-like shape developed because the neck almost entirely disappeared. The forelimbs changed into organs for paddling, while the hind limbs were completely reduced. The main organ for movement is the caudal fin, which is horizontal. Typical representatives include the Greenland whale, the common dolphin, and the blue whale.

Basilosaurus ■

MIDDLE EOCENE – UPPER EOCENE

The genus *Basilosaurus* is included in primitive whales, although these were already completely adapted to marine life. The skull was low and oblong and could grow to a length of 1.5 m (5 ft). There was a small primitive brain inside the skull. The body was slender and a maximum of 20 m (65 ft) long, while the vertebral column consisted of numerous elongated vertebrae. The pelvis was strongly reduced, and the hind limbs had probably lost their function. The genus lived in Africa and North America during the Middle and Upper Eocene. The tooth shown here measures 9 cm ($3^1/_2$ in).

Basilosaurus sp.
Upper Eocene, Fayum, Egypt

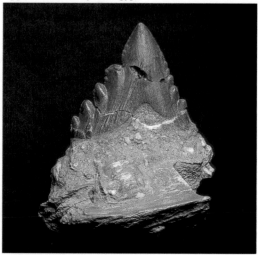

Stratigraphic table

			Period		Epoch
Phanerozoic	Kenozoicum		Quaternary 1.75		Holocene
					Pleistocene
		Tertiary	Neogene 23.5		Pliocene
					Miocene
			Paleocene 65		Oligocene
					Eocene
					Paleocene
	Mesozoic		Cretaceous 135		Upper
					Lower
			Jurassic 203		Upper
					Middle
					Lower
			Triassic 250		Upper
					Middle
					Lower
	Palaeozoic	Early	Permian 295		Upper
					Lower
			Carboniferous 355		Upper
					Lower
		Late	Devonian 410		Upper
					Middle
					Lower
			Silurian 435		Upper
					Lower
			Ordovician 500		Upper
					Middle
					Lower
			Cambrian 540		Upper
					Middle
					Lower
Precambrian	Proterozoic				

Precambrian – period of the creation of the earth's crust up to the beginning of the Cambrian

Phanerozoic – period during which the sediments contained many remains of organisms

Proterozoic
Paleozoic
Mesozoic
Cenozoic – Tertiary + Quaternary

figures in millions of years

Other reading

Barrande, J. (1999): Système silurien du centre de la Bohème : Trilobites. Granit, Prague.

Benton, M. J. (1997): Vertebrate Palaeontology. – 1-452, Chapman & Hall, London.

Cappetta, H. (1987): Chondrichthyes II. In: Handbook of Paleoichthyology . – 1-192, Stuttgart.

Carroll, R. L. (1988): Vertebrate Paleontology and Evolution. – 1-698, W. H. Freeman and Company.

Dance, S. P. (1992): Muscheln und Schnecken. – 1-256, Ravensburger Buchverlag, Ravensburg.

Frickhinger, K. A. (1991): Fossilien Atlas: Fische. – 1-1088, Mergus, Melle.

Gaisler, J. (1994): Úvod do zoologie obratlovců. – 1-275, Masarykova univerzita, Brno.

Gothan, W., Weyland, H. (1964): Lehrbuch der Paläobotanik. – 1-594, Akademie-Verlag, Berlin.

Habětín, V., Knobloch, E. (1981): Kapesní atlas zkamenělin. – 1-288, SPN, Prague.

Kardong, K.V. (1998): Vertebrates: Comparative Anatomy, Function, Evolution. – 1-747, WCB/McGraw-Hill.

Kumpera, O., Vašíček Z. (1988): Základy historické geologie a paleontologie. – 1-568, SNTL and Alfa, Prague.

Mišík, M., Chlupáč, I., Cicha, I. (1985): Stratigrafická a historická geológia. – 1-576, SPN, Bratislava.

Müller, A. H. (1957-1981): Lehrbuch der Paläozoologie I-III. – VEB Gustav Fischer Verlag, Jena.

Nelson, J. S. (1984): Fishes of the World. – 1-477, New York.

Němejc, F. (1959-1975): Paleobotanika I-IV (I-1959, II-1963, III-1968, IV-1975), – Academia, Prague.

Osnovy paleontologii (1958-1964). – J. A. Orlov (ed.), Izd. AN SSSR, Moscow.

Prokop, R. (1989): Zkamenělý svět. – 1-280, Práce, Prague.

Rosypal, S., a kol. (1987): Přehled biologie. – 1-688, SPN, Prague.

Špinar, Z. (1960): Základy paleontologie bezobratlých. – 1-835, NČSAV, Prague.

Špinar, Z. (1966): Systematická paleontologie bezobratlých. – 1-1052, Academia, Prague.

Špinar Z., Burian, Z. (1984): Paleontologie obratlovců. – 1-864, Academia, Prague.

Švagrovský, J. (1976): Základy systematickej zoopaleontológie/I Evertebrata. – 1-581, SPN, Bratislava.

Turek, V., Marek, J., Beneš, J. (1988): Fossils of the World. – 1-495, Paul Hamlyn Publishing, London.

Záruba, B. (2000): Cesta do pravěku / Dávný svět v obrazech Zdeňka Buriana. Granit, Prague.

Index